Regional Development in the 1990s

The British Isles in Transition

Regional Policy and Development Series

Retreat from the Regions
Corporate Change and the Closure of Factories
Stephen Fothergill and Nigel Guy
ISBN 1 85302 101 6
Regional Policy and Development 1

Spatial Policy in a Divided Nation
Edited by Richard T Harrison and Mark Hart
ISBN 1 85302 076 1
Regional Policy and Development 2

The Role of Regional Development Agencies in Economic Regeneration
Michael Danson, Greg Lloyd and David Newlands
ISBN 1 85302 067 2
Regional Policy and Development 3

Local Unemployment Change in Britain
Leaps and Lags in the response to the National
Economic Cycles
Anne Green, Christopher Hasluck, David Owen
and Colin Winett
ISBN 1 85302 160 1
Regional Policy and Development 5

An Enlarged Europe
Regions in Competition?
Edited by Lovis Albrechts, Sally Hardy, Mark Hart
and Anastasios Katos
ISBN 1 85302 188 1
Regional Policy and Development 6

Also published with the Regional Studies Association

Beyond Green Belts
Managing Urban Growth in the 21st Century
Compiled by John Herington
ISBN 1 85302 055 9

Regional Policy at the Crossroads
European Perspectives
Edited by Louis Albrechts, Frank Moulaert,
Peter Roberts and Erik Swyngedouw
ISBN 1 85302 021 4 hb
ISBN 1 85302 024 9 pb

Regional Development in the 1990s

The British Isles in Transition

Edited by Ron Martin and Peter Townroe

Regional Policy and Development Series 4

Jessica Kingsley Publishers
London and Philadelphia

Regional Studies Association
London

First published in the United Kingdom in 1992 by
Jessica Kingsley Publishers Ltd
116 Pentonville Road
London N1 9JB
and
Regional Studies Association

Copyright © 1992 Regional Studies Association and Jessica Kingsley Publishers

British Library Cataloguing in Publication Data
Regional Development in the 1990's:
    British Isles in Transition. – (Regional
    Policy & Development Series;v.4)
    I. Townroe, P. M. II. Martin, Ron
    III. Series
    307.10941

ISBN 1 85302 139 3

Printed and Bound in Great Britain by
Biddles Ltd, Guildford and King's Lynn

Contents

PART VI: EPILOGUE

List of Tables

List of Figures

Preface

In 1983 the Regional Studies Association sponsored the publication of a report by an Inquiry Panel established by the Association[1]. With assistance from the regional branches of the Association, members of the Panel reviewed the regional problems and issues in the United Kingdom at that time, a time when the long standing North-South divide was being highlighted by a deep national economic recession. The report was well received, as providing a convenient updating and overview as well as offering thoughtful conclusions and policy recommendations arising from the discussions of the Panel. The report rapidly sold out, being adopted as compulsory reading on many undergraduate and postgraduate courses concerned with regional problems.

The success of the 1983 publication inspired the Association to update and extend that exercise, in time for a forward look on regional issues into the 1990s The updating was not problematic but the extension was ambitious. Not only was the Irish Branch of the Association brought in to offer a full coverage of the regions of the British Isles, but a series of theme contributions were requested from leading authorities in specialist aspects of regional economic development. Although each contribution of necessity had to be tightly constrained in terms of length, the resulting complexity, involving a total of 47 authors, did delay the final assembly of all of the material. The editors had to crave indulgence from prompt contributors to wait for slower authors to catch up. Once again each regional branch of the Association was involved.

The timing of the publication now follows an election in the United Kingdom, and the formal achievement of the Single Market of the European Economic Community. Regional problems and issues are high on the political agenda, from the question of the significance of regional fiscal transfers across the EEC at a time of a possible single currency and the absence of trade barriers, to new thinking on regional government and mechanisms for securing regional economic regeneration. It is the hope of the editors and the authors that this volume will stimulate discussion on the many issues highlighted, as well as providing a convenient overview of problems and opportunities coming up in the 1990s, region by region.

The editors would like to thank the authors (or most of them!) for their patience. They would also like to thank the Director of the Regional Studies Association, Sally Hardy, for her support and encouragement.

Ron Martin &
Peter Townroe

---

[1] Regional Studies Association (1983) *Report of an Inquiry into Regional Problems in the United Kingdom.* Norwich: Geo Books.

PART I

INTRODUCTION

CHAPTER 1

CHANGING TRENDS AND PRESSURES IN REGIONAL DEVELOPMENT

Ron Martin and Peter Townroe

INTRODUCTION

The past decade and a half has been challenging for regional development in the United Kingdom. The old verities concerning the pattern, causes and cures of the 'regional problem' have been called into question. Throughout the long post-war 'boom' or 'golden age' from 1945 to the early 1970s, there was a broad consensus, academically and politically, surrounding both the nature of 'the regional problem' and the appropriate policy responses directed at its resolution. During this period it was even possible to regard the difficulties of the structurally disadvantaged 'depressed areas' inherited from the inter-war years as marginal in an otherwise buoyant economy. For although the rate of unemployment in the industrial north and periphery of the nation averaged twice that of the south, midlands and east, joblessness everywhere was at an unprecedentedly low level. Since the mid-1970s, however, and especially since 1979, the whole question of uneven regional development has resurfaced with a vengeance.

Over the past ten years or so, regional inequalities in economic growth and welfare have increased dramatically, reaching a scale unparalleled since the 1930s. Moreover, the pattern of inequality has changed in important ways, involving the relative decline of previously prosperous areas and the emergence of problems within the growth regions themselves. Also, the nature of the regional problem has changed. New economic forces and competitive pressures have come to play a key role in shaping the process of uneven regional development. At the same time, partly as a result of these shifts and partly as a result of the major upheavals in political ideology and economic philosophy that have taken place since the mid-1970s, the whole post-war consensus on regional policy thinking has been subjected to critical reappraisal and reformulation. Not since the early 1930s has the debate over policy been as intense. It is probably no exaggeration to claim that there is now a new 'regional problem', although exactly what that problem is and how it should be addressed are contentious issues.

THE CHANGING PROCESS OF UNEVEN REGIONAL DEVELOPMENT

Since the mid-1970s the United Kingdom, in common with other Western industrial countries, has been undergoing an evolving process of economic and social restructuring or reorganisation. What has been gathering momentum is not some mere disturbance of the 'post-war norm', nor simply a trend towards greater cyclical instability of economic growth, but arguably the unfolding of a new phase of uneven economic development (see, for example, Massey and Allen, 1988: Martin, 1988a). Opinions differ as to the precise nature of this new configuration (Martin, 1989a). Some view it as the advent of a new 'post-industrial' information-technology based society (Hall, 1985); others see it as marking the end of a phase of 'organised capitalism' and the onset of a more 'disorganised' phase of development (Lash and Urry, 1987); still others believe we have entered a new 'post-welfarist' era of economic management (Bennett, 1990); a sizable majority are convinced we are witnessing a transition from 'Fordism' to post-Fordist 'flexible accumulation' (Murray, 1989); while some have even suggested the nation is in the throes of a shift from 'modernism' to 'post-modernism' (Cooke, 1991).

But whatever the interpretation, one thing is clear: since the mid-1970s several fundamental processes have been in motion that have had and are continuing to have profound effects on the geography of socio-economic inequality in the country. The first of these has been the large-scale *de-industrialization* of the nation's manufacturing base. The UK manufacturing sector now employs only 4.7 million workers, compared to 8 million two decades ago, and its contribution to Gross Domestic Product (GDP) has declined from 31 per cent to 21 per cent over the same period. And although productivity has been substantially improved, the balance of trade in manufacturing went into serious deficit during the 1980s and continues to be precarious. Many of the nation's long-established manufacturing areas have seen their industrial base undermined and their traditional economic role eroded.

The second is the wave of *technological innovation*, based primarily on microelectronics and various forms of information processing, that began in the early 1970s and which is generating an expanding array of new industries, services and types of employment while increasingly transforming the nature of existing activities and jobs. Access to and the application of the new information technologies are now key determinants of successful regional economic restructuring.

The third new development has been the wave of *tertiarization* or service sector expansion, especially of financial, banking, producer, retail and leisure services. It has been in this part of the economy that capital investment and job creation have been concentrated over the past decade. Arguably, some of this rapid expansion of services, involving an increase in employment of 2 million since 1979, was in excess of that warranted by underlying real conditions in the economy, being encouraged by the unsustainable economic boom during the second half of the 1980s. Nevertheless, it is on this sector and not manufacturing that the regions now depend for new jobs.

The fourth major change, and one that will increase in importance, is the process of *flexibilization*: of production processes, labour utilization, service provision, management, and marketing. In all of these areas of economic activity the new accent is on finding ways of adapting to and indeed promoting rapidly changing and progressively more differentiated ('customized') market demand, and of improving efficiency through the continual manipulation of the quality and quantity of inputs. The different paths to and the costs and benefits of this flexibilization of the economy are regarded by many to constitute a new and potentially far-reaching source of uneven regional development.

Fifth, intersecting with all of these forces is the process of *internationalization*. The flows of capital into and out of the UK economy have expanded dramatically over the past decade and a half. The exodus of direct and portfolio investment capital–due in part to the abolition of exchange controls, in part to the boom in cross-border mergers and takeovers which swept the capitalist countries during the 1980s–has inevitably had important implications for regional development, particularly where, as has often been the case, such outflows have been associated with the disinvestment and ration- alisation of domestic productive capacity. The growth of overseas inward investment in the regions, notably of Japanese investment, is the other side of this internationali- zation process. One result is the progressive disarticulation of local economies, in the sense that they are becoming increasingly linked into and dependent on networks of investment, competition, exchange and technological development that are transna- tional and global in extent.

Sixth, and related to this internationalization process, the next decade will see increasing *economic integration with Europe*. The effects of membership of the Exchange Rate Mechanism, the freeing up of trade and factor flows resulting from the advent of the 'Single European Market' in 1992, and further moves towards monetary union, all will expose the British and Irish regions to new competitive pressures and further restructuring. The expectation is that it will be the south-eastern areas of England, being nearest to the European growth core, that will benefit most from these develop- ments, while other parts of Britain, especially those in the northern and western periphery, will be left behind in their relative economic prosperity. The regional impact, through the European Community, of the economic and political reorganization in Eastern Europe is, however, more difficult to foresee.

The final fundamental change relates to the *reconfiguration of state intervention* that began under Labour in the mid-1970s, but which has been particularly pronounced under the Conservatives since 1979. It is not simply that the aims and instruments of policy have been recast, but rather that those policies–including high interest rates, privatization, employment legislation, deregulation of finance markets, control of local

Table 1.1.1. The North-South Divide in Employment Growth

Absolute change 1979–90 (000s)

	Employees			Self-Employed
	Production and Construction	Services	Total	
South East	-664	846	165	547
East Anglia	-29	150	111	77
South West	-78	256	173	160
East Midlands	-169	190	12	104
'South'	**-940**	**1442**	**461**	**888**
West Midlands	-336	198	-144	130
Yorkshire-Humberside	-279	209	-82	137
North West	-368	119	-250	112
North	-187	58	-133	37
Wales	-127	89	-40	75
Scotland	-240	129	-129	87
Northern Ireland	-57	50	-9	-6
'North'	**-1594**	**852**	**-787**	**572**
United Kingdom	-2534	2294	-240	1460

Source: Department of Employment
Note: Changes measured mid-year to mid-year

Table 1.1.2. The Growing Regional Gap in Output Per Head, 1979–89

GDP per head relative to UK average

	1970	1979	1989	% Change 1979–89
South East	113.7	116.1	120.6	3.9
Greater London	124.5	128.9	129.6	0.5
Rest of South East	105.5	107.4	114.9	6.9
East Anglia	93.6	94.0	99.3	5.6
South West	94.8	90.9	95.6	5.2
East Midlands	96.6	96.1	95.0	-1.1
West Midlands	102.8	96.0	91.7	-4.5
Yorkshire-Humberside	93.3	93.0	88.1	-5.3
North West	96.2	96.5	91.5	-5.2
North	86.9	91.1	86.9	-4.6
Wales	88.3	84.8	83.8	-1.2
Scotland	93.0	95.1	93.1	-2.1
Northern Ireland	74.3	78.1	76.1	-2.6

Source: Economic Trends
Note: Figures exclude the Continental Shelf

Table 1.1.3. The Widening of Regional Unemployment Disparities, 1976–90

	Unemployment rate (%)				Unemployment Differential (Region-UK)	
	1976	1981	1986	1990	1976	1990
South East	3.1	5.5	8.3	4.0	-1.1	-1.8
East Anglia	3.5	6.3	8.5	3.9	-0.7	-1.9
South West	4.7	6.8	9.5	4.4	0.5	-1.4
East Midlands	3.4	7.4	10.0	5.1	-0.8	-0.7
West Midlands	4.3	10.0	12.9	6.0	0.1	0.2
Yorkshire-Humberside	3.9	8.8	12.5	6.7	-0.3	0.9
North West	5.1	10.2	13.7	7.7	0.9	1.9
North	5.3	11.7	15.3	8.7	1.1	2.9
Wales	5.3	10.4	13.5	6.6	1.1	0.8
Scotland	5.1	9.9	13.3	8.1	0.9	2.3
Northern Ireland	7.1	12.7	17.4	13.4	2.9	7.6
United Kingdom	4.2	8.1	11.1	5.8	0.0	0.0

Source: Department of Employment
Note: Historically consistent series used (which take account of the numerous changes in definition made by the Government during the 1980s)

Table 1.1.4. Business Formation by Region, 1981–89

	Stock end-1981 (000s)	Stock end-1989 (000s)	Net gain 000s	% of 1981stock
South East	441.1	593.2	152.1	34.5
East Anglia	54.5	68.3	13.9	25.5
South West	128.3	161.2	33.0	25.7
East Midlands	91.7	113.4	21.8	23.8
West Midlands	116.9	140.9	24.1	20.6
Yorkshire-Humberside	105.2	123.6	18.5	17.5
North West	131.5	149.5	17.7	13.4
North	53.8	62.4	8.6	15.9
Wales	73.0	85.2	12.2	16.7
Scotland	96.2	113.2	17.1	18.3
Northern Ireland	44.8	51.5	6.8	15.1
United Kingdom	1336.7	1662.3	325.6	24.4

Source: Regional Trends 1991
Note: Net gain refers to registrations minus deregistrations (for VAT)

Table 1.1.5. Income Distribution and Welfare Support, by Region, 1988–89

	Proportion of households with average weekly income		average income support per head
	below £60	above £425	UK=100
South East	7.4	31.9	89.0
East Anglia	7.4	21.5	61.5
South West	6.2	21.0	77.9
East Midlands	9.2	18.4	85.3
West Midlands	10.5	19.1	108.5
Yorkshire-Humberside	10.5	14.1	97.9
North West	11.4	18.0	121.0
North	12.2	16.3	118.4
Wales	10.4	15.4	108.8
Scotland	14.0	17.6	118.1
Northern Ireland	17.9	11.6	154.9
United Kingdom	9.7	21.9	100.0

Sources: Family Expenditure Survey and Department of Social Security

Table 1.1.6. Consumer Expenditure 1979–89

	Expenditure £ per head UK=100		
	1979	*1984*	*1989*
South East	113.4	117.4	118.6
East Anglia	98.4	97.0	100.6
South West	92.2	97.8	100.7
East Midlands	93.6	93.2	89.2
West Midlands	97.7	91.6	91.1
Yorkshire-Humberside	91.0	89.3	89.6
North West	95.8	93.5	95.0
North	93.8	86.4	85.3
Wales	91.4	88.8	86.2
Scotland	95.3	96.7	91.8
Northern Ireland	90.7	82.5	81.3

Source: Regional Trends

authority spending, and the commercialization of the remaining public services–have changed how the economy works and substantially altered the economic landscape.

Considered together, then, these seven major forces and shifts are not only forging a new context for regional and urban development in the 1990s, they are reconstituting the very processes of uneven regional development, and as a result the pattern of regional economic problems, possibilities and constraints.

THE CHANGING PATTERN OF UNEVEN REGIONAL DEVELOPMENT

For much of the post-war period, the regional problem was defined in terms of the official 'problem regions' themselves–the relatively depressed 'assisted areas' of South Wales, the North East, Central Scotland and Northern Ireland. Up to about the mid-1970s the gap between these areas and the rest of the UK remained fairly stable, and there was even some convergence in regional industrial structures. But since then, both the pattern and nature of the 'regional problem' have been recast. Not surprisingly, the restructuring of the past decade and a half has been uneven geographically, and spatial disparities have increased as a result.

The most obvious, and most publicly debated disparity has been the opening up of a major North-South divide. Although some, including the Government, have disputed the existence or at least the significance of such a divide, the growth during the 1980s of a distinct gap between the 'southern' regions (the South East, East Anglia, South West and, in most respects, the East Midlands) on the one hand and the rest of the country on the other is beyond question (see Martin, 1988b; Lewis and Townsend, 1989; Smith, 1989). The increasing lead of these southern regions has been particularly marked in terms of employment and output growth (Tables 1.1.1 and 1.1.2), but is also evident across a whole range of economic indicators, such as unemployment rates, new business registrations, incomes, welfare support, and consumer expenditure (see Tables 1.1.3 to 1.1.6). The economic and social disparities that underpin the gap between these 'two Britains' have been mutually reinforcing in their effects. They have also been associated with a redrawing of the political map. Since the mid-1970s, and especially since 1979, the widening of regional socio-economic inequalities has been accompanied by an increased geographical polarisation of political support. Fuelled by its leading role as the growth core of the country during the 1980s, the 'south' became the primary stronghold of the new Conservative politics of competitive individualism, popular capitalism, 'enterprise culture' and low taxes. The Labour vote, by contrast, retreated back into its historical heartlands in the industrial-urban north and Scotland.

However, at the same time as regional inequalities have grown, producing a broad North-South divide in the process, intra-regional disparities have also increased. In every region, whether in the south or the north, local socio-economic inequalities have widened in recent years. In the south, major differences have emerged between the new buoyant areas of high-tech and service sector expansion, and the previously prosperous but now less dynamic towns that were associated with the manufacturing growth of the 1960s and early 1970s. In the north, while the old industrial towns have suffered the brunt of deindustrialization, the major provincial cities and those towns less formerly dependent on manufacturing appear to have been launched on a new service-based wave of growth and regeneration, although as the recession of the early 1990s demonstrated, contrary to what is often assumed, services are far from immune from sharp cyclical downturns. While the majority of the nation's 'boom towns' are in fact in the southern half of the country (Champion and Green, 1987, 1989), and thus part of the North-South divide, nevertheless marked 'north-north' and 'south-south' divides have become distinctive features of the contemporary space economy.

A further local dimension of the increased unevenness of economic development over the past decade and a half has occurred within the nation's major cities. In many ways the metropolitan areas highlight the economic and social dualisms that the national restructuring process has produced. The slump of the early 1980s intensified the economic and social malaise of many inner city areas, leaving them with some of the worst problems of unemployment, poverty and industrial dereliction to be found anywhere in the country. Then, during the subsequent economy recovery from the early 1980s to the end of the decade, a rapid boom in property development–helped by rising rentals and increased government spending and incentives directed at urban regeneration–began to transform parts of metropolitan Britain. New office developments, especially aimed at financial and business services, together with new shopping and cultural complexes, have sprung up in all of the major cities. One measure of this boom in urban property development is that bank lending to property companies rose from less than £7 billion in 1985 to almost £40 billion by 1989, although much of the office space constructed subsequently proved difficult to fill as the economy went into recession in the early 1990s. What these new symbolic urban spaces have done is sharpen the socio-economic and environmental divides between different areas within the major cities.

At all these different levels, one common feature is discernible: a marked increase in the degree of spatial imbalance of economic growth and development. Not only are regional disparities much wider now, there is also much greater local variation within

Table 1.1.7. Inflationary Over-heating in the South and East

% Change
January 1983 to July 1989
in

	Overall cost of living	Average house prices
South East	96.9	203.6
East Anglia	74.8	202.4
South West	72.7	176.4
East Midlands	68.6	191.6
West Midlands	64.8	167.5
Yorkshire-Humberside	59.6	137.9
North West	52.4	117.7
North	45.9	123.1
Wales	63.5	154.6
Scotland	30.2	58.9
Northern Ireland	29.7	37.4
United Kingdom	69.0	158.0

Source: The Reward Group, Cost of Living: Regional Comparisons (Various)
Note: Cost of living is measured by the gross income required to maintain the same standard of living across the different regions. House prices refer to 'asking prices'. Both indices are averages across all socio-economic groups

all of the regions (Breheny, Hart and Hall, 1987; Champion and Green, 1987; SEEDS, 1987). It would certainly seem, as many argue, that economic development within the UK has become spatially more fragmented and differentiated (Cooke, 1989). Adherents of the post-Fordist and flexible specialization schools see this fragmentation as the logical outcome of the decentralization and reconcentration tendencies at work in the transition to flexible accumulation. Post-Fordist flexible accumulation, it is believed, is likely to lead to a patchwork of localized pockets of development because the organizational features of the new system make for the rise of locally specialized production and service networks. There is even talk of the (re)appearance of Marshallian-type 'industrial districts', new growth areas based on local clusters of small and medium-sized firms (Hirst and Zeitlin, 1989). Exaggerated and over-enthusiastic though some of these prognoses are, the idea that the 'regional problem' has become inherently local in complexion and resolution has certainly permeated much recent policy thinking and practice (see CLES, 1990), as will be discussed below.

One undoubted consequence of the spatially imbalanced nature of economic restructuring and development in the UK over the past decade has been its adverse implications for the performance of the national economy and the process of macroeconomic management (Martin, 1989b). During the course of the 1980s, the concentration of economic growth in the south and east of the country fuelled a process of inflationary 'overheating', manifested by skill shortages, fast wage growth and a spiralling of land and house prices (Table 1.1.7). Although in one sense this inflationary pressure was the product of economic success, it was also partly manufactured by the Government's policies of tax reductions and relaxation of monetary controls. The Government nevertheless argued that rising costs and congestion in the south and east would trigger automatic market mechanisms which would diffuse that success to the rest of the country. While there has indeed been some decentralization of economic activity northwards, overall this has been limited and wholly insufficient to relieve the pressures associated with imbalanced renewal between the regions. The problem was that the rapid boom in the south and east strained the limits of supply there (Murray, 1988), setting in motion a wave of inflation that spread to the rest of country and which ultimately undermined the very economic renewal that the Thatcher Government claimed it had wrought. As national inflation increased so the Government was forced to dampen economic growth by a new round of deflationary interest rate rises. The result by the early 1990s was a government-induced downturn into another sharp recession, which unlike that of a decade earlier also hit the service and consumer economy of the south and east. The crucial point is that the increased regional imbalance that has emerged over the past decade or so has imparted an additional inflationary bias to the national economy. Indeed, in this as in other socio-economic welfare respects, the widening of regional disparities during the 1980s casts serious doubt on the Government's claim to have wrought a national economic miracle (Martin, 1991).

THE RECASTING OF REGIONAL POLICY

While the nature and the pattern of the regional problem have been changing, official regional policy has come under the most critical scrutiny and political pressure since it was introduced some sixty years ago. Even if some of the more optimistic estimates of the employment-creation impact of regional policy in the assisted areas during the 1960s and 1970s are accepted (see Moore, Rhodes and Tyler, 1986), by the close of the latter decade it had become clear that traditional regional policy was failing to halt the widening of disparities between the regions. Although this may have been due in part to the sharp cut in real spending on regional policy made by the 1974–79 Labour government, it also reflected the inherent limitations of traditional policy itself, with its preoccupation with manufacturing (which in employment terms was shrinking fast), its concern with regional industrial redistribution rather than development, and its lack of strategic direction or selectivity. In short, arguably never well specified or targeted, regional policy had failed to keep pace with the changing nature and pattern of the regional problem (Martin and Hodge, 1983; Townroe, 1986).

The Thatcher governments' attack on regional policy during the 1980s was, therefore, in one sense justified. The moves to make it more selective and cost-effective, to give much greater emphasis to the service sector, and to incorporate various small firm measures and advisory and consultancy assistance (H.M. Government, 1983, 1988), were certainly improvements. Unfortunately, however, all of these changes were made with the aim of further streamlining expenditure on regional assistance, which currently at under £600 million per annum is now less than half in real terms what it was in the early 1980s (Figure 1.1.1). This has had implications for the UK's access to assistance from the European Regional Development Fund, since much of the aid from the latter is conditional upon being matched by corresponding assistance from the UK government. Furthermore, the lack of a strategic direction to regional policy remained. Instead it was subsumed, like industrial policy in general, under the so-called Enterprise Initiative which was not concerned with shaping national and regional economic growth through some specified development strategy but rather with facilitating the operation of market forces as the means of fostering economic development in the regions (Darwin, 1990). Only a few members of the Thatcher governments seemed to appreciate that market forces are themselves a major source of regional imbalance, and that in the absence of intervention to reduce the enormous 'counter-regional subsidies' that flow to the south-eastern part of the country, the northern regions are likely to remain at a comparative disadvantage, and the south and east to continue to be a potential source of inflationary overheating (Martin, 1989b).

The 'rolling back' of regional policy over the past decade has been accompanied by a distinct shift towards urban assistance, which now makes up half of the government

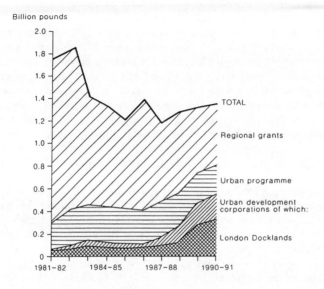

Billion pounds

TOTAL

Regional grants

Urban programme

Urban development
corporations of which:

London Docklands

1981−82   1984−85   1987−88   1990−91

Source: Department of the Environment. Government's expenditure plans

Figure 1.1.1: Government Assistance to Depressed Areas (In real terms, 1990–1991 prices)

aid that goes to depressed areas (Figure 1.1.1). Officially, urban aid is not regarded as part of regional policy, but in reality the expansion of the urban aid programme is part of a general trend towards *central government localism* in area assistance. The urban development corporations, the urban-based enterprise zones, the urban task force areas, and other related schemes introduced in the 1980s, are all locally based. And within regional aid itself, the accent on selectivity of individual projects and on individual enterprise, together with the spatial fragmentation of the map of assisted areas, also signal a shift towards policy localism.

At the same time, as central government regional policy has been restructured and slimmed down, so other locally-based alternatives have sprung up to fill the policy vacuum (Campbell, 1990). Thus the 1980s saw a wave of *local government localism*, a proliferation of economic development initiatives and schemes by local authorities right across the country (Morison, 1988; Bennett and Krebs, 1991). Almost all local authorities now play some sort of active role in promoting and restructuring their local economies, albeit with very limited financial resources. Although they continue to compete for footloose capital by offering financial and other inducements, local authorities have turned increasingly to nurturing indigenous development, by promoting new and small firms and establishing business and science parks, technology transfer centres, enterprise boards and even venture capital funds, often in partnership with the private sector. This new demand-side orientated, entrepreneurial form of local authority economic intervention contrasts quite sharply with local authorities traditional supply-side approach of site provision, cost subsidies, land use zoning and so on.

Alongside this movement, there has also been a surge in *corporate sector localism*. Business has developed a sense of corporate social responsibility, of returning a (small) proportion of profits back into the economic, social and environmental development of the local community. There are now around 300 local enterprise agencies throughout the UK sponsored by national and local firms, and represented by the umbrella organization Business in the Community. Another form of social-economic localism is the burgeoning *voluntary sector* of local community self-help and support bodies, covering everything from unemployment counselling to derelict land reclamation. These private and voluntary sector initiatives form a sort of 'shadow state', stimulated by the lack of governmental response to local socio-economic problems but simultaneously praised by the government as exemplifying the important role local self-help can play. As all of these different forms of local economic intervention multiply it is becoming increasingly difficult to talk of 'regional policy' in any conventional sense.

This shift to an expanding array of local initiatives does have undoubted potential advantages. A local approach allows policies and schemes to be tailored to the specific problems, needs and possibilities of the local area. It also means local interests and resources can be harnessed in the most effective way. And, in principle, it imparts a more democratic and accountable character to local development. But, on the other hand, policy localism has limitations. The progressive internationalization of economic activity, referred to earlier, raises questions about the meaning of the local economy, and hence about the scope and effectiveness of local policy intervention. Equally important, the proliferation of local initiatives and schemes has already reached a point where problems of duplication, integration and co-ordination abound. The case for some sort of regional development agency or body, capable of taking the broader regional view while linking and harmonizing different locally-based policies, is therefore a strong one. The Conservative Party is not attracted to this idea, but both Labour and the Liberal Democrats have promoted regional agencies as part of their political manifestos. A re-organization of local government in the near future, following the Conservative victory in the 1992 general election, it is now a strong possibility.

Perhaps as never before, regional policy has become caught up in the debate between the parties over economic management more generally (Martin, 1989c). The debate over macro-economic policy, in turn, reflects not only different political ideologies but also different interpretations of the changing nature of the UK economy. The restructuring of the economy and the debate over regional policy are thus inextricably linked. The one clear fact must surely be that a more balanced form of regional development is crucial for national growth and renewal over the coming decade, and that it will not occur through the market alone but requires an active and reconstructed regional policy.

ABOUT THIS BOOK

These issues form the context and motivation for this book. The aim of this collection of essays commissioned by the Regional Studies Association is to document the changing nature and challenge of regional development in Britain and Ireland in the final decade of this century. It updates the enquiry carried out by the Association in the early 1980s (Regional Studies Association, 1983). Much has happened to the British regions since that earlier study, which was itself a reaction to processes of regional change in the 1970s. The economic and spatial restructuring that occurred during the 1980s, and which is continuing into the 1990s, has far exceeded that envisaged in the earlier review, and requires a new enquiry and assessment. The present study also differs from its predecessor in being far more comprehensive, both in terms of its regional analyses and its systematic coverage of the various dimensions and processes of change. Based on contributions by leading experts in their respective fields, it provides one of the most detailed and up-to-date surveys of contemporary British regional development.

The next part of the book documents the changes and challenges facing the individual regions of the British Isles. These regional profiles, written by local analysts with close knowledge of their regions, are grouped into five chapters covering southern England (the South East, East Anglia and the South West), the two Midlands regions, northern England (the North West, the North, and Yorkshire-Humberside), the two 'national' regions of Wales and Scotland, and finally Northern Ireland and Eire. No rigid analytical framework was imposed on these regional studies, so as to allow authors to highlight each region's specific trends, problems and policy issues.

The rest of the book adopts a more systematic stance, and examines the differential regional impact and implications of a range of processes and structural developments linked to those outlined earlier in this chapter. Part III looks at the regional dimensions of changes in industrial activity and organization, of new technologies, and of the evolving nature of employment. Part IV considers the impress of national economic and social policy developments on the regions, including infrastructure investment policy, training policies, the social welfare system, housing policy and public services. Part V shifts the discussion to the scope for and limits of specific policies for the regions and cities in the 1990s. The book concludes with some suggestions on what are likely to be the emerging themes of regional development and policy over the next decade.

REFERENCES

Bennett, R.J. (ed) (1990) *Decentralization, Local Government and Markets: Towards a Post-Welfare Agenda.* Oxford: Clarendon.

Bennett, R.J. and Krebs, G. (1991) *Local Economic Development.* London: Bellhaven.

Breheny, M., Hall, P. and Hart, D. (1987) *Northern Lights: A Development Agenda for the North in the 1990s.* Preston and London: Derrick, Wade and Waters.

Campbell, M. (ed) (1990) *Local Economic Policy.* London: Cassell.

Champion, A.G. and Green, A.E. (1987) 'The Booming Towns of Britain: The Geography of Economic Performance in the 1980s.' *Geography,* 72, 97–108.

Champion, A.G. and Green, A.E. (1989) 'Local Economic Differentials and the North-South Divide'. in Lewis J. and Townsend, A.R. (eds), (1989) *The North-South Divide: Regional Change in Britain in the 1980s.* Liverpool: Paul Chapman Publishing. 61–96.

CLES (1990) *Reconverting the Regions, Local Work* (New Series) No. 20. Manchester: Centre for Local Economic Studies.

Cooke, P. (ed) (1989) *Localities: The Changing Face of Urban Britain.* London: Unwin Hyman.

Cooke, P. (1991) *Back to the Future: Postmodernity and Locality.* London: Unwin Hyman.

Darwin, J.(1990) *The Enterprise Society: Regional Policy and National Strategy.* Manchester: Centre for Economic Studies.

Hall, P. (1985) 'Technology, Space and Society in Contemporary Britain', in Castells, M. (ed), *High Technology, Space and Society.* Beverly Hills: Sage. 41–52.

Hirst, P. and Zeitlin, J. (eds) (1989) *Reversing Industrial Decline? Industrial Structure and Policy in Britain and her Competitors.* Oxford: Berg.

H.M. Government (1983) *Regional Industrial Development,* CMND 911. London: HMSO.

H.M. Government (1988) *DTI: The Department for Enterprise,* Department of Trade and Industry, CMND 278. London: HMSO.

Lash, S. and Urry, J. (1987) *The End of Organized Capitalism.* Cambridge: Polity Press.

Lewis J. and Townsend, A.R. (eds) (1989) *The North-South Divide: Regional Change in Britain in the 1980s.* Liverpool: Paul Chapman Publishing.

Martin, R.L. (1988a) 'Industrial Capitalism in Transition: The Contemporary Reorganization of the British Space Economy', in Massey, D. and Allen, J. (eds), *Uneven Re-Development: Cities and Regions in Transition.* London: Hodder and Stoughton. 202–231.

Martin, R.L. (1988b) 'The Political Economy of Britain's North-South Divide', *Transactions of the Institute of British Geographers'*, 13, 389–414. Reprinted in Lewis J. and Townsend, A.R. (eds), (1989) *The North-South Divide: Regional Change in Britain in the 1980s.* Liverpool: Paul Chapman Publishing. 20–60.

Martin, R.L. (1989a) 'The Reorganization of Regional Theory: Alternative Perspectives on the Changing Capitalist Space Economy', *Geoforum*, 20, 2, 187–201.

Martin, R.L. (1989b) 'Regional Imbalance as Consequence and Constraint in National Economic Renewal', in Green, F. (ed) *The Restructuring of the UK Economy.* Hemel Hempstead: Harvester-Wheatsheaf. 80–97.

Martin, R.L. (1989c) 'The New Economics and Politics of Regional Restructuring: The British Experience', in Albrechts, L., Moulaert, F., Roberts, P. and Swyngedouw, E. (eds), *Regional Policy at the Crossroads: European Perspectives.* London: Jessica Kingsley Publishers. 27–51.

Martin, R.L. (1991) 'Has the British Economy Been Transformed? Critical Reflections on the Policies of the Thatcher Era', in Cloke, P. (ed), *Policy and Change in Thatcher's Britain: A Critical Perspective.* Oxford: Pergamon, 123–158.

Martin, R.L. and Hodge, J.S.C. (1983) 'The Reconstruction of British Regional Policy, I: The Crisis of Conventional Practice', *Government and Policy*, 1, 1, 133–152.

Massey, D. and Allen, J. (eds), (1988) *Uneven Re-Development: Cities and Regions in Transition.* London: Hodder and Stoughton.

Moore, B., Rhodes, J. and Tyler, P. (1986) *The Effects of Government Regional Policy.* London: HMSO.

Morison, H. (1987) *The Regeneration of Local Economies.* Oxford: Clarendon.

Murray, R. (1988) *Crowding Out: Boom and Crisis in the South East.* Stevenage: South East Economic Development Strategy.

Murray, R. (1989) 'Fordism and Post-Fordism', in Hall, S. and Jacques, M. (eds), *New Times: The Changing Face of Politics in the 1990s.* London: Lawrence and Wishart. 38–53.

Regional Studies Association (1983) *Report of an Enquiry into Regional Problems in the United Kingdom.* Norwich: GeoBooks.

SEEDS (1987) *South-South Divide.* Stevenage: South East Economic Development Strategy.

Smith, D. (1989) *North and South: Britain's Economic, Social and Political Divide.* Harmondsworth: Penguin.

Townroe, P.M. (1986) 'Regional Economic Development Policy in a Mixed Economy and a Welfare State', *Journal of Regional Policy*, 3, 355–372.

PART II

REGIONAL PROFILES

CHAPTER 2

SOUTHERN ENGLAND

2.1

The South East

Andrew Church, Ian Cundell, Michael Hebbert, Andrew McCoshan,
Derek Palmer, Ricardo Pinto, Al Rainnie, John Sellgren, Peter Wood

INTRODUCTION

The South East has been reviewed as an engine of growth, the benefits from which 'ripple out' into other regions. Regional policy and other mechanisms have sought to transfer from the core to the periphery. It was assumed that the core would continue to generate further growth. In recent years this view has been questioned, and greater attention has been paid to the need to stimulate development within the South East. Yet there still remain within a generally prosperous region areas of considerable disadvantage.

In addition to this, there has been a growing awareness of the negative externalities of excessive and long-standing growth within the South East. These factors are inter-related and manifest themselves in a number of ways, for example in congested transport networks, shortages of housing, pressure on social welfare services, and in labour shortages.

STRATEGIC PLANNING IN THE SOUTH EAST

The scale and complexity of the South East, more than any other Standard Region, require a framework of strategic guidance against which changes in particular aspects of national policy, and within particular sub-regions, can be judged. Such a view, of course, was taken almost for granted between the 1940s and the 1970s. It is still held by most county authorities in the region, judging by the representations made regularly to the Government by the London and South East Regional Planning Conference (SERPLAN), and is even supported by many private sector developers, for whom the current planning environment of the South East is a great cause of uncertainty.

The physical planning problems over which a strategic view might have some influence, such as housing supply, transport investment, or major land use changes in both urban and rural areas, have all remained without any consistent blueprint for change. Exhortation, basically to 'let the market decide', is all that has been on offer. The result has been an endless series of local battles, for example over the future of the green belt, the construction of commuter villages, the alignment of the Channel Tunnel links, or the belated insertion of adequate infrastructure to support London's Docklands development.

The subordination of local government to national direction has also had a particularly marked effect in the South East. This is partly through the loss of the Greater London Council (GLC), and the resources it commanded for London, but also because of the localism that has inevitably resulted from imposed shortages of funding. The priority given to London-wide or regional issues has inevitably become lower.

Meanwhile, the 'Rest of the South East' (ROSE) has been growing too quickly for the liking of many of its residents. The fate of the M25 has perhaps epitomised its dilemma most strikingly. The problem of the rest of the national economy means that too much reliance is being placed on the development of this area. Thus not only is London's legacy of problems now worse than a decade ago, but the environmental and economic impacts of overheating elsewhere in the region have become increasingly significant. As environmental issues come to the fore in the 1990s, the political pressures to constrain and redirect developments will certainly rise.

It can be seen that central government's role has been willfully erratic. The Department of Transport's unsubtle combination of major road-building schemes with real fare increases for public transport users have struck most severely in the South East, which has historically had the most balanced and environmentally friendly transport system of any British region. Some of the Department of Environment's policies, most notably the introduction of the B1 land use class and also the boosterism of its London Docklands Development Corporation (LDDC), have been at odds with the attempts of local planning authorities to balance development demand and environmental protection. The completion of the M25 in 1987 opened up hundreds of square miles of farmland around the built-up edge of London. One interesting new notion to arise in recent years has been the generation of villages and small towns as a policy alternative to urban infilling. These are to be built by the private sector on green field sites. Now that the agricultural surplus has undermined traditional assumptions of farmland conservation, it seems very likely that a sprinkling of new settlements will materialise around the outer South East.

Table 2.1.1 Labour Force in the South East (000s)

	1980	*1981*	*1995*	*2000*
South East	8617	9296	9472	9661
Greater London	4182	4247	4204	4176
Rest of South East	4335	5052	5260	5485

Source: Cambridge Econometrics, 1990

HOUSING

Between 1981 and 1988, the South East region, with by far the largest proportion of the housing stock in the UK, grew in population by 0.3 per cent per annum above the UK average. Owner-occupation in the region increased sharply from 58 per cent in 1981 to 67.5 per cent by 1989. In the same period, the average new dwelling cost has risen from £ 30,000 to £64,000, by far the most expensive in any region. This is naturally reflected in the Building Society borrowers' average dwelling price which stood at £59,600 in 1987 (£14,900 more than the next highest region, the South West).

Between 1981 and 1989, the percentage of local authority housing in the region slumped from 26.8 per cent to 20.9 per cent, representing an absolute reduction in this tenure. The main factor was the Government's policy of creating a 'property owning democracy' through the Right to Buy legislation and its associated discounts in which the South East has proved to be the most attractive region for tenants to purchase. The private rented sector has continued its protracted decline which dates back to the early 1900s. Between 1981 and 1989, the sector shrunk from 12.3 per cent to 8.3 per cent despite government policy and efforts to reverse the trend.

Housing Associations have acquired a key role in providing housing for those in need. However, the sector is small (containing 3% of the national housing stock, as opposed to the 25% in the local authority sector) and severe doubts remain over its ability to expand at the pace and to the extent necessary to meet future demand and needs. This situation is evident in the relatively slow growth of the Housing Associ-ation stock which rose from 3 per cent to only 3.3 per cent of the total housing stock in the South East in the 1980s.

PERSONAL INCOMES AND SOCIAL WELFARE

Analysis of data on national levels of personal income shows that the South East has continued to lead national income levels (Table 1.1.2). It is evident that earnings are up to 16 per cent higher than the national average (Table 1.1.5). However, perhaps more significant are the figures showing the variation between Greater London and ROSE where in 1984 personal incomes were 22 per cent above the national average and by 1987 had grown to 25.4 per cent above. It is suggested by the London Chamber of Commerce (1989) that a slow-down in earnings growth in the City occurred from 1988, and a decline in population in London is estimated to have slowed slightly the growth in consumer expenditure, thus contrasting with the national trend. None the less, the South East leads UK per capita consumer expenditure.

The Family Expenditure Survey (Table 1.1.5) shows that for the year 1987–88 weekly household incomes in the South East were the largest nationally, at £339 per household. This statistic is partly produced by the predominance of very high income households (30.9% having a weekly household income of £400 or more) and relatively smaller proportions in the lower income brackets. However, results from the same survey for 1980–81 and 1987–88 reveal that the differential between average household incomes in the South East and the region with the lowest household income has narrowed.

THE LABOUR MARKET IN THE SOUTH EAST

With around nine million members of the labour force in 1989, the South East is responsible for approximately one-third of total UK employment. Between 1983 and 1988 the area witnessed a 1 million increase in the number of jobs, raising employment levels by around 10 per cent, although a large proportion of the increase consisted of low paid part-time work which amounted to significantly less than 1 million full-time equivalents. However, by 1990 there were signs that the period of growth had come to an end, with the national rise in the underlying unemployment trend being primarily centred on the south of England and East Anglia. Furthermore, concentration of rising levels of company insolvencies in the South East raised further questions concerning the region's job-generation capacity.

In 1987 around 18 per cent of employees were found to be in manufacturing industry, a figure that falls to approximately 14 per cent for Greater London, compared with a national average of 24 per cent. Between March 1988 and March 1989 there was a further 3.7 per cent drop in manufacturing employment in London and the South East, leaving 77 per cent of employees working in the service sector. This figure is expected to rise to 80 per cent by the turn of the century.

Changes in industrial structure and labour process developments are leading to an increase in the demand for managers, professional groups and associated professionals, but also to the removal of complete layers of managerial hierarchy. Demographic changes are expected to increase competition for school-leavers and stimulate employment policies aimed at increasing the participation rates of women returners, people with disabilities and workers from minorities. Labour market difficulties are likely to further accelerate the relocation of organisations (or parts thereof) out of London in particular and out of the region in general.

Between 1987 and 1995 London has the potential to demand 120,000 new jobs, against an expected rise in the city's resident labour force of less than 40,000. Coupled with net migration out of London and house price related difficulties of immigration, current recruitment difficulties will gain in intensity. Employment possibilities for those suffering unemployment, low pay and/or discrimination will be complicated by the geographical and sectoral unevenness of job generation. Manufacturing employment is expected to continue its precipitate decline to less than 9 per cent by the year 2000. Employment is expected to fall in practically every sector except 'other services'. Growth in the 1990s is likely to be concentrated in Inner London, but principally will act to reinforce existing recruitment difficulties for professional staff. The much heralded Docklands development has failed to deliver appropriate employment opportunities to local communities, despite an optimistic scenario which forecast 90,000 office jobs and 25,000 non-office jobs arising from it.

Within ROSE, despite the rhetoric of deindustrialisation, boom counties such as Hertfordshire in 1987 had a higher than national average reliance on manufacturing industry. Of central importance are defence and defence-related sectors. However, changes in the nature and extent of defence expenditure as well as in the nature of weapons and their production systems, and a cyclical downturn in electronics threaten to undermine the health of the region's so-called 'corridors of high-tech development'. To the year 2000, ROSE can expect growth in business service, education and health, and other services. The growth in business services is partly the result of decentralisation from London to suburban centres and to key towns in the rest of the region.

In certain parts of the South East, local authorities have needed to address the problems of high growth pressure, while not constraining indigenous growth in a detrimental manner. In part, the incidence of central government resources has been available to assist some of the most deprived areas of the London metropolitan area. Certain boroughs have been eligible for support under the Inner Urban Areas Act 1978, the Derelict Land Grant, and Urban Programme.

Given the depth and complexity of the labour market problems facing the South East, questions must be raised concerning the ability of the new locally based and private sector dominated Training and Enterprise Councils (TECs) to respond adequately to the challenge facing them. In particular, though the labour market conditions of the 1990s will demand the implementation of extensive Equal Opportunities policies coupled with a fundamental examination of work organisation systems, there is little evidence that these exercises are being undertaken in anything other than a partial and fragmented fashion.

The South East, and London in particular, raise important questions for TECs. At the outset, existing networks of organised business are likely to prove crucial to TECs' initial success but the tradition of business organisation is patchy, both geographically (see Bennett, McCoshan and Sellgren, 1989) and by industrial sector. Because TECs will draw heavily upon public sector resources, their success will also depend on Local Education Authority experience in tailoring education and training to business needs, which is similarly varied.

A problem more peculiar to the South East is the existence of multiple and overlapping labour markets. In London this difficulty is being tackled through the emergence of a central core-radiating wedge structure based on groupings of boroughs. In the ROSE, TECs are being based on counties or parts of counties. This arrangement represents a trade-off between the competing demands of local delivery, the labour market and local provision and overcomes some of the problems inherent in a complex industrial geography. However, the question of how the individual TECs will interface with one another is going to become increasingly important in the South East.

TRANSPORTATION

Strong economic growth in the South East has generated a rapid increase in traffic in the region. All modes have experienced growth; although this has been most notable in air travel, port throughput and road freight, leading to worsening congestion, especially in London, and hence to higher costs for business. Yet the need for a good transport infrastructure is of growing importance to the economy. From 1991 British business will have to compete from the geographic periphery of the Single European Market. The transport network in the South East will be of central importance; not only is the region the largest in the UK, comprising 30 per cent of the nation's population, but it will also provide a major transit route to the Continent. In addition to the Channel Tunnel, due for opening in June 1993, the region contains the UK's largest commercial seaport, London, while Dover is the world's largest international passenger port. Furthermore, the major airports (Heathrow and Gatwick) are central features of the regional economy. And Stansted, London's third airport, is already the fifth largest in the UK.

The Government has recognised the need for more infrastructure expenditure. Expansion of both the road and rail infrastructure is taking place but much controversy surrounds the balance. While a greater commitment to rail infrastructure has become evident, much expenditure is allocated merely for the replacement of ageing stock. No commitment has been made to publicly fund a high speed rail line from London to the Channel Tunnel; and subsidies to Network South East are being withdrawn. Thus further investment will depend on raising revenue from higher fare income. However, the recent slowing of growth has jeopardised several much needed proposed developments, such as new rolling stock. While the forthcoming construction of the Jubilee Line extension will improve access to London's growth area in the Docklands, this will not reduce congestion on existing lines or on the roads.

Congestion in London and the South East is expected to worsen. Since the abolition of the GLC, the tenuous link between land use and strategic transportation planning has been broken. SERPLAN lacks the authority to fill the vacuum. Delays in the planning system and capacity in the construction industry will also impede the provision of new infrastructure.

Since no new airport is to be built in the South East, it is vital that full use is made of the existing resources. Better surface links are needed, especially to Heathrow with the construction of the link to Paddington. Air space can be better utilised by improving terminal facilities to cater for larger planes, for example, by constructing Terminal Five at Heathrow. Runways must also be developed, with the extension of London City Airport's runway and a decision taken on whether to build a second runway at Gatwick or Stansted or a feeder runway at Heathrow.

Traffic management in urban areas needs to be combined with traffic calming measures and improvements to arterial and strategic routes. But congestion is likely to worsen, at least in the immediate future. Demand management needs to be seriously considered and road pricing experiments undertaken to evaluate the potential for reducing congestion and bringing much needed improvements to the environment.

COMMERCIAL PROPERTY

Since 1983 the South East has experienced a property boom as spectacular as any in its history. Whether this boom will turn into an equally spectacular bust is an issue preoccupying many analysts. Analysis of commercial property and regional analysis are, almost by definition, on different wavelengths. Commercial property (the major providers of accommodation for business and, therefore, for jobs) should be at the heart of strategic planning.

Two recent experiences in Central London illustrate the problems presented. The regeneration of London's Docklands was initially seen as being low density and industry led, and the transport planning reflected this (the Light Railway and the Red Brick Road). There was no awareness of the fundamental changes in working practices and conditions about to be sparked off in the City and how these could spill over into Docklands. Whatever research LDDC and government carried out did not identify this. However, just a couple of miles away the developers of the highly successful Broadgate complex sponsored a large body of research not just into the changing local economy and its effect on occupier requirements, but also into the relationships between buildings and people and the local environment. So successful have they been that Hackney Council are said to want the scheme expanded. The same developers did a similarly thorough job at the Stockley Business Park near Heathrow and are using the same approach at King's Cross.

Those issues are being addressed, but only partially. The London Planning and Advisory Committee (LPAC), for instance, has suggested that London should be allowed to 'build up to capacity' for office development, and private sector analysis is tackling some aspects of the problem. But even LPAC has made no real attempt at defining capacity and this must be the next step. Much current discussion about commercial property in the South East is concerned with debating the relative merits of architectural styles or of green belt preservation. However, unless there is a clear understanding of the processes which serve the produce changes in demand in a strategic context, such local discussions will be of little consequence.

Lessons of the London Docklands

The history of London Docklands in the 1980s is well known. Over 1 billion of London Docklands Development Corporation (LDDC) public expenditure (plus another 333 million from land receipts) combined with the national property boom, the credit led growth in owner occupation and the process of industrial restructuring were able to produce an unprecedented spate of physical redevelopment. By 1989 11,000 homes mainly for owner occupation and 0.81 million square metres of commercial and industrial floorspace had been built. Supporters of the development praise the scale of private investment, the massive influx of additional jobs and residents, the new public image of the area and the role office developments like Canary Wharf will play in maintaining London as a leading financial centre. At the same time critics dismiss Docklands as an office location and highlight the property company bankruptcies, the 75 per cent of additional jobs that are transfers from other locations, the heavily congested transport system, the lack of accountability and democracy, the continued loss of industrial jobs, and the 8355 registered homeless and 52,000 unemployed in the five East London boroughs.

The planning lessons are numerous. No strategic perspective was ever developed which related office development in Docklands to that elsewhere, a fact for which certain developers are now paying the price. At the local level the lack of a planned approach to architecture meant that the early intentions of creating an integrated modern Venice based on the water of the docks remain dreams. Predictably, the trickle-down of benefits to local residents has not occurred on any significant scale.

Despite the construction of the Docklands Light Railway, the public and private transport system in Docklands is inadequate. The LDDC and the Department of Transport are proposing to spend £1 billion on public transport and £2.5 billion on roads in and around Docklands. A lack of planning has created extra direct and hidden costs as a result of the disruption while an operational system is upgraded. Consequently the needs of the area and its developers have been given a greater priority than the needs of the 1.2 million people who commute into Central London.

The overall lesson for local planning seems to have been the necessity for consultation and accountability, combined with a specified social remit to ensure that local residents benefit from public sector spending on urban regeneration. Strategically, large scale redevelopment must be planned in relation to the surrounding city. The failure to do this produced negative externalities for Docklands and for London as a whole.

CONCLUSION

Underlying the range of problems currently facing the South East are its future economic prospects. The impacts of intensified European developments are likely to have particular consequences for the South East. The degree of investment needed to maintain, let alone restore, the infrastructure base of the region is likely to be very high. There is as yet no indication that government will be willing to meet this cost. As Britain moves into a more open European market so increasingly localities will be competing to attract capital investment.

The continuing polarisation of the work-force between affluent employees in secure employment and the unemployed together with those employed in low paid jobs is likely to cause increased social segregation within the region. Skill shortages in key sectors, such as construction, repair and maintenance, new technology occupations, and education, coupled with the relatively high costs of housing will increasingly widen the London conurbation commuting catchment. Alterations to fare structures appear likely to lead to increased costs for long-distance commuting. Both of these factors are likely to have national inflationary consequences.

In order to address some of the problems facing the South East there is a need to focus policy initiatives in certain key areas. There are evidently particular problems for training, and it is evident that the South East poses particular problems for the implementation of these measures. Unless these issues are addressed with some urgency, comparisons with practices elsewhere in Europe will become increasingly stark.

Within the South East the decline of manufacturing is likely to continue because of increasing costs of operation. In addition, changes to the Use Classes Order are likely to further displace small manufacturing units. Business and financial services that have grown strongly in recent years are also likely to stabilise or decline in London. Downturns in financial markets can produce rapid shedding of labour in this sector. Technical change, costs of operation, and labour shortages, are likely to crease movement of offices out of London to provincial areas or even to the continent.

There remains little prospect of a coherent approach to public transport provision in London, and little willingness to address the issue of the private car user. This will lead to increasing burdens upon businesses seeking to move goods around and through the region.

There are also potential opportunities in areas of development such as the lower Thames corridor. Development in this location may act as an effective counter to the west of London. A major opportunity exists for large scale strategic planning in this area.

The experience of Docklands has shown that the one-solution approach to the complex problems of the region cannot work. Developments need to be more sensitive to their 'externality' impacts on the local communities, and to the environment. Regional development planning involves anticipating, managing and negotiating such impacts. The abandonment of any attempt to do this in the 1980s has built a range of problems for the 1990s. The outlook does not appear to be optimistic for the South East. However, it is important to remember that the level of capital investment in the region cannot readily be relocated, and thus there will remain a strong interest in finding short-term solutions to the major problems on the part of private capital. It is, however, this 'short-termism' which is likely to prevail in the absence of strategic guidance.

REFERENCES

Bennett, R., McCoshan, A., and Sellgren, J. (1989) *TECs and VET: The practical requirements: organisation, geography and international comparison with the USA and Germany.* London School of Economics, Department of Geography Research papers.

Cambridge Econometrics (1990) *Regional Economic Prospects (update) June 1990.* Cambridge: Cambridge Econometrics.

London Chamber of Commerce (1989) *London's economy: trends and prospects into the 1990s.* London: LCC.

2.2

East Anglia

Peter Townroe

INTRODUCTION

East Anglia is the smallest region in mainland Britain in terms of population. Only Northern Ireland is smaller among the national listing of eleven Standard Regions. The three counties of Norfolk, Suffolk and Cambridgeshire together are also the most sparsely populated of the English regions. However, this region has also been the fastest growing in the country over the past decade, whether looked at in terms of employment, population or output.

The relatively rapid growth rates in the region, compared with national trends, brought East Anglia through the economic recession of the 1970s and early 1980s with unemployment rising to record post-war levels but with the underlying dynamic of growth unimpaired. The sources of growth in the region in the 1980s reach back two decades earlier, providing both structural conditions and a set of market forces that are still at work for the early nineties, and look set to sustain the present growth momentum.

Across the region, the extent of growth in the population in the next decade will depend upon the compromises achieved between developers, planning authorities and public pressure. The number of new houses will broadly determine the size of the resident population in ten years' time. The size and age mix of the population will in turn govern the size of the labour force. Given broadly national trends in productivity, growth in available labour will limit the growth of output in the regional economy. That said, and with an absence of a significant slow-down in the national economy, East Anglia looks set to continue to have the fastest growing regional economy in the United Kingdom over the next ten years.

THE GROWTH REGION OF THE 1980s

The large and richly decorated churches of Norfolk and Suffolk are a valued reminder of the prosperity that came with wool and the trade with the Low Countries in the medieval period. The major engineering works involved in the draining of the Fens in the mid-seventeenth century also point to the value that agriculture had for the regional economy in the past. Agricultural reformers and pioneers, such as Thomas Coke of Holkham in Norfolk, had national and indeed international influence at the end of the eighteenth century. Agricultural activities remained the major part of the economic base of the region up until the early part of the twentieth century. Growth in industries unrelated to agriculture was very limited throughout the nineteenth century. Even the coming of the railways served to link the agriculture of the region to the industrial cities of the nation, rather than to open up the region to industrial development.

By the 1930s, East Anglia had a regional economy that seemed to have been sidelined from the mainstream of the national economy. Population growth was relatively slow and agriculture was very depressed, lacking in incentives to invest in land improvements and in new technology. Such industrial development as there was had largely sprung from the base of the agricultural craft skills and the agricultural engineering industry, together with local services.

The Second World War provided a considerable boost to the regional economy. Not only did the market for agricultural output stabilise and then expand but also, as a glance at the current 1:50,000 scale Ordnance Survey maps will demonstrate, a huge programme of airfield construction commenced. The legacy of this activity remains today, in the large bases of both the Royal Air Force and the United States Air Force in the region.

By the mid 1950s the principal cities of the region seemed to their city fathers to have stable and secure economies. Each had a relatively healthy mixture of prosperous local industrial companies and each fulfilled a role as a sub-regional trading and service centre. But for many second line centres the future did not look so secure. New competition was eating away at their industrial base and the flow of investment going into similar sizes of settlement in the Home Counties around London seemed unattracted to East Anglia. Help then arrived, in the shape of what was then the London County Council, looking to use the 1952 Town Development Act to promote house building and decentralisation, in order to ease the housing demand pressures in the metropolis.

The Town Development Act schemes of the London County Council were concentrated in East Anglia although there were others in what is now called the Outer South East (e.g. Basingstoke, Andover, Aylesbury, Bletchley). They were complementary to the ring of New Towns around London, which were designated in the late 1940s. The schemes in the region included Kings Lynn, Thetford, Huntingdon, St Ives, Bury St Edmunds, Haverhill and Sudbury. With forecasts of severe pressures of population growth in the South East region, these schemes were nearly joined by a major expansion of Ipswich under the 1946 New Towns Act. This proposal was not implemented but one of the other four major towns in the region, Peterborough, was launched onto a major expansion under a New Town Development Corporation. This has more than doubled the population of Peterborough to over 200,000 within 20 years.

The thrust given to the regional economy by these major public sector investments continues today. The growth of these towns, initially with both companies and households moving out from London, has helped to change the economic base of the region. It still provides a dynamic to the growth of the manufacturing sector of the regional economy that surprises many observers from elsewhere. The manufacturing labour force in the region grew from 120,000 in 1965 to 188,000 in 1989, at a time when employment nationally in this sector was declining.

Through the 1970s and 1980s the overall industrial mix of the East Anglia regional economy has developed on a favourable trajectory. The sectoral pattern of employment follows the national breakdown fairly closely. Those sectors that have been growing strongly nationally have been becoming relatively more important in the region. Two specific examples illustrate this.

One is the reinforcement given to the local banking, insurance and finance sectors on the back of national growth in employment and output by the decentralisation of offices from London. Examples of moves of parts of large companies from London include Barclays Bank to Peterborough, Guardian Royal Exchange and Willis Faber to Ipswich, the Sedgwick Group to Norwich; and, in a slightly different category, Her Majesty's Stationery Office to Norwich and the head office of Thomas Cook and a major part of the Passport Office to Peterborough.

Another is the fillip given to the widespread capability in the region in both the hardware and the software of the electronics and computing applications industry by what has come to be called 'The Cambridge Phenomenon' (Segal, 1985). This is the spin-out in and around Cambridge of over 400 small firms over the past 15 years both from laboratories of the university and from government funded research institutes in and around the city (the Computer Aided Design Centre, established in 1969, in particular). These small firms have now been joined by a number of outposts of large established British and internationally-based companies (see review by Keeble, 1989). What has been happening around Cambridge is part of a general strength in the region in what might be termed advanced non-aerospace engineering.

The research capability in electronics in the region has also been strengthened by the presence, since 1975, of the British Telecom research and technology division at Martlesham Heath, just outside Ipswich. Of the 3600 employees, 47 per cent are graduate engineers; and about £55m a year is put into the local economy through contracts, tax revenues and salaries.

Further support for the engineering capacity of the region over the past two decades has come from the stimulus of the development of the gas industry of the Southern North Sea, based in Great Yarmouth. This has been mainly in the equipment and instrumentation areas. Fabrication activity of modules for the drilling rigs and the production platforms has also been important.

Port activity in both Yarmouth and Lowestoft has been sustained by the North Sea gas industry. However the main growth in port tonnage has come at Felixstowe, the largest container port in the United Kingdom, with a fourfold increase in container throughput since 1979; and at Ipswich, although here less than one-fifth the size of Felixstowe. A scheme to build a major extension to port capacity at Yarmouth has not found the necessary finance, but large-scale investment is continuing at Felixstowe, Ipswich and Kings Lynn.

Behind the specifics of the Town Development Act schemes already referred to and strong growth in particular industrial and commercial sectors in the region lies the general benefit to the region of what has been termed the urban-rural shift or 'counter-urbanisation' (see Champion, 1989). Nationally, over the past 40 years or so, the United Kingdom, like other major industrialised nations, has experienced a shift in the trend of its population geography. Households have both led and followed employers away from the largest cities. Between 1951 and 1981 the six large conurbations in Great Britain lost 20 per cent of their working age groups, while small towns and rural areas gained 20 per cent. This shift in population was not just a decentralisation to increase the flow of metropolitan commuters. Of the over two million manufacturing jobs lost nationally between 1951 and 1981, three-quarters were in the conurbations. Many small towns and rural areas, including those in East Anglia, actually gained manufacturing jobs. Overall, employment in East Anglia grew by 38 per cent between 1971 and 1989.

Both push and pull factors lie behind the urban-rural shift trends. The relative significance of the different factors is much debated. However, from the perspective of East Anglia it is possible to point to five factors which have encouraged both house-holds and companies to migrate into the region, largely decentralising from Greater London. These same factors have then assisted companies in their growth once here:

1. The availability of land, with planning permission, for both housing and factory development (including land for subsequent expansion).
2. The relative price of this land and of property in general compared with both inner and outer London and the inner Home Counties.

3. An improving transportation infrastructure, providing fast links back to London by road and rail, with investment also in East-West links and developing the major port of Felixstowe and air links from Norwich and Stansted.

4. Lower property tax rates; and generally lower labour costs in many occupational categories.

5. A quality of living environment that an increasing proportion of the work force seems to be seeking and for which households are prepared to accept relatively lower money incomes (even after allowing for lower housing expenditures).

The impact of these five factors in the region is seen in the recent population growth rates. Four features of the high rate of population increase stand out. First, with both low birth rates and low death rates by national standards, some 90 per cent of the increase can be put down to net inward migration. The migrants are attracted by commuting possibilities, by rural and coastal environments for retirement, and by the availability of local jobs in an uncongested environment. Second, the region is experiencing a growth in the number of residents aged over 75 at rates well above the national trend. Third, the inward movement is overwhelmingly to owner-occupied homes. Only 19 per cent of the region's housing stock is rented from local authorities or new towns compared with 26 per cent nationally. And finally there has been a relative geographical concentration of areas of high population growth within the region: in the Ouse Valley around Huntingdon (where the District Council area gained 18.2 per cent more residents between 1981 and 1988), in the Peterborough area, in the East Cambridgeshire District to the North and East of Cambridge, in West and North Norfolk, and in the coastal area of Suffolk.

Employment growth in the East Anglian regional economy in the past two decades has been broadly based. While reflecting national trends, such as the continuing fall in the significance of employment in agriculture and the rise in significance of producer services, there has been buoyancy in the region in sectors which have been relatively stagnant nationally. And within manufacturing, the relatively high proportion of foreign owned enterprises in the region when compared to all the English regions except the South East, has supported growth without any fears of the region becoming a branch plant economy. Notable also is the high rate of self-employment in the region. At 17.5 per cent of those economically active in 1990, it is three percentage points higher than the national average. The main consequence of the growth overall has been to bring both wages and household incomes up close to national average levels, and to contain unemployment somewhat below the national rate.

PRESSURES OF GROWTH

Throughout the past decade there have been strong pressures for development across the southern half of the region. However in much of Norfolk, in the Waveney Valley of Suffolk and in the Fenland region of Cambridgeshire there was active concern in the early 1980s at the high levels of unemployment and the low levels of job creating investment. After some political hesitation all three County Councils invested in economic development policies and co-operated with the Rural Development Commission to designate Rural Development Areas in order to draw in factory and workshop space investment by English Estates. All of the District Councils also, to a greater or lesser degree, have become involved in job creation policies and in linking the granting of planning permissions more closely with new jobs. Expenditure was £11m. in 1987/88. The Councils have also been involved in Enterprise Agencies, set up to help new small businesses, and they have co-operated with the East Anglia Tourist

Board (for example, in the Tourist Development Action Programme in Norwich, launched in 1988 and also involving the private sector).

Between 1979 and 1986 East Anglia maintained the second lowest regional unemployment rate in the United Kingdom, behind the South East, demonstrating the muted impact of the national economic recession on the region overall. However, the regional unemployment rate did rise to nearly 10 per cent in 1983 and at that time unemployment in places such as Lowestoft, Great Yarmouth, Cromer, Ely and March rose to above 15 per cent in the winter. Even in Norwich, the unemployment rate was still 9.6 per cent in 1987, at a time when it was only 5.6 per cent in Cambridge. The travel-to-work-area rates in the two cities in April 1990 were 4.7 per cent and 2.3 per cent.

By 1988 pressures of growth were being felt all across the region. The winter unemployment rates in Yarmouth and Lowestoft were down to single figures, and in areas across the southern parts of Cambridgeshire and Suffolk there were growing labour shortages. The recession was clearly over. Incomes were rising, participation rates were increasing, and house prices were showing some of the most rapid rates of increase in the whole country.

By 1990 this pressure had eased in the face of high interest rates. Unemployment was rising and the housing market had stagnated. But growth pressure remained to 1991. The conflicts within the region, between those looking to meet or to anticipate demand for new housing and for new industrial and commercial floorspace and those wishing to retain the superior environmental qualities to which they have become accustomed, are imperfectly mediated through the land use planning system. Co-ordination on the pace of new development rests with the regional office of the Department of the Environment (which is located outside the region, in Bedford), the three County Planning Authorities, and with the Standing Conference of East Anglian Local Authorities (SCEALA). The latter body has produced a Regional Strategy which has been endorsed by most of the local authorities in East Anglia and has been received into the Regional Planning Guidance of the Department of the Environment (SCEALA, 1989).

Growth in the region has brought with it not only rural, coastal and urban environmental concerns but also the standard worries about the parallel development of infrastructure and public services. The current road programme, after a lot of political pressure, is now providing by-passes on all of the significant bottlenecks on the major routes through the region: the A10, A11, A12, A45, A47 and A140. Many of these by-passes were designed as single carriageway roads however, much to local indignation. There is now an intention of the Department of Transport to dual these key routes throughout. The A1M1 link motorway, due for completion in 1992, will greatly ease road access across to the Midlands. Rail electrification has now reached Norwich and Cambridge as well as passing Peterborough on the East Coast mainline, and is being extended to Kings Lynn from Cambridge. Services on the cross-country routes have been greatly improved. The main concerns in the area of services remain the level of investment in water supply and sewerage and what is now only a trickle of public funded new housing, to complement the expanding owner-occupied sector. There is a concern that lack of low cost housing might stifle economic growth in some parts of the region.

Pressures of growth are strongest in South Cambridgeshire. This has resulted in severe labour shortages, intense congestion and house price inflation in Cambridge, and a subregional planning dilemma as to how to best accommodate at least part of the growth. In a study for the local authorities involved, the Department of Land Economy of the University proposed a dispersal strategy, possibly to involve six towns in the subregion (Department of Land Economy, 1989). Consortia of private developers have also proposed 'new villages' (Crow Green and Waterfenton) to the north of the city as a way of meeting the housing demand.

Growth in Cambridge has relevance for national economic prosperity as well as for the regional economy, given the cutting edge high technology involved in many of the new small firms. There is also a national interest involved in another major development, which although located just across the southern boundary of the region, will send ripples of development pressure across most of West Suffolk and South Cambridgeshire. This is Stansted Airport. The new terminal opened in 1991, the new rail link is in place, and up to eight million passengers are forecast to be passing through the airport each year by 1995.

THE FUTURE

When looked at alongside the other economic regions of the British Isles, it is difficult to foresee East Anglia having to accommodate major industrial structural changes over the next ten years, or to face dilemmas of national significance in providing for new housing and new commercial and industrial development. Sensitive local planning is what is called for. With that, both prosperity and the quality of life in the region will be enhanced if the 1991 forecasts from Cambridge Econometrics are broadly fulfilled. These envisage a growth rate in population and in the labour force of one per cent per annum between 1989 and the end of the century, and a growth rate of GDP per capita of 2.7 per cent per annum. The population will rise by some 280,000. East Anglia will continue to be the fastest growing region, closely paralleled by the South West.

The uncertainties facing the region are both positive and negative. The impact of 1992 should be positive, given the recent improvements in communications with other British regions as well as across the North Sea. And locally, the Channel Tunnel is not seen as a threat to these links. The urban-rural shift factors, as already noted, will continue to favour the region, perhaps with an extra push from the move to the Uniform Business Rate and the effect this will have on rating differentials between the South East region and East Anglia.

Negative uncertainties include further downward pressure on farm incomes as agricultural support policies become less generous (although only four per cent of employees in the region are involved in agriculture, forestry and fishing). Also, the closure of military airfields and reduction in defence and procurement as part of a general reduction in the defence budget are possible negative factors. Again, the impact of this would be relatively small (Rankin, 1989). Changing patterns of leisure demand have exercised traditional seaside resorts in the region, like Great Yarmouth, Lowestoft, Cromer and Hunstanton, but rising discretionary incomes of both domestic and international visitors should see relevant sectors of the regional economy facing a growing demand for tourist services.

While the future path of the East Anglian economy is dominated by the path of the national economy, with national economic growth the region has every reason to expect low levels of unemployment and rising real incomes in the next ten years. In aggregate terms, the net flow of in-migrants will not place existing households at a disadvantage in the labour market. And the broad industrial and commercial base of the regional economy will be able to ride any temporary set-backs that come from national economic changes while continuing to raise productivity with new investment.

REFERENCES

Champion, A.G. (ed) (1989). *Counterurbanisation: the Changing Pace and Nature of Population Deconcentration*, Edward Arnold, London.

Department of Land Economy (1989), *A Development Strategy for New Industrial Growth in the Cambridge Sub-Region*, Cambridge.

Gudgin, G. (ed) (1991), *Regional Economic Prospects: Analysis and Forecasts to the Year 2000*, Cambridge Econometrics Ltd., and the Northern Ireland Economic Research Centre.

Keeble, D. (1989), High technology industry and regional development in Britain: the case of the Cambridge phenomenon, *Environment and Planning C: Government and Policy*, 7, pp.253-172.

SCEALA (1989), *East Anglia: The Next Twenty Five Years*

Rankins, S. (1989), *United States Military Expenditure in East Anglia*, Economics Research Centre (1989), University of East Anglia.

Segal, N. (1985), *The Cambridge Phenomenon: The Growth of High Technology Industry in a University Town*, Segal, Quince and Partners, Cambridge.

Townroe, P.M. (1988) *Norwich: A Time of Opportunity*, Economics Research Centre, University of East Anglia.

The South West

Peter Gripaios and Paul Bishop

INTRODUCTION

The South West Region comprises the seven counties of Gloucestershire, Avon, Wiltshire, Dorset, Somerset, Devon and Cornwall. It is generally regarded as prosperous by UK standards and as Table 2.3.1 confirms, ranks on average third in terms of the variety of economic indicators listed. The South East is certainly more prosperous in terms of most indicators but there is little difference between the South West and the region which normally ranks second, East Anglia. The South West is then part of the prosperous South but there are nevertheless great disparities between the prosperity of the areas adjacent to the South East in the north and east of the region and those of the far South West. In terms of nearly every economic indicator listed, Cornwall ranks worst of the seven counties in the region. Indeed, it currently has the lowest level of earnings of any county in great Britain and contains a number of the worst unemployment blackspots. The South West then has its own north-south problem, emphasising that for the UK in general the notion of a 'prosperous' South is an oversimplification.

Table 2.3.1. Economic Performance

	Regional Rank SW/UK
GDP per head 1989	3
Average weekly earnings 1991	
Males	5
Females	2
Average Weekly Household Income per head (1989)	2
Cars per 1000 population 1990	2
Unemployment March 1992	4
Economic Activity Rate 1989	
Male	9
Female	6
New Buisiness Registrations 1980–1990/ End 1979 stock	3
% of Professional and Managerial Employees 1988	2
% of Self-employed 1990	3

Source: Consultancy South West (1990)

REGIONAL TRENDS

The South West has suffered much less than many other regions from the restructuring of the national economy as is evident from the picture of labour force growth shown in the tables in Chapter One. The working population grew faster than in the UK generally in the 1980s and female employment also rose faster. Male employment also increased in the South West while declining nationally. Finally the South West had a bigger percentage drop in the number of unemployed over the decade. One important reason for the fact that the South West escaped lightly from the recession of the early 1980s is that the region has never had a high proportion of its work-force in manufacturing. In 1981, 25.7 per cent of South West employment was in the manufacturing sector, compared with 28.5 per cent for the UK as a whole. By 1987 the difference had narrowed to 0.5 of a percentage point with the respective figures being 23.1 per cent for the South West and 23.6 per cent for the UK. However, it is not just a case of manufacturing industry being less important in the South West than the UK. It is also the case that the manufacturing sector in the region has outperformed that in the rest of the country. Traditional manufacturing is not strongly represented and, indeed, one important cause of the differential performance of the region's manufacturing in the 1980s was that many manufacturing jobs were in the sectors of aerospace/defence contracting and other high technology industries. For example, major employers in aerospace are British Aerospace, Rolls Royce, Dowty and Westland, and other high technology companies such as Plessey and Hewlett Packard are also strongly represented. The County of Avon, for example, had a location quotient for high technology jobs of 2.32 in 1981, second in the UK only to Hertfordshire (Hall et al, 1987). For the region as a whole, high technology industry including research and development contributed 5.1 per cent of jobs in 1987. Particular concentrations are in the urban areas in the north and east of the region, such as Bristol, Gloucester, Swindon, Poole and Bournemouth.

It should be stressed, however, that it is not just in manufacturing that the South West has outperformed Great Britain in total.

The South West performed better than Great Britain in total, in both employment and output between 1981 and 1989 in agriculture, manufacturing and private services. There is little doubt that the South West was attracting higher grade service jobs and parts of the region have been major recipients of jobs in producer services. Indeed, in 1987 the South West had one of the highest proportions of employees in producer services (9.6%) of the UK regions. Bournemouth (13.8%), Bristol (13.7%), Cheltenham (13.1%) and Swindon (11.5%), all had figures well above the regional average. The main reason is that the north and east of the region have been favoured in particular by insurance and banking firms which have relocated from London. Bristol, for example, now has part of the head office of Lloyds Bank and the head offices of Sun Life, Sun Alliance, Phoenix, Legal and General and London Life. Abbey Life, American Express, Gresham Life and others are in Bournemouth, while Cheltenham has Eagle Star and Endsleigh. The Registrar's Department of the Bank of England is being moved to Gloucester.

Given the figures on high technology and producer services, it seems clear that the South West in relative terms is prosperous and, indeed, was becoming more so over time. In terms of gross domestic product per head, for example, the South West has jumped up the regional league table. This rose from 91.7 per cent of the UK figure in 1977 to 94.9 per cent in 1990. The result was that whereas the South West ranked ninth out of the 11 UK regions in 1977 in terms of this measure, by 1990 it ranked fourth. Similarly, in terms of average weekly earnings (traditionally low in the South West), there has also been a dramatic improvement. The South West ranked eighth in the UK in 1985 but by 1990 had climbed to third for males and second for females (Table 2.1.5).

Buoyant economic activity would be expected to influence population and, of course, the housing market. An added influence in many parts of the region is retirement. These issues are now examined.

There has been rapid population growth over nearly three decades. The South West has grown faster than the UK and the region's working age population has grown

---

* 'Producer Services' = Banking, Insurance, Finance, R & D, Hiring Services and other Business Services.

faster than the population in total, suggesting that inward migration for retirement is far from the only influence. Indeed, most inward migration to the region, the major reason for the above trends is of persons in the age groups 15–44 most of whom came from the adjacent South East (Plymouth Business School, 1992).

The retirement effect should not, however, be underestimated particularly in the region's more rural parts. This is emphasised by the fact that the region has the highest percentage of pensioners in the UK and also the highest percentage of household income derived from investment, annuities and pensions (Plymouth Business School 1992).

Both economic prosperity and retirement have had a strong impact on the property market. The change in the index of dwelling prices from 1983 to 1989 was above that for the UK in general. The pressure in the housing market in the South West over this period is clearly shown by what happened to the price of housing land. In 1981, the South West had the sixth highest price in England and Wales whereas by 1988 it ranked third.

These statistics demonstrate that the South West is prosperous in national terms and a number of reasons can be advanced to explain this. The most important is probably the proximity of parts of the region to the South East with the result that these areas have attracted spillover expansion and relocation activities. As has been seen above, these include producer services moving from Central London and high technology industry developing particularly along the M4 corridor and in South East Dorset. The region's attraction lies in its good communications with the South East, the relatively lower wage and other cost levels and in its environmental attractiveness.

As noted in the introduction however, intra-regional differences in prosperity are marked and indeed have increased in some instances. For example, earnings in Dorset, Gloucestershire and Wiltshire have been rising relative to the regional average, whereas in Devon, Somerset, and particularly Cornwall they have been falling. In general the level of prosperity falls gradually the further west one travels to the Devon-Cornwall border. After that there is a much more dramatic falling off: West Cornwall stands out as particularly depressed, with Travel to Work Area unemployment rates as a percentage of the workforce of 14 per cent and over. These compare with rates of less than 7 per cent in some Travel to Work Areas in the north and east of the region.

Thus, the far South West has many of the characteristics of a depressed peripheral region. It is distant from major markets, has difficulty attracting sufficient jobs and compares with the problem regions in other parts of the UK. The fact that the South West emerged so strongly from the recession of 1979–82 was largely due to the very strong performance of areas such as Bristol/Bath, Bournemouth, Poole and Gloucester/Cheltenham which, as we have seen, have attracted jobs in producer services and high technology industry. The situation is rather different in the more peripheral areas which have been badly affected by declining agriculture and traditional tourism. In West Cornwall, the collapse of tin prices was an important additional recessionary influence.

Such differential performance between sub-regions is clearly evidenced by indicators such as house prices. At the third quarter of 1991, property prices varied from £58,000 for a semi-detached house in Cornwall to £70,000 for the same house in Avon. Even so, the prices in Cornwall and other rural parts of the region are heavily buoyed by migration for retirement purposes.

THE CURRENT SITUATION IN THE REGION

As has already been argued, the South West benefited from the strong growth of the national economy from 1983–1989. Much of this growth was concentrated in the South East and many of the ensuing constraints on further expansion in this region, such as skill shortages, high labour costs, property prices and shortages of industrial, commercial and residential land, encouraged location in and relocation to the adjacent South West. Much of the early spill-over was concentrated in areas closest to the South East and then rippled westwards with the size of the ripple weakening, the further to the South West it travelled. In any event, there was certainly a surge of economic development in the region with the result that some of the constraints which originally prompted firms to move from the South East became binding in the South West too. Bristol in particular has been a victim of its own success and has expanded to the extent that traffic congestion at peak periods is now severe. There have been proposals including a light railway system to cope with this problem, a matter of some urgency in the opinion of these commentators. Bristol's success was, until the current recession, reflected in increased office rents and also more particularly in skill shortages, in lack of available offices premises and land for commercial and industrial use. Indeed, a TUC report (South West TUC, 1988) suggested that many high technology companies which would have preferred a Bristol location were forced to locate elsewhere. Moreover, relocation is occurring within the commercial sector from Bristol to other areas. Clerical and Medical Insurance, for example, hs moved part of its activities from the city centre out to Clevedon on the Avon coast. Similarly, it was a close decision as to whether Lloyds Bank relocated its head offices to Bristol; it almost chose Cardiff instead.

It should be emphasised, however, that the Bristol experience was far from unique. Cheltenham has also experienced rapid office growth and has had difficulties accommodating this expansion. The Cheltenham and Gloucester Building Society Head Office, for example, recently had to move out of the town to a site closer to Gloucester. The same kind of pressure has been felt in Bournemouth/Poole, Swindon, Taunton, Exeter, Plymouth, Truro and in many smaller areas. The problem is, of course, how to cater for economic expansion without destroying the environment which made firms want to locate in the region in the first place. The situation in Plymouth illustrates the difficulties involved. Unlike many areas in the South West it has higher than UK average rate of unemployment, given that 8000 jobs have been lost in the Naval Dockyard in recent years and further redundancies may follow. Plymouth has had to attract new firms and has been successful in doing so. It has now, however, almost run out of industrial land within the city boundaries. Much of the surrounding area is designated as National Park or area of outstanding natural beauty. There is, therefore, little land that can be developed and even where it can, neighbouring authorities, which are pursuing economic development policies of their own, are extremely reluctant to allow it.

PROSPECTS TO 1995 AND BEYOND

The national recession of the early nineties has had a particularly strong impact on the South West so that overheating is no longer the issue that it was. Indeed, some of the most prosperous parts of the region such as Avon and Dorset have shown the biggest increases in unemployment. The recession may be expected to recover gradually as the brakes come off and the national economy expands. However, there are some special

Table 3.2.2. Forecasts for the South West Region

	1989–1995 change 000s	1995–2000
Population	286	216
Employment		
Total	179	175
Agriculture	-2	-2
Public Utilities	-3	-2
Manufacturing	10	-11
Construction	7	2
Government Services	150	155
		change (%)
Output (1985 prices)		
Total	22.3	19.1
Agriculture	19.2	16.0
Public Utilities	14.8	12.9
Manufacturing	29.9	20.9
Construction	18.7	12.8
Government Services	9.3	11.6
Private Services	26.5	23.7

Source: Cambridge Econometrics (1990)

influences operating this time around which may mean that the South West is considerably less prosperous in the 1990s than it was in the 1980s.

One important factor is cuts in defence expenditure which have already led to significant job losses all over the region. There is little chance that they will be reversed.

A second is that agriculture, like defence, an important industry in many parts of the region, is also in the doldrums as a result of quotas, falling price support, competition from other parts of the European Community and dissatisfaction of the public with modern farming methods.

A third is that financial services, an important regional industry, which have been severely affected by the recession, may show much slower growth in the nineties that they did in the eighties.

A fourth is the increasing importance of the anti-economic development lobby which may only have been temporarily silenced by rising unemployment rates.

A fifth is that an already peripheral region may be disadvantaged by the Channel Tunnel, (with which many parts of the region have poor road and rail links), 1992 and the liberalisation of Eastern Europe.

Nevertheless, some forecasters are reasonably optimistic about the future of the South West as a whole, including Cambridge Econometrics whose 1992 forecast suggested that the South West would continue to be one of the fastest growing regions in the UK.

REGIONAL POLICY AND LOCAL ECONOMIC ASSISTANCE

The revision of the Assisted Areas map in 1984 left only limited areas of the South West with access to regional aid. Five Travel to Work Areas have Development Area status–Falmouth, Helston, Newquay, Penzance and St Ives and Redruth and Cambourne. These are all concentrated in Cornwall reflecting the relative lack of prosperity in the far South West. In addition four areas have intermediate status. Three, Bodmin and Liskeard, Bude and Plymouth are in West Devon and East Cornwall, whilst the fourth–the Gloucestershire part of Cinderford and Ross-on-Wye lies along the border between the South West and the Intermediate and Development Areas of South Wales. In addition Plymouth and Bristol have been designated as Urban Programme Areas.

The total aid received by the South West region from UK central government Regional Preferential Assistance was £14.6m in 1988/89, representing an expenditure of £3.17 per head of population. The South West was ranked seventh (excluding Northern Ireland) in terms of the absolute level of regional aid and received below half the UK average expenditure on regional aid per capita. As a proportion of regional gross domestic product, such aid was smaller at under 0.1 per cent–although clearly this figure would be boosted by taking into account the expenditure of other government agencies which operate in the region.

In addition to government assistance the South West has received an important level of support through the European Community which provides aid to Assisted Areas through the European Regional Development Fund (ERDF) and European Social fund (ESF). In 1986, for example, these funds provided £27.6m of aid to the South West by the UK government (Croxford, 1987). However, the South West has only received a relatively small proportion of European Community funds allocated to the UK. For example, during the period 1975 to 1985, the region received 3.8 per cent of the funds allocated through the ERDF placing it in seventh place of the nine UK regions eligible for aid. This did however represent an expenditure level of £116.5 per person in the Assisted Areas, placing the South West at fifth place in UK regional ranking. In addition the South West receives money from the ESF, representing an additional £639,000 in 1985/86. These funds were used particularly for local authority projects. Indeed from 1984 to 1987 local authorities received over 50 per cent of the allocation of ESF funds to the region. Three authorities, Bristol City Council, Devon County Council and Cornwall County Council have been particularly successful in this area.

Whilst the amount of money spent directly by the UK government on regional aid to the South West is not large, it has increasingly been recognised that a 'hidden' regional policy has effectively operated through the regional impact of defence spending. The South West has been a major beneficiary of defence spending because of the location of many important defence contractors and defence bases in the region.

It can be seen from Table 2.3.2 that such expenditure is high in comparison with regional aid and offsets much of the regional variation in assistance. Indeed, if both types of expenditure are considered simultaneously, the ranking of the regions changes dramatically, with the South West rising from seventh to third between 1983 and 1984,

Table 2.3.2. Expenditure on Defence Equipment and Regional Assistance by Region 1988–9

	Regional Assistance £ (per capita)	Rank	Defence Equiptment Spending £ (per capita)	Rank	Total £ (per capita)	Rank
North	43.2	2	211	2	254.2	1
Yorkshire and	10.2	5	30	8	13.2	10
Easr Midlands	2.3	8	67	7	69.3	7
East Anglia	-	9=	25	9	25.0	9
South East	-	9=	178	3	178.0	3
South West	3.2	7	242	1	245.2	2
West Midlands	5.0	6	80	6	85.0	6
North West	12.8	4	134	4	146.8	4
Wales	51.0	1	17	10	68.0	8
Scotland	29.6	3	110	5	139.6	5

Source: Derived from Regional Trends 1990; BDMI Ltd.

whilst the South East rises from equal last to third place. The 'implicit' regional policy of defence spending hence swamps the much smaller finance available from regional aid.

Nevertheless, whilst the South West as a whole clearly benefits from defence spending, such spending is distributed unevenly within the region. Precise estimates at a sub-regional level are not available, but it is clear from recent research that much defence spending is concentrated in the north of the South West, particularly around Bristol which, as argued above, is an important centre for the aerospace and other defence related industries (Boddy and Lovering, 1986). Of course, particular localities in the far South West, such as Plymouth, also derive benefits from defence spending, but on the whole the expenditure tends to fall outside the Assisted Areas. Intra-regional variations in defence spending may therefore exacerbate the differences in income and employment within the South West and work against the impact of regional aid. It is therefore vital to recognise the spatial impact of defence spending in any appreciation of regional policy in the South West.

At a sub-regional level County Councils now play an important role in economic development in the South West. On average South West County Councils spend less per head on economic development activities than the average for English non-metropolitan authorities. This is perhaps not surprising for a relatively prosperous area. However, there are clear differences between the counties, with the less prosperous far South West counties of Devon and Cornwall spending more per head than their more prosperous neighbours. Wiltshire has recently increased its expenditure, whilst Gloucester, Somerset and Dorset pay less attention to such policies. Overall, however, expenditure is fairly low at approximately £1 per head in 1988-90 compared to £3.17 per head on central government assistance in the South West in 1988/89.

There are considerable similarities in the type of activities supported by County Councils. All of the South West counties attempt to attract inward investment. Devon and Cornwall are particularly active in this respect and coordinate their activities through the Devon and Cornwall Development Bureau (DCDB) which maintains offices in Boston and Tokyo. In 1986/87 the DCDB had a budget of £465,000, £305,000 of which came from the Department of Industry. The Bureau has been particularly successful in attracting mainly North American firms to Plymouth, though the Japanese firms have also been attracted in.

In 1988 DCDB was joined by a new organisation–the Devon and Cornwall Development Company. The DCDC is an umbrella organisation aimed at coordinating and encouraging economic development in the two counties. It has a budget of £250,000 and is constituted as a private sector led organisation perhaps reflecting the emphasis of the present government.

The emphasis of economic development policy in the north of the region is probably somewhat different. The Bristol economy was until recently overheating to such an extent that the Bristol Economic Development Unit saw the retention of existing jobs as a priority and, for example, helped Clerical and Medical Assurance to move part of their operations to Clevedon. Nevertheless, inward investment is certainly still encouraged.

The various county authorities typically provide limited funds for job retention or creation in the event (usually) that funds are not available from elsewhere. In 1987 the Devon Fund, for example, was limited to £50,000 per firm for a three year period. The assistance can take the form of loan guarantees to a bank, direct loans from the fund or indeed grants. Up to March 1987, almost £1.5m had been allocated from the funds, of which only £15,850 involved grants. The Council claimed the retention or creation of 1220 jobs implying an expenditure of £1225 per job. A net loss to the fund of £227,780 was also sustained due to losses on some projects.

Another important area in which some counties are involved is the Rural Development programme. In Devon's case, this programme involves a partnership between the County Councils, District Councils, National Park Authorities, Community Council of Devon, Rural Development Agency and English Estates. It is centred upon those areas of Devon designated as Rural Development Areas (RDAs) by the Development Commission. These cover a wide area of the County. The programme has attempted to develop a strategy for the RDAs and identify projects for which Development Commission support was to be requested. It provides an example of the type of action required to ensure that agencies working in a particular area can coordinate their activities.

There are numerous other areas in which the typical County Council is directly involved or cooperates with other agencies. These include the West Country Tourist Board, Cooperative Development Agencies, the DTI and the Training Commission. Perhaps most important of all, however, is the role which local authorities play in attracting funds from the European Community: a role as seen above in which they have been relatively successful.

Important economic development work at the sub-regional level is also now carried out by district councils, who are engaged in a wide variety of programmes. A survey in 1986 by the Association of District Councils (ADC) on the activities of all member authorities in England and Wales showed that the South West ranks relatively low in terms of regional ranking for the provision of direct financial assistance to local firms. This perhaps reflects two factors. First, the relative prosperity of much of the South West has made district authorities less inclined to seek to directly create new jobs through direct financial assistance to local and/or new firms. Second, the predominance of Conservative authorities in the region has perhaps implied an attitude less favourable towards direct intervention at the local level.

More direct forms of intervention such as providing advice, promotion and advertising have been emphasised by South West authorities. The ADC report speculates that more South West authorities became involved in such activity as the result of the removal of some areas from the Assisted Areas map in 1984. There is evidence from the survey that the level of involvement may be lower in the South West than other areas. For example, the average number of units of premises built by local councils was lower in the South West than any other region during the 1984-87 period.

This may of course reflect not only the lower priority given to such activities in the South West, but also the pressures on the availability of suitable land for development in certain areas. As argued above, the importance of retaining a high quality local environment places substantial difficulties on local authorities. Indeed the tensions between environment and development seem certain to increasingly dominate planners at the local level in the South West.

How effective then have the above measures been in terms of job creation? In the case of Local Authorities it is hard to say, particularly since there is little evaluation by the local authorities themselves. A survey by Barnes et al (1987), of all local authorities in England and Wales with an industrial development officer, concluded that only two of the 68 respondent authorities who provided direct financial assistance to industry, conducted meaningful evaluation of these policies. Most either merely 'checked' that firms fulfilled their technical obligations under the particular aid scheme, or carried out 'limited' evaluation, primarily in the form of crude cost per job calculations.

However, whatever the precise impact of district authority aid, the sums involved in economic development work are fairly small and are likely to have had only a modest impact on employment creation. There is a clear need, however, for a more systematic evaluation of the effect of local authority economic development activities.

What then of regional policy? If this is defined in the narrow sense, the small expenditure in the South West and the narrow areas eligible for assistance probably mean that the impact has been relatively minor. However, as has been seen, other areas of government spending and in particular that on defence have probably been of great importance. Indeed, the current reductions in the defence budget are already having a significant impact upon the south West with a number of major firms announcing redundancies. The issue of diversification away from the traditional defence base is, therefore, likely to be of prime concern to local policy makers in the 1990s.

To sum up, it is clear that the policy decisions of the European Community, national and local government and agencies such as the West Country Tourist Board, the Rural Development Commission and English Estates all have an impact on the region. Indeed a problem is that such a wide range of organisations may operate conflicting rather than complementary policies. This suggests that there is a role for bodies such as the proposed South West Development Agency in contributing to effective regional and local policy making in the region. One encouraging development was the publication in April 1991 of a regional economic development strategy drawn up by the economic development officers of the region's seven counties under the aegis of the South West Planning Conference. Whilst this strategy is primarily aimed at stimulating debate, it could be the precursor to a more coherent and systematic approach to dealing with the economic problems of the region.

REFERENCES

Barnes, I., Campbell, J. and Preston, J. (1987) 'Is Local Authority Economic Intervention a Waste of Resources?' *Public Policy and Administration* Vol 2 No 1, 1–8.

Boddy, M. and Lovering, J. (1986) 'High Technology Industry in the Bristol Sub-Region: the Aerospace/Defence Nexus' *Regional Studies* Vol 20.3, 217–231.

Cambridge Econometrics (1992) *Regional Economic Prospects* Cambridge: Cambridge Econometrics.

Croxford, G. (1987) 'The European Regional Development Fund and the European Social Fund: A Case Study of Local Authorities in South West England', in Gripaios, P. (ed) *South West Economy II*. Plymouth Polytechnic Conference Papers, 126–156

Hall, P., Breheny, M., McQuaid, R. and Hart, D. (1987) *Western Sunrise*. London: Allen and Unwin.

Plymouth Business School (1992) *The South West Economy: Trends and Prospects*. South West Economic Research Centre, Plymouth Business School, Polytechnic South West

South West TUC (1988) *Manufacturing in the South West*

CHAPTER 3

THE MIDLANDS

3.1

The East Midlands

Clive La Court

INTRODUCTION

The East Midlands is a relatively large and diverse region. It has a varied and pleasant, predominantly rural landscape, but also contains a number of large towns and cities including Nottingham, Leicester, Derby, Lincoln and Northampton. These provide the main foci of economic and social life but, unlike other UK regions, none of them is of such size and dominance that it provides a single focus for the whole region.

The diverse nature of the economic base, a robust manufacturing sector and the large number of small to medium-sized firms operating in the area meant that the East Midlands economy was one of the most buoyant among UK regions during the 1980s despite its very poor performance in attracting overseas foreign direct investment. Spatial variations in economic growth, employment and unemployment rates remain apparent within the region however, with particular concentrations of economic problems in declining coalfield areas and some inner city wards. While future economic prospects for the region are generally good these disparities are likely to remain if not increase, at least until the end of the century.

DEMOGRAPHY

The East Midlands has a total population of 3.97 million. The annual percentage population growth of 0.4 per cent between 1981-88 was just above the average of 0.2 per cent for the UK as a whole. The greatest increases were in Northamptonshire and in Lincolnshire. The proportion of males in the East Midlands in 1988 stood at 49.2 per cent, second highest in the UK. Population movements over the past decade have reflected economic performance, as people have moved from regions with slower rates of economic growth to those offering better job prospects. In numerical terms the East Midlands has experienced the third highest total of net inward migration, behind the South West and East Anglia, with a net figure of 72,000, for 1981-88. An analysis of inter-regional population movements for 1987 reveals that 37.7 per cent of the 106,000 in-movers came from the South East, with the two other main 'exporters' of population to the East Midlands being Yorkshire and Humberside (15.1%) and the West Midlands (12.3%).

The cities of Leicester, Nottingham and Derby have reasonably large and diverse ethnic minority populations, the majority located in inner city wards and experiencing disproportionately high levels of economic and social deprivation. The proportion of the population in private households who were members of ethnic minority groups was 4.2 per cent for the East Midlands in 1987; this compares with a figure of 5.3 per cent for England and 4.5 per cent for Great Britain. 67.7 per cent of ethnic minorities were of Indian/Pakistan or Bangladesh origin.

ECONOMIC TRENDS

The East Midlands region is one of contrasts, with the counties not readily forming a composite whole. A striking feature of the economic base is its diversity – extensively agricultural in the east, strongly industrial in the west and heavily dependent on extractive industries, notably coal-mining, in the north. In addition, the cities of Derby and Leicester, and in particular Nottingham, have developed as important regional centres for service activities. The region's economic diversity has had two main consequences. First, the region as a whole has been better placed to withstand some of the effects of fluctuations in national economic trends and hence has generally enjoyed stability and broadly-based growth. Second, in spite of the above, some areas have been particularly hard hit because of their dependence on industries or employers which have been in decline, especially coalfield and inner city communities and some rural areas.

The gross domestic product (GDP) of the region in 1988 is estimated at £25.6 billion or 6.6 per cent of the UK total. The East Midlands GDP per head in 1988 was £6,438, third highest in the UK. Within the region there is considerable variation in GDP per head ranging from 85 per cent of the UK average in Lincolnshire to 106 per cent in Leicestershire at 1987 figures. The major feature of the industrial structure of the region is the high percentage of GDP generated by manufacturing industry which was 32 per cent against a UK average of 25 per cent. This is particularly due to the contribution of lighter manufacturing such as textiles, clothing and footwear. The region also derives an above average proportion of GDP from the energy industries.

During the 1970s the East Midlands growth of GDP, at 2.1 per cent per annum, exceeded that for the UK as a whole (1.2%) and for all other regions with the exception of East Anglia (2.9% p.a.) and the South West (2.5% p.a.). The largest contributions to the region's GDP growth in the 1970s came from the public utilities, education and health and agriculture.

The national economic recession of the late 1970s and early 1980s had a noticeable dampening effect on economic activity in the region although its impact was no more severe than for the economy as a whole and significantly better than that experienced by the West Midlands and Northern regions where manufacturing virtually collapsed. From 1980-83 total GDP in the East Midlands increased at 1 per cent p.a. in line with national trends and only just behind the South East rate of 1.1 per cent p.a. Nevertheless, despite the better than average performance the early 1980's recession accelerated the restructuring of the region's industrial base and led to substantial job losses in the engineering, textiles and mining industries. The region lost 88,000 jobs during 1980-83, 67 per cent of those occupied by men, the majority full-time. The rate of employment loss, at 1.7 per cent p.a., was lower than that for the UK as a whole (at 2.2% p.a.) primarily because job losses in manufacturing and mining were partially offset by modest employment expansion in business services, public sdministration and defence and other services industries.

Assessing change over a longer time period reveals that the process of de-industrialisation, while not absent, has been less marked in the East Midlands than elsewhere. From 1971 to 1986 manufacturing output in the region as a percentage of total output fell from 35.3 per cent to 30.8 per cent and is estimated to have since risen again to 31.4 per cent in 1989, compared with 24.9 per cent for the UK. Changes in manufacturing are of course reflected in changes in employment in that sector, with the East Midlands again performing well by comparison with the rest of the UK. Employment in manufacturing decreased by 17.5 per cent in the region between 1971-83. It has since risen by 3.2 per cent between 1983–89 and currently stands at 516,000 or 28.8 per cent of total employment in the region compared with 21.3 per cent for the UK as a whole and second only to the West Midlands region with 30.3 per cent of employment in manufacturing. Most of the employment expansion in the region over recent years has come from service industries although the manufacturing sector as a whole clearly continues to be a major source of job opportunities. As shown in Table 3.1.1, total

Table 3.1.1: Employment and Output in the East Midlands 1983–1989

Industry	1989 (thousands)	%	Change in 1983–89	%Change in 1983–89	% Change Output 1983–89
Agriculture	53	3.0	3	5.4	+16.5
Mining	35	2.0	28	44.4	1.5
Public Utilities	22	1.2	1	4.3	+37.5
Manufacturing	516	28.8	+16	+3.2	+35.1
Construction	108	6.0	+17	+18.7	+39.6
Distribution	364	20.3	+50	+15.9	+41.4
Transport and Communications	81	4.5	+2	+2.5	+35.3
Business Services	122	6.8	+30	+32.3	+53.5
Public Admin and Defence	141	7.9	+18	+14.6	+14.1
Education and Health	205	11.4	+37	+22.0	+21.9
Other Services	143	8.0	+39	+37.5	+42.3
Total:	1791	100.0	+178	11.0	+29.3

Source: Cambridge Econometrics, *Regional Economic Prospects*, January 1990.

employment in the region increased by 178,000 (11%) during 1983–89, this representing a growth of 11.0 per cent over the period compared with the national figure of 9.8 per cent. Although manufacturing showed a small increase of 16,000 most of this expansion came from the services sector. Particularly strong job growth took place in the other services (37.5% growth), business services (32.6%), education and health (22.0%) and distribution (15.9%) industries. It is important to note that despite the growth of the service sector in recent years, the proportion of employed people working in this sector at 59 per cent in 1989 is still substantially below the national average of 68 per cent. In particular, the rate of increase of employment in business services, one of the UK's fastest growing industries, between 1986–89 continued to be slower than the national average, as it has been since 1980.

The major industries comprising the region's primary sector are agriculture and coal-mining. Employment in agriculture declined steadily during the 1970s and 1980s at a rate of around 1.0 per cent p.a., accounting for 53,000 employed people in 1989. The decline in mining employment has been more acute. The wider introduction of high technology mining, combined with the merging of collieries into pit complexes and the closure of 'high cost' collieries has resulted in heavy job losses. Only 35,000 workers are currently employed in the region's mining industry compared with 74,000 in 1971, a fall of 52.7 per cent. Further job losses in mining and related industries seem likely in the 1990s as the industry moves nearer to privatization.

INWARD INVESTMENT

The impact of inward investment on different regional economies varies considerably. During the 1980s the East Midlands attracted only five per cent of total foreign direct investment into the UK (see Table 3.1.2) amounting to 6812 new jobs with a further 1681 safeguarded. This relatively poor overall performance is in stark contrast to the neighbouring West Midlands and is probably due to two main factors. First, the East Midlands lacks a clear regional identity or image because of its undoubted diversity. Secondly, at present, the region is one of the least directly publicised of all the regions in England. In many other parts of the UK regional development organisations are active in presenting their region's image vigorously to potential overseas investors. In order to address these problems the CBI East Midlands are taking the lead in mounting an East Midlands Investment Campaign to demonstrate and promote the region's strengths as an attractive location for investment and to create a positive image of the East Midlands as a region of both opportunity and achievement. The Campaign is gathering considerable momentum from within both the private and public sectors, spurred on by recent success stories such as the Toyota development in Derby and the relocation of the Inland Revenue and English Heritage to Nottingham.

Table 3.1.2: Inward Investment by Region, 1979–1988

Region	Projects	% Share of UK
Scotland	420	17
Wales	350	14
Northern Ireland	176	7
North East	227	9
North West	220	9
Yorkshire-Humberside	137	5
West Midlands	302	12
East Midlands	**125**	**5**
South East	454	18
South West	100	4
Total	*2,511*	

Source: *Hansard,* February 1990.

THE LABOUR FORCE

Shifts in the industrial structure of the East Midlands region together with demographic trends have given rise to changes in the size and composition of the labour force. The civilian employed labour force of the region stood at 1.9 million in 1989, an increase of 5.8 per cent on the 1980 figure. Between 1988 and 2000 the civilian labour force is projected to increase by seven per cent, (139,000) to 2,134,000, the third highest increase after the South West (14%) and East Anglia (13%) and marginally above the Great Britain average of 4 per cent. The current composition of the labour force will not remain unchanged during this period however, largely because of the effect of the so-called 'demographic time-bomb'. This refers to the forecast sharp decline in the number of young people entering the job market, a trend which will continue until 1994, after which the numbers will increase slightly to 2000. The numbers of young people in the labour force will still be well below the levels of the early 1980s. The number of 16–24 year olds in the labour force is expected to fall by 21 per cent (94,000) between 1988 and 2000, comparable with the GB average of 22 per cent. The counties of Nottinghamshire and Derbyshire are expected to experience sharper rates of decline however. In common with all regions in Great Britain this sharp fall will be counter-balanced by an increase in the adult work force.

The male/female composition of the work force has also been changing in response to the increase in part-time employment associated with the expansion of the services sector in the region. In 1981 the employment ratio in the East Midlands was 59 per cent male and 41 per cent female; by 1989 the ratio was 55%:45%. The region has the third highest female economic activity rate (51.9) in the UK after the South East and East Anglia. The male economic activity rate of 74.5 in 1988 was the third highest after the South East and the West Midlands.

Self-employment has experienced a strong upward trend in the East Midlands. The region is widely regarded as having a strong entrepreneurial tradition. In contrast to the North, the East Midlands is far less dominated by large manufacturing plants and has a stronger small business sector which may be an important contributory factor in explaining its better economic performance overall. In March 1989 there were 217,000 people self-employed in the East Midlands. This represents 11.3 per cent of the employed civilian workforce. The growth in self-employment in the region between 1976–1989, although strong (77.9%), did not match that achieved in East Anglia, the South East, or the South West. There is mounting evidence that the region's small firms sector is being particularly hard hit during the recession of the early 1990s due to a combination of depressed domestic demand and high interest rates. Together with the South West, the East Midlands recorded the highest rates of increase in business failures in the first nine months of 1991. The East Midlands had 1575 business failures over the period according to Dan and Bradstreet; an increase of 90 percent on 1990. This follows a decade of significant not new firm formation.

UNEMPLOYMENT

Unemployment in the East Midlands increased rapidly in the late 1970s and early 1980s from a rate of 3.5 per cent in 1976 to a peak of 9.9 per cent in 1985. As the regional economy expanded in the late 1980s so the rate exhibited a downward trend reaching 6.2 per cent in 1989, just below the UK average of 6.3 per cent but equal to the average rate for the English regions. The marked down turn in economic activity in the early 1990s resulted in significant job losses in both the manufacturing and service sectors. The seasonally adjusted rate of July 1991 was 7.6 per cent comprising 110,400 men and 36,400 women. The unadjusted total looks set to continue to rise steadily, but not dramatically, at least until mid–1993.

There are strong variations in terms of unemployment levels within the region, with the counties in the southern half faring considerably better than their northern counter-parts. In particular, Northamptonshire recorded a rate of 6.4 per cent in July 1991 which compares with 8.9 per cent in Nottinghamshire. Within major cities such as Leicester and Nottingham long term unemployment, particularly among ethnic minorities, is a major problem with some inner city wards recording rates of 40 per cent for males. A contributory factor behind these trends has been the shedding of labour in traditional industries such as textiles and clothing which has not been adequately compensated for by an increase in service sector employment accessible to relatively unskilled inner city residents.

REGIONAL AND LOCAL ECONOMIC ASSISTANCE

The region is well served by a large and diverse network of economic development agencies and programmes operating within the public, private and voluntary sectors.

Much of the economic development effort is targeted at the local level, there being no regionally based development agency and only limited partnership arrangements between the constituent areas. The East Midlands region of the Department of Trade and Industry covers Derbyshire (except the High Peak District), Leicestershire, Lincolnshire, Northamptonshire and Nottinghamshire. The Assisted Areas as of 1990 are:

Development Areas (the travel-to-work-areas of):

- Corby;
- Scunthorpe (the parts in Lincolnshire);

Intermediate Areas (the travel-to-work-areas of):

- Coventry and Hinckley (the parts in Leicestershire);
- Gainsborough;
- Grimsby (the parts in Lincolnshire);
- Sheffield (the parts in North East and West Derbyshire Districts).

Grants and incentives are available in the Assisted Areas of Corby, Dronfield, Gainsborough and Hinckley. The principal form of help is Regional Selective Assistance. Between 1980 and 1988 the East Midlands received £30.2 million in selective financial assistance from the Government, the lowest figure for any eligible region with the exception of the South West. In Corby and Dronfield firms employing less than 25 employees are eligible for Regional Enterprise Grants for innovation and investment projects, where the project is taking place in the Development Area.

The cities of Derby, Leicester and Nottingham are designated as Inner Urban Areas. These Programme authorities have made much use of their enhanced powers to assist urban regeneration and the extra resources made available under the Department of Environment's Urban Programme. City Grant, introduced in 1988, is paid direct by the Government to support private sector capital projects which benefit run-down urban areas and which cannot proceed without public assistance. City Grant will be paid on projects for which the total value exceeds £200,000. Priority for City Grant is given to three Urban Programme areas in the East Midlands. Up to 31 March 1991, DoE City Grant offers for property developments project amounted to £19.0m in the East Midlands, 27 projects having received approval and creating in excess of 4500 jobs (York Consulting Limited, 1992).

In April 1988 a City Action Team (CAT) was formally set up covering Nottingham, Leicester and Derby. The CAT co-ordinates the multi-million pound inner city programmes of the Departments of Trade and Industry, Environment and Employment. In the relatively short time since its inclusion in the local urban regeneration scene the CAT has developed good working links with other key economic actors including the local authorities, enterprise agencies, the CBI and representatives of the private sector (e.g. Chamber of Commerce, Nottingham Development Enterprise). Only one Task Force remains in operation in the region based in Nottingham, this is expected to 'exit' in 1993. A varied portfolio (including skills audits, customised training, support for start-ups through a Development Fund) in excess of 120 projects has so far been approved by The Government's Nottingham Task Force with a committed spend of £2.5m. In addition, these projects have levered in £5.1m composed of £1.2m private, £3.3m public sector and £0.6m in other funds. The Task Force estimate that these projects combined have created 490 new jobs, provided over 2000 training places and assisted in the start-up and growth of 300 firms.

Seven Training and Enterprise Councils (TECs) have been established in the region as part of the Government's proposals for training within the White Paper 'Employment for the 1990s'. Each TEC will assume responsibility for designing and delivering the bulk of the Government's training and enterprise programmes from an employer-led and locally orientated perspective and has a budget of between £20m and £40m a year.

The East Midlands has a considerable number of local enterprise agencies (LEAs) which offer advice and other support for new and growing businesses. The majority are supported by local/central government and prominent ones include Nottinghamshire Business Venture, Derby and Derbyshire Business Venture, Leicestershire Business Venture and Nottinghamshire Co-operative Development Agency. All East Midlands LEAs receive private sponsorship from several companies (including financial institutions) and local authorities. In addition, they have access to assistance from the Employment Department's Regional Enterprise Unit. In some areas a number of different business support agencies have been brought together under one roof to provide a one-stop-shop for business advice and support for example, The Nottingham Business Bureau which houses several such agencies together, each contributing to local business development in different but complementary ways.

Senior executives of regionally based companies have shown their willingness to form or join various city-based business leadership groups to stimulate private sector interest in inner city revival and to develop better partnership arrangements around development ideas and schemes involving the public (both central and local) and private sectors. Nottingham Development Enterprise (NDE) for instance, was established on the initiative of the private sector and is active in partnership with the public sector in stimulating projects designed to improve Nottingham's physical, social and economic performance. NDE's board is drawn from the chairmen of major city companies and representatives from the Chamber of Commerce, the City and County Councils, and the Government's Task Force.

Local authority economic development services are provided by the majority of Council's in the region. Nottingham, Leicester and Derby, together with the County Councils have been especially active although even smaller district and borough councils have in recent years become more involved in mainstream economic development activities (the provision of financial assistance to start-ups, managed workspace, selective training initiatives, support for tourism development and industrial promotion). Most local authorities in the East Midlands have tended to adopt a more pragmatic and private-sector orientated approach to economic regeneration in comparison to other regions in the UK. This commitment to private sector led regeneration may be one of the reasons which explains why an Urban Development Corporation (UDC) has not been imposed by the Government.

THE EUROPEAN DIMENSION

The advent of the Single European Market marks an important change for relationships between European countries and between those countries in the Single Market and those elsewhere, whether in the European Free Trade Area such as the Scandinavian countries, America or the Far East. The overall impact of the Single Market on the East Midlands will in part be determined by the readiness and ability of local industries to adapt to an expanded European market, and this response will in turn affect the employment prospects and standards of living of local residents.

In view of the region's heavy reliance on lighter manufacturing, especially textiles and clothing, its under developed business and financial services sector, and its poor accessibility to the Channel Tunnel, the region does not appear to be well placed to gain maximum benefit from the Single Market. On the other hand, the continued diversification of manufacturing industries and developments in the retail and office sector provide grounds for optimism. Moreover, the East Midlands' strategic location on the edge of the over developed South East and its reasonably good (and improving) communication links with other regions makes it an attractive proposition for companies seeking a foothold in Europe. On the policy side, Nottingham and Leicester appear to have become aware of the need to adjust quickly to this new economic environment. In Nottingham, for example, the University has established a European Documentation Centre and the Chamber of Commerce has received EC funds to help establish and equip a European Information Centre which provides advice and information on a regional basis for companies who are assessing the implications of 1992 or seeking to gain access to various forms of financial support. In addition, the City and County Council's have both established European Liaison Teams who are giving a European dimension to their respective economic development strategies.

The East Midlands Regional Operational Programme (EMROP) Area comprises the Chesterfield, Gainsborough, Mansfield, Retford and Worksop TTWAs, the Nottingham Urban Programme Area and the part of the Scunthorpe and Grimsby TTWAs which are in the region. The partners in the EMROP have successfully obtained European Commission support for a regeneration Programme. The overall aim of the Programme is to maximise the benefit of the European Regional Development Fund in conjunction with other financial instruments, including the European Social Fund, to act as a catalyst to stimulate the economic regeneration of the region. The EMROP can expect to receive a total of £13m ERDF and 3.25m ESF support during the two year period 1990-91, considerably less than was originally envisaged by most eligible authorities in the region.

Finance from the European Community also comes through loans at preferential interest rates from the European Coal and Steel Community. The DTI may arrange in certain cases to exchange risk cover on these loans. The eligible areas for loans are the counties of Derbyshire and Nottinghamshire, the areas around North West Leicestershire, Corby and a small area in North West Lincolnshire.

Coal-mining areas within the region, of which there are several, are also likely to be eligible for EC support under the RECHAR Programme. This initiative aims to support the economic conversion of mining areas which have been confronted by substantial problems arising out of the restructuring and rationalisation of the coal industry. Support, in the form of grants or loans, is available for a range of projects including construction of new advance factory units, environmental improvements, the promotion of enterprise and tourism development.

FUTURE PROSPECTS

The medium term prospects for the East Midlands economy are likely to be determined by the inter-play of various forces and trends at the national and international as well as the regional level. Several factors which may adversely affect the continued recovery of the region include:

- lack of good quality industrial land (particularly in coalfield and some inner city areas);

- the continuing over dependence on declining primary and manufacturing industries such as coal mining, agriculture, textiles and heavy engineering in some parts of the region (particularly the north and east);
- the lack of a strong regional identity may limit the full realisation of the region's economic potential, particularly in markets for large overseas inward investment;
- under-representation in key growth sectors, especially business and financial services, high technology and knowledge-based industries.

Despite these constraints the region possesses considerable potential for economic and employment development in the medium term. Major strengths include:

- the region's central position within the UK and its good communications links, thus enabling it to benefit from any growth induced 'rippling-out' effect from the South East;
- a reasonably large and adaptable labour force which contains a high proportion of women workers;
- a diverse and fairly robust industrial base much of which is based on a vibrant small business sector;
- environmental and heritage assets which should assist in the promotion of tourism and the attraction of new job generating investment;
- a large and well developed institutional infrastructure serving to promote local economic development and raise the region's profile in the UK and overseas.

FORECAST TRENDS

Reflecting the normal pattern in a recovery, employment is forecast to grow more slowly than output, with some further decline in employment in 1992 and a gradual picking up in the labouring market in 1993 followed by more buoyant growth there-after. Overall growth of 1.3 percent pa in employment in the East Midlands is forecast for the years 1992–93, associated with an increase in the labour force.

Within the region there has been increasing interest in developing international ties with major overseas undertakings and the siting of Toyota's £700m European manu-facturing plant in Derbyshire represents the biggest success in this respect. It is likely that by the end of the1990s the investment will have generated about 7000 permanent jobs in Derbyshire. There will be positive knock-on effects for other countries in the region and adjacent West Midlands.

Overall, the region's manufacturing industries can be expected to grow consistently faster in the next century than the UK as a whole with particularly strong growth in GDP from 1995 onwards. Employment in manufacturing will follow the long term downward trend although once the immediate problems of the 1990–92 recession have passed, jobs losses will be at a slower rate than for the UK as a whole with only some 9000 jobs going between 1992 and 2005. The losses will, however, be spreading unevenl across industries, with an increase in engineering employment from the nadir of the early 1990s being more than offset by continued decline in Textiles, Clothing and Footwear and in Food, Drink and Tobacco.

In the past the region has seen relatively few high-technology developments, the only science part being at Nottingham University. However, the siting of the Gas Research Centre and the creation of a science part of Loughborough, point to the prospect of greater success in the area.

The overall economic outlook for the East Midlands to the end of the century appears reasonably promising both in terms of economic and employment growth. The region's diverse economic base, robust manufacturing sector and strong small business sector should help consolidate its position as one of the top UK performers. The extent to which the benefits of growth will be equally distributed throughout the region is clearly open to question however, given its economic diversity and the existing patterns of inequality which have become deeply embedded. Inner city, coalfield and rural communities in particular will continue to suffer from economic and social hardship for some time to come. Even with the prospect of further economic growth, there is a distinct possibility of a marked 'North-South Divide' emerging within the region as it moves towards the end of the century. Redressing that trend is likely to prove no easy matter.

REFERENCES

York Consulting Ltd. (1992) *City Grant and Urban Registration*. February.

The West Midlands

Michael Marshall

INTRODUCTION

During the past decade the West Midlands has experienced a series of dramatic swings in its fortunes. The region is traditionally regarded as Britain's manufacturing heartland, centring on the conurbation of Birmingham, Coventry and the Black Country and encompassing the surrounding shire counties of Shropshire, Hereford and Worcester, Staffordshire and Warwickshire. The region suffered an unprecedented economic collapse during the recession of the early-1980s. In contrast, during the second half of the decade the West Midlands enjoyed a remarkable economic revival, with the region expected to display a more resilient performance during the challenges of the 1990s.

LONG-TERM BACKGROUND

The sharp swings in the West Midlands' economy over the past decade continue the cyclical dynamism which has characterised the region's 200-year industrial history. This dynamism has rested on an industrial base of diverse but interlinked metal-based manufacturing sectors which have developed and evolved through successive periods of economic change and adaptation (Marshall, 1987, p.115).

The initial development of the regional economy from the late-eighteenth to mid-nineteenth centuries was founded on coal, iron and steel together with a complex of metal-working trades. Birmingham emerged as the industrial, financial and commercial focus of the region while the neighbouring Black Country developed a network of metal-working industries meeting the demands of Birmingham manufacturers for materials and semi-finished products.

A distinctive characteristic of industrialisation in the West Midlands throughout this period was the predominance of small-scale workshop production and craft skills. This gave the area a degree of economic and social cohesion which contrasted with other industrial areas where large-scale, mechanised production in factories was more widespread.

The Great Depression of the 1870s and 1880s marked the first major transition in the West Midlands' industrial and social organisation. Some of the older metal trades, such as wrought iron and nail-making, contracted during the depression under the impact of foreign competition. However, many of the old trades were consolidated into new and expanding sectors, such as cycles, electrical engineering and machine tools which, by 1914, had stimulated the emergence of further new industries, most importantly motor vehicles. The rise of these new industries was accompanied by the growth of large-scale factory production, breaking up the traditional craft-based workshop system which had survived until the 1870s.

The flexibility and adaptability of the region's industry and skill base continued to insulate the West Midlands from the worst effects of the recession in world markets after the First World War. Although there were pockets of severe distress in the Black Country, unemployment rates during the 1930s were lower on average than in most other parts of Britain. Moreover the region's recovery from the depression, led by armaments production in the 'shadow' factories, was more rapid.

The West Midlands' economic dynamism continued into the region's post-war heyday. Employment fluctuations during the economic cycles of the 1950s and 1960s were generally less intense in the West Midlands than other regions. Protected from structural unemployment, West Midlands skilled male manual workers were the highest paid in Britain. The region remained an area of relative labour shortage, attracting black and Asian workers from Commonwealth countries.

FROM BOOM TO SLUMP

The world economic slowdown from the mid-1960s exposed the underlying competitive weaknesses of UK manufacturing which had been masked during the post-war boom. These weaknesses were compounded by an over-valued pound which inhibited British exports while assisting overseas producers to increase progressively their share of UK markets.

The vulnerablity of the West Midlands to this decline in UK manufacturing competitiveness was compounded by the concentration of large multinationals in the region. The jungle of small workshops that had once characterised the region's industrial structure had ceased to be the dominant feature. The process of capital concentration and merger had created an economy which was heavily dependent upon a relatively small number of giant plants in a narrow range of engineering industries. By 1977 ten major multinationals – GEC, Lucas, GKN, Tube Investments, Glynwed, Dunlop, BSR, Cadbury-Schweppes, Delta and IMI – employed 27 per cent of their UK work-force in the West Midlands, while nationalised industries and state holdings, such as British Steel and British Leyland (forerunner of Rover), occupied pivotal positions in the regional economy (Gaffikin and Nickson, 1984).

The growth of large-scale mass production in giant plants, especially in the car industry, was accompanied by a new mass trade unionism which earned West Midlands workers a reputation for militancy which was alien to their earlier tradition (Spencer et al, 1986, pp.26–8). There seems little doubt that this acted as a 'push-factor' in the disinvestment from the region by some major companies while the corporate strategies pursued by some key companies, notably British Leyland under the Edwardes Plan, were partly aimed at undermining trade union organisation in their West Midlands plants.

Underlying the West Midlands' deteriorating industrial performance was a long-term record of under-investment. This was particularly severe among the West Midlands' substructure of locally-owned, medium-sized component manufacturers and engineering subcontractors which supplied the region's leading producers. Dependence upon a single market for their products left them vulnerable to contraction in demand and lacking the capability to diversify. Not surprisingly, many went to the wall in the recession of the early-1980s.

The long-term record of under-investment was reflected in the technological backwardness of much of West Midlands industry. Between 1968 and 1983 the number of industrial R&D units in the region fell from 82 to just 27 (Buswell et al, 1985, p.43). On the process side, in 1982 over 30 per cent of metal-working machine tools in the West Midlands were over 35 years old while only 1 per cent were modern CNC models (Metal Working Production, 1983, pp.59–60).

Under-investment by the region's manufacturers was paralleled by low levels of public sector investment and resource allocation. During the late 1970s the West

Midlands suffered the highest deficit on government expenditure and transfers of all UK regions (Cambridge Economic Policy Group, 1980, p.34). Lack of public investment was compounded by the operation of regional policy during the 1960s and early 1970s when the West Midlands, along with the South East, was treated as an industrial donor expected to forego expansion in favour of the Assisted Areas.

THE IMPACT OF RECESSION IN THE EARLY 1980s

While these problems had been recognised since at least the recession of 1974–75 it was not until the onset of the 1979–81 recession that they became fully apparent. Prior to the recession, in 1978 some 45 per cent of the West Midlands work-force were employed in manufacturing compared to 32 per cent in Great Britain.

Between 1978 and 1984 the West Midlands suffered a 30 per cent decline in total manufacturing employment compared to 25 per cent nationally. The region's key vehicles, metals and engineering sectors were particularly badly affected with a 34 per cent decline in employment over this period. Industrial job losses combined with relatively low rates of service sector growth led to a rapid rise in the regional unemployment rate which tripled from around 5 per cent in 1978 to almost 15 per cent by 1983.

Rising unemployment was accompanied by declining relative income levels and living standards. West Midlands male manual workers fell from top of the ten-region pay ladder in 1972 to eighth a decade later while it was estimated in 1983 that one in three households in the metropolitan area lived in poverty conditions (West Midlands County Council EDC, 1983).

Underlying this decline was a process of corporate restructuring by the West Midlands' leading manufacturers in response to changing markets and intensifying international competition (Gaffikin and Nickson, 1984; Spencer et al, 1986, Ch.5). The effects of this restructuring on the wider regional industrial complex are well illustrated by the example of the motor and components industry.

The region's major vehicle manufacturers and assemblers, most importantly Rover and Land Rover in Birmingham and Jaguar and Peugeot-Talbot in Coventry, are supported by a diverse substructure of components and equipment suppliers. Among the components firms, the larger and more sophisticated supply car components and sub-assemblies while the smaller firms supply basic castings, forgings and fabrications. Equipment producers supply metal cutting and forming machine tools as well as mechanical handling and processing equipment. It was estimated in 1984 that 60,000 jobs in 4000 firms within the West Midlands conurbation were directly dependent upon Austin Rover which itself employed a further 17,600 workers (Bessant et al, 1984, p.54).

From the mid-1970s the industry suffered a major contraction of output, capacity and employment. Within the West Midlands conurbation, redundancies announced by the major companies between 1979 and 1985 included 28,000 by Austin Rover, 3000 by Peugeot-Talbot, 8500 by GKN, 10,000 by Lucas and 4000 by Dunlop.

THE LATE 1980s REVIVAL

From 1983 the West Midlands experienced a marked revival of its economic fortunes, evidenced by the sharp reversal of the former trend in unemployment.

While the West Midlands suffered the steepest increase in unemployment of all UK regions during the early 1980s, the region subsequently enjoyed one of the fastest reductions with the regional unemployment rate falling back to the national average in March 1989 for the first time during the decade.

Restructuring of the manufacturing sector was central to the region's recovery. Despite the closures and contractions of the early 1980s, manufacturing continues to generate over one-third of total West Midlands GDP, the highest share of all UK regions. While the metal manufacturing sector has declined considerably in importance following the closure of all primary steel-making capacity in the region, the motor vehicles, metal goods and engineering industries remain leading sectors of region-wide significance. Other long-established sectors continue to play a key role in particular localities, such as ceramics in the Staffordshire 'Potteries', carpets in Kidderminster and crystal glassware in Stourbridge. Elsewhere, the inner urban areas of Birmingham and Coventry have experienced a dramatic expansion of predominantly Asian-owned clothing businesses in the aftermath of the recession.

Between 1983 and 1990 West Midlands manufacturing output increased by an estimated 29 per cent while employment declined by 39 per cent, implying an almost 80 per cent increase in productivity. Many of the region's traditional metals and engineering groups have pursued far-reaching shifts in product and market strategies, often with a stronger orientation towards export markets. Firms like Glynwed and IMI, which are traditionally regarded as metals groups, now earn less than half their turnover from their non-ferrous metals activities. Lucas has diversified strongly into aerospace through a programme of US acquisitions while GKN has been transformed into an international automotive, defence and industrial services group bearing little resemblance to the original conglomeration of fasteners businesses.

Overseas investment has played an increasingly important role in the restructuring of the regional economy with the West Midlands' share of total foreign direct investment in the UK rising from only 5 per cent of projects in the early 1980s to around 20 per cent by the end of the decade (Coventry Polytechnic Centre for Local Economic Development, 1989, p.15). This has involved transfer of ownership of existing businesses as well as new, greenfield developments. Examples include the acquisition of Dunlop tyres by Sumitomo; Lucas' transfer of its batteries plant to Yuasa and its electrical components plant to Magneti Marelli; the Rover Group's sale of its Black Country foundry operation to Eisenwerk Brühl; the Thyssen steel group's acquisition (via Blue Circle) of the former Birmid foundry businesses; and, perhaps most significantly of all, Ford's acquisition of Jaguar and British Aerospace's sale of a 20 per cent stake in the Rover Group to Honda.

Overseas investment in new, greenfield capacity has been most prominent in the New Town of Telford which has attracted over twenty Japanese companies including Hitachi-Maxell cassette tape, Ricoh copiers, NEC computers and Epson printers, culminating in the 1990 announcement by Toyota's Nippondenso subsidiary of its intention to establish an electrical component plant supplying the parent company's new Derbyshire car assembly facility.

The restructuring of West Midlands manufacturing has been accompanied by a sharp acceleration in the rate of service sector growth with total regional service employment expanding by 3 per cent a year between 1983 and 1990 compared to less than 0.5 per cent per annum in the 1980–83 period. Recycling of derelict industrial sites has led to rapid growth of out-of-town retail and leisure facilities, including the Merry Hill complex in Dudley Enterprise Zone on the site of the former British Steel Round Oak works, and Festival Park in Stoke-on-Trent on another disused steel site as well as a number of smaller scale developments along the M5 and M6 motorways.

The region has enjoyed particularly strong growth in banking, financial and business services with a 47 per cent increase in employment in these activities between 1983 and 1990. A number of major institutions have relocated offices to the West Midlands from the South East, notably the TSB's retail banking arm, and several Japanese banks have established a regional presence.

These developments have made an important contribution to the wider business revival in the region with corporate reorganisation in the manufacturing sector strongly linked to the expansion of West Midlands 'producer services' (Marshall, 1989). Since the early 1980s the number of financial institutions in Birmingham providing development capital for industry has increased from just three to over ten with the city becoming a major provincial centre for corporate finance and related services (Smith, 1991).

POLICY RESPONSES

Central government responses to the West Midlands' economic decline in the early 1980s were widely perceived as piecemeal and unco-ordinated. One of the first Enterprise Zones was designated in Dudley in 1980 and a further Zone later added in Telford at that time an area of high unemployment. After much eleventh-hour lobbying, Birmingham Airport was included in the ill-fated freeport programme announced in early 1984. In the run-up to the 1983 General Election, Coventry MP John Butcher was given special responsibility for the region at the Department of Trade and Industry (DTI). However, it was not until November 1984 that the region's decline was formally recognised when a large part of the West Midlands, including the whole of the metropolitan county, achieved Assisted Area status.

Prior to 1984, the European Commission had recognised Urban Programme areas in Birmingham, Coventry and the Black Country as eligible for support from the European Regional Development Fund, acknowledging that the out-dated UK map of assistance failed to encompass the West Midlands. ERDF awards to the region increased significantly after 1984 with the West Midlands attracting 17 per cent of total UK allocations over the next six years.

While central government was slow to respond to the West Midlands' decline, as early as 1974 the West Midlands County Council published 'A Time For Action', suggesting that the former dynamism of the regional economy was coming to an end. From 1981 the County Council pioneered a range of economic and employment initiatives including the formation of the West Midlands Enterprise Board which provides long-term development capital for medium-sized manufacturing businesses. Several of these initiatives survived the County Council's abolition in 1986 when the metropolitan district councils began to take a more active role in economic development (Marshall and Mawson, 1987, pp. 112–20).

The shire County Councils and New Town Development Corporations were active throughout the 1980s in developing industrial and commercial sites while promoting their areas' attractions. Efforts were increased from 1983 by the West Midlands Industrial Development Association (since renamed the West Midlands Development Agency), formed on the initiative of the regional Confederation of British Industry (CBI) with DTI and some private sector funding to promote inward investment to the region.

Urban regeneration remained the central theme of strategic land-use planning policies throughout the 1980s, despite the inherent tension between the needs of the conurbation and development pressures in the shires (West Midlands Joint Data Team, 1990). The continuing objective of regeneration was reiterated in the Department of the Environment (DoE's) 1988 Strategic Guidance while recognising that acute shortages of premium industrial sites in the conurbation will necessitate release of land for development on the urban periphery.

Local government partnerships with the private sector expanded as the regional economy recovered from the mid-1980s, most notably in Birmingham where the City Council, educational institutions, Chamber of Commerce, developers and other private institutions have partnered a wide range of business development, employment and training projects, notably Aston Science Park and the Heartlands development programme in East Birmingham (Carley, 1991). In 1985 the City Council launched an ambitious Economic Development Strategy for the city which included promotion of business tourism through the National Exhibition Centre and flagship International Convention Centre complex.

Elsewhere, the Black Country Development Corporation has taken the leading role in partnership with the private sector in recycling derelict industrial sites for residential and commercial as well as industrial use. This includes the planned Black Country Spine Route aimed at modernising the area's highway links with the surrounding motorway network.

LIMITS OF THE REGION'S RECOVERY

While the West Midlands enjoyed a radical transformation in its overall economic performance during the late 1980s, the region's recovery from recession remained highly uneven both socially and spatially. The growth of houshold incomes and consumer spending failed to match the region's revived performance measured by other economic indicators. West Midlands income per head remains about ten per cent below the UK average while consumer spending in the region lagged behind UK growth during the spending boom of the late 1980s.

The West Midlands conurbation bore the brunt of manufacturing job losses in the 1980s while the surrounding shire counties benefited from the strongest growth in services. The total regional population has remained broadly static at 5.2 million over the past decade, but the population of the metropolitan county fell by 2 per cent between 1981 and 1988 while growing by between one and five per cent in the four surrounding shires.

Despite the overall reduction in the West Midlands jobless total, unemployment in the urban centres remained well above average. While the UK and regional unemployment rates converged at seven per cent in 1989, unemployment remained in excess of ten per cent in Birmingham, Coventry and Wolverhampton with male rates of over 30 per cent in several inner urban wards.

In addition, the regional manufacturing sector continued to suffer a range of underlying weaknesses. This was well illustrated by the rate of technological advance with a widening investment gap between the larger industrial groups and smaller regional companies (Mackie, 1990). In 1985 an estimated 62 per cent of West Midlands manufacturing plants had introduced microelectronics in product or process applications. This compared poorly with the national average of 71 per cent and remained the lowest proportion of all UK regions (Northcott, 1986, p.121).

The adoption of new technologies had been particularly constrained by under-investment in the skilled workforce, traditionally one of the West Midlands' strongest assets. The intake of new engineering apprentices, for example, slumped by almost 60 per cent between 1978 and 1986 as companies cutback on training and recruitment. The effects of these cutbacks were felt sharply by the end of the decade with companies persistently reporting skill shortages as a key obstacle to business expansion (Lewis and Armstrong, 1986).

Some of these problems were undoubtedly masked by buoyant national economic growth during the late 1980s with booming domestic demand and export markets. The five successive years of record UK car markets from 1985, for example, imparted a strong stimulus to the West Midlands motor and component industries while the retailing, construction and business finance booms were visibly well-represented in the area. By the end of the decade, mounting inflationary pressures and a widening trade deficit showed that the UK economic boom was unsustainable. A return to the conditions of the early 1980s with sluggish demand combined with high interest rates and exchange rates threatened the West Midlands' revival, undermining expansion of service industries while severely testing the manufacturing sector's resilience (Wardlow, 1990).

PROSPECTS AND POLICIES FOR THE 1990s

As we enter the 1990s, the West Midlands faces recession for the second time in a decade. During the UK economic slowdown of 1988–89, the West Midlands held up strongly relative to the southern regions. West Midlands consumers and services were less vulnerable to the economic squeeze of high interest rates than the southern regions, while buoyant manufacturing exports partially offset weak domestic demand. However, from mid-1990 industry began to feel the economic squeeze more severely while the Gulf crisis, high oil prices, rising sterling and slower world growth sharply undermined manufacturing exports. By 1991 the West Midlands was rapidly sliding into recession with the region's manufacturers embarking on a further wave of redundancies leading to a renewed sharp rise in unemployment.

Although the West Midlands' short-term outlook appears gloomy, there are grounds for optimism over the medium-term. The region continues to command an impressive array of indigenous strengths including its location at the centre of the UK transport network, proximity to markets and suppliers and availability of a skilled labour pool while the region remains a relatively low cost location by UK and West European standards (West Midlands Region CBI, 1989). These strengths have been demonstrated by the scale of inward investment to the region, from both overseas and elsewhere in the UK, over recent years.

However, these strengths are unevenly distributed across the region with marked contrasts between the conurbation and outlying shires and between the north and south of the region (West Midlands Joint Data Team, 1990, p.11). Intra-regional contrasts are likely to be accentuated by any further drift of growth northwards from the South East to the M40/M42 corridors which present a strong counter-attraction to the north of the region.

The region as a whole remains acutely dependent on wider national and international developments. The West Midlands is more exposed to foreign trade and competition than most other regions, exports generating an estimated 35 per cent of total GDP (Business Strategies Ltd, February 1991, p.5). The Single European Market will bring mixed benefits to the region. International restructuring, as North American and Japanese as well as European companies position themselves within European markets, has already had far-reaching implications for the West Midlands. This is especially true of the car industry where Nissan, Honda and Toyota have selected UK locations for their European production base, attracting parallel investment by foreign component suppliers as well as presenting opportunities and threats for indigenous producers in the West Midlands (West Midlands Enterprise Board, 1990). In other sectors where the West Midlands suffers comparative disadvantages, such as domestic ceramics and some of the metals and engineering industries, European market integration poses serious competitive threats (Begg, 1989).

During the 1990s the West Midlands' economic performance is expected to mirror its geographic position at the centre of Britain's North-South Divide with regional GDP growing at around the national average (Cambridge Econometrics/NIERC, January 1991; Business Strategies Ltd, February 1991).

Forecasts suggest that a medium-term growth path for the UK economy lies in the range of two to three per cent per annum. Annual average growth of less than two per cent would imply that the economy was growing below its productive potential, one sign of which would be persistently high unemployment. Growth of greater than three per cent a year would serve only to reproduce the overheating pressures of the late 1980s boom which precipitated the 1990–91 recession.

Full UK economic integration with the EC will require convergence of UK growth rates and inflation with the European average. This will necessitate a protracted period of adjustment with industrial production expanding faster than consumer services and investment growing faster than consumption.

The relative contraction of the UK manufacturing base has become a major structural constraint on the growth of the whole economy. Hence, the regeneration of West Midlands manufacturing is vital not only to the region's future performance but for the UK economy as a whole. This is a matter for policy prescription rather than econometric projection.

Macro-economic management alone is unlikely to resolve the remaining competitive problems of UK and West Midlands industry. Direct measures to promote investment in key technologies and skills will be required through a revived regional industrial policy involving a new institutional apparatus.

The existing West Midlands agencies and initiatives launched by local authorities, educational institutions, government departments and the private sector have already made an important contribution. However, the economic problems and potential of the West Midlands are so large-scale and inter-related that isolated initiatives pursued by individual agencies can have only a limited impact. There is an urgent need for a co-ordinated framework to fill the vacuum left by the progressive dismantling of strategic planning during the 1980s.

REFERENCES

Begg, I. (1989) 'Assessing the impact of the Single Market'. Paper presented at Cambridge Econometrics/Cambridge University Department of Applied Economics conference on The Regions, the Tunnel and 1992, July, Cambridge.

Bessant, J., Jones, D., Lamming, R. and Pollard, A. (1984) 'The West Midlands automobile components industry: recent changes and future prospects'. *West Midlands County Council Economic Development Unit Sector Report No. 4.* Birmingham: WMCC.

Business Strategies Ltd (February 1991) *Regional Outlook Volume 1: Summary and Analysis.* London: Business Strategies Ltd.

Buswell, R.J., Easterbrook, R.P. and Morphet, C.S. (1985) 'Geography, regions and research and development activity: the case of the United Kingdom', in Thwaites, A.T. and Oakey, R.P. (eds) *The Regional Economic Impact of Technological Change*, 36–66. London: Frances Pinter.

Cambridge Econometrics/Northern Ireland Economic Research Centre (January 1991) *Regional Economic Prospects: Analysis and Forecasts to the Year 2000*.Cambridge: Cambridge Econometrics.

Cambridge Economic Policy Group (1980) 'Urban and regional policy with provisional regional accounts for 1966–78'. *Cambridge Economic Policy Review* 6 (2).

Carley, M. (1991) 'Business in urban regeneration partnerships: a case study in Birmingham'. *Local Economy* 6(2),100–115.

Coventry Polytechnic Centre for Local Economic Development (1989) *Overseas Investment to the West Midlands Region: Second Report to West Midlands Industrial Development Association.* Birmingham: WMIDA.

Gaffikin, F. and Nickson, A. (1984) *Jobs Crisis and the Multinationals: The Case of the West Midlands.* Birmingham Trade Union Group for World Development.

Lewis, J.A. and Armstrong, K.M. (1986) 'Skill shortages and recruitment problems in West Midlands engineering industry'. *National Westminster Bank Quarterly Review* November, 45–57.

Mackie, I. (1990) 'Small firms, technology transfer and a rapidly changing Europe'. *West Midlands Enterprise Board Quarterly Economic Commentary* July, 8–10.

Marshall, J.N. (1989) 'Corporate reorganization and the geography of services: evidence from the motor vehicle aftermarket in the West Midlands region of the UK'. *Regional Studies* 23 (2), 139–50.

Marshall, M. (1987) *Long Waves of Regional Development.* London: Macmillan.

Marshall, M. and Mawson, J. (1987) 'The West Midlands', in Damesick, P. and Wood, P. (eds) *Regional Problems, Problem Regions and Public Policy in the United Kingdom* 95–124. Oxford: Oxford University Press.

Metal Working Production (1983) *The Fifth Survey of Machine Tools and Production Equipment in Britain.* London: Metal Working Production.

Northcott, J. (1986) *Microelectronics in Industry: Promise and Performance.* London: Policy Studies Institute.

Smith, A. (1991) 'Birmingham: financial centre'. *Investors Chronicle* 24 May, 53–8.

Spencer, K., Taylor, A. Smith, B., Mawson, J., Flynn, N. and Batley, R. (1986) *Crisis in the Industrial Heartland: A Study of the West Midlands.* Oxford: Clarendon Press.

Wardlow, A. (1990) 'High interest rates have ended the seven fat years, but what will follow?'. *West Midlands Enterprise Board Quarterly Economic Commentary* February, 2–4.

West Midlands County Council Economic Development Committee (1983) *Family Income Trends: Report to the Economic Development Committee.* Birmingham: WMCC.

West Midlands Enterprise Board Ltd. (1990) *Automotive Sector Review: Components Manufacturers.* Birmingham: WMEB.

West Midlands Joint Data Team (1990) *West Midlands Planning Trends: Annual Monitor 1989.* Solihull Metropolitan Borough Council.

West Midlands Region CBI (1989) *Regeneration of the Region: Change and Challenge in the West Midlands* (report by Coopers & Lybrand and York Consulting). Birmingham: West Midlands CBI.

CHAPTER 4

NORTHERN ENGLAND

4.1

Yorkshire and Humberside

Christine Leigh and John Stillwell

INTRODUCTION

The economy of Yorkshire and Humberside, in common with that of other industrial regions of the United Kingdom, has undergone a major transformation during the 1980s. The region's traditional primary and manufacturing industries have shed labour rapidly as a consequence of severe rationalization and extensive restructuring. The extent of deindustrialisation can be gauged by the fact that in 1989, there were 66,000 fewer jobs in primary industries (including coal-mining) and over 74,000 fewer jobs in manufacturing industries than in 1981. In contrast, the growth in service sector activities has been emphatic, with the tertiarization process creating 194,000 more jobs between 1981 and 1989. Various signs of the new forms of investment that have taken place in the region are now visible and there is evidence to suggest that the economy experienced an upturn at least in parallel with that occurring in the national economy during the second half of the 1980s. Demand for vacant office space in the region's major cities began to outstrip supply. The cities of Leeds, Bradford and Sheffield have been at the forefront of this resurgence, but patterns of outward growth towards rural hinterlands are also evident. A short profile of the region is presented in the following sections which documents the extent of changes occurring in the region's economic structure, summarizes primary elements of support for development and draws attention to future issues of regional significance.

DEMOGRAPHIC AND WORK-FORCE CHANGES

Official sub-national mid-year estimates indicate that the population of Yorkshire and Humberside (around 4.9 million) declined in size by 19,000 persons between 1981 and 1986. This fall of 0.4 per cent compares with an increase in the population of England and Wales of 0.9 per cent. However, North Yorkshire experienced a significant growth of 3.4 per cent, an increase which is predicted to continue through to the end of the century and will offset the further projected losses of population in South Yorkshire and Humberside to generate a regional population gain of 17,500 in total between 1986 and 2001.

The changing structure of the population is only partially explained by fluctuations in past levels of fertility. Aggregate net out-migration between 1981 and 1986 of over 35,000 outweighed the positive natural growth component of 16,700. Thus, it is evident that the region overall has not been particularly successful in retaining its population, although data from the National Health Service central register provides new evidence that the region's overall net migration balance had turned positive by the end of the decade (Stillwell, 1990). It is changes in demographic structure which present one of the most demanding challenges to those concerned with strategic planning and the provision of services. A major reduction in the number of young people reaching working age has significant implications for employers, employee training and educational agencies in the region. Changes in Yorkshire and Humberside are predicted to follow the national picture whereby the working younger age groups (15–29) will have much reduced numbers by 2001, whilst the older groups (30–64 for males and 30–59 for females) will experience increases but on a smaller scale. West Yorkshire is projected to lose over 100,000 persons aged 15–29 by 2001 but to gain 85,000 in the older working age range. It is clear from the projections for the working age population as a whole in the region up to the year 2001 (Table 4.1.1), that Humberside and South Yorkshire will face the largest shortfalls in contrast to North Yorkshire, where few demographic constraints on development should exist.

Table 4.1.1: Working Age Population Projections to 2001, by County

County	1985	Working Population Aged 16–60/65 2001	1985–2001	
	(000)	(000)	(000)	(000)
Humberside	516.6	492.0	-24.6	-4.8
North Yorkshire	425.7	474.4	+48.7	+11.4
South Yorkshire	802.9	766.4	-36.5	-4.5
West Yorkshire	1246.6	1233.9	-12.7	-1.0
Yorkshire & Humberside	2991.8	2966.7	-25.1	0.8

Source: Employment Gazette

The balance between different components of the labour force has changed markedly during the 1980s. A net gain of 128,000 female jobs contrasts with a net loss of nearly 67,000 male jobs between 1981 and 1989. Similarly, a loss of 37,500 full-time jobs was offset by a gain of 99,000 part-time jobs. Although fluctuations during the 1980s saw some diminution of the erosion of the labour force, it is a telling commentary on the nature of contemporary labour market dynamics that the only part of the workforce to grow consistently, and increasingly rapidly, across the region was the part-time component. Growth in this part of the labour force was particularly strong for women in North Yorkshire and for men in South Yorkshire. In 1987, for the first time, female part-time employment exceeded female full-time employment in both North Yorkshire and Humberside. It is also important to identify an increase in the demand for labour willing to take various forms of non-standard employment, mostly of a part-time nature, but also short contract, deregulated or casual work. This demand was frequently gender-specific, particularly in the traditional industries of textiles, clothing and food and drink manufacture.

In January 1990, 167,348 people were registered as unemployed in Yorkshire and Humberside, an unemployment rate of 7.2 per cent which compares favourably with rates in other northern regions but is still well above the unemployment rates to be found in the south of the country. Unemployment rates for the region's counties, which have all fallen appreciably since 1986, have been consistently high in South Yorkshire and low in North Yorkshire throughout the 1980s. Humberside began the decade with the worst rates but was overtaken during 1985 by South Yorkshire whose rates have remained relatively high ever since. Rotherham and Mexborough and Barnsley and Doncaster hold the distinction of being the Travel-To-Work Areas (TTWAs) with the worst unemployment rates, and the TTWAs with the highest rates of long-term unemployment.

SECTORAL AND STRUCTURAL COMPONENTS OF CHANGE

Not surprisingly, the spatial distribution of manufacturing industry in Yorkshire and Humberside today maintains a close resemblance to its historical geography (Leigh, Stillwell and Wilson' 1990), but by the end of the 1980s, it had become apparent that the mix of industries in the region was much closer to that of the nation as a whole than it was in 1981. The sectoral demands on labour, however, have fluctuated quite markedly during the decade. Using the time periods, 1981–84, 1984–87 and 1987–89, it is possible to trace the course of restructuring as it affected major sectors. First, there was a catastrophic and accelerating decline in both coal-mining and metal manufacture. Second, a decelerating decline occurred in the traditional regional industries of textiles and food, drink and tobacco. Third, and most importantly, there has been a turnaround in net employment in metal goods, clothing, paper, printing and publishing, and most dramatically of all, in mechanical engineering, which shifted from a loss of 26,000 jobs in 1981–84 to a net gain of nearly 6000 jobs in the 1984–87 period. Growth in the service industries has been particularly strong in financial, public and other services, whilst leisure and medical services have been less buoyant.

The changing situation of nationalised industries has been particularly important to the labour markets of the region because of the influence of major actors like British Coal and the British Steel Corporation. Coal-mining, once such a dominant component of the local economies of South and West Yorkshire, now employs only 2 per cent of the region's labour force (although this represents nearly 30 per cent of national employment in the industry). More redundancies are expected in the future related to nuclear fuel development and, more significantly, the privatisation of the electricity industry, which many believe will mean increased coal imports via the Humber ports.

British Steel was also active in restructuring in the late 1970s and early 1980s when a number of major closures took place in Rotherham, Sheffield and Scunthorpe. BSC rationalised those activities that overlapped with the private sector and disposed of businesses and investments outside its main areas of activity. In South Yorkshire, this led to the creation of new companies like Sheffield Forgemasters, for example, as an amalgamation of former BSC companies. What is left of British Steel in Yorkshire and Humberside is now undoubtedly successful, concentrating on stainless steel production in Sheffield (producing for 40 per cent of the UK market), and a highly efficient Scunthorpe plant which has set new European productivity records but again at enormous costs to the labour markets of the region.

Almost all the major manufacturing categories employed many more people in the region than might be expected as their national share. In these terms, therefore, the massive job losses that have occurred in the industrial base of Yorkshire and Humberside have not diminished the region's relative contribution to the industrial work-force of the country. The job losses and gains for dominant sectors of each county's economy have been matched against the performance of these sectors nationally for 1981–87 by Leigh et al (1990) using shift share indices. The largest positive differential shift values show 'other services' to be both absolutely and competitively buoyant in each of the four counties whilst the negative differential shifts for 'financial services', which were underperforming in each county despite job gains across the region up until 1987, were performing much more competitively by 1989.

The role of high technology in generating regional economic growth is recognised, but Yorkshire and Humberside, with only 2.2 per cent of the national share of high technology activities, ranked eighth in the regional league table in 1987. High technology, even taking the most liberal definition to include pharmaceuticals, telecommunications, electrical and electronic engineering, aerospace industries and research and development, made only a 1.7 per cent contribution to employment in the region in 1987.

The total number of businesses in Yorkshire and Humberside grew from 103,100 in 1980 to nearly 114,000 in 1986, but this increase is lower than that occurring in other regions of Great Britain apart from the North West. The changes within particular sectors display considerable diversity and confirm that North Yorkshire is the most successful county, outperforming the GB average in most sectors. In each of the constituent counties, firms employing less than 100 people make up at least 92 per cent of the business population but provide only about one-third of the employment. An important feature of the region is its higher than average share of companies with 100-500 employees and its lower than average share of very large companies (Leigh, Stillwell and Wilson, 1990).

Self-employment rose from just over 6 per cent of all employment in 1983 to 11.6 per cent in 1987. At the same time, Yorkshire and Humberside moved up the national ranking as a result of rapid rates of growth (nearly 40 per cent), assisted by the introduction of initiatives such as the Enterprise Allowance Scheme in 1983. Self-employment grew faster in this period than in any other region except for the South East, and the momentum has continued since 1987. This may suggest the existence of a strong entrepreneurial culture in Yorkshire and Humberside but it is more likely to owe something to the depth of recession in the early 1980s which affected certain parts of the region so adversely. Undoubtedly, many unemployed workers used their redundancy payments to set up their own, usually low order, businesses.

Yorkshire and Humberside retains an economy strongly supported by indigenous companies. It has the smallest proportion of foreign-owned manufacturing firms in the UK. In 1984, foreign manufacturing enterprises in the region employed 39,000 people, only 5.4 per cent of the UK total and well below the region's expected national share. The region cannot, therefore, be described as a branch plant economy. However, there have been some important indications of increasing interest in inward investment (Roberts and Leigh, 1990), not least from Japanese firms. Citizen, for example, has located in Scunthorpe, Nikken engineering has established its UK headquarters in Barnsley, and Pioneer has located in Wakefield. Since 1985, some of the most notable losses of indigenous control include Rowntrees of York, Burtons of Leeds, Johnson and Firth Brown of Sheffield, and the Yorkshire Bank. On balance, however, there are more new PLCs based in the region than moved their headquarters elsewhere. Thus, notwithstanding sizeable areas of depressed economic and social health, particularly in the south of the region, at least parts of Yorkshire and Humberside recovered from the recession of the early 1980s and had begun, by the end of the decade, to realise the potential based on nearness to European markets and to take advantage of good communication links with the rest of the UK. These trends are likely to continue as the nation diverts its attention away from its westward connections with the New World and the Commonwealth and towards emerging eastward connections with trading partners in the European Community and Eastern Europe.

SUPPORT FOR DEVELOPMENT

Large parts of the region are now eligible to receive European support for industrial and infrastructure development, although certain areas suffering high rates of unemployment (e.g. Castleford and Pontefract TTWA) failed to win recognition of the need for assistance from Brussels until 1989, when agreement on the designation of Objective 2 areas in Yorkshire and Humberside was finalised. North Yorkshire fails to meet the

NUTS II criteria and therefore Whitby TTWA continues to receive no EC funding despite recording one of the highest unemployment rates in the country. Between 1983 and 1988, over £150 million of European Regional Development Fund (ERDF) quota resources were commited to infrastructure projects in the region, with South Yorkshire receiving 48 per cent and Humberside 37 per cent of the grant approvals across all sectors. Despite recent ERDF reforms leading to a reduction in support for infrastructure expenditure, a high priority has been given to 'integrated development operations' schemes which aim to have greater impact by tackling the infrastructure and employment problems of a particular locality simultaneously. In December 1988, it was announced that part of the Steel Closure Area in South Yorkshire and Humberside would receive £108.7 million from the ERDF and a further £16.8 million from the European Social Fund (ESF) by 1992. A scheme for Bradford was also approved, involving a commitment of £43 million from the ERDF and £8 million from the ESF over the period 1988–92.

The role of EC funds in the financing of infrastructure development within Yorkshire and Humberside has become increasingly important during a decade which has witnessed a decline in regional policy expenditure provided by Central Government as well as a large reduction in the area scheduled to receive assistance. Yorkshire and Humberside has received between 5 and 7 per cent of total government expenditure on regional preferential assistance to industry, with firms in the Rotherham and Mexborough, Scunthorpe and Whitby TTWAs receiving around £25m in Regional Development Grants between 1984–1985 and 1987–88.

English Estates has been the only major developer of advance factories in much of the area of Yorkshire and Humberside designated to receive assistance. With a surge in demand in the late 1980s. Evidence suggests a greater involvement of the private sector in some of the better locations, particularly where much of the initial infrastructure investment had already been put in place. Considerable investment in the diversification of the economy of rural Yorkshire and Humberside occured during the 1980s through the Government's Rural Development Programme, under which most of North Yorkshire and large parts of Humberside were designated as Rural Development Areas.

As inner city problems have risen up the political agenda, the Government has responded with a battery of new initiatives focusing within the region on eight Urban Programme authorities. By 1990, the local authorities concerned had received £167m to improve sites and buildings, to encourage individual enterprise and to promote joint ventures. The majority of the funds have been allocated to the larger cities of Bradford, Hull, Leeds and Sheffield. Central to the Government's approach has been the establishment of partnerships with the private sector, through initiatives such as the Urban Development Grant (UDG) and the Urban Regeneration Grant (URG), both of which were superseded in 1988 by the City Grant and have been used to assist, for example, the £80 million redevelopment of Hull's Victoria Docks into a complex of shops, leisure facilities and homes.

Increasingly, the Government has taken a more direct role in inner city regeneration in the region, most notably through the establishment of 'third generation' Urban Development Corporations (UDCs) in Sheffield and Leeds in 1988. The Sheffield UDC covers part of the Lower Don Valley, the industrial corridor running between Sheffield and Rotherham, where the problems of obsolescent industrial building and land dereliction are particularly severe. The UDC was created with a budget of £50 million and an anticipated life span of seven years. One of the major developments within the area, in addition to the infrastructure for the 1991 Student Games, is the Meadowhall regional shopping centre, which will provide 1 million square feet of retail space and 250,000 square feet of leisure facilities. The Leeds UDC, covering parts of the Aire Valley at Kirkstall and a larger area to the south of the city centre, was given an initial allocation of £15m and has an anticipated life span of five years.

Local authorities at both county and district level have become increasingly concerned to facilitate the processes of economic development. One significant feature of change has been the formation of local authority companies. In 1984, West Yorkshire County Council, recognising the gap in the provision of equity capital, set up the West Yorkshire Enterprise Board Ltd (WYEB) as a development and venture company offering risk finance in equity and loan packages ranging from £25,000 to over £1m to companies based in West Yorkshire. After metropolitan county abolition in 1986, WYEB expanded its geographical area to cover the whole of the region and shortly thereafter became known as Yorkshire Enterprise Limited (YEL). YEL now has six joint venture capital companies operating with different local authorities in the region.

New partnership relationships between local authorities and the private sector have also been set up to develop sites and premises. In Leeds, for example, Leeds City Development Company has been established to develop appropriate schemes on land held by the Council. The board of the company, which includes city councillors and leading business representatives, has secured substantial backing from the private sector. Partnerships between private and public sector institutions have manifest themselves in a variety of different forms and each development project tends to have a different financing structure. In Wakefield, regeneration of the district is now being tackled through the local authority working in partnership with AMEC, a large construction company, in such a way that the authority retains a critical degree of control and the profits from more successful developments are used to cross-subsidise less profitable projects.

Within the region, a variety of organisations are responsible for stimulating or regulating the processes of development. The structure, functions and autonomy of each of these agencies fluctuate over time. Significant changes have taken place in the regional offices of central government, for example, in order to improve their co-ordination. All the regional bodies have a number of common interests, particularly in the area of infrastructure development. In the absence of a Regional Economic Planning Council, the four representative bodies (Regional CBI; Regional TUC; Association of Chambers of Commerce; and Yorkshire and Humberside Regional Association (YAHRA)) together with the region's promotional agency for attracting new investment, the Yorkshire and Humberside Development Association (YHDA), have established the Regional Partnership as a forum to identify and take action on common issues affecting the region (Leigh and Green, 1990).

ISSUES FOR THE FUTURE

What then are the future prospects for the region? Past evidence and analysis of the underlying structure of the regional economy suggest that, overall, development will reflect what happens in the national economy. It is reasonable to assume that the most prosperous areas (Leeds and parts of North Yorkshire, for example) will show growth rates comparable with many areas in the South East, whereas the least prosperous areas (especially parts of South Yorkshire) will show some of the smallest gains in the country.

A major determinant of the region's economy will be the performance of the existing indigenous manufacturing industry (Monck, 1990), under pressure to make further quality and delivery improvements, as well as to reduce costs. Companies that anticipate 1992 and establish a European or global marketing strategy are more likely to achieve levels of growth that are necessary to justify the new investment required to improve efficiency. One likely effect of the creation of the Single European Market for Yorkshire and Humberside is an increase in the level of mergers and takeovers as foreign firms attempt to acquire additional production capacity and market share. Another important effect of the Single Market is an increase in the level of inward investment as foreign firms seek to establish their production or distribution operations within the Market. The region is also likely to benefit from the in-migration of companies from other parts of the UK, particularly from the South East. Faced with increased congestion, labour shortages and rising property values, there are signs that an increasing number of firms in the South, especially in low value-added activities, are looking to expand or to relocate to new areas. There are a number of factors on the supply side that will also influence the future prosperity of the regional economy. One of these is the availability of human resources and the changing demographic structure of the work-force. It is widely held that the skills gap will widen as the needs of industry continue to outstrip the provision of training (Campbell, 1991). The role of the Training and Enterprise Councils (TECs) will of course be particularly important in the 1990s in this context.

Another important influence on future economic development involves the provision of suitable sites and premises. Constraints on land availablity are particularly apparent in West and South Yorkshire and around Hull. A balance will be required between alternative methods of making both 'brownfield' and 'greenfield' sites available. An upsurge in demand in the last few years and its impact on rental growth has led to renewed interest by the private sector in industrial and commercial property. Whilst new speculative development by private sector developers is still confined to the most prosperous parts of the region around Leeds, the M62 corridor and selected sites close to the M1, there has been a surge of interest to acquire tenanted properties for investment purposes. This is leading to an uneven provision of industrial and commercial premises in those areas which are able to command higher rents and secure greatest rental growth.

The quality of the link between Yorkshire and Humberside and the Channel Tunnel will be one of the most important issues during the next few years. It will be essential that a reliable and low cost freight service is developed to link the region with key locations on the continent. However, British Rail anticipate that only a relatively small proportion of the region's trade will use the Tunnel, whilst the majority of general cargo will continue to use the Humber ports. Further investment in port facilities is now being made, in anticipation of growth in trade with Northern Europe, as new industrial investment is attracted to the eastern side of the country.

Over the past decade, government initiatives in Yorkshire and Humberside have been many and varied, resulting in an increasing number of overlapping activities which only partially address the underlying problems and, in some cases, have led to competition and rivalry at the local level. Central government has striven to encourage participation by local industry and commerce whilst curtailing the role of local authorities in local economic management. These changes have contributed to reducing the coherence of the region at a time when the European Commission, in contrast, has increasingly looked to the regions and to regional bodies in those parts of Europe facing major structural difficulties to develop properly researched long-term strategies and economic programmes. The recognition of the need for a common voice for Yorkshire and Humberside has led to the creation of the Regional Partnership, whose effectiveness in the 1990s will depend on its ability to outline the case for key priorities and then undertake the necessary lobbying and promotion in a forceful way.

ACKNOWLEDGEMENT

The authors wish to acknowledge the material, ideas and comments received from various individuals and organisations in the region in the course of preparing this profile.

REFERENCES

Campbell, M. (1991) 'Trends and prospects in the regional labour market'. *The Regional Review* 1(2), 16–17

Leigh, C.M. and Green, H. (1990) 'The strategic imperative: the role of agencies in the region's development'. *The Regional Review* 1(0), 2–3

Leigh, C.M., Stillwell, J.C.H., Wilson, A.G. and Monck, C.S.P. (1990) *Yorkshire and Humberside: Economic Development and Future Prospects* Leeds: Yorkshire and Humberside Development Association.

Leigh, C.M., Stillwell, J.C.H. and Wilson, A.G. (1990) *Manufacturing under Pressure: Yorkshire and Humberside in Profile*. Leeds: Yorkshire and Humberside Regional Observatory.

Monck, C.P.S. (1991) 'Regional economic prospects: the basis for optimism'. *The Regional Review* 1(2), 2–3.

Roberts, P. and Leigh, C.M. (1990) 'Turning the tide? Overseas inward investment into Yorkshire and Humberside'. *The Regional Review* 1(0), 12–13.

Stillwell, J.C.H. (1990) 'Yorkshire and Humberside net migration turns positive'. *The Regional Review* 1(0), 4.

The North West

M. Clark, D. Gibbs, E.K. Grime and C.M. Law

INTRODUCTION

Any simple examination of performance indicators will suggest that North West England is a problem region. Population and employment are declining, unemployment is high, incomes are low and the region's residents have poor health. Further, the image of the region, which is not completely out of line with reality, is one of a poor urban fabric and pollution. Of course, such indicators need to be treated with care. For a region which is the most densely settled in Britain, some 'thinning out' might be considered desirable. Then again, lower incomes may be acceptable given lower living costs and do not necessarily suggest lower living standards. Finally, we should be wary of dubbing the whole of the region as a problem. It consists of many parts from the highly urbanised Manchester and Merseyside conurbations, to the more rural north Lancashire and south Cheshire, and the coastal resorts of the Fylde and Morecambe. Problems and opportunities may vary considerably. However, we believe that the state of the economy and the high level of unemployment do give real cause for concern and is one that should be tackled in a national review of spatial policy such as the RSA is encouraging.

In this brief report we shall review the assistance given to the region, population changes, economic and employment trends and unemployment. We shall give regard to the variations which exist within the region, and finally we shall suggest how government policies should be changed to solve the region's problems.

NATIONAL ASSISTANCE TO THE REGION

The economic history of the region, the rise of the cotton textile industry and associated activities, is well known and need not be repeated here. The relative economic importance of the region probably reached a peak just before the First World War after which the staple industries began to decline. Thus, whilst the focus of this paper is on changes and problems during the last ten years, it would be intellectually false not to place contemporary difficulties in the context of over 70 years of decline. Similarly, economic changes in recent years partly reflect the Government's response to regional problems, and thus a brief resume of urban and regional policies is appropriate at this point.

For various reasons which have never been fully explained, the region received no formal assistance under the 1934 Special Areas Act during the 1930s. However, just before and during the Second World War the region did benefit from the movement to and encouragement of industry in 'safe' western areas, most notably witnessed in the growth of the aircraft industry around Preston. After the war in, 1946, south Lancashire (St. Helens - Wigan - Leigh) was designated a Development Area, followed by Merseyside in 1949 and north east Lancashire in 1953. With the revival of regional policy in the late 1950s various parts of the region received assistance – most notably Merseyside, which around 1960 attracted several motor vehicle plants. By the mid-1970s, when regional policy was at its height, all the region received assistance;

Merseyside as a Special Development Area and the rest of the region as an Intermediate Area.

Since the Conservative government came to power in May 1979, regional policy has been cut back, both in the amount of assistance and in the geographical areas covered. Initially, much of the region lost Intermediate Area status, but in the changes announced in November 1984, this was restored to Blackburn, Accrington, Rossendale, Rochdale, Oldham, Bolton, Bury and central northern Manchester. At the same time, Special Development Area status was abolished, but Merseyside, Chester, Halton, St. Helens and Wigan were designated Development Areas. Since 1987 automatic assistance has been abolished – it is now all selective, with more chance of success and higher rates in the Development Areas.

This pattern of designation within the region needs to be placed in the wider geography of assistance. The adjacent area of north east Wales has been a Development Area for many years, as have parts of Cumbria and the rest of northern England. Thus southern industrialists wishing to move north have had considerable choice in this part of the country. The highest benefits have been consistently available in the north east Wales–Merseyside Area, which has gained much more from industrial movement than, say, the Greater Manchester area which had only intermittently been designated, and then only with a low level of assistance. Indeed it has been suggested many times, with at least some evidence, that firms have been moving from the eastern part of the region to Merseyside and north east Wales to gain the higher grants (examples include Brother Industries, Kelloggs and Sharp's). This highlights the question of the basis on which areas should receive assistance. Traditionally this has been unemployment, which has discriminated against the textile areas where net outward migration has reduced unemployment rates to near national levels.

The New and Expanded Town programme is another aspect of national policy which has impinged on the region. One of the prime objectives of these programmes was to plan the decentralisation of population from the conurbations using the ideas of Ebenezer Howard concerning green belts and satellite towns. In the first phase of this policy in the late 1940s no new towns were designated in the region, although thought was given to the designation of green belts. Later, with an upsurge in population growth, new towns were designated for Merseyside at Skelmersdale in 1962 and Runcorn in 1964, and, partly to serve Greater Manchester as well as other regional strategies, Warrington in 1968 and Central Lancashire in 1970. By the time the latter became effective, population relocation had ceased so that they merely served as growth points. The increase of population at Ellesmere Port, Widnes (both receiving Liverpool overspill population) Runcorn and Warrington served to reinforce the notion of a Mersey Corridor, elaborated in the 1973 Strategic Plan, and this corridor also benefited from the construction, during the 1970s, of the M62 and M56 motorways.

Whilst there were several town expansion schemes in the region, the only effective and significant one which resulted in long distance population movement was at Winsford. From the late 1970s the New and Expanded Town Programme became unpopular owing to the slow down in population growth and the rising importance of the 'inner city problem'. Accordingly, the New Town Corporations were wound up in 1985 for Central Lancashire and Skelmersdale, and 1989 for Warrington-Runcorn (the two corporations had been merged in later years).

Although inner city policies can be traced back to the late 1960s, current high profile policies began in 1978 with the passing of the Inner Urban Areas Act. Under this Act, Urban Programme funds became available to the Inner City Partnerships established in Liverpool and Manchester/Salford, to Programme Areas at Bolton, Oldham, Rochdale, Wirral, Knowsley and Blackburn, and to other designated districts at Sefton, St. Helens, Wigan, Burnley and Trafford (Old Trafford area only till 1987). The new Conservative government introduced the idea of Enterprise Zones and Urban Development Corporations. EZs were located at Salford/Trafford (1981), Speke (Liverpool) (1981) and north east Lancashire (1983). A Merseyside Development Corporation to revitalise the derelict docklands was established in 1981, to be followed by corporations for Trafford Park in 1987 and Central Manchester in 1988. In the early 1980s the then Secretary of State for the Environment, took a personal interest in Liverpool, calling himself the Minister for Merseyside, and establishing a special task force in 1981. This idea of task forces later became national, with forces located in Moss Side and Hulme (Manchester) (1986), Rochdale (1987), Preston (1987–90) and Granby Toxteth (Liverpool) (from 1989). In 1985 City Action Teams which co-ordinate government policy were established in Liverpool and Manchester/Salford. There have been many other initiatives, including a Freeport at Liverpool and Education Compacts in many Urban Programme areas.

POPULATION

As mentioned in the Introduction, the key feature as regards population is that there has been decline. This is shown in the table below:-

Table 4.2.1: Population Change in the United Kingdom and North West

	Population (000s)	
	UK	NW
1979	56,227	6498
1988	57,065	6364
Change (%)		
1979–84	0.4	-1.6
1984–88	1.1	-0.5
1979–88	1.5	-2.1

Regional population has been declining since the early 1970s. The rate of decline was highest in the early 1980s when the national population was growing slowly and there was severe economic recession. Decline slowed down in the mid-1980s when the economy began to grow and the national population increased more rapidly. Between 1981 and 1987 there was a small natural increase of 34,800 but this was offset by a large outward migration which resulted in a net decline of 124,200.

The main area of decline has been in the conurbations, and particularly in the inner cities. Large losses have been experienced in inner Manchester and Salford, although the rate of decline is now much less than it was in the 1960s and 1970s. Liverpool has been losing many people and the rate of decline appears to be continuing. Core area decline is often part of a process of decentralisation, which reveals itself in increases in peripheral areas. However, unusually in the North West there is very little evidence of this, most of the outer urban areas having a stable population. In the case of Greater Manchester, this may be because some of the outer areas are old cotton towns. In general these have shown a slight tendency to decline, continuing a long-term process. In the case of Merseyside, some of the outer areas such as Knowsley, also experienced decline. Only a decade or two ago these were the main expansion areas for the conurbation.

The principal area of growth in the region has been Warrington where an active Development Corporation has, for twenty years, exploited the town's good location at the intersection of the M62 and the M6. There were small gains in Congleton, which could be connected with the Potteries overspill, and in Vale Royal. In Lancashire the main area of growth was Chorley, perhaps a beneficiary of the policies of the Central Lancashire New Town. Elsewhere the Fylde conurbation and Lancaster, two coastal areas, showed a small increase in the period, with inward migration compensating for natural decrease.

EMPLOYMENT

Population changes might be expected to largely reflect employment trends, so it is to the economy that we now turn. The figures below show the trends for the region.

Table 4.2.2   Employment Change in Great Britain and North West

	Great Britain	Change %	North West	Change %
		Employees in Employment (000s)		
1978	22,218		2640	
1981	21,067	-5.4	2418	-8.4
1984	20,846	-2.2	2296	-6.5
1987	21,271	2.0	2345	2.1
1990*	22,491	6.7	2464	5.7

Source: Department of Employment Estimates

These figures reveal very clearly the poor performance of the economy. In the period 1978–84 when national employment was contracting decline was more severe in the north west, and when the national economy picked up and created new employment, it was not strong enough in the north west to stop further job losses. Overall, in the period 1978–88 over 300,000 jobs have been lost, representing 15 per cent of employment in 1979. To further understand these changes the two main sectors, manufacturing and services, can be separately considered. The figures below (Table 4.2.3) show the situation for manufacturing.

Table 4.2.3:Manufacturing Employment Change in Great Britain and North West

	Great Britain	Change %	North West	Change %
		Employees in Employment (000s)		
1978	7120		994	
1981	5968	-16.2	801	-19.4
1984	5327	-12.1	671	-14.0
1987	5107	- 4.1	663	- 1.2
1990	5096	0.9	679	3.3

Source: Department of Employment Estimates. 1987–90 change figure based on 1987 and 1990 estimates.

Nationally in this period over 2 million jobs were lost in this sector representing almost 30 per cent of employment in 1978. In the north west, where in 1978 manufacturing was more important in the structure than nationally, (31.8% against 28.4%) the rate of decline was worse. Over 300,000 jobs have been lost, equivalent to 32 per cent of employment in 1978. Thus the importance of and condition of manufacturing in the region has been a primary factor in the poor employment performance. However, it is interesting to note that the performance of manufacturing employment has been better since the mid-1980s. The figures for the service sector are given in Table 4.2.4

Nationally the service sector continued to expand, even during the recession, and since the mid-1980s has grown rapidly. In the North West the performance of the sector

Table 4.2.4: Service Employment Change in Great Britain and North West

	Great Britain	Change %	North West	Change %
		Employees in Employment (000s)		
1978	12,858		1448	
1981	13,091	1.8	1464	1.1
1984	13,542	3.4	1438	-1.8
1987	14,344	5.9	1507	4.8
1990*	15,644	9.8	1619	7.4

Source: epartment of Employment Estimates. 1987–90 change figure based on 1987 and 1990 estimates.

is much worse than nationally, but overall for the period there has been some growth, but this is so small as to make hardly any overall impression given the size of the decline in manufacturing. Some employment in this sector is related to consumer services, and clearly the decline of population will have affected any change of growth in this segment. Other employment in this sector is connected with producer services, which have proved a force for growth in London and the South East. However, the evidence in the North West is that whilst there has been some growth in this segment, it has been slower than nationally.

Table 4.2.5: Total Employment Change 1978–87

	1978	1987	Chnage %
	Employees in Employment (000s)		
Great Britain	22,218	21,271	-4.2
North West	2,640	2,345	-11.2
Cheshire	356	360	+1.1
Greater Manchester	1,136	1,017	-10.5
Lancashire	526	489	-6.6
Merseyside	618	478	-22.6

Sources: Censuses of Employment

For changes within the region figures are only available for the period 1979–87 (see Table 4.2.5). Nationally, employment declined by over 4 per cent, but declined at more than twice that rate within the region. Merseyside county experienced a decline of nearly 23 per cent, Greater Manchester of 10 per cent, Lancashire of nearly 7 per cent and Cheshire a small increase. However, these county figures conceal considerable variations. Within Cheshire, Chester and Macclesfield experienced growth, whilst Congleton (next to Macclesfield) had a 14 per cent loss. Ellesmere Port, Wigan, Manchester and Salford also had high rates of decline, as did the North East Lancashire area from Blackburn to Pendle. Within Lancashire, Lancaster and the West Lancashire District experienced growth. This varied pattern is difficult to interpret. It partly reflects the economic structure of areas, with those highly dependent on manufacturing suffering most. However, it also reflects other factors illustrated by decline in inner city areas and growth in peripheral and nodal areas (Warrington, Macclesfield and West Lancashire). These points can be further illustrated by reference to the manufacturing and service sectors (Tables 4.2.6 and 4.2.7).

Overall the region lost nearly one-third of its manufacturing jobs in the period 1978–1987. The highest rates of decline were in the Merseyside area (including Ellesmere Port), inner Manchester and Salford, North East Lancashire and Preston. Only Macclesfield and the Ribble Valley experienced an increase. Without detailed knowledge of local areas the variations in rates of decline are difficult to explain. Textile areas, inner city areas and new industrial estates with branch plants all suffered.

Table 4.2.6: Manufacturing Employment Change 1978–87

Employees in Employment (000s)

	1978	1987	Change %
Great Britain	7119	5107	-28
North West	997	672	-33
Cheshire	142	112	-21
Greater Manchester	437	293	-33
Lancashire	216	164	-24
Merseyside	202	104	-48

Source: Censuses of Employment

Table 4.2.7: Service Sector Employment 1978–87

Employees in Employment (000s)

	1978	1987	Change %
Great Britain	12,858	14,334	+11
North West	1448	1507	+4
Cheshire	178	219	*+22
Greater Manchester	616	653	+6
Lancashire	271	283	+4
Merseyside	373	343	-8

Source: Censuses of Employment
* This figure may be exaggerated due to boundary changes

Table 4.2.7 shows the situation for the service sector. The small overall increase in services in the region included a decline in Merseyside. This probably represented the continuing loss of jobs in the port and related activities. Elsewhere there were general increases in service employment, with the exception of inner Manchester and Salford and some eastern textile towns. The greatest increases in service employment occurred in areas such as Warrington, Vale Royal, Chorley, West Lancashire and Bury where either the population was increasing, creating a demand for services, or warehousing (near motorways) was developing rapidly.

UNEMPLOYMENT

Table 4.2.8: Unemployment Totals – Unadjusted North West (thousands)

Date	Male	Female	Total Unemployment rate	% of work-force
1988 March	253.5	104.6	358.1	11.9
June	233.5	96.0	329.4	10.9
September	231.1	98.2	329.3	10.9
December	211.5	81.3	292.8	9.7
1989 March	207.1	77.9	285.0	9.5
June	188.4	68.3	256.8	8.2
September	182.0	68.6	250.6	8.0
December	176.4	60.2	236.6	7.6
1990 March	177.8	59.8	237.5	7.6
June	167.9	55.1	223.0	7.2
September	175.3	59.5	234.8	7.5

Source: Department of Employment

As in other regions the figure has been falling partly because of small increases in the availability of jobs but mainly through reductions in those eligible to claim benefit and outward migration. The annual average for 1989 was, for example, 262,300 (8.4%) while in March 1988 it was as high as 358,100 or 11.9 per cent. Even the 7.5 per cent is unacceptably higher than the 5.9 per cent for Great Britain, and as such constitutes as real problem.

There are wide sub-regional variations. Examining the 18 travel to work areas (Table 4.2.9) in the North West (excluding Cumbria) we find that rates vary from 13.7 per cent in Liverpool down to 2.8 per cent in Clitheroe, an essentially non-urban area in north-east Lancashire. Wigan and St Helens (10.1%) and the Wirral and Chester (10.0%) are particularly badly affected, while Widnes and Runcorn (9.2%) is little better off.

Table 4.2.9: Unemployment: by Travel to Work Area in the North West – August 1990

	Total	Per Cent Unemployed
Accrington & Rossendale	3104	6.2
Blackburn	5297	8.0
Blackpool	6747	6.2
Bolton & Bury	14,334	8.2
Burnley	2850	6.8
Clitheroe	281	2.8
Crewe	2818	5.7
Lancaster & Morecambe	3559	7.9
Liverpool	61,242	13.7
Macclesfield	2027	3.6
Manchester	58,123	7.7
Pendle	1841	5.9
Preston	8956	5.9
Rochdale	5686	8.9
Warrington	4217	5.4
Widnes & Runcorn	5125	9.2
Wigan & St. Helens	17,159	10.1
Wirral & Chester	20,557	10.0

Source: Employment Gazette, September 1990

The towns immediately to the north of Manchester such as Rochdale (8.9%), Bolton and Bury (8.2%) and Blackburn (8.0%) all have above average rates and even Lancaster and Morecambe (7.9%) can be described as a problem area. The Manchester Travel To Work Area (7.7%) is only fractionally above the regional average, however.

The areas which are below average are the commuting zones surrounding the Merseyside and Greater Manchester conurbations. Macclesfield with 3.6 per cent does particularly well and Crewe (5.7%), containing much of Cheshire, has a low score. Warrington at 5.4 per cent is actually the third best area in the North West, probably reflecting the success achieved in the past by the Development Corporation. These Travel To Work Areas provide a first approximation in our analysis of the problem. They are rather unsatisfactory geographical units mainly because of their unequal size, but they give a flavour of the range of values involved.

Some of the most acute unemployment problems are hidden by taking such large geographical units. Inside what is probably regarded as a 'good' area like Cheshire, for example, certain areas in the north of the county experience very high rates of unemployment. The district of Halton, which includes Runcorn, had a rate of 10.8 per cent in January 1990, but seven of its seventeen wards were above this figure, with the highest, Castlefields, standing at 18.4 per cent. Greater Manchester displays similar variations. Manchester with 13.3 per cent has the highest district rate but the range in the city is quite extreme. Inner city Hulme fared worst with almost one-third (32.2%) of its resident population out of work while the southern ward of Didsbury recorded only 6.4 per cent. Similar, but perhaps not quite so extreme, conditions can be found in most, if not all, of the districts of Greater Manchester, Merseyside and Lancashire.

If we take a non spatial view of unemployment the greatest concern should be with the length of time people have remained out of work. Some 54 per cent (132294) have been unemployed for more than six months and 27,815 (11.4%) for more than five years. Over half (52%) of the long-term unemployed are over 45, indicating how difficult it is to break back into the labour market at an older age. In spite of the fact that in October 1988 all those under 18 who had not succeeded in entering the labour market were guaranteed a YTS place, and the consequent loss of entitlement of young people to claim unemployment benefit, 22,601 or 9.3 per cent were recorded as unemployed.

Geographically there is wide spatial variation in unemployment which is largely a reflection of the socio-economic status of the resident population. Paradoxically areas of low unemployment usually have few local employment opportunities because a high proportion are commuting to urban areas where jobs for them are available. Policies to increase jobs in inner city areas appear to be reenforcing this situation.

Table 4.2.10:Unemployment in North West England by County – June 1990

United Kingdom	1,555,610	5.5
North West	233,001	7.2
Cheshire	21,636	5.5
Greater Manchester	89,440	7.6
Lancashire	34,177	6.2
Merseyside	78,748	13.4

EVALUATION

We begin by examining some of the weaknesses of the economy. North West England is an old manufacturing region. It has suffered, and this shows to a lesser degree from a higher than average proportion of declining industries. Again it has a relatively high proportion of its employment in manufacturing industries. These two factors are important in explaining the employment decline that it has experienced in recent years. It has also suffered from the centralisation that has taken place within the British economy during the twentieth century. For industry this has meant that increasingly its firms have become parts of national (or multinational) organisations with their headquarters and other higher management functions including research and development, often based in London and South East England. When the region has benefited from an inflow of manufacturing capacity, as Merseyside did in the 1950s, 1960s and 1970s, these have usually been branch plants. Overall there has been a tendency for a branch plant economy to develop with lower skill and lower paid jobs in the region. Coupled with the decline of indigenous industry this has weakened business services in the region. If the role of government in research development and procurement is also considered, these functions mainly taking place in southern Britain, then it can be seen that the region has suffered from being distant from the centres of power, decision making and high technology. We must be careful not to overemphasize these points, because as we shall indicate below the region still has some strengths.

The region also suffers from the legacy of its early industrial development. There is a high level of pollution of air, water, sea and soil. Many of its buildings are old, obsolete and unaesthetic. There is much derelict land. They give a poor image to the region, one that is often picked up by the media and greatly exaggerated. This often frustrates the region in its attempts to attract visitors and new activities.

The region has also suffered from division and fragmentation. At every level it seems divided. Liverpool versus Manchester and Manchester versus Salford. It has been difficult to get the various interests of the region together to agree on policies for change and then to take them to those with power in the country. The recently formed Inward organisation is an example of this process, with many districts not being members. Earlier we discussed government assistant to the region. Here again the region was divided with substantial areas, principally the textile districts, either receiving little or no assistance. We believe that this has harmed regional development.

In recent years the position of this region in the north west of the country has increasingly become a disadvantage as Britain looks more and more to Europe. The decline of the Port of Liverpool is one example of this effect. There is a natural concern that with the approach of 1992 and the completion of the Channel Tunnel in 1993 this shift towards the south and east will be accentuated and the region will suffer further problems in its economy.

Finally and more controversially, there is some concern about the 'Liverpool' effect on the region. The confrontational approaches of many on Merseyside may well have done real damage to that part of the region. More importantly, the Merseyside image may have weakened not only that area but other parts of the region in its abilty to attract new investment.

Having mentioned the weaknesses of the region, it is appropriate to give some corrective by mentioning some of its strengths. North West England whilst small in area is large in population and economic activity. There are many sectors of its economy which are still large and relatively independent: chemicals, aerospace, and electrical engineering including computers. These employ skilled workers at several levels and of different types. There is a diversity in the region which is good: large cities, medium-sized towns, rural areas, each with their own advantages.

The peripheral location of the region should not be exaggerated. It is in fact central within the British Isles and close to other industrial regions such as the West Midlands, Yorkshire and North East England. Manchester is only 180 miles from London. There are good communications to and within the region, although these of course need to be constantly upgraded. In Manchester Airport is has the only international gateway outside South East England (other than the poorly used Prestwick).

Among the strengths of the region should be mentioned its academic institutions. There are five universities and three polytechnics, most with good links to industry and commerce. Taken with the research and development laboratories of industry within the region, these should offer some potential for the development of high tech industry. Another strength of the region is the size of its business services sector, particularly in Manchester. This is evidenced by the 22 foreign banks found in the city.

One final advantage of the region is the relatively low living costs compared to the South East. Wages may be lower, thus attracting firms, but because of lower costs living standards are just as high.

Given this list of advantages and disadvantages for North West England what is its future? We believe that if assistance can be given and the constraints removed there is considerable potential for development, much if not more than for any other region in the country outside the South East. Only the West Midlands could challenge the region. Given the tendency for South East England to overheat, for prices to rise in that region and then be passed on to the rest of the country, as witnessed in 1988, there is a good argument for diverting growth away from the South East. Given the high unemployment rates in many peripheral regions, including the North West, there is still a social argument for diverting growth away from the South East.

The opportunities for the region lie in three areas. First, in high technology industries, based on existing activities, labour skills and the institutions of higher education. Second, in the development of business services, particularly in the Manchester area, based on the existing industry and the potential that might be there if Manchester Airport is allowed to develop. Third, there is a potential in tourism, which is just beginning to be realised in cities like Liverpool and Manchester, as well as in the traditional localities.

PRESCRIPTION

How is this potential going to be realised? What policies by government are necessary? First, there must be a positive effort by government to decentralise and support regional government. This will affect very many areas from the arts, higher education, support for tourism, traditional regional policy to relocating as many of its own activities as possible, including research and development. This end could be furthered most significantly if regional government could be established, an idea which has wide political support outside the Conservative Party.

Many of the difficulties experienced in the North West and other regions are the result of the centralisation of the economy in London and the Greater South East. There is a need to break down this centralisation (to decentralise) and provide positive incentives in the regions. In the past, regional policy operated on the basis of sticks and carrots, the stick being controls in the South East. Whilst this was important in encouraging firms to move to the peripheral regions, given the present integration of the UK into Europe, such a policy is not feasible today. Instead, government must decentralise its activities, firms must be encouraged to locate in the peripheral regions through an enhanced regional policy and there should be some devolution of government.

There is now widespread support amongst non-Conservative parties for administrative devolution, which we also support. Regional government plus district authorities (some enlarged from their present size) would form a more suitable system of administration. Regional government would be responsible for strategic planning and a Regional Development Agency would enhance capital investment, including equity participation in new and expanding firms, especially those based in the region. The agency would attract and promote inward investment, the development of factories and estates, and development activity at strategic sites (such as is now partly being undertaken by Urban Development Corporations). This Regional Development Agency would receive some funds direct from central government as well as through local taxation. One of the current weaknesses in the North West is the fragmentation of structures and the competition which exists between authorities. Regional government would be a way of bringing the region together to achieve greater results than at present. The regional development agency would operate both in the manufacturing and service sectors. We regard the development of the latter as significant. It would include the enhancement of head office roles, business services, tourism and cultural activities, many of which are presently underdeveloped in the region.

The improvement of communications both to and within the region is extremely important if the region is to develop. Integration of Europe could leave the region more isolated unless efforts are made to improve basic transport and communications infrastructure. This would involve improved railway links and services to take advantage of the Channel Tunnel, enlarged and more motorways and the continued development of Manchester International Airport. Restrictions on routes should be removed. The provision of telecommunications and fibre optic channels is also important.

Finally, through both tiers of government there must be funds to clean up the rivers, to clean beaches, to reclaim derelict land and to generally upgrade the environment.

CONCLUSION

The above account has illustrated that the North West has suffered serious absolute and relative decline, and that this is especially acute in particular districts. We do not hold that because a region is growing less rapidly than the country, or declining faster, that this necessarily constitutes a problem. However, given the high unemployment and poor health record we believe that there is cause for concern. In spite of a period of growth within the national economy, the full effect has yet to be felt in many parts of the North West region. This suggests that positive interventionist policies are necessary of the kind described above. These policies are also desirable because of the overheating of the South East economy and its wider inflationary effects. The national economy would be more efficient if there were a greater spread of activity.

The Northern Region

Fred Robinson with members of the RSA Northern Branch

INTRODUCTION: THE NORTH REBORN?

At the end of the 1980s, many people in the North had begun to believe that the economic recession might, at last, be over in the region. Signs of new economic growth were clearly evident: a wave of Japanese inward investment; large-scale retail development; and waterfront redevelopments planned on the Tyne, Wear and Tees. Nissan's car plant at Washington, the MetroCentre retail complex in the Gateshead Enterprise Zone and the proposed redevelopment scheme for Newcastle Quayside became well-used symbols of the region's rebirth. Unemployment had been falling, house prices continued a belated rise. Most people in work enjoyed rising standards of living and shared in an unprecedented consumer boom. The North's 'moaning minnies', harangued by Mrs Thatcher in a legendary outburst on a rare visit to the region in 1986, became almost silent. The region's economic development agencies, the local authorities and the media were busy spreading optimistic 'hype' about economic recovery in 'The Great North'.

But the cold winds of recession are now blowing the region off course once again. The 'boom', such as it was, proved to be short-lived; nevertheless, it is argued that the region's industries – now leaner, fitter and more diverse – are better able to withstand recession than in the early 1980s. The impact of the present recession is difficult to forecast but further traumatic changes may well be in store. Sustained economic prosperity still seems an elusive goal for the North.

FROM ECONOMIC CRISIS TO PARTIAL RECOVERY

Overview

The Northern region is a textbook example of nineteenth-century industrialization based on 'carboniferous capitalism'. Coal-mining stimulated the establishment of iron and steel making, the development of railways, shipbuilding and heavy engineering. In the region's economic heyday – from the mid-nineteenth century until the end of the post-war boom in the early 1920s – its economic power was virtually unparalleled; in particular, it was a world leader in shipbuilding and heavy engineering, and the North East coalfield was one of the most productive in the country.

Subsequently, the region's traditional industrial base was hard hit by the depression of the inter-war years. The new consumer industries developed in the South, not the North; unemployment became a severe problem and the Northern region, a victim of outdated industrial specialization, was to become a testing ground for a succession of regional policies. At the end of the 1930s, rearmament revived the traditional industries and the 'long boom' of the 1950s served to maintain them until decline again set in from the early 1960s.

From the mid-1960s to the mid-1970s, a period of relatively strong regional policy and also investment in infrastructure, the North did gain many new branch plants in manufacturing industry which helped to offset the severe contraction of coal-mining and the continuing decline of traditional heavy manufacturing activity. As elsewhere, there was also substantial growth in public sector services in this period. Nevertheless, these sources of employment growth were insufficient to stem rising unemployment in the 1970s; even before the recession, the region was evidently experiencing serious economic difficulties.

The severe recession of the late 1970s and early 1980s undoubtedly had a catastrophic impact on the region, with massive job losses in all manufacturing industries. During 1980 and 1981 there were more than 66,000 redundancies, mainly in the manufacturing sector. The traditional industries witnessed a sharp decline, with the closure of steelworks (Consett, Workington), shipyards (on the Tyne, Tees and Wear) and engineering plants, coinciding with job-displacing capital investment in the Teesside chemicals industry. At the same time, the 'branch plant economy' – factories established with regional policy support – proved vulnerable to corporate restructuring prompted by the recession. This generated a steady exodus of many British-based multinationals, like Courtaulds, Dunlop, Plessey, TI, RHM and WD & HO Wills. The coal-mining industry also witnessed further contraction and, more recently, another wave of closures following the 1984/5 strike. The recession checked the long-term growth of the service sector as well, principally owing to public expenditure restraint.

Thus, between 1978 and 1983 the number of employees in employment in the Northern region fell by 185,000, a decline of 14.9 per cent. Most of this loss comprised full-time jobs, about three-quarters of them held by men, predominantly in manufacturing industry. Over the same period, regional unemployment increased by 100,000 to 225,000, rising from a rate of 9.3 per cent in 1978 to 16.3 per cent in 1983 – in spite of both changes to the methods of calculating the unemployment figures and the growth of Manpower Services Commission (MSC) schemes.

Since the mid-1980s there has been some recovery in the region's economy. Unemployment in the region fell steadily from 1985 until mid-1990, down to 116,800 by June 1990, a rate of 8.3 per cent compared with a national rate of 5.3 per cent. Since then, however, unemployment has been rising once again, edging upwards as the effects of the latest national economic recession begin to be felt in the North. High unemployment is regarded as endemic in the region and the North has, for many years, recorded the highest regional rate of unemployment in mainland Britain.

Economic and Employment Trends

The number of employees in employment in the North is estimated to have increased from 1,061,000 in June 1986 to 1,119,000 in December 1990 – an increase of 58,000, or 5.5 per cent. This is, of course, a welcome trend, but there is still a long way to go to make up for the losses of the early 1980s and, indeed, to tackle the region's unemployment problems. Moreover, employment is now falling as a consequence of the present recession.

Nearly all the recent employment growth has been in the service sector of the economy. The decline of manufacturing jobs continues: the number of manufacturing jobs in the North fell by more than 30 per cent between 1979 and 1990. In a sense, the kinds of jobs being created by the MetroCentre – around 6000 jobs, mainly part-time, low paid female employment – are more typical of recent trends in the economy than are the incoming Japanese branch plants.

The region has undergone a profound process of *deindustrialization*: only 24 per cent of jobs are now in manufacturing industry, compared with 33 per cent ten years ago. The near-extinction of shipbuilding – now represented, since the recent closure of Sunderland's yards, by just two remaining yards, at Barrow and on Tyneside – is perhaps symbolic of the final destruction of the old industrial order. So, too, is the decline of the other great staple industry, coal-mining, now reduced to a mere five pits: coal-mining employment in the region has fallen from 125,000 in 1960 to under 6000 by 1992. The potential for *reindustrialization* is not yet clear but, so far, it remains much more limited than the media 'hype' would suggest: Japanese plants in the region currently employ only about 10,000 people, for example (and their contribution is outweighed by disinvestment by the region's American-owned companies over the last decade). The growth of the service sector has led to the further 'tertiarisation' and, with it, 'feminisation', of the economy: women now comprise 47 per cent of the region's employed work-force, largely concentrated in public and private service sector jobs. There has been a welcome increase in job opportunities for women and female activity rates have been rising – resulting in labour force growth despite net out-migration.

To what extent has the 'enterprise culture' taken root in the North? To take one measure, there has been a steady increase in the number of self-employed people in the region over the last ten years, but it is interesting to note that the rate of growth of self-employment in the North slowed significantly in the second half of the 1980s. In the country as a whole, self-employment has really 'taken off' but the North appears to have fallen well behind the national rate of self-employment growth: self-employment in the region grew by just 26 per cent between 1976 and 1989, compared with 66 per cent nationally, and from a much lower base. Only 7.9 per cent of the workforce was self-employed in 1989 in the North, well below the UK figure of 11.5 per cent. One might well be drawn to the conclusion that the great efforts to encourage self-employment in the region over the past few years have, in fact, made relatively little difference and have not had much real impact. It could also be concluded that the North, with its economic problems and particular economic structure (large plants, nationalized industries, public sector dependence) has provided a rather hostile environment for the small entrepreneur.

After employment, either in terms of employees or self-employment, a third element in labour demand is the provision of training or temporary employment through government schemes. This is especially important in a region where the majority of 16-year-old school leavers join the Youth Training scheme (YT) because jobs are simply not available. In August 1991, 26,000 youngsters in the region were on YT – an increase of nearly 7500 since 1985. In 1990, 23,300 adults were on Employment Training, 10,000 more than on the previous scheme, the Community Programme, in 1985. Aside from the obvious effect of these schemes on the unemployment figures it is worth remarking that their significance and growth underlines the region's weakness and the continuing failure to generate sufficient 'real' jobs in the economy. Moreover, this failure is not just a question of numerical supply and demand: many of the unemployed are either unskilled or have redundant skills in traditional industries, while the new jobs being created are part-time and low paid or in the white-collar service occupations. This mismatch is still not being seriously addressed, either through training initiatives or economic development policy.

Social Trends

The North-South divide in the economy and in employment prospects is paralleled by a similar divide in social circumstances and well-being. Certainly, Northerners have the advantages of lower house prices and often less stretched public services than in the overcrowded South. There is easy access to fine coast and countryside and the region has some very 'liveable' towns and cities. For those in secure and well-paid jobs there is a good 'quality of life' and there are parts of the region which are quite affluent.

Notwithstanding this, however, the North is a poor relation to the South with, on average, lower standards of living and poorer 'life chances'. Various indicators can be cited to demonstrate this:

Income Average weekly household income in the Northern region is now the lowest in the UK, at nearly 19 per cent below the national average and the region's relative position has deteriorated over the 1980's. The North has a higher proportion of low income households (below £80 p.w.) than any other region and the third lowest proportion of households with incomes over £400 pw. This situation stems both from high unemployment and a consequent reliance on benefits and also a growing problem of low pay. Tax cuts to high earners, cuts in the relative value of benefits and labour market deregulation have further disadvantaged the North.

Education and Training Fewer young people continue in education after 16 in the region. In 1988/89, 43 per cent of 16-year-olds stayed in full time education at school or college, compared with 48 per cent in Great Britain as a whole, but this does represent a marked improvement in recent years. Nevertheless, the lack of job opportunities, coupled with traditional attitudes on the value of education, appear to discourage extended education and encourage youngsters to enter the labour market competition early. The Youth Training scheme (YT) has very largely replaced apprenticeships and the conventional youth job market; in September 1989, 42 per cent of 16 and 17-year-olds in the North were on YT, compared with 25 per cent of this age group in Great Britain.

Health The North's Standardised Mortality Ratio, at 111 (UK = 100) for males in 1988, is the highest of any region in England and well above that of the South East (92) or East Anglia (89), for example (see Table 4.3.1). This links to a wide range of factors, including deprivation and occupationally-related disease. At the same time, health service expenditure per head is well below the national level and the average number of persons per GP remains higher in this region than elsewhere. There remains an overwhelming reliance on NHS services: in 1987 only 4 per cent of males and 3 per cent of females aged 16 and over were covered by private medical insurance in the region compared with national (GB) figures of 10 per cent and 8 per cent respectively.

Housing Differences in house prices and house price inflation confer both advantages and disadvantages: Northerners need spend less on housing but find severe difficulties in moving to another region and buying a house there. But, above all else, regional house price differentials are a manifestation of the North – South economic

Table 4.3.1: Standardised Mortality Ratios By Region – 1988

	Index : UK = 100	
	Males	Females
United Kingdom	100	100
North	111	110
Yorkshire & Humberside	104	102
East Midlands	98	99
East Anglia	89	92
South East	92	94
South West	90	91
West Midlands	102	102
North West	109	108
England	98	98
Wales	102	100
Scotland	114	111
Northern Ireland	113	109

Source: Regional Trends, 25 (1990)

divide, with much lower prices in the region reflecting its lack of economic buoyancy. The price gap widened considerably in the mid-1980s, with some subsequent convergence as regional house prices inflated and prices in the South slumped. By 1989 the average price of a house in the North was 71.7 per cent of the UK average – almost the same differential as in 1985.

In addition to these indicators, it is also worth making reference to the 'culture' and attitudes in the region. Above all, while the region's promotional agencies are anxious to cast off the cliché of 'cloth caps and whippets', the North does remain strongly 'traditional working class' in terms of outlook and lifestyle. The North remains faithful to the Labour Party: at the 1987 general election, 46.4 per cent voted Labour in the region, compared with only 30.8 per cent in the UK and 72 per cent of the region's employees were in a trade union in 1984, compared with 58 per cent nationally. Things are changing – witness the acceptance of single union agreements and no-strike deals in new factories – but Thatcherism did not properly take hold. The vast majority of people still look to the public sector to provide education and health services, for example, and still retain at least a degree of class consciousness and cohesion.

THE CURRENT STATE OF THE REGION: KEY ISSUES

Patterns of Inequality

Northerners may feel a great loyalty to their area and feel satisfied with their quality of life but materially, at least, they are worse off – on average – than most of their counterparts in the rest of Britain. On nearly all economic and social indicators, the Northern region comes off badly. A sense of grievance or injustice is further provided by the relative powerlessness of the region's institutions and people. Its industries are largely the 'global outposts' of national or multi-national companies headquartered elsewhere: around 80 per cent of manufacturing employment is in externally owned and controlled companies, including about 16 per cent in foreign-owned businesses. At the same time, the powers of its (predominantly Labour) local authorities have been increasingly curtailed by the (Conservative) central government, leaving the region cast in the role of a colony governed by a distant and unsympathetic government in London.

But, in addition to inter-regional differences, there are significant inequalities *within* the North, differences as great as any North-South divide. There are prosperous 'county' towns, for example, such as Hexham in Northumberland (unemployment rate just 3.7 per cent in September 1990) as well as places with severe problems such as South Tyneside (with an unemployment rate of 14.3 per cent in September 1990, the highest of any TTWA in mainland Britain).

It has become apparent that the various economic, social and political changes of the last ten years have led to increasing inequality, indeed increasing polarization, not only between North and South but between socio-economic groups or classes. In turn, these inequalities are manifested in intra-regional spatial variations. In the North, those in secure, well-paid, white-collar jobs have reaped further rewards and advantages, while the unemployed, the low paid, the 'claiming class', the poor, are being left further and further behind.

Economic development policies

The region has tried and tested – sometimes to destruction – almost every kind of economic development policy option available within the context of a 'mixed economy'. Policy fads and fashions have come and gone, each leaving a layer of policy and a set of institutions. The region consequently has a plethora of economic development policies and agencies, each with a range of objectives and each hardly evaluated, if at all.

Government (DTI) regional policy remains in operation, though pruned through revisions in 1984 and again in 1988. Gone are the automatic subsidies (Regional Development Grant) on capital investment, most of which used to go to the big capital-intensive industries, notably ICI, British Steel and British Nuclear Fuels. Now, the emphasis is on selectivity, aiding smaller job-creating companies and inward investment projects from overseas. In 1988–89, the region received £133.7m in regional preferential assistance. Here, as elsewhere, companies may also receive support for consultancy services and innovation from the DTI's 'Enterprise Initiative', provided at a preferential rate in the Assisted Areas.

While regional policy has declined in importance, both financially and politically, urban and local policy has become much more prominent. The Urban Programme, (covering local authorities in Tyne and Wear and Cleveland), together with the European Community, has helped local authorities to maintain and even expand economic development policy initiatives in spite of expenditure cuts and, in some cases, rate-capping. While economic development policy is generally on a larger scale in the urban areas, it is also pursued by nearly all the other local authorities throughout the region; only in relatively affluent rural commuter areas is development resisted; elsewhere it is anxiously sought. Local authority economic development policies in the North tend to be somewhat conventional, the uncontroversial products of a right-wing Labourism, mainly involving the provision of sites, premises and financial assistance, most often to smaller businesses.

The region has four Enterprise Zones established in the 1980's (Tyneside, Hartlepool, Middlesbrough, Workington) due to end their leases of life in the early 1990s. A fifth EZ – quite possibly the last – was designated in Sunderland in 1990 to counter the effects of recent shipyard closures. The EZs, the most spatially-targeted element of the Department of Environment's urban policy, have had limited success. In the main they have served to distort local property markets and/or promote short-distance moves. The distortion effect is evident in the location of retail developments including Gateshead's MetroCentre and 'Retail World' schemes, both of which might otherwise have taken place elsewhere in the Tyneside conurbation. The EZs have also promoted substantial environmental improvements by bringing back into use derelict and despoiled sites. They have not, however, stimulated the creation of many new manufacturing jobs.

The region also has a considerable number of local enterprise agencies. Most of these are financially supported by local and/or central government. Some have been funded by the job-creating subsidiaries of British Steel, British Coal and British Shipbuilders in the wake of large-scale redundancies. Private sector support is rather limited – unsurprising, perhaps, in a branch plant economy. Examples of these agencies and initiatives include the Tyne and Wear Enterprise Trust, Cleveland's CADCAM Centre and, in Cumbria, Workington's Moss Bay Enterprise Trust. At the regional level there are some similar, but more specialized, agencies: the Northern Region Co-operative Development Agency and the North East Media Development Trust, for example.

Central government, uneasy about local authority economic development activities, has sought more control over such policies and initiatives through the creation of Urban Development Corporations. Two UDCs were established in the region in 1987, covering riverside areas in Tyne and Wear and in Cleveland, and they are now of major importance in the region: unlike the local authorities they have massive resources to spend on urban regeneration – but unlike the local authorities they are not subject to local democratic control. Both UDCs have placed heavy emphasis on property development as the key to regeneration and have announced several major development schemes to be undertaken by the private sector with substantial UDC grant subsidy. Retail and leisure schemes, housing and some office development are planned (e.g. at Newcastle Quayside) and also marinas (e.g. on the Tyne and at Hartlepool docks). Unlike some cities subject to regeneration policies, in these derelict areas of the North there is little to displace or gentrify and few 'yuppies' but, even so, these developments are clearly not aimed at the unemployed, the poor or, more generally, the 'working class'. At this point, the impacts of UDC activities must remain uncertain since, in both conurbations, most schemes are either under construction or still on the drawing board, but some success has been achieved, notably the Newcastle Business Park. The recent collapse of the property market – the effects of which are now belatedly being felt in the North – now adds uncertainty about which schemes will actually go ahead in the future.

The next step forward from UDC-style regeneration may be an even more privatized approach led by the private sector itself, rather than by an intervening quango. The Government has certainly been keen to promote such a shift of responsibilities directly onto the private sector. Out of this 'privatization' of economic development policy has come 'The Newcastle Initiative' (TNI), a private sector-led organization concerned to stimulate regeneration which originated from a CBI 'Inner Cities Task Force'. Working with Newcastle City Council and the UDC, TNI has largely devoted energy to promotional activities rather than action, with emphasis on promoting the regeneration of the city's Victorian Grey Street, encouraging the creation of a 'Theatre Village' and fostering further links with the Japanese. Sunderland has followed with a similar organization, 'The Wearside Opportunity' and Teesside has recently followed suit with 'Teesside Tomorrow'. The recent introduction of the Training and Enterprise Councils represents yet a further move to 'privatize' economic development policy, but the new 'City Challenge' initiative suggests a partial shift back to public sector intervention.

TNI and its Wearside and Teesside counterparts form a part of a now vigorous pro-business, pro-development lobby concerned with 'talking-up' and 'selling' the region, a lobby which embraces the local authorities, the UDCs, the regional TUC and CBI and also the region's inward investment promotional agency, the Northern Development Company (NDC). The NDC, the latest in a long line of promotional agencies, is an interesting case of pro-business consensus since it was founded and is supported by both local and central government and both the CBI and the TUC. All these organizations, along with the region's media and the local 'elite', are now embarked on promoting 'The Great North', a campaign aimed at changing the image of the region to attract inward investment. Ten years ago, the call was for public sector infrastructure and financial support for industry; today, in stark contrast, the new regionalism is about image building, marketing opportunities and hiding from view the region's problems.

The European Dimension

In the North, membership of the European Community (EC) has, until recently, largely been seen as providing a source of funding for various programmes to alleviate the region's problems. Certainly, this remains a significant and beneficial aspect of membership, and may well assume even greater importance in the future. But, in addition to these support measures, EC membership is now increasingly being recognized as a major economic challenge in relation to the Single European Market. The opportunities – and threats – associated with 1992 are being considered and debated in the region, with an expectation that EC integration will have a considerable impact on the region's economy.

The region's local authorities in particular have come to be familiar with the EC and its operations, drawing mainly on the Regional and Social Funds, most commonly to support investment in infrastructure such as roads and industrial estates. Both Shildon in County Durham and the Tees Corridor receive innovative EC programme funding for a wide range of projects to deal with especially severe problems while other areas affected by closures in steel, shipbuilding and coal mining have also been targeted for special assistance. Most of the region is eligible for assistance in the future under Objective 2 of the new Structural Fund Regulations. Two areas, embracing a large part of the region, have established long-term assistance programmes: 'Integrated Development Operations Programmes', covering Durham/Cleveland and Tyne and Wear/South East Northumberland. In addition, such schemes as the Kielder reservoir and the Tyne and Wear Metro have received grants from the EC and a substantial part of the activities of the MSC/Training Agency have been funded from Europe. Public sector agencies, particularly the local authorities, have thus responded positively to the EC and would not find difficulty with the notion of a 'Europe of Regions' involving direct negotiation between the region and Brussels, sidestepping an often unenthusiastic central government. The private sector response has, however, perhaps been less enthusiastic; few of the region's firms have sought to benefit from EC technology initiatives, for example.

There are well-grounded fears that, on balance, the North will lose more from the Single European Market than it will gain. Stronger competition will apply further pressure on firms hit hard by two deep recessions within a decade. There is a general concern, too, that the North will suffer even more from the disadvantages of peripherality within Europe, distant from a relatively fast-growing core and distant, also, from the Channel Tunnel. On the other hand, the North has succeeded in attracting branches (often 'screwdriver plants') of companies based outside the EC which are anxious to have a presence within post-1992 Europe.

THE FUTURE OF THE NORTH

Is the North now set on course for revival and regeneration? Will the North-South divide be seriously reduced? Can the North develop a self-sustaining, balanced and growing economy? Above all, can there be a return to 'full employment' in the North?

Looking ahead over the next few years, say to the mid-1990s, there are grounds for optimism – but also for pessimism. It may realistically be expected that the region's economy will continue to have problems which may well be exacerbated by intensifying competitive pressures:

- Further decline of what remains of the traditional industries can be expected. There will almost certainly be further pit closures, while shipbuilding and heavy engineering could well experience further contraction. Privatization of the electricity generation industry (stimulating further imports of cheap coal) and the Single European Market (opening up defence procurement) will put severe pressure on these industries.

- Increasing takeover activity may further weaken the position of indigenous companies and downgrade the status of existing branch plants in the region.

- Job-displacing investment is to be expected both in manufacturing and in the service sector. In manufacturing, there are still opportunities to displace labour by capital investment especially in the labour-intensive assembly operations so well-represented in the region (and also in such areas of production as bulk chemicals). The region has also some dependence on 'clerical factories' doing routine work and further developments in information technology could well reduce labour demand here.
- The move towards regional pay differentials and local wage bargaining might well, ultimately, dampen down growth in disposable incomes, with deleterious knock-on effects in retailing and other parts of the private sector services.
- More generally, the trend is towards an even greater 'peripheralization' of the North, distant from the core of the EC Single Market and gaining little or no benefit from the Channel Tunnel.

Countering these tendencies and trends, there are some important prospects for growth and regeneration in the region's economy:

- There are likely to be further relocations of non-EC branch plants, taking advantage of the Single European market, and a supply of low wage labour.
- Some activity can be expected to be relocated from the South to the North, including routine clerical work in the private sector and also in the public sector (e.g. civil service jobs) as well as some manufacturing activity. This very much depends, however, on economic conditions in the South: recession reduces the impetus to move as the once overheated economy cools and labour becomes more easily available in the South.
- The region's two Urban Development Corporations, to remain in business until the late 1990s, are subsidizing property development which may help stimulate growth – of office employment, for example. They have also been successful in attracting new private sector investment. Sunderland's recently established Enterprise Zone should also prove attractive, especially since other Zones are now reaching the end of their designation.
- There appear to be reasonable prospects for some growth in new sectors, notably in tourism which is clearly underdeveloped in the region.

It is difficult to form a view on the overall balance between these positive and negative trends in the economy. Assuming no really massive national economic collapse, the region's economic fortunes do appear more hopeful over the next five years than they were back in the early 1980s. But it is to be expected that unemployment will remain at an historically high (and unacceptable) level. No-one, case hardened by the experience of the early 1980s, could confidently predict a return to 'fifties-style full employment in the region within the foreseeable future. The continuation of high unemployment, together with the growth of low-wage, casualized private sector services, emphasizes again the need for ameliorative social policies to deal with the widening economic and social divides within the region itself. There is a real danger that a permanent 'underclass' is being established. Regional policy must take on board this social dimension to guard against polarization within regions as well as tackling the North-South divide.

It is far from clear that the North's economy is moving towards balanced and self-sustaining growth. One of the lessons from the last few years is that a branch plant economy is in a vulnerable position – and the region is, once again, re-creating a branch plant economy. Are the new foreign-owned plants now coming to the region likely to be more permanent than those which came in the 1960s? Or will we see a mass exodus of Japanese plants in the late 1990s, with movement to other locations in the 'United States of Europe'?

The hard truth is that the region's relative position in the mid-1990s will probably be much the same as it is today. What the region needs is a degree of power and autonomy – regional devolution – to grasp new opportunities rather than merely react to events, coupled with social policies to cope with the consequences of a harsh competitive climate: in other words, a set of policies which fundamentally transcends conventional regional policy.

CHAPTER 5

THE CELTIC NATIONS

5.1

Wales

R. Ross Mackay

Wales remains a land of contradiction. A country of great beauty, remembered for industrial and mining landscapes. A nation proud of language and culture, but lacking the independent institutions which ensure voice and influence. A people with a strong sense of Welsh identity, but unwilling to embrace devolution. A territory which was once the centre of the iron and steel industry, with techniques copied by every developing country, but which remained dependent on external capital. A country divided between south and north. A developed region whose internal transport links have been compared unfavourably with those in Third World countries. Recent and planned improvements in North and South Wales concentrate on improving links to England. They do not address the problem of contact between North and South Wales.

And finally Wales is an industrialized region which has lost much of its industrial base. Until recently, important industrial areas within Wales were dominated by coal and steel. As the dominant industries and employers declined, it has become more difficult to identify and differentiate the Welsh economy. In a time of general change the steep decline in major sectors of the Welsh economy has few parallels in Europe. Half the jobs in Welsh steel disappeared between 1977 and 1980. Between 1979 and 1986 employment in industrial units with over 1000 employees fell to one-third of the 1979 level. Employment in coal-mining has been halved since the miners' strike of 1984, continuing a decline that has seen the loss of 8 out of 10 miners' jobs in Wales over the last two decades.

A recent review of unemployment (Piore 1987) claims that modern unemployment takes its characteristic form from the employment relationship within large, (apparently) permanent manufacturing (and mining) units. Employment required a clear separation between formal and informal economy – a clear divide between work and household activity. With employment ties of this kind lost, there is a gap in the community and around the individual which is the essence of present unemployment. That gap, or space, is not confined to Wales, but it is evident in a region where local labour markets were often dominated by major employers.

This review of economic performance will (1) provide a picture of the recent past of major industries in Wales (the period covered includes the major recession of the post-war years and subsequent recovery), (2) indicate why Wales has had particular problems in recovering from deindustrialization, (3) explore unemployment, concealed and open, (4) stress that the potential and problems of Wales must be seen in a wider context (economic performance in Wales links to trends in the national and international economy), (5) consider the forms of policy that are important to Wales. It is people who form the dynamic agents in economic development. But the release of their potential depends on key, strategic decisions which can only be made by government.

INDUSTRIAL OUTPUT

The period since the mid 70s has been one of rapid socio-economic change. Many of the changes can be traced to the economy where there has been a far-reaching restructuring of the economic base. In industrial developed economies, output normally grows. Capital accumulation and innovation in product and process move the production possibility frontier outwards. However, in spite of notable improvements in productivity, output in the production industries of Wales remained well below 1979 levels in 1987. The shift away from manufacturing and disappointing performance in manufacturing is not confined to Wales, but there are important contrasts. In Great Britain industrial output falls from 1979, but recovers from 1981 and returns to 1979 levels by 1985. In Wales industrial output falls from 1979 to 1984 and is still 9 per cent short of 1979 level in 1987. The recession was deeper in Wales, the recovery less impressive.

Given improvements in productivity, falling (or stable) real output implies (1) a transfer to service employment (2) unemployment or (3) hidden unemployment. All three have taken place, but the major shifts involve unemployment (open and concealed).

EMPLOYMENT CHANGE

Welsh service employment (employment outside of the production industries, agriculture and construction) fell by 5000 (less than 1%) between 1979 and 1987. Service employees have grown as a proportion of total employees, but this follows from decline in industrial employment. The important shifts sum to a notable reduction in jobs (a 16% decline in employees in employment between 1979 and 1987). Table 5.1.1 provides detail on sectoral shifts. In all production industries employment declines: in important sectors decline is rapid. In the service industries additional employment in banking, insurance and finance is less than jobs lost in transport and public administration. Table 5.1.2 shows employment change for males and females. In the eight year period, which included the major recession of the post-war years and subsequent recovery, one in

Table 5.1.1 Welsh Employment Changes by Sector 1979–87
(Employees in Employment)

Sector	% change	Change in Employment (000s)
Metal, Manuf., Chemicals	-46	-49
Coal, Energy, Water Supply	-45	-28
Metal Goods, Engineering, Vehicles	-44	-51
Construction	-30	-18
Transport and Communication	-29	-17
Ag., Forestry and Fishing	-16	-2
Public Admin	-14	-14
Other Manuf.	-10	-9
Education, Health and Social Services	+1	+2
Distribution, Catering	+4	+7
Banking, Insurance, Finance	+32	+17
Total	*-16*	*-162*

Source: Employment Gazette, Historical Supplements, No.1 and No.2

five male jobs were lost to the Welsh economy. Female full-time employment also declined.

Table 5.1.2 Welsh Employment Change:
Male and Female Employees in Employment 1979–87

	% change	Change in Employment (000s)
Male	-22	-134
Female (full-time)	-19	-48
Female (part-time)	+14	+21

Source: As for Table 5.1.1

Employment decline has been severe, particularly for males and even more notably for those employees who relied on the major employers within Wales. In 1979 there were 50 manufacturing establishments with over 1000 employees: by 1986, only 18. The forms of employment which identified and defined industrial and mining communities disappeared. The major employers created local economies: without them community and economy lack direction.

OUTPUT AND CONSUMPTION

Reduction in employment does not imply falling output, income, or consumption in the overall Welsh economy. Access to the 'necessaries and conveniences of life' continue to improve, at least for those in employment. Real value added within the Welsh economy (including services), after tax income and consumption levels all grow in the 1980s (see Table 5.1.3). There are two important provisos. Improvement is slow by the standards set in earlier years. And we see a change in trend. In the 1970s (see Table 5.1.3) the economic indicators show Welsh income and consumption levels converging on those in the rest of the United Kingdom. In the 1980s the gap between Wales and other parts of the United Kingdom grows.

Table 5.1.3 Output, Income and Consumption in Wales

Real percentage Change Between 1979 and 1986 in:

Gross Domestic Product per Head			Personal Disposable Income per Head			Consumption Expenditure per Head		
+5%			+2%			+9%		
Wales as % of UK Average			Wales as % of UK average			Wales as % of UK average		
1971	1979	1986	1971	1979	1986	1971	1979	1986
88	90	86	91	93	89	91	93	88

Source: Welsh Economic Trends, Economic Trends

Less than 60 per cent of Welsh household income comes from wages and salaries, a rather lower proportion than in the UK as a whole. For those in employment, average earnings are close to UK levels (roughly 97%). A larger proportion of income (close to one-fifth by 1986) comes from social security benefits. The increasing importance of these benefits is a natural consequence of high unemployment (open and concealed) rather than growing generosity from Welfare State.

DECLINE AND RECOVERY

There is a view of economic adjustment which essentially sees 'shake-out' and employment decline as providing the opportunity for employment growth in alternative industries. Some economists believe that there are strong forces at work which tend to restore a market economy to full employment. No matter the shock to the economy, no matter the degree of change – unemployment and output loss are seen as temporary.

They involve transitional adjustment as resources released from declining industries discover more profitable employment.[1] In such a convenient economy, choice in work is treated no differently from choice in consumption: the realities, the complexities of the labour market are ignored, its imperfections and segmentations are denied.

Market clearing has been described as an act of faith. It rests on assumptions which are seldom admired for realism. The 1980s are difficult to reconcile with either market clearing, or rapid transfer to alternative employment. Male unemployment in the United Kingdom averaged 2.2 per cent from 1955 to 1966 and 14 per cent 1980 to 1988. In the earlier years 1 in 45 of the male working population failed to find work: in the later years just under 1 in 7. High unemployment emerges against the background of a growing opportunity gap within Britain.

In the eight years from 1979 to 1987 male employment (employees and self-employed) falls by 15 per cent in Outer Britain (Wales, Scotland, North, North West, Yorkshire and Humberside): over the same period male employment falls by only 1 per cent in Inner Britain (West and East Midlands, South West, East Anglia, South East). At one extreme of employment loss are Wales and the North West(18% decline): by contrast male employment in East Anglia grows by 14 per cent.

The region by region results demonstrate a surprisingly uniform pattern. The more severe the employment loss in recession (1979–83), the more disappointing the record in recovery (1983–87). Severe employment decline does not provide the ideal background for transfer of resources (including labour) to expanding sectors.

There is a pattern to regional economic change. The pattern implies that employment opportunity is differentially distributed throughout the United Kingdom; the opportunity gap is growing. That pattern is reinforced by trends in service employment. Service employment gain is distributed so that the major employment increases concentrate on the regions where loss of manufacturing jobs is limited. In Wales with a fall in industrial employment of 45 per cent, service employment also falls (between 1979 and 1987). East Anglia, with close to no decline in industrial employment, shows a gain of 27 per cent in service employment. In Outer Britain the gain in service employment is 11 per cent (970,000), the loss in industrial jobs 24 per cent (1,080,000); the figures for Outer Britain are service employment gain 2 per cent (128,000), industrial job loss 37 per cent (1,281,000). On average an extra 1 per cent decline in industrial employment in a region reduces service employment growth by 0.6 per cent. If the enterprise society relies on the service sector for recovery, success is more obvious in Inner Britain.

UNEMPLOYMENT – OPEN AND CONCEALED

The broad regional comparisons conceal considerable local variation. There are pockets of high unemployment and economic decline in the Inner Regions and there are prosperous localities in the Outer Regions. Like regional differentials, intra regional differences have widened dramatically in response to economic pressures and restructuring. The major regional contrasts remain important.

Those contrasts are indicated by the growing male unemployment gap between Wales and the Inner Regions. The gap takes an annual average of 1.6 percentage points from 1959 to 1966, 6.5 percentage points from 1980 to 1988. By 1988 an extra 7 out of 100 males are unemployed when we compare Wales with Inner Regions.

The unemployment gap indicates differences in measured unemployment. The official definition of unemployment is widely held to understate true unemployment; frequent revisions to the unemployment count ensure that it is an increasingly selective statement. Concealed unemployment is indicated by low participation (or activity) rates. A participation rate counts the proportion of the relevant group in the working population (either employed, self-employed or classified as unemployed). As male unemployment rates climb in the 1980s, male participation falls in all regions.

In 1979 the activity or participation rate gap between Wales and Inner Regions (for males of working age) is 2 percentage points: by 1987 the participation gap is 9 percentage points. In 1979 close to 9 out of 10 Welsh males of working age were part of the working population. By 1987 only 76 per cent of males of working age were in the working population.

In 1979 82 per cent of males of working age in Wales were in employment (the employment gap between Wales and the Inner Regions was 4 percentage points). By 1987, 64 per cent of males of working age in Wales were in employment (the employment gap between Wales and the Inner Regions was 15 percentage points). In Wales, to a greater extent than in other regions, loss in opportunity is only inadequately recorded by the 'claimant count' of unemployed. Fall in male participation has been greater than growth in unemployment.

REGIONAL POLICY – REDUCED EMPHASIS AND DIMINISHING RETURN

There is evidence that the absence of clear commitment to regional policy contributes to divergence. The 1950s are years of weak regional policy; the years 1963 to 1976 are years of active regional policy; the years 1977 to 1988 are years of reduced regional policy. In real terms regional aid loses two-thirds of value between 1975 and 1985. IDC (Industrial Development Certificate) control (control over the location of industrial expansion) is abandoned in 1981. At 0.2 per cent of GDP in 1985 (and falling) regional aid is not a significant charge on the public purse. It does not involve a major dispersion of wealth or opportunity to communities and areas with high unemployment. It no longer involves a significant response to the problem of differentially distributed, structural decline.

There have been major contrasts between the three policy periods within Wales. There is a clear employment deficit (fall in Welsh share of UK employment) in the 1950s and from 1977. The employment deficit takes an annual average of 5000 in the years of weak regional policy (1954–62) and over eight thousand in years of reduced regional policy emphasis (1977–1987). This is in significant contrast to the years of active regional policy (1963 to 1976). In these years there is an annual employment surplus (rise in Welsh share of UK employment) of over 4000. The results suggest that regional policy was important to Wales, with location contributing to success in attracting mobile industry.

A DIFFERENT FORM OF REGIONAL POLICY?

A true assessment of the difficulties facing regional policy must touch on the process of restructuring. Progress involves creative destruction, the introduction of new production possibilities which displace existing employment and introduce new. From 1965 manufacturing has lost 3.2 million jobs (38%), most of this decline taking place since 1979. No region is immune, but loss concentrates on Outer Britain. The decline in manufacturing contributes to spatial inequality and has a negative effect on the traditional instruments of regional policy. It implies fewer mobile investment projects and increasing competition for them. The mobile projects tend, on average, to provide fewer jobs. Those jobs fall over time rather than multiply. Regional policy increasingly resembles an attempt to fill a doubtful tank from a tap of diminishing cross-section. There is a need for different emphasis.

From 1965 employment in government and private services has increased nationally by 4.4 million (41%). Expansion, particularly in recent years concentrates on the private sector; many of the new jobs are in finance, banking and producer services. The stronger the decline in manufacturing employment, the slower the growth in service employment. Deindustrialization and limited growth of service jobs go together. It is in Inner Britain (notably the South East outside London, the South West and East Anglia) that high technology and service industries have grown most rapidly.

A regional element has to be injected into national recovery, if the high unemployment regions are to win a reasonable share of new jobs. This implies a greater interest in employment trends in the service sector and an understanding of the constraints on location within that sector. The emergence of an effective regional policy in the post-war years was, in part, a response to detailed studies of relocation cost. There is a lack of knowledge and understanding of the long-term influences on service sector location. One or two points are clear. London is not always the most economic location. A recent study (Ashcroft and others, 1989) of relocation of part of the Overseas Development Administration (ODA) from Central London to East Kilbride identified substantial relocation costs. In spite of these, the transfer breaks even within six years.

In spite of wage costs above the national average, the public sector in London faces skill shortages and turnover problems: wage and salary levels fail to meet the standards set by the private sector. The London allowance in the private sector is over double the allowance in the public sector. High labour costs, high rents and skill shortages have prompted a number of service companies to consider relocation. Most relocations are short distance, but a number involve moves outside the South East. Lloyds Bank have transferred 1400 jobs from the City of London to Bristol, for example. They calculate the pay-back period at between two and three years.

The Government seeks a form of regional policy which delivers growth from within the region. This self-generating growth will apparently reduce disparities on a stable, long-term basis. One possible problem is that the key institutions of the United Kingdom are overwhelmingly concentrated in and controlled from London. In addition to the concentration of private headquarters and government employment in the capital, the pattern of state purchasing is channelled towards the Inner Regions. Moreover, London has increased its dominant position as the country's leading financial centre and money market with the dramatic growth of international finance, the influx of foreign banks and deregulation of the Stock Exchange.

There is one law of economic development which we can accept, almost without question. It comes from Adam Smith and has been amply verified. If we compare the 'state of a nation', or a region at different points of time and find annual product improved, we may be sure that 'its capital must have increased'. At regional and national level improvement in the quality and quantity of the capital stock is a key source of economic growth. We enjoy higher living standards not because of longer hours in work, or greater sacrifice while in employment, but because we work with and against the background of an increasingly effective private and public capital. Part of the problem in Wales and other Outer regions is that an appreciable proportion of their industrial capital lost relevance in a remarkably brief period of time. To take an extreme example, decline in mining leaves little of value to other industries, while it creates substantial problems in terms of environment, dereliction and location.

One important function of capital is to provide a new sense of direction, given industrial decline. Our financial system, it has been suggested, is part of the problem and that applies at national and regional level. British banks and other financial institutions have adopted an arm's length relationship with industry. The City's world role has encouraged it to demand independence in its relationship with domestic industry. Compared to other nations, the United Kingdom financial sector has traditionally been less inclined to investment in domestic industry, preferring overseas financial trading and investment, or speculation in property and take-overs. The banking sector has been more reluctant to provide long-term finance and generally the degree of integration between industry and finance has remained limited. Loans in forms unsuitable for long-term investment (e.g. overdrafts) have discouraged long-term planning and contributed to under-investment and slow industrial growth.

The national problem has been identified as a contributory factor in UK deindustrialization and has, in itself, had serious repercussions for the revival of the nation's industrial regions. At another level the location and operation of the financial, banking and investment capital sectors favours the known South East rather than the 'remote', 'high risk' Outer Regions. An over- centralized and (in some respects) over-cautious financial system may involve a bias which works against Outer Britain. In 1985, only 17 per cent of venture funding went to the five regions of Outer Britain (40% of the population). There is a high degree of localization: 80 per cent of all investments were located within 120 miles of the source. The case for closer integration between finance and industry is taken from countries where the financiers seek a deep familiarity with the industries they intend to finance. If the links are developed within Britain, they must reach the regions – see Martin (1989).

Our second law of economic development is that human capital is a key resource. Adam Smith's definition of capital includes 'the acquired and useful abilities of all the inhabitants'. Human capital, like physical capital, expands productive capacity: the skills, qualifications and resources of the labour force may be even more important than physical capital, though human capital is not recognized in regional and national accounts.

In the UK economy there is both a substantial labour surplus and a shortage of the skills and qualities which contribute to economic development. The argument applies with particular strength to Wales and other Outer Regions. The labour problem is, in part, a product of the pace and severity of industrial decline. Abrupt structural decline implies capital and human obsolescence: new trades have to be learned, new habits to be acquired, a different range of occupations and skills is required. The individual is given little indication of the forms of investment (training, retraining, job search) which will yield a return. The principle type of human investment is education and training. Increased personal productivity involves a lifetime process in which education and training are the formal phase and learning by doing is the test of development potential in a given occupation.

In spite of unprecedented unemployment, the economy remains short of skilled, trained manpower. The real development gap, it has been suggested, is that our working population is under-educated, under-trained and under-skilled. To these continuing problems is added the present danger of myopia. Over two-thirds of British children leave school at 16, as compared with only 4 per cent in Japan and about 10 per cent in Germany. Studies at international level have suggested that qualitative changes in labour are as important to growth as quantitative changes in capital. Research indicates that British children in the lower half of the ability range are as much as two years behind their German equivalents in mathematical skills. A National

Institute Study compared similar plants in Britain and West Germany. Notably lower productivity in Britain was attributed to lack of technical expertise: training was the major bar to better performance by British plants. The difficulties were linked to lower levels of achievement at school for 'non-academic' pupils: the absence of numerical, or mathematical skills, being particularly important.

British education standards appear to compare favourably with other countries for a privileged minority; one question to ask of change is whether it extends the reach and range of education by encouraging higher standards among those who are not identified as academically gifted. The question appears to be of particular importance in Wales, not just because of pace of structural decline, but because Welsh schools demonstrate considerable spread in achievement levels. The Welsh education system produces the largest proportion of young people who leave school without any academic qualifications and is a leader in the production of 'A' level passes and entrants to full-time further education. In Wales (as well as Scotland) there is a tradition of academic attainment and there does appear to be a group who place a high value on education, tending possibly to see education as an insurance policy, or as a gateway to financial security. The gate often implies migration and is, perhaps, particularly important to those in rural Wales. The picture that emerges indicates an education system which does well by the abler, younger people and poorly by the less able, so perpetuating and exacerbating broader deprivations.

In the United States the success stories of local and regional regeneration often emphasize the contribution made by higher education and the links between educational institutions and the industrial and business community. The UK Government emphasizes the importance of self-generating growth, while pursuing a higher education policy which contributes to uncertainty, particularly in the regions. Detrimental to Wales is the underlying presumption that university excellence in research derives from concentration of resources in large departments (or large universities). The argument has merit in particular disciplines, but is exceedingly dangerous as a generalization applied to all subject areas.[2]

CONCLUSION

Socially and economically the United Kingdom is still a surprisingly uniform country. Productivity differentials as between regions are by no means major. Consumption and living standards are reasonably even[3] Disparities in social provision are less significant than in many other countries. Britain has no equivalent to the problems of rural depopulation and decay in Southern Italy. In measures of regional disparities, provided by the EEC, the regions of the UK tend to cluster. Other countries demonstrate a wider spread of regional performance. The absence of contrast is, in part, a product of geography. Within a limited land area there is relatively little variation in climate and natural resources (apart from North Sea Oil), transport costs are low and contact is easy. The nation is informed, if not united, by a national press and broadcasting service. Another influence is early industrialization, with a strong manufacturing presence developed in all regions of the UK. Industrialization and the diffusion of its income and influence to all parts of the UK provided a degree of uniformity as between regions and helped to limit dissent and conflict between centre and periphery.

That lack of contrast is relative rather than absolute. The UK remains a multi-national state. Cultural and national traditions have given Welsh and Scottish life, in particular, a different and distinctive character. In addition to separate national identities it has become clear that deindustrialization involves a growing imbalance as between Inner and Outer Regions. Productivity differences may be relatively small as between regions, but unemployment differences are not. When we allow for concealed unemployment, the opportunity gap is significant. It involves substantial costs. These are not confined to the burden of unemployment benefit and national assistance. The economic divide is reflected in political voting patterns. The Conservative Governments of the 1980s took their comfortable parliamentary majorities from Inner Britain.

In the 1980s, as in the 1930s, the Outer Regions show the most marked decline in recession and the least impressive record in recovery. A pattern emerges of a more unequal society; the majority remain part of a prosperous country, a substantial minority experience more difficult social and economic conditions. That pattern is not unique to Wales, or the Outer regions, but there is a reality to the growing economic and political divide at regional level.

In December 1983 (in the White Paper on Regional Industrial Development) the government called for a regional policy which would 'focus on encouraging new and indigenous development in the Assisted Areas, rather than simply transferring jobs from one part of the country to another'. This clarion call for self-improvement failed to identify the competitive disadvantages facing the Outer Regions. Encouraging indigenous growth requires an approach which is broadly based. The logic of self-generating growth suggests that government must decentralize when possible. To develop an economy, regional or national, and to disregard the needs of its people can only lead to unbalanced development.

According to the Government, 'imbalances in employment between areas in employment opportunities should in principle be corrected by the natural adjustment of labour markets' (Department of Trade and Industry, 1983). The approach is essentially market-orientated. The principle rests on assumptions which are convenient rather than realistic. 'Natural adjustment' is easier to identify in the textbook than in reality. The real economy operates differently from an economy where spatial inequalities are temporary, or minor. There may even be a vague and reluctant recognition that there are problems in achieving wage flexibility and labour mobility of the form required to achieve regional balance. And there is an underlying contradiction. In the market tradition inequalities between regions are blamed on rigidities, without any attempt to understand why these inflexibilities emerge in all market economies. The simplified hypothesis of rapid adjustment is identified as health, the complexities of the real world are regarded as disease.

The government strategy involves reductions in regional aid; reliance on general, economy-wide policies designed to encourage response to market signals; local interventions which are initiated by central government. Some aspects of this strategy have met with success. There are, however, four consistent forms of bias. First, government policies have made least progress at the lower end of the income scale. Second, the signals to which the market reacts are short-term. Third, the approach appears to be more effective in the prosperous parts of the country. Fourth, the regions are increasingly remote from where power is.

Markets operate under institutional conditions which vary between countries. As far as the regions are concerned there are three outstanding priorities for policy. First, a longer term perspective from the market. Second, and connected, higher levels of productive investment (including education and research and development). Third, a recognition of what the market cannot do and a degree of independence for the organizations which administer non-market activities. The intermediate institutions, whose criterion of action is the public good as they understand it, are essential to participation and to indigenous development. By dividing power they ensure that priorities different from those of central government remain important. Those priorities are important to Wales. Indigenous growth requires active involvement at local and regional level. Centralized control is remote, ill informed and in essence non-democratic. Development from within is impossible without the active participation of those for whom it is meaningful.

Finally, as emphasized earlier, the other side of the economic development coin is human development – in the context of this review, education, training and retraining of the labour force. No sustained economic development is possible without simultaneous human development. Traditionally regional development consists of so called 'hardware' investment tools such as financial incentives and infrastructure investment in order to create jobs. Very little attention, if any, was paid to the need to develop 'software' development tools, that is job skills to support and encourage a momentum that may require capital investment. It is people who form the dynamic agents in economic development. In Wales there are indications that we need to back traditional Welsh pride in education with a policy which ensures greater opportunity for larger numbers.

NOTES

1. For a critical review of this belief, see MacKay and Jones (1989).

2. There is a broader theme. The targets for education cannot be set in terms of immediate financial benefits. Ideas may well be, as Marshall (p.780) claimed, 'the most real of the gifts which each generation receives from its predecessors', but he added, 'the wisdom of expending public and private funds on education is not to be measured by its direct fruits alone'. There is no logical reason to believe that profit-maximizing firms will provide sufficient support for basic research. Ideas may be the most important gifts, but the risks are always substantial and the returns are often general rather than local: they do not necessarily concentrate on individual industries and firms. There are strong elements of the public good in education: self-interest is not sufficient as an organizing device. The need for public funds does not necessarily imply increasingly detailed and centralized government control. If loss of independence for universities comes in this way it is the result of government choice.

3. According to the Family Expenditure Survey, expenditure per head (1986–87) on goods and on services is lower in Wales than in any other region. Expenditure per head comes to 70 per cent of the South East level and 80 per cent of the Inner Britain level. Given reasonable growth (say 2.5% p.a.) Wales would reach Inner Britain's 1987 level of goods and services consumption by 1996. Sustained, more or less continuous, improvement in living standards dates from about 1700. On this rough estimation, 296 years improvement in Wales equals 287 in Inner Britain.

REFERENCES AND SOURCES

Ashcroft B., Holden D., Smith J., Swales K. (1988) 'ODA Dispersal to East Kilbride: An Evaluation'. Industry Department for Scotland ESU Research Paper No.14.

George K.D. and Mainwaring L. (1988) *The Welsh Economy*. Cardiff: University of Wales Press.

MacKay R.R. and Jones D. (1989) *Labour Markets in Distress: The Denial of Choice*. Aldershot: Gower Press.

Marshall A. (1920) *Principles of Economics*, 8th edition. Basingstoke: Macmillan.

Martin R. (1989) 'The Growth and Geographical Anatomy of Venture Capitalism in the United Kingdom'. *Regional Studies*, Vol 23 (5) 389–403.

Moore B., Rhodes J. and Tyler P. (1986) *The Effects of Government Regional Economic Policy*. London: Department of Trade and Industry, HMSO.

National Institute (1985) 'Productivity, Machinery and Skills in a Sample of British and German Manufacturing Plants'. *National Institute of Economic Review*, (111) 48–61.

Piore M.J. (1987) 'Historical Perspectives and the Interpretation of Unemployment'. *Journal of Economic Literature*, XXV 1834–1850.

Smith A. (1776) *The Wealth of Nations*. Ed E. Cannan, London: Methuen (1904).

Trade and Industry (1983) *Regional Industrial Development*, Cmnd 9111, December 1983.

Scotland

M. Danson M.G. Lloyd and D. Newlands

INTRODUCTION: SCOTLAND ON THE PERIPHERY

In general terms the evidence reproduced below suggests that the Scottish economy, in common with much of northern Britain, has lagged further behind the country as a whole over the last decade. The evidence shows that unemployment has remained higher and incomes and expenditure have risen more slowly than in the south of the country. Furthermore, the degree of external ownership and control of Scottish industry has continued to increase together with a relative brake on the rates of new firm formation and indigenous economic development. Concomitantly, output, trade and investment have become more narrowly dependent on a limited number of key industrial sectors. In particular, office machinery and whisky now account for almost half of all non-oil exports and, with, chemicals, have commanded 45 per cent of manufacturing investment in recent years. It is important to note, however, that although these sectors are increasing in importance in terms of output they are employing less people both in relative and absolute terms. The narrowing of the industrial base and the growing dominance of branch plants have had and must continue to have profound implications for the performance of the Scottish economy. The deepening of this divide should also make it ever more clear that the policy prescriptions for an inflationary south-east of England are inappropriate in the context of an embattled and regressing north.

CHANGING ECONOMIC CIRCUMSTANCES, 1978–1988

There are a range of possible indicators available to measure the quality of life and performance of a regional economy. Unfortunately, as will be evident from the other chapters in this volume, many statistics in the United Kingdom are now discredited through inadequacies in data sources, discontinuities in time series, untimely revisions of bases and increasing lags in publication. In this context, the Standing Commission on the Scottish Economy (1989) stated that the case for provision of a better database of Scottish economic statistics, publicly available through official sources, seemed inarguable. It would permit more informed discussion of Scottish economic performances and prospects and it would aid in enhancing efficiency in policy prescription and evaluation. As a consequence, while we present a statistical review of the health of the Scottish economy, the qualitative commentary which accompanies it provides stronger evidence of the state of the nation, its recent economic history and its possible future development.

Over the two main periods of the last business cycle: recession (1979–83) and recovery (1983–89), Scotland has performed poorly in the national and international contexts. In the international context, for example, by 1987, Scotland's Gross Domestic Product (GDP) per head was 15 per cent below the average for the developed world (OECD) and within Western Europe only Greece, Ireland, Spain, Portugal and Turkey were poorer. This from the world's first industrialized nation!

In the national context, Scotland has performed badly relative to the country as a whole. The increasing prominence given to GDP as a measure of relative living standards prompts us to start with an analysis of recent trends in national prosperity and income. With an average income of £6387 in 1988 Scotland was in fourth position in the UK national league, behind the South East, East Midlands and East Anglia. The data also suggest that the average standard of living in Scotland is 6 per cent below the national average and 8 per cent lower than the average for England. It is therefore noteworthy that Scotland's relative living standards have declined steadily since 1982, falling from 2.4 per cent below the national average to 6.1 per cent below over the six year period. In crude terms, in 1988 every man, woman and child in Scotland was, on average, some £10.31 per week worse off than their UK equivalent. As the regional economies of the North and North-West of England, Yorkshire and Humberside, Wales and Northern Ireland have also fallen behind the southern part of the country, this suggests that systematic forces have been at work in the 1980s which have deepened the North-South divide.

A particular feature of Scotland's relative decline, however, is obscured by presenting the region's position in terms of income per head. Throughout the 1980s there was a constant haemorrhaging of the Scottish population, which declined by 1.3 per cent between 1981 and 1988, to 5.1 million. This is primarily because of the exceptionally high level of migration, in net terms over 150,000 of the younger, more skilled and more dynamic people leaving during the decade. This has masked a parallel decline in the relative size of the Scottish economy during this period. So, whereas 9 per cent of all UK economic activity took place in Scotland in 1982, by 1988 that had fallen to 8.4 per cent.

We should point out that North Sea oil production and revenue estimates are excluded from these calculations. Obviously, the impact on relative nominal prosperity would be marked if they were to be included. In terms of the sectoral breakdown of the Scottish economy, services now dominate, contributing 67 per cent of GDP in 1988. Whilst, in aggregate, the primary and manufacturing sectors are now of far less relative importance, a number of other industrial sectors have grown over the decade. The critical positions held by high technology and whisky cannot be ignored, although, as is explained below, growth in these sectors should not be accepted uncritically. The evidence also demonstrates the relatively high dependence of Scotland on state service sectors such as health, education and public administration together with the less prominent contribution of the financial and business services sector, the latter being more heavily concentrated in and around London.

Since 1979, employment in Scotland has declined from 2.108 million to 1.917 million (June 1989), representing a fall of over 9 per cent, with manufacturing bearing the brunt of the collapse. The comparable fall in Britain as a whole was only 3.4 per cent, much of this difference in performance occurring in the latter half of the 1980s. In particular, Scottish employment continued to decline between 1984 and 1987, whereas there was a 2 per cent growth in the country overall with all regions apart from Scotland benefiting from this turnaround. Whilst Scottish jobs increased in numbers subsequently after 1987, the pattern has been somewhat erratic with no suggestion of strong, long term sustainable growth.

In detailed terms, between 1984 and 1987 trends in Scotland broadly followed the UK pattern. Service sector employment increased by 2.7 per cent, and manufacturing employment fell by 6.2 per cent. Male employment fell by 4.1 per cent and female employment rose by 5.9 per cent. Part-time female employment rose to 8.2 per cent. Within the service sector, employment grew by 8.9 per cent in banking and finance and by 5.8 per cent in other services. Within manufacturing only 'other manufacturing' showed any increase (2.1%). All other industry divisions showed a decrease in employment including agriculture, forestry and fishing (21.6%), energy and water supply (12.3%) and construction (9.4%).

As in previous trade cycles, Scotland seemed therefore to do relatively well during periods of recession, with its unemployment rate rising at a slower rate than the South East, but in the upturn the traditional pattern is re-established. So by the end of the 1980's Scottish unemployment relative to the remainder of the national economy was higher than at any other time during the previous two decades, (about 70% higher than the corresponding Great Britain rate), although it had declined to only 20 per cent above in 1983.

Aggregate Scottish output (Gross Value Added) of the production industries has been stagnating since 1979, with output some 9 per cent lower in 1987 than in 1973. While certain sectors have grown markedly since the early post war period, only electrical and instrument engineering have maintained that pattern of development in a consistent way to the late 1980s. This is to be contrasted with a number of other sectors, such as chemicals and whisky, which demonstrated a pattern of long-term growth but which have performed rather more erratically in recent times. Conversely, the traditional industrial heart of Scotland, the metal and metal using industries such as steel, mechanical engineering, shipbuilding and transport equipment have all experienced decline over the past 30 years. The last decade has not witnessed a recovery in their fortunes, the opposite in fact being the case, often as a result of the Government's privatization and deregulation programmes.

The restructuring of Scotland's industrial base has been accompanied by other equally significant changes. While the traditional industries were predominantly indigenously owned and controlled, the new industries of electronics, computers and chemicals and, to a lesser extent, whisky and paper, are characteristically branch plants of multinational corporations. Decision-making powers concerning research and development, finance and marketing have therefore been lost from the Scottish economy. This has important implications for the ability of Scotland to secure self-generating growth through locally initiated redevelopment (Ashcroft et al, 1980; Boyle et al, 1989; Danson, 1986).

The shift to a narrower industrial base has been exacerbated by the process and forms of exploration for the exploitation of North Sea oil and gas resources. The mixed effects of North Sea oil on the Scottish economy are highlighted by the more localized impact on Aberdeen and Grampian (Harris, Lloyd and Newlands, 1988). Although North Sea oil- and gas-related industries have created significant regional benefits they have also intensified the penetration of Scottish companies, markets and industries by non local capital. To illustrate the increasing dislocation of industrial linkages within Scotland, we may observe the endemic crises in the steel and heavy engineering industries at the very time when the offshore investments represented tremendous opportunities for Scottish participation and growth. So, by 1987 the value of output in these two activities was 65 per cent and 72 per cent respectively of their 1954 levels.

Data inadequacies prevent a complete analysis of Scotland's trade position although there are limited manufacturing surveys of non-UK trade (Scottish Council (Development and Industry) 1989). These figures show that although Scotland's economy is relatively export intensive, its share of UK trade has been falling over a long period. In geographical and sectoral terms, exports are relatively concentrated with four countries (United States of America, Germany, France and Italy) and two commodities (office machinery and whisky) accounting for almost half of all foreign earnings. Given the dominance of foreign ownership in these sectors and the relative instability of the exchange rate, there are grounds for concern as to the stability of an economic development strategy that encourages this degree of dependence.

Recent trends compound this difficulty. Manufacturing investment, for example, has favoured a deepening of the importance of a limited band of sectors. Thus, office machinery, electronics, chemicals and whisky have accounted for greater than half of all net investment in recent years. These sectors have failed to establish linkages with the rest of the regional economy, being typical branch plant operations and furthermore have tended to develop in isolation from each other within their individual sectors. As a consequence, there have been limited opportunities for agglomeration economies to be established or for significant transfers of technology to the indigenous sectors to take place.

Underpinning and reinforcing this process of under-development we can discern three principal weaknesses of the Scottish economy. First, a continuing dependence on heavy manufacturing industries with poor growth prospects and endemic decline. Second, an unmet need for internally generated growth, particularly through small and medium-sized enterprises. Finally, an absence of high technology growth sectors within Scotland and a poor rate of technological innovation in the established industrial base.

The justification for taking this very general perspective of Scotland's economic position is borne out by the figures reproduced here. The 1987 Census of Production, for example, continues to show a heavy concentration of activity in a relatively few industrial sectors, and these are themselves based on a narrow band of sub-sectors. Moreover, the so-called 'Silicon Glen' phenomenon is less apparent in real terms when we consider that employment in electronics and electrical engineering represents a lower proportion of Scottish employment than in the country as a whole. The evidence on new firm formation from business registrations for Value Added Tax, also shows a laggardly situation with a relatively low rate of company start-ups in Scotland.

The picture of a Scottish economy progressively more dependent on external decisions in both the public and private sectors is reproduced and reflected in the trends of incomes and earnings since 1980. For all regions of the UK, the largest contribution to national income estimates is derived from 'earnings from employment'. The slower growth from this source accounts for the overall relative decline in GDP per head in Scotland. It is interesting to note, however, that 'profits' in Scotland have nevertheless tended to increase at a rate faster than the national average. In terms of an alternative measure of living standards, 'household income', Scotland is not only poorly ranked, seventh out of ten regions and declining relative to the nation as a whole, but it is also highly dependent on wages and salaries and social security benefits, with relatively small contributions from self-employment. To a greater extent than in the south, low incomes from the labour market are reproduced through poverty, unemployment and retirement. This evidence would further suggest that a greater proportion of Scottish families are on very low incomes, with 24 per cent on less than £80 per week in 1987–8 compared with 18 per cent in the UK as a whole.

It would seem, therefore, that Scotland's relative position and relative decline can be traced to a slower growth in wages. For men and women, Scotland appears in fourth place in the regional rankings, in 1989 of average earnings for full time workers on adult rates of pay, as with GDP per head figures, but again the position has been declining relatively. Thus, for instance, although in 1988 only the South East surpassed Scotland in earnings, the rate of increase of wages and salaries for men over the period 1988–89 was 7.8 per cent in Scotland – the lowest in the country and compared to a national average of 9.5 per cent. For men and women taken together, earnings were the fifth highest in Britain, with the equal lowest rate of increase over the year. Again, Scotland had the highest proportion of lowest paid workers: 45 per cent received less than £180 per week whereas in the country as a whole, 38 per cent were in this position of relative poverty.

As earnings are the major component of total income, we believe that the long-term relative decline in Scotland's GDP per head will have continued after 1988. This would probably take Scotland further down the league table of regions and have the effect of deepening the divide in living standards between Scotland and the South-East. Likewise, as there is a higher proportion of people on social security benefits in Scotland and as benefits have been increasing at a lower rate than wages since 1988, the pressure on GDP per head from this component of income will also have been downward.

In 1977, on the basis of an analysis of the censuses of population up to 1971, it was suggested that Scotland is now more working class vis-a-vis England than at any other time since the First World War (Payne, 1977). Over the last two decades, we have argued, the economic forces and tendencies underlying their assertions have undoubtedly intensified.

PUBLIC POLICY CHARACTERISTICS AND ISSUES IN SCOTLAND

A consequence of Scotland's relatively disadvantaged economic position within the national economy is the extent to which successive governments have intervened in the form of policy initiatives and assistance (Randall, 1987). Thus, throughout the greater part of the post-war period, Scotland was eligible for a considerable range of incentives under the conventional regional policy framework in an attempt to address its structural and locational disadvantages.

In general terms, and in common with the remainder of the economy, the regional policy framework has been modified in line with the present government's liberal market philosophy. This has involved the rationalization and restructuring of the public policy framework for economic development in Scotland. At the present time there are three principal characteristics to the policy framework: the role played by the Highlands and Islands Development Board (HIDB) and Scottish Development Agency (SDA) in organizing economic development initiatives: the increased role of the private sector in terms of policy formulation and implementation; and the diminished contribution of local authorities to the economic development process.

First, economic development policy implementation in Scotland is dominated by the HIDB and SDA. The latter, in particular, plays a critical role in organizing local area specific initiatives throughout Scotland. The enhanced role of the development agencies is a consequence of the Government's restructuring of regional policy. The origins and subsequent development of the HIDB and SDA is given elsewhere in this volume. In general terms, however, the agencies' remit has been modified to conform more rigourously with the governments ideology. As a consequence the HIDB and SDA are much more commercial and selective in terms of their support to industries and areas in Scotland. This approach is illustrated by the findings of a review of the SDA carried out by the Industry Department for Scotland (1987). This concluded that the SDA should only be involved where the market alone will not produce the outcome desired by policy; and its intervention should wherever possible seek to achieve its ends by improving the working of the market and should not create dependence.

As a consequence of its modified remit, the SDA has embarked on an aggressive strategy of establishing public-private sector partnerships in Scotland. The main aim of this strategy is not only to increase the role of business in public policy but also to replace public resources with private sector investment (Boyle, 1988). Thus, in terms of urban renewal initiatives, the SDA has stated that it will pursue renewal in partnership with other organizations in both the public and private sectors to unlock the commitment and contribution of all parties. 'At the core of the approach, the Agency plays a vital pro-active role, identifying, packaging and promoting opportunities to the private sector and negotiating the support of local authorities' (SDA, 1989). It is evident from this that the public-private partnerships are not an equal coalition of the interests involved.

Over time the SDA has developed an expansive portfolio of area specific initiatives. These include comprehensive urban renewal projects such as the Glasgow Eastern Area Renewal project; Task Forces, which are a form of 'fire-brigade' role in areas of immediate economic distress; Integrated Area Projects; and self-help initiatives, which are largely facilitated through a network of local enterprise trusts (Gulliver, 1984). This experience has led the SDA to be given a key role in the implementation of urban policy in Scotland (Lloyd and Newlands, 1989a). 'New Life for Urban Scotland' sets out the policy context for regeneration in inner cities and selected peripheral public sector housing estates in Scotland. The SDA has the responsibility for organising these measures through partnerships with the private sector. The SDA led partnerships are intended to enable the private sector to make additional resources available so as to help people in the designated areas escape from the dependency on the state and the isolation from markets which is held to be characteristic of the problem areas (Scottish office, 1988).

Similarly, the SDA has been instrumental in securing the designation of a fourth enterprise zone in Inverclyde, as indeed it was involved in the earlier zones in Clydebank, Tayside and Invergordon. In all four instances, the enterprise zone designation was a political response to a localized crisis in Scotland and an extension to an established SDA-based programme of support. Thus, the Clydebank zone followed the closure of the Singer Sewing Machine Co. factor, which had been one of the largest employers in the area (Brownrigg, 1983). The Tayside zone formed part of a SDA led initiative – the Dundee Project, which was designed to address the endemic problems of decline in the local economy. The Invergordon enterprise zone was designated in the wake of the closure of the British Aluminium Co. smelter in Easter Ross.

The Inverclyde enterprise zone is located some 20 miles west of Glasgow, on the south bank of the Clyde. It forms part of the Port Glasgow-Greenock-Gourock area of the regional economy. Despite its proximity to Glasgow and the Upper Clyde shipbuilding industry, Inverclyde forms a distinct labour market in terms of its own local history. In the 1980s, the local economy experienced a sharp decline in its traditional industrial base. This is reflected in its local unemployment rate which increased from 12.8 per cent (1980) to 21.4 per cent (1987). Despite this marked deterioration in the local economy, the public policy response was initially sluggish (Lever, 1986). In 1985, however, the SDA, in conjunction with Strathclyde Regional Council and Inverclyde District Council, established the Inverclyde Initiative. This public sector partnership set out to diversify the local industrial base, activate local training and develop new enterprises in the area. It also provided the immediate basis for the designation of the Enterprise Zone (Lloyd and Danson, 1991).

Notwithstanding the Government's apparent confidence in the HIDB and SDA, particularly after it had effected modifications to their respective remits and objectives, the Government has embarked on the radical transformation of the two agencies. In December 1989, the Government published its Enterprise and New Towns (Scotland)

Bill which provided for, amongst other things, the dissolution of the HIDB and SDA and the establishment of Scottish Enterprise and Highlands and Islands Enterprise. The new agencies will effectively integrate the responsibilities for the provision of training, previously discharged by the Training Agency, with business development and environmental improvements, the previous functions of the HIDB and SDA. The new bodies will be charged with the long-term objective of securing self-sustaining economic development and the growth of enterprise in Scotland. The delivery of the integrated services will be provided by means of a network Local Enterprise Companies (LECs). These local business led bodies will be responsible for assessing local labour markets, arranging the delivery of national training programmes, developing training for specific local needs and raising private sector funds (Danson, Fairley, Lloyd and Newlands, 1990).

The second characteristic of economic development policy in Scotland is the increasingly active role played by the private sector in public policy formulation and implementation. This can be illustrated in a number of ways. The arrangements for the winding-up of the Scottish New Towns, for instance, involves the direct privatisation of the New Town assets to private individuals and firms. This approach differs from that in England and Wales and represents a deliberate attempt to shift responsibility from the public to the private sector (Lloyd, 1989).

Enterprise Trusts also illustrate the increasing influence of the business community over economic development. Scottish Business in the Community (ScotBIC) was formed in 1982 with the intention of promoting enterprising solutions to local problems in Scotland by encouraging greater participation by business in partnerships with the public sector. By the end of the 1980s, there were forty enterprise trusts in Scotland, the majority based on a partnership arrangement with local business interests and local authorities. Although the trusts are designed as partnerships, they are dominated by the private sector but rely to a considerable extent on public sector support (Keating and Boyle, 1986). Furthermore, ScotBIC tends to confirm its interest in terms of the formation of trusts to localities where there is evidence of support by the local business community. It will not assist established groups nor devote attention to areas where there is poor interest from the private sector.

The private sector has also been active in terms of designing a number of individual local development initiatives in Scotland. 'Glasgow Action', for example, was formed by local business people in 1985, with the tacit support of the SDA, although the leadership, control and direction of the group has remained firmly with the private sector. Glasgow Action has subsequently acted as a catalyst for property development schemes in the city (Boyle, 1989). Similarly, 'Aberdeen Beyond 2000' was set up by a self appointed ad hoc committee of business people in 1987. It was a response to the concern felt by the local business community as to the over-dependence of the city on the oil industry reflected in the localised impact of the fall in oil prices in 1985 (Lloyd and Newlands, 1989b). It established an agenda for action with the longer term objective of securing the diversification of the local industrial base. This was to be achieved through complementary strategies concerned with economic development and property development.

The Scottish Enterprise and Highlands and Islands Enterprise proposals will further extend the role and influence of the private sector in local economic development through the LECs. These will be based to some extent on existing enterprise trusts and, furthermore be given responsibilities for a wider sphere of activities, including training and environmental improvement.

Finally, economic development policy in Scotland is characterized by the diminished or constrained role played by local authorities. This is particularly the case with respect to local economic development initiatives. In common with local authorities in England and Wales, Scottish authorities do not have a specific general power for devising, financing and executing local initiatives. As a result, their strategies are a composite of measures derived from a diverse range of individual powers, such as planning, infrastructure provision and land use zoning. Furthermore, Scottish authorities were able to utilise s.83 of the Local Government (Scotland) Act 1973 as a source of finance for the purposes of local development. By the mid-1980s, there was evidence to suggest that Scottish local authorities were actively engaged in a range of business support and marketing measures (Lloyd and Rowan-Robinson, 1988). A favoured arrangement for securing local economic development was through partnerships with the SDA and private sector. Recent legislative proposals, however, suggest that the future for such initiatives is not an optimistic one (Hayton, 1989). Increasing centralisation, the transfer of responsibility for economic development to the private sector and the restrictions on the ability of authorities to engage in such activity will confine Scottish local government to small scale, pump-priming measures in the community.

It is important to note, however, that one of the most important areas of local authority activity continues to be the education and training of young people. As such, through primary, secondary and further education and through YTS and European Social Fund supported schemes, the Regional Councils have a key role to play in this aspect of business development. Although Scottish Enterprise, Highlands and Islands Enterprise and the, as yet limited, proposals for centralisation and privatisation of education and training threaten to diminish this position, local authorities will undoubtedly maintain at least this essential component of local economic development largely under their own control.

CONCLUSIONS

Oft repeated during the last election, and re-affirmed in Glasgow in February 1989 by Mrs Thatcher, is the Government's claim that 'Scotland is advancing and prospering. You (sic) see it in the highest standard of living after the south-east of England – a level of prosperity which is enabling much more to be devoted to protecting the weak'. In conclusion, and contrary to the Government's view, we have argued that Scotland has been suffering relative decline for most of the decade when compared against the remainder of the economy, Europe and the developed world. Looking behind the statistics we also believe that this decline will continue to be progressive and cumulative. Although it is difficult to forecast the future of the wider European economy, whatever evolves between now and the end of the century will see Scotland as an increasingly peripheralised region of a declining national economy. As the Scottish economy has been progressively destructured – losing ownership, control and decision making functions, suffering further net migration of its younger, more skilled population, so we would expect further falls in living standards in Scotland. The balance of economic trends and pressures in the next decade suggest an intensification of this pattern of decline.

De-industrialization, destructuring and selective depopulation, as well as the brutal restructuring of public policy and the re-alignment of responsibility for public policy to the private sector, are together undermining the ability of the Scottish people to turnaround the economy and achieve self-generating and self-sustaining growth. Far from the Tory Government creating an advance in relative prosperity in Scotland, it has presided over a catastrophic degeneration in relative standards of living with higher and more persistent unemployment, poverty and deprivation. For some, this period has meant improved salaries, opportunities and quality of life; for the majority, however, their relative position has deteriorated. Election claims should not, therefore, divert us from recognising the truth that lies behind the economic statistics.

REFERENCES

Ashcroft, B. et al (1980) *The Economic Effects of Inward Investment of Scottish Manufacturing Companies, 1965–1980*. Edinburgh: Industry Department for Scotland.

Boyle, R. (1988) 'The Price of Private Planning', in McCrone, D. and Brown, A. (eds) *The Scottish Government Yearbook 1988*. Edinburgh: Edinburgh University Press, 183–199.

Boyle, R. (1989) 'Partnership in Practice. An Assessment of Public-Private

Collaboration in Urban Regeneration: A Case Study of Glasgow Action'. *Local Government Studies* 15, 17–28.

Boyle, S. et al (1989) *Scotland's Economy – Claiming the Future*. London: Verso.

Brownrigg, M. (1983) 'Clydebank. The Economics of Decline'. *The Planner* 69, 85–87.

Danson, M. (ed) (1986) *Redundancy and Recession: Restructuring the Regions?* Norwich: Geobooks.

Danson, M., Fairley, J., Lloyd, M. G. and Newlands, D. (1980) 'Scottish Enterprise: An Evolving Approach to Integrating Economic Development in Scotland', in Brown, A. and Parry, R. (eds), *The Scottish Government Yearbook 1990*. Edinburgh: University of Edinburgh Press, 168–194.

Gulliver, S. (1984) 'The Area Projects of the Scottish Development Agency'. *Town Planning Review* 55(3), 322–334.

Harris, A., Lloyd, M. G. and Newlands, D. (1988) *The Impact of Oil on the Aberdeen Economy*. Aldershot: Avebury.

Hayton, K. (1989) 'The Future of Local Economic Development'. *Regional Studies* 23(6), 549–556.

Keating, M. and Boyle, R. (1986) *Remaking Urban Scotland*. Edinburgh, Edinburgh University Press.

Lever, W. (1986) 'From Ships to Chips in Greenock-Port Glasgow', in Cooke, P.(ed), *Global Restructuring, Industrial Change and Local Adjustment*. London: ESRC, 195-200.

Lloyd, M. G. (1989) 'Privatisation and Economic Development in the Scottish New Towns'. *Town and Country Planning* 58(11), 302–304.

Lloyd, M. G. and Danson, M. (1991) 'The Inverclyde Enterprise Zone. A Continuing Experiment in Regeneration'. *Scottish Geographical Magazine* 107(1), 58–62.

Lloyd, M. G. and Newlands, D. (1989a) 'Recent Urban Policy Developments in Scotland: The Rediscovery of Peripheral Housing Estates'. *Scottish Geographical Magazine* 105(2), 116–119.

Lloyd, M. G. and Newlands, D. (1989b) 'Aberdeen: Planning for Economic Change and Uncertainty'. *Scottish Geographical Magazine* 105(2), 94–100.

Lloyd, M. G. and Rowan-Robinson, J. (1988) 'Local Authority Responses to Economic Uncertainty in Scotland', in McCrone, D. and Brown, A. (eds), *The Scottish Government Yearbook 1988*, Edinburgh: Edinburgh University Press, 282–300.

Payne, G. (1977) 'Occupational Transition in Advanced Industrial Societies'. *Sociological Review* 25, 387–427.

Randall, J. (1987) 'Scotland', in Damesick, P. and Wood, P. (eds), *Regional Problems, Problem Regions and Public Policy in the United Kingdom*. Oxford: Clarendon Press, 218–237.

Scottish Council (Development and Industry) (1989) *Exports Survey 1987–1988*. Edinburgh: SCDI.

Scottish Development Agency (1989) *Partnership in Economic and Environmental Renewal*. Glasgow: SDA.

Scottish Office (1988) *New Life for Urban Scotland*. Edinburgh: HMSO.

Standing Commission on the Scottish Economy (1989) *Final Report*. Glasgow: STUC.

CHAPTER 6

IRELAND

6.1

Northern Ireland

Mark Hart and Richard T Harrison

INTRODUCTION

Within the context of an emergent North-South Divide in the economic prosperity of the United Kingdom since the early 1980s, Northern Ireland provides an extreme example of its widening nature in a period of national economic boom. Any comparison of Northern Ireland with the other UK regions serves only to highlight the continuing problems of the region. The sad truth is, despite this remarkable period of growth in the national economy since 1983, employment in the Northern Ireland economy has grown more slowly than in all the other regions while its labour force has grown much faster.

In stark terms, the socio-economic position of the Province at the start of the 1990s can best be summarised as follows: unemployment remains high at around 14 per cent; out-migration continues at persistently high levels; participation rates are low, and incomes are falling even further behind the national average. Even more disturbing than this gloomy assessment of the Northern Ireland economy is the fact that such trends have developed against a background of substantial public sector intervention. The purpose of this brief profile of the Northern Ireland economy is twofold. First, to examine the nature and extent of economic change in Northern Ireland in the last decade, and assess the possible reasons why the region has missed out on the most expansionary six year period in UK post-war history. Second, to evaluate the efficacy of previous policy initiatives in Northern Ireland and to explore possible new directions for regional economic policy in the 1990s.

ECONOMIC TRENDS IN THE 1980s

The Recession Years

The post-war Northern Ireland economy has been characterised by persistent structural weaknesses in the manufacturing sector (Bull and Hart, 1987; Teague, 1987). By the start of the 1980s, national and international recessionary influences exacerbated these weaknesses and plunged the Province into severe economic crisis. For example, between 1981 and 1983 the manufacturing sector experienced a net decline of 16,000 employees (6.6%). A more detailed investigation of the gross changes reveals that 14,000 jobs were lost in externally controlled branch plants and firms in the two years of 1980 and 1981 (Gudgin et al, 1989). In particular, the closure of five major plants in the man-made fibres industry provided a significant proportion of that total (Harrison, 1986a; Gudgin et al, 1989).

Thus, despite a small measure of employment growth in the private services sector in this period of recession in the early 1980s, Northern Ireland experienced a rapid rise in the level of unemployment from just over 10 per cent in 1980 to 17 per cent in 1983. Whilst the high level of job loss in the manufacturing sector was primarily responsible for this rise, high rates of natural increase in Northern Ireland's population of working age have greatly exacerbated the labour market imbalances brought about by the recession. It should, however, be noted that high levels of out-migration (averaging between 5000 and 7000 a year since the early 1980s) and low participation rates (75% of the working age population in 1981) by UK standards, have served to disguise a more realistic assessment of the unemployment situation throughout the recession. For example, it has been argued that the level of unemployment in Northern Ireland would have been at least twice as high without the safety valve of migration (Gudgin and Roper, 1990).

The recession of the early 1980s clearly had a major effect on Northern Ireland and confirmed its position on almost every measure of economic welfare as the poorest region of the UK and one of the poorest regions in the European Community. However, of particular interest in this assessment of the Northern Ireland economy in the 1980s, is the nature of its performance during the period of national economic recovery from 1983 to 1989.

Recovery Phase: 1983–89

It has now become widely recognised that the UK economy has been experiencing a sustained period of growth since 1983 which has gone far beyond a simple cyclical recovery from recession (Cambridge Econometrics/NIERC, 1990; Gudgin and Roper, 1990). The details of the phase are explored elsewhere in this book and will not be repeated here. From the perspective of the Northern Ireland economy the task in the remainder of this section is to investigate the extent to which the region has shared in this overall recovery.

Table 6.1.1: Economic Changes in Northern Ireland 1983–89

	Northern Ireland (% change)	United Kingdom
GDP	22.5	26.5
GDP/annum	3.4	4.0
Total Employment	3.1	9.7
: Financial & Business Services	17.3	41.9
: Manufacturing	-2.3	-5.6
Unemployment	-0.5	-4.0
Participation Rates	-1.5	+1.7

Source: Cambridge Econometrics/NIERC (1990)
Gudgin and Roper (1990)

Table 6.1.1 provides an overview of the performance of the Northern Ireland economy since 1983. In terms of output the Province experienced a 3.4 per cent per annum increase in GDP over the period 1983–89. Although this represented an improvement on previous periods it was still considerably lower than for the UK economy as a whole. A worrying feature of this trend is that after following broad national trends until 1986, GDP in Northern Ireland has expanded much more slowly. As a consequence growth in Northern Ireland has been slower than all the other regions of the UK except Scotland and the Northern Region (Gudgin and Roper, 1990). The existence of a large public sector experiencing slow growth in spending in the 1980s, together with a relatively small Financial and Business Services sector at the start of the period has,in general, prevented GDP growth in Northern Ireland following national trends.

The stark reality of the gap in economic performance between Northern Ireland and the national economy is clearly illustrated by the pattern of employment trends since 1983 (Table 6.1.1). Total employment in Northern Ireland has grown by 3.1 per cent in the total UK employment. From an inter-regional perspective, therefore, apart from Scotland (3.9% growth) Northern Ireland lags considerably behind all the other UK regions (Cambridge Econometrics/NIERC, 1990).

One of the most significant factors driving this trend and which serves to 'detach' the Province from the experience elsewhere in the UK is the performance of the Financial and Business Services sector. Starting from a very small base in 1983 this sector in Northern Ireland has experienced the slowest growth of all the regions. Between 1983 and 1989 employment in this sector expanded by 17.3 per cent compared to 41.9 per cent nationally. Overall, nearly 900,000 jobs were created nationally in this sector while only approximately 18,000 materialised in Northern Ireland. The most plausible explanation for this trend would appear to be a combination of the absence of gains due to the decentralisation of main offices (especially in insurance) together with the high degree of external control leading to the diminution of local sourcing of service functions within Northern Ireland. However, there is an urgent need to establish the precise reasons for this employment shortfall.

With respect to the manufacturing sector, Table 6.1.1 reveals that since 1983 employment has declined by approximately 2.3 per cent (or just over 2000 jobs). By national standards this was a modest decline but reflects both the rapid contraction that had already taken place in the early 1980s, and the continuation of a very high level of public subsidy. This latter point is further underlined when one realises that this trend in the manufacturing sector was taking place at a time when the two industrial development agencies in the Province Industrial Development Board (IDB) and Local Enterprise Development Unit (LEDU) were claiming to have promoted just over 50,000 manufacturing jobs since 1983. The fact that the manufacturing employment level remained at approximately the same level throughout the 1980s clearly illustrates the substantial level of support being given to existing manufacturing firms and jobs. A more detailed examination of industrial development policy in Northern Ireland will be presented in the following section.

Overall, therefore, Northern Ireland's disappointing trends in output and employment relative to other regions in the UK, when set beside the persistent chronic excess of labour supply over labour demand, have served to reinforce the three long-established labour market characteristics of the region. Furthermore, with birth rates currently the highest in Western Europe this trend will remain a significant characteristic of the labour market in Northern Ireland for many years.

Unemployment remains the highest in the UK at approximately 14 per cent and throughout the period 1983–89 its differential with the UK unemployment rate widened. At the beginning of the period the gap was 5.5 percentage points but, due to a more rapidly falling unemployment rate in the UK, by 1989 the differential was significantly higher at 9.1 percentage points (Cambridge Econometrics/NIERC, 1990).

From an already high level by UK terms net out-migration from Northern Ireland increased between 1983 and 1989 to 7,000 per annum (Gudgin and Roper, 1990). Nevertheless, as noted above this has not prevented unemployment trends in Northern Ireland diverging from the national pattern since 1983. Indeed, as argued earlier, this level of net out-migration deflates the level of unemployment in Northern Ireland, and disguises the real underlying weaknesses of the economy. Recent forecasts indicate that this high level of net out-migration will fall in the latter half of the 1990s to approximately 3500 per annum (Gudgin and Roper, 1991). Therefore, these forecasts, in the absence of any significant increase in labour demand within the province, point towards the continuation of high levels of unemployment in the 1990s.

Finally, apart from Wales, participation rates in Northern Ireland are the lowest in the UK and disguise yet again the 'true' extent of the unemployment problem in the region (Gudgin and Roper, 1991).

Recession: 1990–91

It is now widely recognised that the national economy is in recession for the first time since the early 1980s and that the decade of the 1990s will be characterised by a period of slow growth (Gudgin and Roper, 1991). However, although the signs of the current recession were visible in the South East as early as January 1990 through rising unemployment, it was only towards the end of the year (November) that seasonally adjusted unemployment began to rise in Northern Ireland. The chief reason for this would appear to be that the province's economy did not share in the expansion experienced elsewhere in the UK in the late 1980s. In particular, the dominance of the public sector in Northern Ireland whilst curtailing growth during the credit boom will now serve to protect the economy against the worst effects of the recession.

It has emerged in recent months that due to revisions to the official employment and self-employment statistics, there were 36,000 new jobs created in the Northern Ireland economy since 1986, mostly in private services (Gudgin and Roper, 1991). However, despite this seemingly optimistic note it must be stressed that the deep-rooted labour market problem of persistently high unemployment remains unresolved as the region now begins to feel the effects of national recession.

In the light of this situation in Northern Ireland, and faced with a decade of slow growth in the national economy, it is pertinent to consider the most appropriate policy response for the 1990s. However, before doing so it should be noted that continued rapid growth of the labour force will dictate for many decades the nature and extent of the employment shortfall in the Province. Policies, therefore, designed to stimulate labour demand at the regional level may well be effectively constrained by this unique feature of the Northern Ireland economy.

ECONOMIC DEVELOPMENT POLICY

Background

The response of a succession of regional and national governments to the economic problems of the Northern Ireland has been the development and implementation of a considerable public expenditure programme. Indeed, government expenditure in 1986–87 at £4597m represented just over 60 per cent of the Province's GDP and reflected the general trend of the 1980s (Gudgin and Roper, 1990). This high level of public spending does much to alleviate low levels of spending from the private sector but total domestic spending still remains considerably lower than in the UK. More import- antly, public expenditure within Northern Ireland is far in excess of what can be financed locally and therefore, a subvention (transfers from Great Britain Exchequer Funds) is required which in recent years has been equivalent to over 20 per cent of GDP (Gudgin and Roper, 1990).

In comparative terms government expenditure in Northern Ireland on a per capita basis is 43 per cent above the national average (35% excluding 'extra' amounts under the Law and Order heading), although much of the difference is accounted for by variations in population age structures and other measures of 'need' (NIEC, 1984). This pattern of expenditure holds true for all categories of spending except transport. Clearly, without this level of public spending the economic performance of the Northern Ireland economy would diminish sharply and irrevocably. Even after 11 years of a Conservative administration, with its inherent allegiance to public expenditure constraint, the social, economic and political problems of Northern Ireland defy any attempts to seriously reduce the level of government expenditure.

However, such an acknowledgement does not imply that a strategy to simply maintain the 'status quo' in terms of public expenditure will best serve the interests of the Northern Ireland economy. The evidence of the previous section is testament enough to the deepening economic problem confronting the Province at the start of the 1990s, and a radical re-think of public policy is urgently required. This is best illustrated with reference to the budget of trade, industry, energy and employment which is central to the strategic debate on employment creation. The level of proposed spending per capita under this heading in 1987/88 was two and a half times that in the UK as a whole and over 50 per cent greater than in Scotland and Wales (Gudgin and Roper, 1990).

Industrial Development Assistance

Industrial Development (ID) policy in Northern Ireland is administered locally by the Department of Economic Development (DED) in conjunction with its two agencies (IDB and LEDU). A more detailed review of the evolution of ID policy in Northern Ireland within the context of national regional policy can be found elsewhere (Harrison, 1990a; 1990b; Hart and Harrison, 1990).

The DED and its two ID agencies are highly active in attempting to attract new inward investment (IDB), in assisting companies already established within the Province (IDB and LEDU), and in promoting new indigenous firm formation (LEDU). Total expenditure on industrial assistance in Northern Ireland is currently £214m and has run at similar levels in real terms throughout the 1980s (Gudgin et al, 1989). The instruments of ID policy are a combination of national programmes, regional assistance available in all UK assisted areas and specifically local schemes.

One major form of financial assistance, until its abolition in 1988, was Standard Capital Grant (SCG) given automatically at a rate of 20 per cent for investment in manufacturing (Harrison, 1986b; Harris, 1991). In addition, Selective Financial Assistance under a range of schemes covering grants for capital investment, start-ups of new firms. Loans and equity participation are also available. Increasingly, over recent years both the IDB and LEDU have augmented the financial assistance schemes to provide advice, grants and assistance to increase the operational competitiveness of firms.

Impact of ID Policy

In recent years there have been a vast array of studies published which directly or indirectly provide an assessment of the impact of ID policy in Northern Ireland (Bull and Hart, 1987; Gudgin et al, 1989; Harrison, 1990a; 1990b; Hart and Harrison, 1990; Hitchens and O'Farrell, 1987; 1988; Hitchens and Birnie, 1989; NIEC, 1985a; 1985b; 1990; Teague, 1987; 1989). Rather than summarise here the findings of these studies the reader is left to pursue them through independent inquiry. By way of illustration, however, the most recent direct study of the impact of ID policy discovered that of the 23,000 jobs promoted in 305 firms assisted by the IDB between 1982 and 1983 and 1987–88 less than 10,000 jobs were in place at the end of the period: an attainment ratio of job creations to promotions of 40.5 per cent (NIEC, 1990).

The overwhelming conclusion to emerge from all these studies is that, despite many decades of substantial public sector support to both large- and small-scale indigenous and externally controlled firms in Northern Ireland, the result has not been the creation of a competitive local economy capable of generating sufficient jobs for its labour force. This is not to say that past and current levels of financial assistance are ineffective. It may well be the case that job losses in firms operating in Northern Ireland would have been much greater in the absence of assistance. Furthermore, some of the assistance is likely to be offsetting the negative impact of the 'Troubles'. Nevertheless, it has been estimated that industrial structure and the effects of the 'Troubles' are not sufficient in themselves to account for the massive employment shortfall in Northern Ireland (Gudgin et al, 1989).

The weak competitive basis of locally owned firms in Northern Ireland has been identified as a major factor in understanding the poor performance of the manufacturing sector. This is not to ignore the detrimental effects of inward investment on the performance of the Northern Ireland economy, but rather to acknowledge that it is a common feature of economic development in the 1980s throughout all peripheral economies in the UK, and furthermore, beyond the control of local policy-makers.

Northern Ireland owned manufacturing possesses a level of productivity only four-fifths that of Great Britain in the first half of the 1980s (Hitchens and Birnie, 1989). Once again, this position emerges across a wide spectrum of industries and is not, therefore, a simple function of industrial structure. Differential energy and transport costs and the smaller average size of factories in Northern Ireland are thought not to provide a full explanation of the productivity gap. Arguably, it is the quality of labour and management which explain the failure in physical productivity in Northern Ireland and thus an ID policy based upon simple capital subsidization may not be the most appropriate.

Hitchens and O'Farrell's inter-regional comparative work on small firms sheds further light on this issue by demonstrating the low product quality and price competitiveness of Northern Ireland firms (Hitchens and O'Farrell, 1987). Poor management and labour force skills, experience and attitudes were identified as the major explanation of this finding. Evidence on the poor employment performance of the indigenously owned small firm sector in Northern Ireland over the period 1973–86 would tend to provide further support for this conclusion (Gudgin et al, 1989). With respect to larger indigenously owned Northern Ireland firms similar results emerged when they were compared with their counterparts in Germany (Hitchens et al, 1989).

ID Policy: the way forward?

ID policies are kept constantly under review and the most recent was initiated under the heading of the 'Pathfinder Process' (DED, 1987). In essence, this exercise has concentrated on the ways in which indigenous potential can be harnessed in the regeneration of the Northern Ireland economy. In particular, the proposals include the stimulation of a more positive attitude to enterprise; changing attitudes to competitiveness; encouraging export activity; exploiting the strengths of the public sector and the better targeting of public funds.

The concentration upon indigenous potential and enterprise creation seemingly at the expense of any co-ordinated policy on inward investment has attracted some comment. First, the level of enterprise created in the manufacturing sector in Northern Ireland has been shown to be as high as in other better performing regions and probably above average for the UK (Gudgin et al, 1989). The problem in Northern Ireland appears to be not in the creation of new firms but in their survival and subsequent growth. Second, and following on from this, the potential of small and large firms in the indigenous sector to create substantial numbers of new jobs has been seriously questioned (Gudgin et al, 1989; Hitchens and Birnie, 1989). Over the period 1973–86, and despite massive public sector support, the indigenous sector quite simply failed to provide sufficient jobs to counteract the job losses in existing Northern Ireland firms. Finally, Teague (1989) has argued that inward investment cannot be ignored on the grounds that, in the short-term at least, it offers important employment opportunities and provides an opportunity for diversification and multiplier effects in the regional economy.

More generally, there is certainly a case from the evidence presented above for continuing the process of redirection of financial assistance begun with the abolition of SCG in 1988. Grant aid should be more carefully designed to raise competitiveness and growth, rather than just employment, and may well require, therefore, a higher degree of conditionality in targets directed specifically at competitiveness: for example levels of output for employee, proportion of output sold outside Northern Ireland, and levels of investment in marketing, design and product development. It is vitally important that progress in achieving these targets be monitored on a regular basis. Unfortunately, this has not been a particularly important priority in the past within IDB and LEDU with respect to their job creation activities (NIEC, 1990).

Finally, the future role of development agencies such as the IDB has been called into question by the changing responsibilities for the provision of ID policies. Nationally, the adoption of monetarism and supply-side economics has led to the substantial erosion of the conventional regional policy framework. As a result policy delivery has shifted away from national government level to the supra-national (EC) scale of the one hand to the local and sub-regional scale on the other (Armstrong, 1991). Development agencies in the UK, as constituted in the 1970s and restructured and repositioned in the market place in the early 1980s, now find themselves caught between two major approaches to regional policy which differ in terms of their strategies, mechanisms, orientations and dynamics (Stöhr, 1989). In the Northern Ireland case the IDB is very much in the mould of a centralised state-sponsored agency, and as such is firmly rooted within Stöhr's (1898) traditional regional policy. There is, therefore, a conflict between this role and that required in the emerging regional policy, which emphasizes decentralised bottom-up rather than top-down policy taking and delivery.

In the light of this progressive shift in the content and context of spatially designated economic development policies, as delivered both at the national level (as in the DTI Enterprise Initiative) and at regional and local level it appears that policy in Northern Ireland is evolving less rapidly and with less assurance than elsewhere not only in Britain but throughout Europe (Bachtler, 1991).

Since the initial impetus given by 'Pathfinder' there has been a great deal of activity in the last year by those responsible for the design and delivery of industrial policy in Northern Ireland. In the first instance a major redirection of industrial policy was signalled by the Department of Economic Development in their document 'Competing in the 1990s' (DED, 1990). Following on from this the three industrial development agencies, IDB, LEDU and the new Training and Employment Agency, have each published strategy documents designed to put into practice the principles of the DED statement. Of central concern to each of these documents is the overall move towards improving industrial competitiveness as a means of stimulating economic growth. Quite how the agencies intend to address this objective at an operational level is still somewhat unclear, although this should evolve in the coming months.

CONCLUSION

This brief review has clearly demonstrated the extent to which the Northern Ireland economy has become 'detached' in the 1980s from the economic performance of the rest of the UK. The unique features of the regional economy have meant that there has been little evidence of Northern Ireland participating in the period of rapid growth in the national economy between 1983 and 1989. This situation has arisen despite very high levels of public sector support to the economy as a whole, and industry in particular. In a very real sense, therefore, the recession of the early 1980s has become transformed into a period of slow growth in Northern Ireland relative to the rest of the UK. This situation has become further exacerbated with the onset of another national recession in 1990–91.

Recent forecasts published by the NIERC for the Northern Ireland economy for the period up to 2000 would tend to suggest that the situation is not likely to change in the medium-term (Gudgin and Roper, 1991). Set within a context of recession followed by slow growth in the national economy it is predicted that, for example, GDP in Northern Ireland will lag behind the rest of the UK and that unemployment will remain at or around the already high level of 14 per cent.

Even if Northern Ireland were to experience a significant increase in the demand for labour brought about by increases in the level of inward investment and / or through genuine job creation from established firms in the Province, the scale of the employment shortfall outlined above mitigates against a speedy solution. It would appear that very high unemployment may have become a permanent feature of the Northern Ireland economy.

This very pessimistic assessment for the Northern Ireland economy clearly demands a radical response from both the private and the public sectors. A more carefully targeted ID policy, as outlined in recent policy statements by the three agencies responsible for the delivery of industrial policy, fully extended to involve the key growth industries in the service sector, may yield some benefits in terms of job creation in the short to medium-term. However, this on its own will clearly not be sufficient to resolve the chronic problem of unemployment.

As a result, more radical solutions to this problem have been recently aired which involve policies designed to increase the already high level of out-migration from Northern Ireland (Gudgin and Roper, 1990; 1991). Whilst it is difficult to refute the 'cold' statistical analysis and logic behind this viewpoint the implementation of such a strategy is fraught with difficulties. In particular, the self-selecting nature of the process might well produce a more damaging effect on the Northern Ireland economy by even further reducing the stock of actual and potential labour skills. The knock-on effects that this might have on inward investment, the job creation potential of established and indigenous and externally controlled companies, levels of new firm formation and overall confidence in the Northern Ireland economy are clearly difficult to quantify by extremely worrying nonetheless.

The sad truth is that even with a period of national economic growth combined with massive public sector support the social and economic welfare of the Northern Ireland economy remains in a critical condition. Consequently, the economic future of Northern Ireland is closely related to continual public sector intervention in terms of ID policy, direct employment and a supportive benefit system for low income families. This obviously should involve a radical review of the efficient use of public sector funds. Although such a review is currently under way in Northern Ireland the detailed strategies have yet to emerge.

REFERENCES

Armstrong, H. (1991) The Conflict between District Councils and Regional Policy in England and Wales. In Harrison R.T. and Hart M. (eds) *Spatial Policy in a Divided Nation*. Jessica Kingsley Publishers: London (forthcoming).

Bull, P. J. and Hart, M. (1987) Northern Ireland. In Damesick, P. and Wood, P. (eds) *Regional Problems, Problem Regions and Public Policy in the United Kingdom*, Oxford Clarendon Press.

Bachtler, J. (1991) Regional Policy: European perspectives and the comparative experience. In Harrison, R.T. and Hart, M. (eds) *Spatial Policy in a Divided Nation*. Jessica Kingsley Publishers: London, (forthcoming).

Cambridge Econometrics/NIERC (1990) *Regional Economic Prospects: Analysis and Forecasts to the Year 2000 for the Standard Planning Regions of the UK (Abridged Version)* NIERC: Belfast.

Department of Economic Development (1987) *Building a Stronger Economy: The Pathfinder Initiative*. HMSO: Belfast.

Department of Economic Development (1990) *Competing in the 1990s*. HMSO: Belfast

Gudgin, G., Hart, M., Fagg, J., D'Arcy, E. and Keegan, R. (1989) *Job Generation in Manufacturing Industry, 1973–1986: A Comparison of Northern Ireland with the Republic of Ireland and the English Midlands*. NIERC: Belfast.

Gudgin, G. and Roper, S. (1990) *The Northern Ireland Economy: review and forecasts to 1995*. NIERC: Belfast.

Gudgin, G. and Roper, S. (1991) *Economic Forecasts for Northern Ireland, 1991–2000*. NIERC: Belfast.

Harris, R.I.D. (1991) Automatic Capital Incentives and Company Investment Decisions in Northern Ireland. In Harrison, R.T. and Hart, M. (eds) *Spatial Policy in a Divided Nation*. Jessica Kingsley Publishers: London (forthcoming).

Harrison, R.T. (1986a) Industrial development policy and the restructuring of the Northern Ireland economy. *Environment and Planning: Government and Policy*, 4, 53–70.

Harrison, R.T. (1986b) The standard capital grants scheme in Northern Ireland: a review and assessment. *Regional Studies*, 16, 267–85.

Harrison, R.T. (1990a) Industrial Development in Northern Ireland: the Industrial Development Board. In Connolly M. and Loughlin S. (eds) *Public Policy in Northern Ireland: Adoption or Adaptation*. Policy Research Institute: Belfast.

Harrison, R.T. (1990b) Industrial Development Policy. In Spencer J. et al (eds) *The Northern Ireland Economy: a comparative study in the economic development of a peripheral region*. Longman: London.

Hart, M. and Harrison, R.T. (1990) Inward investment and economic change: the future role of regional development agencies. Local Economy, 5, 196–213.

Hitchens, D.M.W.N. and O'Farrell, P.N. (1987) The comparative performance of small manufacturing firms in Northern Ireland and S E England. *Regional Studies*, 21, 547–53.

Hitchens, D.M.W.N. and O'Farrell, P.N. (1988) The comparative performance of small manufacturing firms in South Wales and Northern Ireland. *Omega*, 16, 429–38.

Hitchens, D.M.W.N. and Birnie, J.E. (1989) *Manufacturing Productivity in Northern Ireland: a comparison with Great Britain*. NIERC: Belfast.

Hitchens D.M.W.N., Wagner, K. and Birnie, J.E. (1989) *Northern Ireland Manufacturing Productivity compared with West Germany: statistical summary of the findings of a matched plant comparison*. NIERC: Belfast.

Northern Ireland Economic Council (1984) *Public Expenditure Priorities: An Overall Review*. NIEC: Belfast.

Northern Ireland Economic Council (1985a) *The Duration of LEDU Assisted Employment*. NIEC: Belfast.

Northern Ireland Economic Council (1985b) *The Duration of Industrial Development Maintained Employment*. NIEC: Belfast.

Northern Ireland Economic Council (1990) *The Industrial Development Board for Northern Ireland: selective financial assistance and economic development policy*. NIEC: Belfast.

Stöhr, W. (1989) Regional Policy at the Crossroads: an overview. In Albrechts, L. et al (eds) *Regional Policy at the Crossroads*. Jessica Kingsley Publishers: London.

Teague, P. (1987) Multinational Companies in the Northern Ireland economy: an outmoded model of industrial development? In Teague P (ed) *Beyond the Rhetoric: Politics, the Economy and Social Policy in Northern Ireland.* Lawrence and Wishart: London.

Teague, P. (1989) Economic development in Northern Ireland: has Pathfinder lost its way? *Regional Studies,* 23, 63–9.

The Republic of Ireland

Jim Walsh

This chapter examines the regional dimensions of recent patterns of economic adjustment in the Republic of Ireland. Following a brief review of both the EC and domestic macro-economic contexts there follows an assessment at the regional level of recent demographic and labour force trends. The remaining sections consider the ways in which approaches to regional development in Ireland have developed with particular attention to some recent initiatives.

The Republic of Ireland is the most seriously disadvantaged region in the northern periphery of the European Community (Commission of the European Communities, 1987,1991.). There are a number of particularly serious problems which make the task of achieving economic growth relatively more difficult than in other regions of the EC. These include major structural weaknesses in all sectors of the economy; a very high level of public debt with related high servicing charges amounting to one-quarter of current government expenditure in the mid-1980s; a steady decline at about 2 per cent per annum in gross fixed capital formation up to 1986; a very high level of economic dependency amongst a small relatively sparsely distributed rural population and a highly primate form of urban system (over 30% of the population resides in the area in and around Dublin); a rapidly expanding labour force; a very centralised system of public administration, and a high level of peripherality with respect to the major European markets. Among the outcomes from the 1980s which can be partially attributed to some of these factors were a decline of almost 50,000 (4%) in the number of persons at work (up to 1988), a trebling between 1980 and 1992 in the number employed, and a net emigration of approximately 208,000 between 1981 and 1991 which is equivelant to an annual average of 5.8 per 1000 population.

CHANGING REGIONAL PATTERNS IN IRELAND

It is against the background outlined above that one must consider the regional dimensions of adjustment. A number of key demographic indices are set out in Table 6.2.1. Despite a rapid decline in fertility and a very high level of net emigration the total population increased by almost 94,000 (2.8%) between 1981 and 1986 (Walsh, 1988). In keeping with long established trends nearly one-half of the total increase occurred in the East region. However, within this region a decline of approximately 8500 per annum was recorded for the Dublin county borough area while most of the growth took place in the expanding suburbs. Elsewhere in the state there were large losses in remote rural areas particularly in the Northwest where prospects for agricultural development are extremely limited and urbanisation is at a very low level.

The impact of emigration was most severely felt in Dublin which in the first half of the decade accounted for over two-fifths of the total net emigration from the state. Furthermore up to 1988 there was a very significant decline in inter regional migration and especially in migration to the East (Walsh, 1991a). Since 1986 the scale of emigration has increased considerably, especially from rural areas, so that by 1991 the total population was some 17,200 (0.5%) less than in 1986 (Walsh, 1992a). The excess of net

Table 6.2.1: Regional Demographic Indices

Region	Total Population 1991 (000s)	Population Change 1981–91 (000s)	%	Net Emigration 1981–86 (000s)	Net Emigration 1986–91 (000s)	Percentage in towns >10,000 1986
East	1350	59.6	4.6	31.8	44.5	76.4
Southwest	532	6.3	1.2	10.1	19.3	37.6
Southeast	383	8.4	2.3	8.0	15.4	26.6
Northeast	195	1.2	0.6	4.6	9.0	27.6
Midwest	311	2.3	0.7	7.2	14.4	29.2
Midlands	255	- 1.9	- 0.7	5.4	14.6	10.8
West	291	4.2	1.5	5.0	10.1	16.0
Northwest*	208	- 0.2	- 0.1	4.6	9.2	8.5
Total	3523	80.0	2.3	75.3	136.5	44.2

Northwest includes county Donegal, * Industry includes building and construction,
** = population not at work per 100 persons at work.

emigration over natural increase has resulted in widespread population decline, with increase confined mainly to the immediate hinterlands of the cities (Walsh, 1991b).

Table 6.2.2 presents a summary of the regional structure of the labour force towards the end of the 1980s. Almost two-fifths of the total number at work resides in the East where 70 per cent of all employment is in the services sector. In the remainder of the state agriculture continues to account for over one-fifth of all employment in each of the remaining regions, reaching a maximum of 28 per cent in the West. It should be noted that within the agricultural sector there is a marked gradient in prosperity away from the Southeast and South towards the Northwest and West reflecting variability in farm sizes and enterprise specialisation. Employment in industry, especially manufacturing, is now more evenly distributed between regions due to a combination of significant declines in the older industrial areas and a highly successful programme of industrial dispersal based largely on mobile inward investments since the 1960s (Drudy, 1991). The scale of employment losses especially in manufacturing and the construction sector combined with high growth rates in the labour force resulted in an increase in unemployment from 91,000 in 1980 to 232,000 in 1987. While there was a modest reduction in 1988 the overall unemployment rate in that year was 16.7 per cent which varied from a low of 12 per cent in the West to a high of 22 per cent in the

Table 6.2.2: Regional Labour Force Characteristics 1988

Region	Total at work 1988 (000s)	Agri-culture	Indus-try#	Ser-vices	Total Unemployed 1988 (000s)	Economic Dependency Ratio** 1988
East	429.5	3.5	26.2	70.2	90.1	211
Southwest	160.3	20.6	27.8	51.6	31.1	235
Southeast	111.2	23.3	29.6	47.1	25.3	247
Northeast	58.4	20.0	32.5	47.4	14.3	240
Midwest	100.6	22.3	26.8	50.9	16.2	212
Midlands	81.9	23.8	29.7	46.5	12.8	220
West	92.8	28.4	24.2	47.4	12.8	216
Northwest*	56.6	20.7	30.0	49.3	15.9	275
Total	1091.2	15.2	27.5	57.3	218.6	224

(percentage at work engaged in)

* Northwest includes county Donegal, Industry includes building and construction
** = population not at work per 100 persons at work,

Data Source: Labour Force Survey, 1988, CSO, Dublin.

Table 6.2.3: Regional Employment Changes 1961–1988

Region	Absolute change			percentage change		
	1961–71	1971–81	1981–88	1961–71	1971–81	1981–88
East	+44027	+64011	-23100	+12.8	+15.5	-5.1
Southwest	-2126	+8489	-9100	-1.3	+5.3	-5.4
Southeast	-3041	+6078	-6500	-2.7	+5.4	-5.5
Northeast	-2081	-1209	-5000	-3.1	-1.9	-8.0
Midwest	-1066	+7203	+300	-1.2	+7.7	+0.3
Midlands	-9786	+2606	-1400	-10.8	+3.2	-1.7
West	-13290	-147	+2300	-12.8	-0.2	+2.5
Northwest	-10267	-4043	-3900	-13.7	-6.3	-6.4
Ireland	*+2300*	*+83000*	*-46600*	*+0.2*	*+7.9*	*-4.1*

Northwest. The 90,000 unemployed in the East represented over 17 per cent of the regional labour force and over two-fifths of the total unemployed in the state.

The trends of the last decade need to be viewed in relation to patterns established over previous decades, Table 6.2.3. The total employment increase of only 2300 in the 1960s resulted from an increase of over 44,000 in the East and declines in every other region, and most especially in the Midlands, West and Northwest. In these regions the very high outflows from agriculture which were associated with increasing mechanisation were only partially offset by modest gains in manufacturing. In the 1970s over three quarters of the total increase of 83,000 took place in the East, but there were also gains in four other regions leaving only the Northwest, Northeast and West as regions experiencing net declines. Most of the growth in the East came from expansion in the tertiary sector, while in the other regions much of the expansion resulted from the high level of success achieved by the IDA and others in dispersing throughout the state a large number of internationally mobile manufacturing projects. In the 1980s expansion was replaced by a net decline of 46,600 in the number at work, of which almost half occurred in the East and another 44 per cent in the Southwest, Southeast and Northeast. These regions contained disproportionate shares of the older indigenous industrial firms in sectors such as textiles, clothing and footwear, and some parts of the food industry which found it most difficult to survive in a recessionary period especially in the face of imports from other EC states which increased after thethe ending in 1978 of the transition period of accession (NESC, 1989). In contrast to the performance of the older industrial regions there was some growth in employment in both the West and Midwest which can be partially attributed to the presence in these regions of significant concentrations of strategic high growth sectors such as electronic and instrument engineering as well significant numbers of producer services. Shift and share analysis points to the existence of significant factors of comparative advantage in these regions especially around Galway city and Limerick-Shannon (Walsh, 1991c). One outcome of these contrasting regional performances has been a significant narrowing of the gap in average household income levels and unemployment rates between the East and other regions. It should be noted that the trends just described refer to regions, which in some cases are quite diverse in terms of their internal structure. Thus for example the decline in total employment in the East was confined to Dublin, while in the West and Midwest most of the growth took place in Galway and around Limerick/Shannon respectively.

TRADITIONAL MODELS OF REGIONAL DEVELOPMENT IN IRELAND

In attempting to account for the regional adjustments noted above one can, for convenience, distinguish between events which took place prior to 1980 which left some regions better able to adapt, and some policy initiatives with regional implications which have emerged in recent years. Throughout the 1960s and 1970s there was a strong commitment to regional planning which relied heavily on industrial policy (Breathnach, 1982; Walsh, 1989). Throughout much of this period very little assistance was given to manufacturing in the Dublin area while in other regions there was significant expansion (Gillmor, 1985) as Ireland became more incorporated into the new international division of labour (Breathnach, 1988). Rural regions became increasingly polarized as agriculture became more influenced by the Common Agricultural Policy (CAP). While dairy farmers and cereals growers in the South and Southeast benefited from high levels of price supports (Walsh, 1985-86) there was an increasing level of marginalization of small farms (Kelleher and O'Mahony, 1984). Perhaps, the principal weakness in the approach to regional development in the 1970s was the absence of a coherent policy in relation to the tertiary sector (Bannon, 1989) which resulted in excessive concentration in Dublin, and also many problems in relation to physical planning.

NEW MODELS OF REGIONAL DEVELOPMENT

Over the past decade there have been a number of significant changes in the conceptualization of approaches to regional and local development. Stohr (1989) has noted a shift in strategy from growth to innovation, and a replacement of a centralized state-sponsored organisational structure with one which is characterised by greater decentralisation where there is greater regional and community involvement. Some other characteristics of the new models are a greater emphasis on the 'software' of development, (e.g. technical skills, knowledge, entrepreneurial attitudes); a broadening of approach from reliance on manufacturing only, to one which also encompasses business services, a switch from single projects to programmes, and more reliance on small and medium sized firms. In terms of dynamics there is a recognition that problem regions are no longer geographically stable and that the targets of policies ought to be more flexible so as to be able to respond to 'spontaneous' local resource mobilization. In summary, the new approach emphasises a broadly based strategy involving mobilisation of indigenous regional and local resources through a programme approach which is facilitated through partnerships between individuals, institutions and agencies at different geographical scales. Many of these ideas are reflected in the 1988 reform of the Structural Funds, (Commission of the European Communities, 1989), and also in the model of local development prepared for the EC sponsored LEDA programme (Martinos 1989).

RECENT INITIATIVES IN IRELAND

Throughout most of the 1980s there was a steady decline in interest in regional development in Ireland, partly due to the over-riding macro-economic problems, but probably also due to an increasing dependence on the EC especially in areas such as agriculture and infrastructural investment. However, in recent years there have been a number of initiatives, often at the instigation of the EC, that are worth noting (Walsh, 1991). In 1989 the government submitted a National Development Plan 1989–93 to the European Commission in support of its request for aid from the Structural Funds. The process of plan preparation generated a considerable amount of controversy, most of

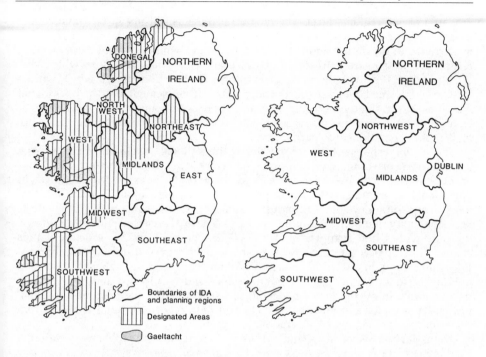

Figure 6.2.1a: Planning Regions and Designated Areas   *Figure 6.2.1b: Regions for Programmes for EC funding*

which was centred on the partnership principle. The difficulties here arose from the absence of a regional level consultative/advisory framework following the abolition in autumn 1987 of the nine Regional Development Organisations, and the curtailment of the development potential of local authorities in the late 1970s under a revision of financing arrangements. The preparation of the plan necessitated the establishment of a new regional framework involving seven regions, (Figure 6.2.1.). The new regions did not represent any attempt to harmonise the variety of regional frameworks already in existence (as might have been expected in the preparation of a plan which was meant to show evidence of integration), but instead resulted in a rather curious selection of boundaries in some places, such as around Dublin where reliance on the county boundary has resulted in an unsatisfactory identification of the country's largest and most complex functional region. An innovatory aspect of the preparation process was the establishment in each of the subregions of two committees: one representing the European Commission, relevant government departments and state agencies, and the local authorities, while the other, which was designated as an advisory group, consisted of all the main representative bodies with an interest in development. This latter group made recommendations to the first group who were responsible for preparing a programme for each region. While this particular administrative and consultative innovation was designed to meet the partnership principle advocated by the European Commission it was subject to considerable criticism particularly from local interests who were excluded from the formal consultative procedure and also because of uncertainty concerning the real influence which the sub-regional level contributions would have on the final submissions made to Brussels. In the event this apprehension was well founded since the final plan bore little resemblance to the submissions prepared at sub-regional level. The new arrangements did not in fact involve any transfer of responsibility for regional and local development from the national government, much to the disappointment of the European Commission and Parliament. In response to pressure from Brussels the two sets of sub-regional committees which were established in 1988 have been merged to form Review Committees which will be 'regularly informed and consulted concerning the implementation of operational measures in, or significantly affecting, the subregions concerned' (Department of Finance, 1989). It remains to be seen whether this initiative represents anything more than a token commitment to partnership.

The official response of the Commission to the National Development Plan was set out in the form of a Community Support Framework (CSF). This provides for assistance of about IR£2860m for Ireland over the period 1989–1993 to be expended through eight operational programmes with specific priorities given to agriculture, fisheries, forestry, tourism and rural development; industry and services; measures to offset the effects of peripherality, and human resource measures. The total projected public expenditure up to the end of 1993 is approximately IR£4772m, of which the EC Structural Funds contribution represents 60 per cent. A notable and welcome feature of the Operational Programme for industrial development is a shift from supporting capital to non-capital investment in areas such as marketing, science and technology, and management development. In overall terms the combined support from the ESF and the ERDF towards non-capital assistance amounts to over 72 per cent of the total available from these sources for the industry operational programme.

The industrial sector in Ireland suffers from a number of problems including a predominance of small firms, weak marketing and management systems and very low levels of investment in research and technology development. The limited amount of Research and Development (R&D) activity is localised, though not as much as in other parts of the EC periphery. In 1988 37 per cent of the total expenditure on R&D by business firms was by firms located in the East region. The shares in the Midwest and Southwest were 19 per cent and 15 per cent respectively, which in the case of the Midwest is largely a reflection of the high concentration there of foreign owned firms. Over the past decade a number of items of new infrastructure, including science parks, industrial and business innovation centres, and incubator units have been established in Dublin, Limerick, Galway and Cork. Recently similar initiatives have been taken in the towns where the Regional Technical Colleges are located. Probably the most advanced application of this approach is the Plassey Technological Park which was developed in 1984 by the University of Limerick in consultation with the regional development agency (SFADCo) and local high-tech enterprises. The importance of this initiative and those in the other university cities is reflected in the data on employment trends. In 1987 the Southeast region was selected as the location for an EC sponsored Pilot Technology programme. One of the outcomes has been the appointment of industrial liaison officers to Carlow and Waterford Regional Technical Colleges which has resulted in the establishment of closer links between the colleges and over 60 firms in the region. Such links are particularly important for small and medium sized firms, many of which are trying to supply niche markets. In a recent review it has been noted that the small industry sector can make a significant contribution to 'balanced regional and rural development' (Department of Industry and Commerce, 1990).

There have been a number of other initiatives relating to regional development which are briefly summarised in the remaining sections. Almost two-fifths of the total population resides in rural areas at an average density of less than 20 persons per square kilometre. The Government's objectives for such areas are to relieve social deprivation and create viable rural communities. Since the problems relating to low incomes in the poorer agricultural regions cannot be solved by relying solely on agriculture (Commission of the European Communities, 1988) there have been a number of proposals to encourage alternative activities. These include horticulture, forestry, agri-tourism and integrated rural development programmes.

In relation to urban areas there has been much concern over the decline in the quality of the physical environment in some parts. There have been a variety of responses to this problem culminating in the 1986 Urban Renewal Bill. Significant financial incentives are now available for industrial, commercial and residential developments in designated areas of Dublin, Cork, Limerick, Waterford and Galway in an effort to attract private enterprise back into the city centre. This initiative, involving a joint effort between the State which provides tax incentives, local authorities who are direct promoters and co-ordinators, and the private sector, has been extended to another 17 towns. In terms of both regional and national impacts the most important of the designated areas is the Custom House Docks area in Dublin, part of which has been designated as an International Financial Services Centre with an attractive range of taxation reliefs that are comparable to those provided to the manufacturing sector. Already over one hundred companies are committed to establishing operations in the Centre. This initiative represents a significant addition to the International Services programme operated by the IDA since 1981 which has resulted in the establishment of over 300 companies providing approximately 5000 jobs. While the high quality of the telecommunications system has facilitated the establishment of some service companies who are mainly involved in routine data processing operations in a number of small towns, the majority of the jobs assisted through this programme have been in Dublin, Cork, Limerick and Galway. At the same time there are severe problems of unemployment and poverty in many urban areas which require new responses (Combat Poverty Agency, 1991) – which has at last been officially acknowledged (Government of Ireland, 1991).

CONCLUSIONS AND PROSPECTS

The 1980s was a decade of difficult adjustment for most sectors of the Irish economy which resulted in significant modifications of the geography of development in the state. Many of the traditional approaches to regional development were found to be inadequate and have recently been replaced by initiatives which are more in accordance with trends in other parts of Europe. Over the next decade there are likely to be many more adjustments, especially as a result of increasing European integration (NESC,1990; Walsh, 1990a). The completion of the internal market may in fact assist the further expansion of overseas controlled firms who will save in exports to a barrier-free EC. This will be particularly important for electronics and pharmaceuticals firms which are mostly located close to international airports and third level colleges. The indigenous manufacturing sector will probably undergo further restructuring in an attempt to remain competitive. In the tertiary sector there is likely to be considerable expansion of producer services with a high level of polarization between relatively high skilled forms of employment in Dublin and a few other cities, and more routine and less well paid employment which may be distributed among smaller towns. Already a large part of the more specialist producer services sector is dominated by international organizations (e.g. accountancy). This trend is likely to continue. However, the competition for foreign direct investment in both manufacturing and services is likely to increase, particularly from Spain and eastern Germany. Apart from the effects of the internal market programme the agricultural sector will have to adjust to the requirements of a new CAP, a process which will be particularly difficult in the western regions (NESC, 1992; Walsh, 1991d). There will be an ongoing need for high levels of financial support from the EC, which will become even greater in the context of an Economic and Monetary Union.

There will continue to be a major problem in relation to unemployment and emigration mainly due to very high levels of growth in the labour force (NESC, 1991). Since 1987 there has been some growth in employment, and a gradual reduction in unemployment though this positive trend has recently been reversed due to a sharp reduction in net emigration and an increase in return migrants. This adjustment can be related to the effects of recession in the UK and US economies. At the regional level recent trends in employment and internal migration, particularly of highly qualified personnel, point towards a renewed focus on Dublin and to a lesser extent on Galway, Limerick and Cork cities (Walsh, 1992b). This trend is likely to continue, and therefore needs to be considered within the context of a national settlement strategy which would also consider the needs of regions which currently lack the facilities and amenities available in the larger urban areas. Many other problems remain including the need to clarify the level of priority given by government to reducing regional disparities within Ireland given the magnitude of the disparities between the state and the more prosperous parts of the EC, the definition and harmonization of regional systems, the allocation of functions between different spatial levels of government and the identi- fication of appropriate structures to facilitate local and regional involvement in the preparation and implementation of national programmes for development (Walsh 1992c). Recently there has been a resurgence of interest in some of these issues(Bar- rington Report, 1991; Culliton Report, 1992), which is strongly supported and encour- aged by the Irish Branch of the Regional Studies Association in its most recent policy document (RSA, June, 1990).

REFERENCES

Bannon, M.J. (1989) 'Development planning and the neglect of the critical regional dimension'. In Bannon M. J. et al *Planning: the Irish experience 1920–1988*. Dublin: Wolfhound Press.

Barrington Report (1991) *Local Government Reorganisation and Reform*, Dublin: Stationery Office

Breathnach, P. (1982) 'The demise of growth-centre policy: the case of the Republic of Ireland'. In Hudson, R., and Lewis, J. (eds.) *Regional Planning in Europe*. London: Pion.

Breathnach, P. (1988) 'Uneven development and capitalist peripheralisation'. *Antipode*, 20 (2) 122–144.

Combat Poverty Agency (1991) *Urban Poverty, the Economy and Public Policy: Options for Ireland in the 1990s*. Dublin.

Commission of the European Communities. (1987) *The Regions of the Enlarged Community – Third Periodic Report on the Social and Economic Situation and Development of the Regions of the Community*. Luxembourg: Office for Official Publications of the European Community.

Commission of the European Communities (1988) *The Future of Rural Society*. Luxembourg: Office for Official Publications of the European Community.

Commission of the European Communities (1989) *GUIDE to the Reform of the Community's Structural Funds*. Luxembourg: Office for Official Publications of the European Community.

Culliton Report (1992) *A Time for Change, Industrial Policy for the 1990s*, Dublin: Stationery Office

Department of Finance (1989) *Reynolds outlines Community Support Framework*. Dublin: Government Infor- mation Services.

Department of Industry and Commerce (1990) *Review of Industrial Performance 1990*. Dublin: Stationery Office.

Drudy, P.J. (1991) 'The regional impact of foreign investment in Ireland'. In McAleese D. and Foley, A. (eds.) *Overseas Industry in Ireland*. Dublin: Gill and Macmillan.

Gillmor, D.A. (1985) *Economic Activities in the Republic of Ireland*. Dublin: Gill and Macmillan.

Government of Ireland (1991) *Programme for Economic and Social Progress*. Dublin: Stationery Office.

Kelleher, C. and O'Mahony, A. (1984) *Marginalisation in Irish Agriculture*. Dublin: Teagasc.

Martinos, H. (1989) *The Managemant of Local Employment Development Strategies*. London: LRDP.

NESC (1989) *Ireland in the European Community: Performance, Prospects and Strategy*, Report No. 88. Dublin: Stationery Office.

NESC (1990) *A Strategy for the Nineties: economic stability and structural change*. Dublin: Report No. 89, Stationery Office.

NESC (1991) *The economic and social implications of emigration*, Report No. 90. Dublin: Stationery Office.

NESC (1992) *The Impact of Reform of the Common Agricultural Policy Report No. 92*, Dublin: Stationery Office.

Regional Studies Association (Irish Branch) (1990) *Towards a regional development strategy for Ireland*. Dublin.

Stohr, W. (1989) 'Regional Policy at the Crossroads: an overview'. In Albrechts, L. et al (eds.) *Regional Policy at the Crossroads: European Perspectives*. London: Jessica Kingsley Publishers.

Walsh, J.A. (1985–86) 'Uneven development of agriculture in Ireland'. *Geographical Viewpoint*, 14, 37–65.

Walsh, J.A. (1988) 'Components of demographic change in the Republic of Ireland'. *Geographical Viewpoint*, 16, 45–59.

Walsh, J.A. (1989) 'Regional Development Strategies' in Carter, R. W. G., and Parker, A.J., (eds.) *Ireland; a Contemporary Geographical Perspective*. London: Routledge.

Walsh, J.A. (1990a) 'Regional Implications of a Single Market European Community'. *Geographical Viewpoint*, 18, 43–58.

Walsh, J.A. (1991a) 'Inter-regional migration in the Republic of Ireland: patterns and processes'. In King, R. (ed.) *Contemporary Irish Migration*. Dublin: Geographical Society of Ireland Special Publications No. 6.

Walsh (1991b) 'The turn-around of the turn-around in the population of the Republic of Ireland', *Irish Geography*, 24, (2) 116–124.

Walsh, J.A. (1991c) Regional and Local Development in Ireland in the 1990s', in Walsh, J.A. (ed.) *Local Economic Development and Administrative Reform*, Dublin: Regional Studies Association (Irish Branch).

Walsh, J.A. (1991d) 'A regional analysis of enterprise substitution in Irish agriculture in the context of a changing Common Agricultural Policy', *Irish Geography*, 24, (1) ,10–23.

Walsh, J.A. (1992a) 'Economic Restructuring and Labour migration in the European periphery: the case of the Republic of Ireland', in O'Cinneide, M., and Grimes, S., (eds.) *Planning and Development of Marginal Areas.*, Galway: UCG.

Walsh, J.A. (1992b) 'Education, Migration and Regional Development'. In Davis, J. (ed.) *Education, Training and Local Economic Development*, Dublin: Dublin Regional Studies Association (Irish Branch).

Walsh, J.A. (1992c) 'Regional Planning for the 1990s', in *The Regions, Partnership and Planning*, Dublin: Chambers of Commerce of Ireland,

PART III

DIMENSIONS OF REGIONAL ECONOMIC DEVELOPMENT

INDUSTRY, TECHNOLOGY AND EMPLOYMENT

CHAPTER 7

INDUSTRIAL ACTIVITY AND THE REGIONS

7.1

Corporate Reorganisation in the Manufacturing Sector

H. D. Watts

Throughout the 1980s the 100 largest manufacturing enterprises in the UK maintained their share of manufacturing net output at around 40 per cent and they played an important role in the shaping of regional economies through the re-organisation of production activities. These re-organisations were accompanied by significant employment losses in the manufacturing sector. Although the firms were responding to changes in the macro-economic environment, it was the decisions of the firms themselves that led to job losses (and in some cases job gains) in particular places. For many communities the loss of jobs was seen to arise from the policies of major firms, rather than from the changes in the global and national contexts within which the firms were operating.

CORPORATE RE-ORGANISATION

Each site within a multi-locational firm is characterised by an activity mix and in response to external circumstances a firm can add and delete sites from the system and can change the mix of activities on sites that are retained (Healey and Watts, 1987). These sites are, of course, located in particular places and the decisions to open, shut or change activities can have important repercussions for the communities in which the plants are, have been or will be sited. The establishment of entirely new sites by large UK firms was less common in the 1980s than had been the case in earlier decades and changes in activity mixes at particular sites have escaped detailed attention.

However, considerable interest was raised by corporate shut-downs and an under-standing of the causes of selection between places in corporate re-organisation are better understood (Watts, 1991). When the choice is between plants undertaking similar activities in different locations, the dominant elements in choosing a plant for closure are related primarily to the plant itself, but local environmental influences include local government attitudes and local labour relations. Plants in regions perceived to have hostile local administrations and difficult labour forces may be selected for closure.

Among the plants that have remained in operation some writers have identified a move towards a more flexible labour force and interpreted this as a move from a Fordist to a post-Fordist (neo-Fordist) organisation of production. Each firm, it is argued, is re-organising its activities such that there is a group of primary (core) workers usually permanent staff, often skilled, and with a full range of employment benefits. To complement this group are secondary (peripheral) workers, often on limited contracts, usually unskilled and with few, if any, employment benefits. The primary workers are associated with functional flexibility seen for example in the UK pottery industry where those workers once employed on single tasks are now employed on a range of jobs (Imrie, 1989, p.16). In contrast, the secondary workers are associated with numeri-cal flexibility being, often, part-time, temporary or casual workers.

The extent to which firms are moving towards this dual labour market is difficult to assess but an indicator might be increases in the proportion of part-time, temporary or casual workers in the manufacturing sector. Certainly from 1971–1981 full-time jobs fell more rapidly than part-time jobs (Townsend, 1986); while from 1981 to 1987 evidence from older industrial regions suggests increases in both numerical and functional flexibility are taking place (Morris, 1988; Hudson, 1989). In contrast, Pinch, Mason and Witt (1989) found a relative lack of labour flexibility in the Southampton region.

Overall, the regional implications of changes in labour practices within large firms still need detailed evaluation but there is considerable debate about both the extent and causes of change. Quantitative assessments indicate that the changes in both functional and numerical flexibility are not as great as some commentators suggest. Further, while some have argued these changes reflect a move from Fordist to post-Fordist production systems others are not so sure. Hudson (1989, p.24) sees the changes as best interpreted as 'part of strategies by capital to preserve old modes of accumula-tion' while Sisson (1989, p.30) argues 'the growth of non-standard forms of employ-ment does not so much represent a conscious and changing strategy to the employment relationship on the part of British management...but a response to changes in the labour supply...and a growing realization of the need to find alternative sources of labour, particularly from among the ranks of middle-aged married women'. The 1990s may, however, be very different. Many future managers are now being taught 'the concept of core and periphery workforces is an essential feature of human resource management' (Torrington, 1989, p.61).

SUB-CONTRACTING AND MANAGEMENT BUYOUTS

Although some parts of the labour force may have been marginalised, they do, at least, remain on the payroll of the firm. Marginalisation of the secondary work-force in its most extreme form sees the 'buying-in' of services and goods formerly provided 'in-house'. As Shutt and Whittington (1987, p.18) observe 'sub-contracting takes work out of the stable and expensive internal labour markets of large firms into the insecure, low-waged and non-union employment of small firms. It also gives large firms flexibility in times of fluctuating demand.' This process is seen in the case of a commerical vehicle manufacturer based in Leyland (Lancs) where from 1979–1983 no less than ten different activities were out-sourced including the supply of petrol tanks, upholstery, pattern-making and cleaning services. The employment effects of out-sourcing strategies may be marked. The example of Chloride (also in the North West) shows that the labour force in the new firms set up to supply the firm was smaller than the number employed in the activities when they were within Chloride. It was 50 per cent less in the case of a joinery operation and 25 per cent less in the case of printing activities.

In contrast to this evidence of fragmentation, Milne (1989) shows the opposite process at work in part of the electronic consumer goods industry where some firms are bringing formerly sub-contracted work in-house. It is argued that this is a cheaper solution than out-sourcing since the overheads and profits of the suppliers are not added on to the price the large firm has to pay. What is more, delivery times can be more closely controlled and component development carefully integrated with overall product development. Clearly, the disadvantages of in-house capabilities may have been over stressed.

The regional implications of these changes to the boundaries of a firm's activities are problematical. Obviously, movement of activities in-house/out-sourced create/destroy jobs within the firm making the decision but the implications for suppliers/former suppliers are more difficult to measure. Moves to 'in-house' production may have little effect if the supplier is acquired, but if a supplier is abandoned job loss may result, especially if the supplier is unable to obtain alternative markets. Out-sourcing may retain jobs in a region, (possibly fewer in number, as in the case of Chloride, and at lower rates of pay) but if the contract is met by a firm outside the region the jobs are lost. It is possible that out-sourcing will produce regional swarms of suppliers particularly if the just-in-time delivery systems are implemented but Morris (1988, p.314) convincingly demonstrates that this is only likely to occur 'in particular place-specific, industry-specific and situation-specific instances'.

One scenario which may encourage local swarming is when a firm encourages managers of activities it wishes to 'out-source' to 'buy-out' the current activities of the firm. Some management buyouts (MBOs) can increase a firm's dependence upon sub-contracting activities but not all MBOs are of this type. Some involve the sales of major parts of diversified organisations to their managers, a notable example being Cadbury Schweppes which reversed an earlier diversification programme and repositioned itself with a focus on confectionery and drinks (Watts, 1990). Examination of MBOs in all sectors (not only manufacturing) shows that most MBOs (whether arising from out-sourcing or repositioning) come from divestment by firms still trading, less than 10 per cent from receivership of the parent. Although MBOs are stressed here, some activities are transferred (sold) from one firm to another (Healey, 1983, p.337).

MBOs increased in the 1980s and this may have helped local economies in one of three ways. First, it may help to save jobs in that the parent is willing to consider buyout proposals whereas in the past run-down or closure was a more likely option. Second, a buyout may offer an opportunity for a plant to escape restrictive policies and financial practices imposed by head office. Third, by returning a plant to local control the prospect of rationalisation or shut-down by a distant head office is reduced. These benefits should be seen as *potential* gains for, equally, the new owners could implement major job losses (Lovejoy, 1988). Contemporary regional variations in the extent of MBOs and their effects still await detailed investigation but the evidence for the early

1980s suggests one region of marked over-representation of MBOs is the West Midlands where buyouts have been concentrated in the manufacturing sector.

TAKEOVERS AND MERGERS

Rather more detailed information is available relating to the extension of a firm's boundaries through acquisition. Within the largest firms, acquisitions often involve the purchase of smaller firms based mainly in UK regions outside the South East. For example, of the North's 16 firms manufacturing in *The Times 1000* of 1971 only four survived in the 1984 list, with acquisitions accounting for nine of the twelve non-survivors. Smith (1985–6, pp.31–32) argues that acquirers placed a relatively high value upon these firms suggesting they were performing satisfactorily at time of takeover. Similar trends can be seen in other areas. In Sheffield, Britain's fifth largest city, the 22 *Times 1000* firms of 1976 had been reduced to 13 by 1989 primarily through acquisition (Watts, 1989).

Such acquisition processes tend to reduce the white collar jobs in the regions in which firms are acquired and help maintain or increase the jobs in the regions in which the corporate head offices are located. Further white collar jobs can be lost through centralisation of sub-corporate head office activities. In the Sheffield case, Unilever's decision to focus the administration of many of its food companies in Croydon, resulted in the shut-down and loss of 300 jobs in the Sheffield headquarters of Batchelors Foods.

Acquisitions have played a major part in increasing the level of external control in particular regions. Although the economic disadvantages of external control have perhaps been overstressed, corporate financial restructuring through acquisition does still cause concern in regions with high levels of external control, especially where national interest groups (notably in Wales and Scotland) raise awareness of the issue (Watts, 1981). The sensitive nature of this issue was recognised when Elders IXL, in an abortive bid for Edinburgh-based Scottish and Newcastle Breweries, offered to relocate the global headquarters of their brewing division to Edinburgh (Fagan, 1990, p.664).

The effects of takeovers on the manufacturing sector have been explored in detail in Scotland (Ashcroft, 1988; Ashcroft and Love, 1989; Love, 1990). Whereas the overall effects on company performance were beneficial, for example, through improved sales performance, the wider effects on the regional economy were less favourable. Many of the firms reduced their links to the Scottish economy, especially those for services. Examples were the switching of road haulage to the acquirer's own transport services in England and the changing of auditors from a Scottish to an English firm. Overall, 72 per cent of the acquired firms transferred business to suppliers outside Scotland.

Although regional outcomes of acquisition activity can be established, the regional interest in UK merger policy is confused. In deciding whether to refer proposed acquisitions to the Monopolies and Mergers Commission (MMC) regional interests *may* be ignored, but once the referral has taken place MMC rules make clear that the regional interest must be considered. From a regional viewpoint, there appears to be considerable strength in the argument of Ashcroft and Love (1988) that the MMC should examine all qualifying takeovers where the party to be acquired has its headquarters or substantial part of its operations in a peripheral region. Further, the size threshold above which acquisitions can be referred should be lowered as relatively few regional firms are above the present size threshold selected on competition grounds.

CONCLUSION

Certainly, in the 1980s, large corporate organisations have faced a changed task environment and have responded accordingly. Whether the adjustments they have made reflect a marked shift from one form of production to another or a response to different labour and market environments is a matter for debate. What is clear is that in such a period of change teasing out any well researched regional implications is fraught with difficulty.

REFERENCES

Ashcroft, B. (1988) External takeovers and Scottish manufacturing industry: the effect on local linkages and corporate functions. *Scottish Journal of Political Economy*, 35, 129-148.

Ashcroft, B.K. and Love, J.H. (1988) The regional interest in U.K. mergers policy. *Regional Studies*, 22, 341.

Ashcroft, B. and Love, J.H. (1989) Evaluating the effects of external takeover on the performance of regional companies: the case of Scotland, 1965-80. *Environment Planning* A, 21, 197-229.

Healey, M.J. (1983) Components of locational change in multi-plant enterprises. *Urban Studies*, 20, 327-41.

Healey, M.J. and Watts, H.D. (1987) The multi-plant enterprise, in Lever, W.F. (ed.) *Industrial Change in the United Kingdom*, Longman, pp.149-166.

Hudson, R.L (1989) Labour market changes and new forms of work in old industrial regions: may be flexibility for some but not flexible accumulation. *Environment and Planning* D, 7, 5-30.

Imrie, R.F. (1989) Industrial restructuring, labour and locality: the case of the British pottery industry. *Environment and Planning* A, 21, 3-26.

Love, J.H. (1990) External take over and regional linkage adjustment: the case of Scotch Whisky. *Environment and Planning* A, 22, 10-118.

Lovejoy, P. (1988) Management buyouts and policy responses in the West Midlands. *Regional Studies*, 22, 344.

Milne, S. (1989) New forms of manufacturing and their spatial implications. *Environment and Planning* A, 21, 211-232.

Morris, J.L. (1988) New technologies, flexible work practices and regional socio-spatial differentiation: some observations from the United Kingdom. *Environment and Planning* D, 6, 301-319.

Pinch, S.P., Mason, C.M. and Witt, S.G. (1989) Labour flexibility and industrial restructuring in the U.K. 'Sunbelt': the case of Southampton. *Transactions*, Institute of British Geographers, NS 14, 418-434.

Shutt, J. and Whittington, R. (1987) Fragmentation strategies and the rise of small units: cases from the North West. *Regional Studies*, 21, 13-23.

Sisson, K. (1989) Personnel management in transition, in Sisson, K. (ed.) *Personnel Management in Britain*, Blackwell, pp.22-52.

Smith, I. (1985/6) Takeovers, rationalisation and the Northern Region Economy. *Northern Economic Review*, No.12, 30-38.

Torrington, D. (1989) Human resource management and the personnel function, in Storey, J. *New perspectives on human resource management*, Routledge, pp. 56-66.

Townsend, A. (1986) Spatial aspects of the growth of part-time employment in Britain. *Regional Studies*, 20, 313-330.

Watts, H.D. (1981) *The Branch Plant Economy*. Longman.

Watts, H.D. (1989) Non-financial head offices: a view from the North in Townsend, A. and Lewis, J. *The North-South Divide*, pp.157-174.

Watts, H.D. (1990) Manufacturing, the corporate sector and locational change, *Geography*, 75, 358-60.

Watts, H.D. (1991) Plant closures, multi-locational firms and the urban economy: Sheffield, UK *Environment and Planning* A, 23, 37-58.

Overseas Inward Investment in the UK Regions

Clive Collis

INTRODUCTION

The content of this contribution is confined to the role that overseas inward companies play in the regions of the UK. It therefore does not discuss the inter-regional movement of indigenous companies nor the outward investment activities of UK-owned companies. The type of overseas investment discussed is direct rather than portfolio investment. The term overseas inward investment is used to cover the activities of what are variously called multinational enterprises or transnational companies. The theory of overseas direct investment is not explicitly reviewed, nor are particular paradigms such as restructuring and the international spatial division of labour referred to specifically. However, the first section reviews the main evidence from the early 1960s to the early 1980s derived from a variety of sources. The second section concerns itself with the most recent trends in the flow of overseas inward investment to each of the UK regions while the third section consists of case studies of selected regions. Finally, an attempt is made to highlight some issues likely to be of particular relevance to the 1990s.

OVERSEAS-OWNED COMPANIES AND THE UK REGIONS: Early 1960s to Early 1980s

There is a considerable amount of evidence on the role of overseas-owned companies in the UK regions. A recent review (Young, Hood and Hamill, 1988) has drawn together the contributions of numerous authors* from whose work a number of interesting conclusions emerge. These conclusions relate mainly to the period between the early 1960s and the early 1980s and are:

(i) From the early 1960s to the early 1970s employment in the overseas-owned manufacturing sector grew much more in the Assisted Areas than in the South East of England. However, from the mid-1970s to the early 1980s both the Assisted Areas and the South East performed similarly in the context of a downward trend in overseas-owned manufacturing employment. This pattern also applied to individual assisted regions: for example employment in overseas-owned manufacturing companies peaked in Wales in 1979 and then fell in the early 1980s. These more recent trends reflect a situation in which closures affected the Assisted Areas more than the South East and the location of acquisitions by overseas-owned companies focused on the South East but new overseas-owned investment projects were concentrated in the Assisted Areas.

(ii) On the whole, overseas-owned companies have shed employment at a lower or similar rate to that of indigenous companies. This is not unexpected given the representation of the former in high technology and growing sectors. However, there are some regional variations: the Northern region has been susceptible to closures from externally-owned plants and in Scotland the concentration of closures has been

---

* The space constraint for the section prohibits individual attribution and a consequential lengthy bibliography. A long list of authors and their contributions is to be found in Young, Hood and Hamill, 1988, pp.150–53.

in a small number of large overseas-owned enterprises. Much of the regional variation in job losses reflects differences in the industrial mix of overseas-owned investment.

(iii) In 1979 there was a stock of 3651 overseas-owned manufacturing units in the UK of which 2332 originated from North America, 734 from the European Community countries and 585 from the Rest of the World. The South East had the largest share of the stock overall (34%) and from each source. In the Assisted Areas the North West had the largest share (12.5%), followed by Scotland (9.9%).

(iv) Between 1979 and 1981 the flows of overseas inward investment to the traditional Assisted Areas favoured Scotland which in 1981 received 21 per cent of all overseas investment projects and 35 per cent of all new jobs. Wales and the North West of England also each increased their share of the flow of projects and jobs between 1979 and 1981. This was in part at the expense of the North East and Northern Ireland but the main decline in shares of the flows of both projects and jobs took place in the Rest of the UK.*

(v) For companies from the USA and Continental Europe, market access has been the main factor in the choice of the UK as a location but regional assistance, particularly the Regional Development Grant, has been important in the choice of location within the UK. While regional assistance has also been of significance to Japanese companies, the main reasons for their switching from exports to manufacturing in Europe have been tariff and non-tariff barriers and the high value of the yen.

(vi) With respect to the impact of regional policy assistance, overseas-owned mobile companies have been more responsive to the financial incentives than have indigenous mobile companies. Moreover, Regional Development Grants were as important to expansions as in attracting initial investment from overseas-owned companies.

(vii) Aside from the employment effects, overseas-owned companies may help regional competitiveness. During the 1970s the productivity performance of overseas-owned manufacturing companies in the Assisted Areas was superior to that of all such companies in the UK and in 1981 net output per employee in the Assisted Areas was higher in overseas-owned manufacturers than in all manufacturing. In Wales and Scotland in 1983 net output per employee in overseas-owned manufacturers was at a similar level to that of the South East, these three regions being well above the UK average for overseas-owned manufacturers. Moreover the overseas-owned sector accounted for a growing share of net capital expenditure in manufacturing in the Assisted Areas during the late 1970s and early 1980s.

(viii) While overseas-owned companies have created jobs and contributed to increases in investment and productivity, concern has been expressed about the branch plant nature of much overseas-owned manufacturing investment in the Assisted Areas. This concern relates not only to closures, but to lack of integration into regional economies through their input purchasing policies and their contribution to the concentration of head office functions and research and development facilities in the South East of England. On the other hand it has been argued that branch plants of overseas-owned companies have helped diversify the industrial structure of the Assisted Area regions and that acquisitions by overseas companies have led to the introduction of new management practices. Also overseas-owned companies may engender a more rapid spread of new technologies and working practices. The evidence that exists is varied: for Scotland the evidence, particularly with respect to

---

* These particular conclusions are based on IBB data which has a number of deficiencies (see Note 2 to Table 7.2.1 below).

acquisitions, is that beneficial effects have not been predominant but for the West Midlands some beneficial effects are emerging from the presence of overseas-owned companies.

(ix) The bulk of the evidence relates to overseas-owned manufacturing with less evidence available on the role of overseas-owned companies in the service sector. However, in the West Midlands region it is known that distribution is strongly represented in the overseas-owned sector. With respect to banking, there is, not unexpectedly, a predominance in the South East concentrated in Central London. There is also a presence of overseas-owned banking and business service companies in Scotland, in this case related to North Sea oil developments.

(x) A key sector for the future economic development of regional economies is the electronics industry. This role derives from its position as the main user and supplier of core technology. While the UK indigenous sector of industry is weak, the UK is a favoured location for overseas-owned investors, particularly from the USA. The hierarchy in the regional representation of the electronics industry is first the South East, then Scotland followed by Wales. In Scotland in 1984 nearly half of the electronics industry employment was in overseas-owned companies. While in Scotland the companies from the USA are dominant within the overseas-owned electronics sector, in Wales it is the Japanese companies that are dominant.

FLOWS OF OVERSEAS INWARD INVESTMENT TO THE UK REGIONS, 1983-1988

A more complete regional coverage of overseas investment project and job flows is provided for the period 1983 to 1988 in Table 7.2.1 below. On the basis of this data it appears that by the late 1980s the South East of England's share of both projects and jobs, particularly the latter, had declined markedly. On the other hand the West Midlands had emerged as a strong competitor for both jobs and projects and had come to rival Scotland and Wales.

The data in Table 7.2.1 indicate that during the first nine months of 1988 the South East attracted only 15 per cent of projects and 8 per cent of jobs and that Scotland, Wales and the West Midlands each attracted a larger number of projects and jobs than the South East. Not only is the South East becoming less attractive to new overseas investors, there are examples of overseas-owned companies relocating from the South East to the adjacent West Midlands and to Wales.

Locational advantages and disadvantages help explain these trends. The characteristics which constitute 'overheating' are clearly affecting adversely the South East as a location for new and existing overseas investment. For the West Midlands the main advantageous locational factor is that it is central with good international, national and local transport networks. For Wales, the main locational factors can be summarised as 'stability and welcome'. Scotland benefits from the concentration of academic institutions which contribute to the flow of professional, technical and skilled labour.

REGIONAL CASE STUDIES

In order to provide an understanding of the role of overseas inward investment in the three regions which are currently the main hosts for new overseas investment, short case studies are provided for the West Midlands, Wales and Scotland.

Table 7.2.1: The Regional Distribution of the Flow
of Overseas Inward Investment, 1983–1988

% *Shares of UK Total Projects and Jobs.*

Regions	1983 Projects (%)	Jobs (%)	1985 Projects (%)	Jobs (%)	1988 (first 9 months) Projects (%)	Jobs (%)
West Midlands	6	14	17	15	16	25
East Midlands	5	3	5	2	5	4
North East	8	6	8	8	7	5
North West	9	6	8	8	4	5
South East	25	18	23	21	15	8
South West	4	3	4	3	2	2
Yorkshire and Humberside	4	3	4	12	5	6
Scotland	21	28	15	18	22	20
Wales	13	13	12	8	18	19
Northern Ireland	5	6	4	5	6	6
Total	100	100	100	100	100	100
UK Total Numbers	236	30800	377	44400	224	25887

Notes: 1. The jobs are those associated with projects over the long term and are the total of new and safeguarded jobs.
   2. In addition to the long-term or 'hypothetical' nature of jobs, there are other problems associated with IBB data, particularly for inter-regional comparisons: lack of consistency in methods of counting projects and jobs and varying levels of interest in counting projects accurately.
Source: Extracted from Roberts, Noon and Irving (1988) and Collis, Noon, Roberts and Gray (1989). Derived from IBB data.

The West Midlands

Over the period 1983–88 the West Midlands region improved its share of overseas investment project flows from 6 per cent to 16 per cent and its share of jobs from 14 per cent to 25 per cent. The West Midlands has thus emerged as a powerful competitor amongst the UK regions for overseas inward investment. IBB data for the first nine months of 1988 show the three major recipients of projects and jobs to have been Scotland, Wales and the West Midlands.

While the main source of overseas inward investment project flows to the West Midlands has been North America, the latter's importance as a source declined towards the end of the 1980s by which time European Community countries had become more important. In the later 1980s the Far East had emerged as an important and growing source of inward investment projects. By 1989 the stock of overseas inward investors in the West Midlands was made up from the following sources: North America 37 per cent, European Community 39 per cent, Other European 14 per cent, Far East 6 per cent, Rest of the World 4 per cent.

Broadly representative survey results reveal that the predominant activities of North American inward investors in the West Midlands are in metal goods, engineering and vehicles. The dominant activities of West German and Japanese inward investors in the region are in distribution.

The most prevalent functions of overseas investors in the West Midlands region are sales and marketing, and warehousing and distribution followed by assembly and manufacturing. Some 35 per cent of the overseas-owned companies now carry out some research and development functions although this is not prevalent amongst Japanese-owned companies located in the West Midlands. The large majority of overseas-owned inward investors in fact carry out multiple functions at their West Midlands location. However, there is a discernable sequence over time from distribution activities to assembly and manufacture and then some research and development activities. Japanese companies are entering the cycle at a later stage, as assemblers and manufacturers, replacing exports because of tariff and non-tariff barriers and the completion of the Single European Market in 1992.

There are intra-regional differences of note: the West Midlands 'county' area and Hereford and Worcester appear particularly attractive to North American companies, Staffordshire to European Community companies, Shropshire (mainly Telford) to Far Eastern companies (particularly the Japanese), and Warwickshire to other European companies, particularly Swedish. The main sector of manufacturing located in the West Midlands is metal goods, engineering and vehicles and it is heavily represented in both the conurbation and each of the shire countries. Distribution is important in all sub-regions. Recently banking and business services have been activities in which Japanese and North American companies are increasing their presence in the region.

To date there is only preliminary data on the quality of overseas inward investment in the West Midlands as a whole, based on a survey of 99 companies (Collis, Noon, Roberts, Berkeley, 1990). Survey evidence shows that overseas companies have increased employment threefold since locating in the region and that training and retraining the workforce is extensively undertaken. Over 70 per cent of the overseas-owned companies source some inputs locally, most extensively in metal goods, engineering and vehicles. Of the Japanese companies, however, only 40 per cent source locally. While 65 per cent of surveyed companies said component supplies already existed when the locational choice was made, some 55 per cent say that new component suppliers have emerged. In addition there is an extensive amount of local purchasing of capital equipment. Also there is considerable use made of local business services, although not by Japanese-owned companies. With respect to markets, of those companies surveyed, 77 per cent sell final products to the West Midlands, 95 per cent sell to the rest of the UK and 65 per cent export. North American companies are the most export-oriented but for European Community companies selling final products, the main market is the UK. Other European Country companies undertake some exporting as well as supplying the UK market. Overall, there is evidence that overseas-owned companies are providing some benefits to the West Midlands region but there is need for greater integration into the regional economy and indigenous companies must seize the opportunities as they become available.

The locational factors of importance in attracting overseas companies to the West Midlands as a whole are: a central location with good national, regional and local transport communications, the availability and cost of premises and land, the availability of financial assistance and the promotional activities of the West Midlands Development Agency. Some of these factors are being reinforced while others are becoming less of a pull. For example, with the extension of the motorway network and the development of Birmingham International Airport the transportation benefits are being reinforced while skilled labour in particular is becoming scarcer.

Wales

The take-off period for overseas inward investment in Wales occurred in the mid- to late 1960s. In 1971 overseas-owned companies employed 35,500 people in manufacturing, 11 per cent of the total of manufacturing employment in Wales. While the numbers employed in overseas-owned manufacturing peaked in 1979, at 53,200, the overseas-owned share of all manufacturing has risen steadily reaching over 22 per cent by 1986 (44,500 manufacturing jobs). Nearly 60 per cent of manufacturing jobs in the overseas sector in 1986 were in North American companies with European Community companies accounting for 12 per cent and Japanese companies for almost 10 per cent.

At the beginning of 1988 there were 259 overseas-owned manufacturing plants in Wales, employing 47,000 people and accounting for 20 per cent of the manufacturing workforce.

From Table 7.2.1 above it is evident that during the 1980s the flow into Wales of all overseas inward investment projects has been high but there has been some volatility in jobs. However, in 1988 for both projects (18%) and jobs (19%) Wales was, along with Scotland and the West Midlands, attracting a high proportion of the flow of overseas inward investment into the UK.

At the sub-regional level, Mid Glamorgan and West Glamorgan (plus Llanelli) had a disproportionately high share of foreign-owned employment in 1983. Over the period 1983–87 while the attractiveness of Mid Glamorgan persisted, Gwent and Clwyd improved their positions markedly. Over that period these three counties together, with a combined share of population of less than 50 per cent, gained nearly 80 per cent of projects associated with projects flowing from overseas.

While successful in attracting overseas inward investment projects and jobs there are question marks about the quality of such investment in Wales. There has been a spatial concentration of overseas inward investment, with Dyfed, Gwynedd and Powys being noticeably unsuccessful in attracting such investment. Employment in assembly plants, particularly in electronics, is low paid and these poor quality mainly female jobs have not helped solve the male unemployment problem. Overseas-owned plants have integrated into the Welsh economy to only a limited extent. Nor have overseas-owned companies established high level research and development functions in Wales.

The locational factors important in attracting overseas inward investment to Wales have been summarised as 'stability and welcome': a stable population of existing overseas investors, stable attitudes to work and stable industrial relations, and a welcoming approach by national and local authorities. In addition, the availability of premises and sites and of regional financial assistance have been factors. However, shortages of professional, technical and skilled labour generally are emerging, premises and sites are becoming scarcer, there are problems in relation to the availability of component supplies and weak service structure and Regional Development Grants are no longer part of the regional policy package. While promotional agencies, particularly WINvest, have been active, concern has been expressed that Wales has not presented a clearly defined and coherent image to companies in potential source countries. On the other hand, Scotland has presented a clearly defined image.

Scotland

The build-up of overseas-owned companies in Scotland accelerated in the early 1960s and the period 1965–1975 was the most important for new openings of USA-owned companies. The USA was the most important source country and in 1975 accounted for 14 per cent of total manufacturing employment in Scotland. In total there were 280 overseas-owned units, employing 108,200 people. A growth in the numbers of Continental European manufacturing units took place in the 1970s, including many acquisitions of indigenous companies. However, during the period 1976–1981 there were a number of closures in overseas-owned manufacturing units which at their maximum employment provided 45,000 jobs in Scotland. Most of the jobs lost were in a small number of large well-established companies. The closures were concentrated, sub-regionally, in Strathclyde and, sectorally, in electrical and mechanical engineering. The reasons for these closures were complex but the performance and corporate perception of that performance, particularly with respect to labour, had a major impact in a number of cases (Hood and Young, 1982). The position by 1981 was that in total there were 288 units employing 80,457 people. By the beginning of 1988 there were 344 overseas-owned manufacturing plants employing 70,300 people, over 18 per cent of total manufacturing jobs in Scotland.

With respect to the current situation, a number of contrasts can be made with the Welsh experience (Young, 1989). There is a difference in the relative importance of Japanese-owned companies: whereas in Scotland Japanese-owned employment accounts for only 2 per cent of manufacturing employment, in Wales it accounts for 10 per cent. There are contrasts in the quality of investment: while Wales has been performing better recently in attracting new overseas-owned projects, the quality of Scottish overseas-owned investment is regarded as higher. In the electronics sector Wales is a branch-type region whereas Scotland is in an intermediate position between the South East of England and Wales. The investment in this sector by Japanese-owned companies is of low quality in Wales. A further contrast relates to the promotional agencies: both WINvest and Locate in Scotland have been subject to recent scrutiny (Welsh Affairs Committee, 1988; National Audit Office, 1989) and Locate in Scotland appears to be the better regarded. However, it is the case that WINvest has had fewer resources and powers than Locate in Scotland.*

OVERSEAS INWARD INVESTMENT IN THE UK REGIONS IN THE 1990s

A number of trends and issues are relevant to the 1990s. First, the UK as a whole is faced with increasing competition with respect to the attraction of overseas direct inward investment. Competition for USA-owned manufacturing projects is strengthening from other European countries, such as Ireland and Germany, and the UK is in danger of losing its predominant position in Europe. However, UK regions, particularly Scotland, may remain popular locations for USA electronics companies. Moreover, the UK is competitive for USA-owned investment in banking and for this the South East of England is likely to remain attractive. With respect to inward direct investment from other European Community countries, the trends are not favourable. While outward direct investment from the EC has been rising the main beneficiary has been the USA. However, within Europe, the UK is a favoured location for Japanese direct inward investment and there is considerable potential for the UK regions from this source. As well as Japan, other Pacific Rim countries are likely to become increasingly important in the 1990s. In general, however, a number of factors and perceptions affect the competitiveness of the UK and its regions in attracting overseas direct investment: these include adverse perceptions about the work force, concerns over infrastructure provision, and the fact that the Regional Development Grants are no longer part of the regional policy package.

Second, a sector of growing importance in international direct investment is services, in particular banking and finance and business services. While there is a concentration of overseas-owned banking in the South East of England and this is likely to continue, a wider regional dispersal may take place. However, there is a greater danger than in manufacturing that overseas-owned service firms will cause a displacement effect since they will be competing more directly with indigenous service companies.

---

* On 1 May 1990, WINvest, an arm of the Welsh Development Agency became Welsh Development International. Locate in Scotland now operates as part of Scottish Enterprise, a newly formed agency resulting from the amalgamation of the Scottish Development Agency and the Training Agency (1 April 1991). The English Unit at the DTI (established November 1989) promotes England as a location for inward investment projects working in close partnership with the eight English regions.

Third, as well as direct investment there are other forms of overseas inward investment, such as licensing, joint ventures and other collaborative agreements between companies and these are likely to increase in importance. Thus regional organisations responsible for the attraction of overseas inward investment will need to take on board these new developments and their relative success, as with direct investment, will influence their regional distribution. However, the industrial structure of regions will be important since collaborative ventures are likely to benefit regions where there is a strong base of suitable indigenous companies with which to collaborate.

Fourth, while the creation of the Single European Market in 1992 presents opportunities for overseas inward investment to the UK and its regions there are dangers. It is possible that the attractiveness of the London-Paris-Hamburg 'golden triangle' will be reinforced and that this will be exacerbated by the completion of the Channel Tunnel.

Finally, with the development of the globalisation of business, whereby companies' strategies take on a world wide rather than a national market perspective, recent research (Young, Hood and Dunlop, 1988) has adopted a corporate strategy approach to analysing the role of overseas investment in Scotland. In the 1990s this approach to research is likely to be developed and applied to other UK regions.

REFERENCES

Collis C., Noon D., Roberts P., Berkeley N. (1990) *Benefits of Inward Investment to the West Midlands Region*, West Midlands Development Agency, Coleshill, Warwickshire.

Collis C., Noon D., Roberts P., Gray K. (1989) *Overseas Investment to the West Midlands Region (Second Report)*, West Midlands Industrial Development Association, Coleshill, Warwickshire.

Hood N. and Young S. (1982) *Multinationals in Retreat The Scottish Experience*, Edinburgh: Edinburgh University Press.

National Audit Office (1989) *Locate in Scotland*, Report by the Comptroller and Auditor General, House of Commons, London: HMSO.

Roberts P., Noon D., Irving P. (1988) *Overseas Investment to the West Midlands Region*, Coventry Polytechnic, Coventry, Warwickshire.

Welsh Affairs Committee (1988) *Inward Investment into Wales and its Interaction with Regional and EEC Policies*, First Report Session 1988-89, House of Commons, London: HMSO.

Young S. (1989) Scotland v Wales in the Inward Investment Game, *Fraser of Allander Quarterly Economic Commentary*.

Young S., Hood N. and Dunlop S. (1988) Global Strategies, Foreign Multinational Subsidiary Roles and Economic Impact in Scotland, *Regional Studies, Vol 22 No.6*.

New Firm Formation and Growth

Colin Mason

TRENDS IN NEW FIRM FORMATION

One of the major features of the 1980s was the remarkable rise in the rate of new business formations in the United Kingdom. The number of businesses registering for value added tax (VAT) rose from 158,000 in 1980 to 255,000 in 1989, falling back slightly in 1990 to 235,000, and the surplus of businesses registering (i.e. new businesses) over those deregistering (i.e. closures) increased from 16,000 to 66,000 over the same period (Table 7.3.1). VAT data give only a partial indicator of trends in business start-ups since at least half of the self-employed are not registered for VAT, usually because their annual turnover is below the registration threshold. However, trends in the self-employed population confirm the increase in new business activity in the UK, with the number of people who were self-employed in their main job increasing between June 1980 and June 1990 by 1.3 million to almost 3.3 million, an increase of 64 per cent (Skills and Enterprise Network, 1991). Most of this growth has comprised one-person businesses without employees: only one-third of the self-employed had employees.

Table 7.3.1. New Business Registrations and Deregistrations in the UK, 1980–90 [a]

year	stock at start of year	registrations	deregistrations	net change	stock at end of year [b]
		(thousands)			
1980	1289	158	142	16	1305
1981	1305	152	120	32	1337
1982	1337	166	145	21	1357
1983	1357	180	145	35	1392
1984	1392	182	152	30	1422
1985	1422	182	163	19	1441
1986	1441	191	164	27	1468
1987	1468	209	167	42	1510
1988	1510	237	171	66	1576
1989	1576	255	172	83	1659
1990	1659	235 [c]	185	50	1709
1980–90	1289	2147	1727	420	1709

Source: Daly (1991)
Notes: [a] the pattern of registrations and deregistrations may have been affected by disturbances in the regular processing of register amendments because of industrial action in 1979 and 1981; [b] row totals may not add up due to rounding; [c] includes an allowance of 15,000 for the effect of changes introduced in the 1990 Budget.

The vast majority of new businesses have been established in the service sector (Table 7.3.2). More than one in every six businesses registering for VAT between 1980 and 1990 was in the retail sector; however, retailing was one of only two sectors (agriculture being the other) in which deregistrations exceeded registrations. The other services sector accounted for 18 per cent of registrations, with construction comprising a further 16 per cent. Manufacturing accounted for only 10 per cent of new registrations. The sectors which recorded the largest percentage net increases in VAT-registered busi-

Table 7.3.2. New Business Registrations and Deregistrations in the UK, 1980–90, by sector

sector	registrations	deregistrations	net change as percentage of stock at start year
	(thousands)		
Agriculture	68.5	69.9	-0.8
Production	204.5	166.5	+31.3
Construction	335.0	245.7	+49.4
Transport	97.4	79.6	+32.0
Wholesale	176.1	145.3	+32.1
Retail	375.6	383.6	-3.0
Finance, property & professional svs	188.1	104.9	+105.4
Catering	206.4	195.2	+9.6
Motor trades	102.7	89.0	+20.2
Other services	393.0	247.3	+115.7
Total	2147.4	1727.0	+32.6

Source: Daly (1991)

nesses were other services (116%) and finance, property and professional services (105%) (Table 7.3.2). The latter sector includes information-based business services which had a faster increase in formation rates during the 1980s than any other sector (Keeble et al, 1991).

This rising trend in new business formation has been accompanied by an increase in both the diversity of forms of enterprise and in the social composition of small business owners and the self-employed (Mason and Harrison, 1985; Curran, 1986). The number of co-operatives increased from around 300 to nearly 2000 between 1978 and 1989 and the number of franchising units doubled from 8000 to 16,000 between 1984 and 1988 (Skills and Enterprise Network, 1991). The number of self-employed women increased by 101 per cent between 1980 and 1990, compared with a 51 per cent increase for men, although in numerical terms the growth of self-employment amongst men was much greater (850,000 compared with 386,000). The proportion of the ethnic minority work force who are self-employed is 16 per cent compared with 13 per cent among the white population. However, there is considerable variation within the ethnic minority population, ranging from 23 per cent of the Pakistani/Bangladeshi population in self-employment to just 8 per cent of those of West Indian/Guyanese origin (Skills and Enterprise Network, 1991).

EXPLANATIONS FOR RECENT TRENDS IN NEW FIRM FORMATION

Four broad sets of factors have been proposed to explain this growth in new business formation (Mason and Harrison, 1990; Keeble, 1990a). However, their significance varies considerably between sectors, between regions and over time, and their impact is often felt in combination rather than in isolation (Keeble, 1990a). Moreover, the amount of empirical support for each of these factors varies.

(i) *Recession-related factors.* Redundancy, rising unemployment and job insecurity have either forced many individuals into setting up their own businesses because of the lack of alternative job opportunities or have provided the stimulus to put into effect a long-held ambition to start their own firm (Harrison and Hart, 1983; Hamilton, 1986; Hudson, 1987; Mason, 1989a, Storey, 1991). In addition, the shedding of peripheral activities by large firms has created market opportunities for new businesses (Shutt and Whittington, 1987), while the availability of cheap second-hand plant and equipment and premises as a result of plant closures and company liquidations has reduced start-up costs (Binks and Jennings, 1986).

(ii) *Corporate restructuring*. Large firm fragmentation stategies, involving the subcontracting of production and production-related activities and the externalisation of various business and ancilliary services, all aimed at reducing costs and increasing flexibility, have also created market opportunities for small businesses (Shutt and Whittington, 1987; Morris, 1988). New enterprises have also been created as a result of spin-outs of existing activities from large firms to become independent businesses, for example, through management buyouts (Howells, 1989; Wright et al, 1990). Externalisation processes are widely thought to be particularly important in explaining the large increase in start-ups in the business services sector, although there is contradictory evidence on their significance in explaining the increase in new manufacturing firm start-ups (Keeble, 1990a). However, it is probable that the main driving force behind the increase in start-ups in the business services sector is simply growing demand by organisations of all types (large and small, private and public) for specialist services in an era of economic turbulence and rapid technological and regulatory change (Keeble et al, 1991).

(iii) *Income growth*. Rising real incomes, along with related lifestyle changes, have had two effects which, in turn, have contributed to the increase in new business formations. First, it has resulted in an increase in the amount of income spent on discretionary items such as tourism, leisure and entertainment and upon 'quality of life' goods and services (e.g. education- and health-related goods and services). Second, it has resulted in a break-up of the mass market as demand has increased for more varied, customised and sophisticated goods and services. As a consequence, numerous market niches have appeared which small firms have been better able to exploit than large enterprises.

(iv) *Technological change*. The technological revolution, based around micro electronics and computers, has stimulated the formation of new technologically advanced businesses by highly qualified entrepreneurs who have been able to identify and exploit new opportunities for advanced products and technological applications more rapidly than larger organisations. In addition, the application of new technologies to process technologies has created equipment especially well-suited to small batch production, thereby reducing entry barriers for new, small businesses in many sectors (Carlson, 1989).

A further two factors have facilitated new business formation. First, there has been a rise in the *social esteem* in which the small business owner-manager is held (Bannock, 1987). Second, *Government support* for the small business sector, notably through schemes to improve the availability of finance (e.g. Loan Guarantee Scheme, Enterprise Allowance Scheme) and through the provision of enterprise training and advice and counselling, has reduced many of the constraints on new business formation and growth and, more generally, has contributed to the creation of an 'enterprise culture'.

NEW FIRM FORMATION AND REGIONAL DEVELOPMENT

The growth in the number of new business formations during the 1980s has been distributed very unevenly between regions and sub-regions. At the regional scale, new firm formation rates (as measured by VAT registration statistics) exhibit a north-south divide. Formation rates are highest in the South East, South West and East Anglia, and are lowest in Scotland, the North and Northern Ireland (Table 7.7.3). The South East, South West and East Anglia also have rates of self-employment above the national average, while the North and Scotland have the lowest rates (Creigh et al, 1986). Superimposed upon this geographical pattern is an urban-rural contrast: new firm

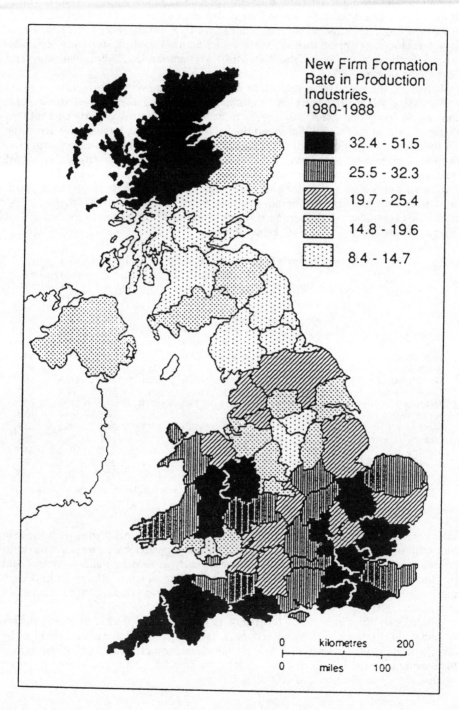

Figure 7.3.1. *New Firm Formation in the UK, 1980-88 (source: Department of Employment unpublished VAT statistics).*

formation rates are highest in rural and semi-rural areas, notably, mid and North Wales, South West England, the outer South East, non-metropolitan West Midlands and much of eastern England. Most urban-industrial areas, by contrast, have low rates of new firm formation: examples include Merseyside, South Yorkshire, Tyneside, Teesside, central Scotland, south Wales, the West Midlands conurbation, Nottinghamshire and Derbyshire (Figure 7.3.1).

However, there are some important differences in new firm formation rates by sector (Table 7.3.3). In particular, manufacturing exhibits the clearest urban-rural contrast in formation rates. Highest rates are in less urbanised parts of southern England, central and North Wales and the Scottish Highlands; lowest rates are in the conurbations. This contrasts with the pattern of new firm formation rates in the finance, property and professional services sector which exhibits a clear north-south contrast but only a limited urban-rural distinction. Counties with the highest rates of new firm formation are concentrated along the M4, M3/M27 and M11 corridors, along with outliers in Cheshire and Grampian. Business formation rates in the 'other services' sector are also highest in the southern regions, with the highest rate in the South East region outside Greater London (Keeble, 1990b).

Table 7.3.3. New Business Registrations, 1980–88, by Region and Sector

	Production Industries		Finance, Property, Professional Services		Other Services		All Industries and Services	
	no.	rate	no.	rate	no.	rate	no.	rate [a]
Greater London	33.0	44.8	35.6	40.8	72.6	76.1	296.1	83.0
Rest of South East	31.4	29.4	32.8	38.5	73.8	114.0	353.2	96.0
East Anglia	5.7	28.9	4.4	31.0	9.6	89.7	60.9	89.4
South West	12.2	28.5	9.1	26.9	22.1	84.7	147.0	95.1
West Midlands	17.7	20.7	7.5	21.6	20.1	68.6	139.6	68.7
East Midlands	13.0	20.8	5.4	20.7	14.4	81.4	107.4	73.2
Yorkshire-Humberside	11.7	16.8	6.1	17.3	15.4	58.6	121.4	65.9
North West	16.5	19.0	9.7	19.4	22.4	54.1	160.4	65.4
North	5.1	12.5	4.2	19.9	7.1	39.0	59.2	52.9
Wales	6.1	20.4	3.2	15.9	7.5	44.1	71.6	76.4
Scotland	8.2	14.3	8.2	18.7	14.4	40.8	102.2	51.5
Northern Ireland	2.5	19.2	1.2	10.6	2.7	26.2	31.4	64.7
United Kingdom	163.1	23.7	127.4	27.5	282.0	71.9	1650.4	75.7

Note: [a] New business registrations are in thousands. Rates are new registrations per 1,000 employees in that sector in 1981.
Source: Keeble (1990b)

There are also clear regional differences in growth rates of small firms, with those in the south of England performing better than those in peripheral regions. Production-related issues affecting firm competitiveness, such as design, quality control and product positioning are suggested as lying at the heart of such differences in performance (Hitchens and O'Farrell, 1987; 1991; O'Farrell and Hitchens, 1989; Gallagher and Miller, 1991).

Spatial variations in new firm formation and growth are a product of a wide variety of social, cultural, structural and economic factors which combine to influence the emergence of new firm firm founders. Explanations for these spatial variations in new firm formation rates can be grouped under three broad headings: industrial structure, occupational composition and economic factors.

Industrial structure

Most studies of new firm founders have noted that they tend to set up their business in the same industry in which they previously worked, and were previously employed in small and medium-sized rather than large firms. Two geographical implications arise from these features of the new firm formation process. First, because industries differ in their ease of entry, new firm formation is likely to be low in areas that are dominated by industries with high barriers to entry. Second, new firm formation is likely to be depressed in areas where a high proportion of employment is concentrated in large plants. Shift-share type analyses (e.g. Storey and Johnson, 1987a) have found that substantial spatial variations in new firm formation rates still exist even after controlling for the effect of industrial structure. However, there is considerable evidence, at least for the manufacturing sector, that new firm formation is lowest in large-plant dominated regions and sub-regions and is highest in areas in which most employment is provided by small and medium-sized enterprises (e.g. Fothergill and Gudgin, 1982).

Occupational composition

Studies of the new firm formation process have also noted that most new firm founders have either managerial or skilled manual class backgrounds. Such studies have also noted that firms started by those with management backgrounds show the fastest rates of growth. Consequently, the occupational composition of regions and localities (which in turn is a product of the spatial division of labour within large enterprises) also helps to explain the geography of new firm formation and growth. Specifically, new firm formation rates are highest in those areas, such as the 'Greater South East', which have a high proportion of those managerial, professional and technical occupations with the highest propensity for entrepreneurship, and are lowest in areas such as northern England and central Scotland with a high proportion of manual employees (Gould and Keeble, 1984; Whittington, 1984). Migration flows of managerial, professional and technical workers to environmentally attractive less urbanised parts of southern England and peripheral rural areas such as Devon and Cornwall and mid-Wales have enhanced the pool of potential entrepreneurs in such areas (Keeble, 1990b). A significant proportion of the new businesses established in rural areas have been founded by in-migrants (Keeble and Gould, 1985; Westhead, 1989). Simultaneously, such migration flows are draining the origin areas notably – large cities and urban-industrial regions – of their entrepreneurial talent.

Economic factors

Spatial variations in new firm formation are also associated with local/regional demand and with the availability and cost of factors of production. As most new firms tend, at least initially, to serve a restricted geographical market, differences in the size, nature and growth of local and regional demand for goods and services is an important factor in determining start-up rates in different areas. This factor is particularly important in accounting for geographical variations in service sector start-ups, since many services are not easily tradeable over space and therefore require to be located close to sources of demand. The concentration of high income groups in the South East and adjacent counties and the above average growth in personal incomes in this region helps to account for the high rates of new firm formation in consumer service industries in southern England.

Industrial and commercial demand for both products and services also exhibits spatial variations. Market opportunities for small businesses are limited in regions with declining industrial complexes. Conversely, rapid growth regions and localities contain considerable market opportunities for small firms to supply goods and services to other firms: for example, the rapid growth of financial and business services in London and the South East during the 1980s has provided market opportunities for new firms in these sectors (Keeble, 1990b). A second source of spatial variation in intermediate demand arises from the ownership structure and functional composition of industrial establishments in different regions. In northern regions of the UK much of the industrial base is characterised by externally-owned establishments with limited purchasing autonomy and, in the case of manufacturing plants, the mass production of relatively standardised products (Thwaites, 1978). Consequently, intermediate demand is limited and largely confined to low value components, subcontracting and services (Peck, 1988). Conversely, in southern England where establishments have much greater autonomy over purchasing decisions and are commonly engaged in activities at an earlier stage in their life cycle, market opportunities for small firms are much greater.

Spatial variations in new firm formation and growth are also associated with the availability of factors of production. New firm founders in the South East have the greatest access to start-up finance. Most new businesses are started largely or exclusively on the basis of the financial resources of the founder: per capita incomes and savings are highest in the South East. Since many new firm foundes raise start-up capital either by taking out a second mortgage or by using their home as security against a bank loan, the low levels of owner-occupation in northern England and Scotland deny many aspiring entrepreneurs the collateral from which they might be able to obtain a loan. Similarly, the high house prices in the south of England raise the level of personal capital available to new firm founders in these areas. Moreover, the supply of external sources of finance (such as venture capital) is also greatest in the South East region (Mason and Harrison, 1989; 1991; Martin, 1989).

Although new firms in areas of contrasting economic prosperity and unemployment rates encounter skill shortages (Lloyd and Mason, 1984) those in the south of England may also encounter fewer recruitment difficulties. In the economically buoyant south of England such shortages are associated with high demand for labour, whereas in northern regions such shortages are caused by the limited supply of skilled labour. Large, externally-owned branch plants often dominate local economies in peripheral regions. The employees of such plants are often inappropriate for small businesses because they tend to be oriented towards maintenance rather than production, be narrowly specialised and lack sufficient flexibility (O'Farrell and Hitchens, 1988). In addition, because of the lack of high level corporate functions in such plants, workers with technical and managerial skills are in short supply. Given the limited initial labour requirements of most new businesses such labour shortages may not impinge on the start-up decision; however, in those predominantly northern regions with the most limited supply of skilled labour the growth and performance of new businesses (e.g. quality of product, competitiveness) is likely to be adversely affected (O'Farrell and Hitchens, 1988).

The superior availability of information in the south of England is also likely to be associated with its higher rate of new firm formation. The ideas around which an entrepreneur establishes a new business, which stem from his awareness of new developments in technologies, techniques, equipment, materials and markets, emerge from a mixture of information derived from a diverse range of sources. As most of the contact sources of any individual are within half-an-hour's travelling time. it follows that the quality of information available to an entrepreneur is dependent upon the wealth of the stock of knowledge in the locality. In areas with a poor stock of knowledge it is much harder for the potential entrepreneur to perceive a business opportunity because of the cost and time penalties in searching for appropriate resources and developing a response or input from the resource (Sweeney, 1987). In the UK the stock of knowledge is greatest in the London region on account of the location of national government and the concentration of corporate decision-making functions and other information-intensive functions, and in the remainder of southern England which is rich in technical information on account of the concentration of corporate research, development and design activity, consultancy and technological institutes and organizations, and 'leading-edge' activities of multi-plant companies. Conversely, in northern regions of the UK new business formations are inhibited by the low stock of knowledge which arises as a result of the dominance of sectors with mature technology and externally-owned plants with declining levels of best practice and information networks that are oriented to centres outside the region (Sweeney, 1987).

NEW FIRM FORMATION AND UNEVEN DEVELOPMENT IN THE UK

To what extent do such geographical variations in new firm formation and growth contribute to contemporary patterns of local and regional development in the UK? Certainly, there is evidence that spatial variations in job creation are greater than spatial variations in job losses (Fothergill and Gudgin, 1982; Birch, 1979). The implication is therefore that the job generation performance of regions and localities depends more on their ability to create new jobs than their success in retaining existing jobs. However, new businesses have a high failure rate; according to VAT data half of all new firms have closed by their fifth year (Ganguly, 1983). In addition, the majority of the businesses which survive for any length of time remain small. The contribution of new firms to other aspects of local and regional economic development is also limited. They are not concentrated in growing or profitable sectors, tend to replicate an area's industrial structure rather than acting as a diversifying force, and are dependent on local markets (Mason and Harrison, 1990; Turok and Richardson, 1991). Thus, over the short term, spatial variations in new firm formation have been of minor significance in contributing to the north-south divide and the urban-rural shift.

But over the longer term, spatial variations in new firm formation and growth have undoubtedly been a major factor in local and regional development (Fothergill and Gudgin, 1982). However, this longer term impact is largely a function of the very small minority of new businesses which achieve rapid growth. These businesses make a significant contribution to local and regional economic development, notably in terms of employment (Gallagher and Miller, 1991), innovation (although by no means all are in high-tech sectors), industrial diversification, regional and national export orientation and local multiplier effects (Mason, 1987). Hence, it is spatial variations in the locational distribution of these firms – which are overwhelmingly concentrated in the south of England (Mason, 1985; 1989b) – rather than the overall geography of new firm formation which is of greatest significance in contributing to contemporary patterns of local and regional development in the UK.

Even though the 1990s are predicted to be a more hostile environment than the 1980s for self-employment and small scale enterprise (Curran and Blackburn, 1990), new firm formation is likely to remain at a relatively high level and small firms will continue to play an important role in the economy. As the major factors which account for spatial variations in new firm formation and growth – the most important of which, according to multivariate analysis, is the occupational structure of different areas (Whittington, 1984) – seem unlikely to decline in significance over the next decade, the important contribution of new firms to uneven local and regional development over the longer term is unlikely to diminish. Consequently, there is a clear need for a regionally-focused small firms policy (Mason and Harrison, 1986). However, it is not sufficient for such a policy simply to be concerned with increasing the number of business start-ups in economically depressed regions and localities. Rather, such a policy must seek to improve the 'quality' of start-ups (Turok and Richardson, 1991) in order to promote the emergence of rapid-growth new enterprises in such areas. But whether such an approach can be successfully designed and implemented remains a matter for debate (Storey and Johnson, 1987b; Hakim, 1989).

REFERENCES

Bannock, G. (1987) *Britain in the 1980s: Enterprise Reborn?*, London: Investors in Industry.

Binks, M. and Jennings, A. (1986) New firms as a source of industrial regeneration, in Scott, M., Gibb, A., Lewis, J. and Faulkner, T. (eds) *Small Firm Growth and Development* Aldershot: Gower, 3–32.

Birch, D.L. (1979), *The Job Generation Process*, Cambridge, Mass: MIT Program on Neighbourhood and Regional Change.

Carlsson, B. (1989) The evolution of manufacturing technology and its impact on industrial structure: an international study, *Small Business Economics*, 1, 21–37.

Creigh, S., Roberts, A., Gorman, A. and Sawyer, P. (1986) Self-employment in Britain: results from the Labour Force Surveys 1981-84, *Employment Gazette*, 95, 183–192.

Curran, J. (1986) *Bolton Fifteen Years On: A Review and Analysis of Small Business Research in Britain 1971–1986*, London: Small Business Research Trust.

Curran, J. and Blackburn, R. (1990) *Small Business 2000: Socio-Economic and Environmental Factors Facing Small Firms in the 1990s*, London: Small Business Research Trust.

Daly, M. (1991) VAT registrations and deregistrations in 1990, *Employment Gazette*, 99, 579–588.

Fothergill, S. and Gudgin, G. (1982) *Unequal Growth: Urban and Regional Employment Change in the UK*, London: Heinemann.

Gallagher, C. and Miller, P. (1991) The performance of new firms in Scotland and the South East, *Royal Bank of Scotland Review*, 170, 38–50.

Ganguly, P. (1983) Lifespan analysis of businesses in the UK, 1973-82, *British Business*, 12 August, 838–845.

Gould, A. and Keeble, D. (1984), New firms and rural industrialization in East Anglia, *Regional Studies*, 18, 189–201.

Hakim, C. (1989) Identifying fast growth small firms, *Employment Gazette*, 97, 29–41.

Hamilton, R.T. (1986) The influence of unemployment on the level and rate of company formation in Scotland, 1950-1974, *Environment and Planning* A, 18, 1401–1404.

Harrison, R.T. and Hart, M. (1983) Factors influencing new business formation: a case study of Northern Ireland, *Environment and Planning* A, 15, 1395–1412.

Hitchens, D.M.W.N. and O'Farrell, P.N. (1987) The comparative performance of small manufacturing firms in Northern Ireland and South East England, *Regional Studies*, 21, 543–553.

Hitchens, D. and O'Farrell, P. (1991) Comparative performance of small manufacturing firms located in South Wales and two English regions, *International Small Business Journal*, 9 (2), 64–70.

Howells, J. (1989) Externalisation and the formation of new industrial operations: a neglected dimension in the dynamics of industrial location, *Area*, 21, 289–299.

Hudson, J. (1987) Company births in Great Britain and the institutional environment, *International Small Business Journal*, 6 (1), 57–69.

Keeble, D. (1990a) Small firms, new firms and uneven regional development in the United Kingdom, *Area*, 234–245.

Keeble, D. (1990b) New firms and regional economic development: experience and impacts in the 1980s, in Cameron, G., Nicholls, D., Rhodes, J. and Tyler, P. (eds) *Cambridge Regional Economic Review, (Department of Land Economy, University of Cambridge)*, pp. 62–71.

Keeble, D., Bryson, J. and Wood, P. (1991) Small firms, business services growth and regional development in the United Kingdom: some empirical findings, *Regional Studies*, 25, 439–457.

Lloyd, P.E. and Mason, C.M. (1984), Spatial variations in new firm formation in the United Kingdom: comparative evidence from Merseyside, Greater Manchester and South Hampshire, *Regional Studies*, 18, 207–220.

Martin, R. (1989) The growth and geographical anatomy of venture capitalism in the United Kingdom, *Regional Studies*, 23, 389–403.

Mason, C.M. (1985) The geography of 'successful' small firms in the UK, *Environment and Planning* A, 17, 1499–1513.

Mason, C.M. (1987) The small firm sector, in Lever, W.F. (ed) *Industrial Change in the United Kingdom*, London: Longman, 125–148.

Mason, C.M. (1989a) Explaining recent trends in UK new firm formation rates: evidence from two surveys in South Hampshire, *Regional Studies*, 23, 331–346.

Mason, C.M. (1989b) Where are the successful small businesses? A geographical perspective, in Foley, P. and Green, H (eds) *Small Business Success*, London: Paul Chapman Publishing 11–26.

Mason, C.M. and Harrison, R.T. (1985) The geography of small firms in the United Kingdom: towards a research agenda, *Progress in Human Geography*, 9, 1–37.

Mason, C.M. and Harrison, R.T. (1986) The regional impact of public policy towards small firms in the United Kingdom, in Keeble, D. and Wever, E. (eds) *New Firms and Regional Development in Europe*, Beckenham: Croom Helm, 224–255.

Mason, C.M. and Harrison, R.T. (1989) The north-south divide and small firms policy in the UK: the case of the Business Expansion Scheme, *Transactions Institute of British Geographers*, ns 14, 37–58.

Mason, C.M. and Harrison, R.T. (1990) Small firms: phoenix from the ashes? in Pinder, D. (ed) *Western Europe: Challenge and Change* London: Bellhaven Press.

Morris, J.L. (1988) New technologies, flexible work practices, and regional sociospatial differentiation: some observations from the United Kingdom, *Environment and Planning D: Society and Space*, 6, 301–319.

O'Farrell, P.N. and Hitchens, D.M.W.N. (1988) Alternative theories of small firm growth: a critical review, *Environment and Planning* A, 20, 1365–1383.

O'Farrell, P.N. and Hitchens, D.M.W.N. (1989) The competitiveness and performance of small manufacturing firms: an analysis of matched pairs in Scotland and England, *Environment and Planning* A, 21, 1241–1263.

Peck, F. (1988), *Manufacturing Linkages in Tyne and Wear*, Newcastle upon Tyne: Tyne and Wear County-Wide Research and Intelligence Unit.

Shutt, J. and Whittington, R. (1987), Fragmentation strategies and the rise of small units: cases from the North West, *Regional Studies*, 21, 13–21.

Skills and Enterprise Network (1991) *Labour Market and Skills Trends*, Sheffield: Employment Department Group, Chapter 4.

Storey, D.J. (1991) The birth of new firms – does unemployment matter? A review of the evidence, *Small Business Economics*, 3, 167–178.

Storey, D.J. and Johnson, S. (1987a) Regional variations in entrepreneurship in the UK, *Scottish Journal of Political Economy*, 34, 161–173.

Storey, D.J. and Johnson, S. (1987b) *Job Generation and Labour Market Change*, Basingstoke, Hampshire: Macmillan.

Sweeney, G.P. (1987) *Innovation, Entrepreneurs and Regional Development*, London: Frances Pinter.

Thwaites, A.T. (1978), Technological change, mobile plants and regional development, *Regional Studies*, 12, 445–461.

Turok, I. and Richardson, P. (1991) New firms and local economic development: evidence from West Lothian, *Regional Studies*, 25, 71–83.

Westhead, P. (1989) A spatial analysis of new manufacturing firm formation in Wales, 1979-1983, *International Small Business Journal*, 7 (2), 44–68.

Whittington, R.C. (1984) Regional bias in new firm formation in the UK, *Regional Studies*, 18, 253–256.

Wright, M., Thompson, S. and Robbie, S. (1990) Management buyouts: achievements, limitations and prospects, *National Westminster Bank Quarterly Review*, August, 40–53.

Financing Regional Enterprise: The Role of the Venture Capital Market

Ron Martin

INTRODUCTION: FINANCING ENTERPRISE BRITAIN

A central plank in Mrs Thatcher's market-based approach to the restructuring and regeneration of the British economy during the 1980s was the promotion of a new national 'enterprise culture' (Department of Trade and Industry, 1988; Young, 1990; Burrows, 1991; Martin, 1991). One of the main symbols of this new 'enterprise Britain', and certainly the most commonly used measure of its progress, has been the small business sector, and in particular the rate of new firm formation. Available data indicate that there has indeed been a sharp rise in new business registrations over the past decade, from around 150,000 per annum in 1980 to nearly 275,000 by 1989 in England alone. However, the recent boom in new firm formation has not been a nationally uniform phenomenon, but one biased in favour of the southern regions (South East, South West and East Anglia), where new firm registration rates have typically averaged almost twice those for northern Britain (Keeble, 1990; Mason, 1991 and in this volume).

These regional differences obviously reflect the impress of a range of local characteristics, including the inherited economic and industrial structure of an area, its skill, educational and social-class composition, its previous history of small firm development, its pre-existing firm size distribution, and the local market opportunities for new enterprises. In addition, another feature frequently invoked to explain spatial disparities in new and small business activity, and an issue of some debate, is the geographical variation in the availability of start-up and expansion investment finance. Areas with low rates of new firm formation tend to be handicapped, it is claimed, by a relative lack of available risk capital, that is by the existence of regional 'equity gaps'.

A long-standing criticism of British financial markets has been that they provide an inadequate supply of risk capital for new and small business ventures. The Macmillan Committee in the early 1930s (HM Government, 1931), the Bolton report in the early 1970s (HM Government, 1971), and the Wilson Report in the late 1970s (HM Government, 1979) all identified such a gap in the provision of capital, and the issue surfaced again in the 1980s (NEDC, 1986). This gap has been attributed to several factors: the historical domination of the capital market by the Stock Exchange, with its preference for large established companies and international business; the short-termism of British capital and financial markets; the high fixed costs of evaluating and monitoring new and young firms, which by their nature entail considerable uncertainty; and the traditional reluctance of the banks to commit long-term funds or 'patient money' to risky investment in industry and commerce. And to add to these criticisms, it has frequently been argued that the national equity gap for the new and small business sector is itself regionally uneven, with northern and depressed parts of the country, those where new enterprise is particularly needed, being noticeably disadvantaged as compared to southern areas with respect to the supply of risk capital.

Since the early 1980s, however, as the numbers of new and small firms have expanded so there have been parallel developments in the provision of small business finance. In line with its ideology and promotion of 'enterprise', the Government itself has introduced or enlarged a number of schemes to increase the flow of loan and equity capital from the general public and financial institutions into the small enterprise sector, for example the Business Start-Up, Loan Guarantee, and Business Expansion Schemes. At the same time, encouraged by Government exhortation and by the rapid economic boom and relaxed monetary conditions of the second half of the 1980s, the major clearing banks have adopted a more proactive and positive attitude towards assisting new and small enterprises. Even allowing for the flood of media and marketing hype issued by the banks, their financing of the new enterprise culture expanded considerably during the late 1980s, arguably excessively so. The main result of these various developments has been to increase the supply of *loan* capital. While this is welcome, it has been achieved at the expense of raising the gearing of many small firms and increasing their vulnerability to high interest rates. However, there have also been important developments in the supply of *equity* capital. The restructuring and de-regulation of the investment finance market itself (see Rybczynski, 1988) has led to new institutional forms, such as the Unlisted Securities Market and the Third Market, that are aimed specifically at increasing the supply of equity capital to new and small businesses. But probably the most interesting innovation in this sphere has been the emergence of a rapidly expanding venture capital industry.

THE GROWTH OF A NEW CIRCUIT OF ENTERPRISE FINANCE:
THE VENTURE CAPITAL MARKET

Venture financing is the activity by which investors support entrepreneurial business ventures with equity funds and management skills to exploit market opportunities with the aim of making long-term capital gains rather than running income (see Shilson, 1984). A primary virtue stressed by venture capitalists is their opportunity to choose with broad discretion where to commit their clients' capital across what Braudel (1982, p.381) refers to as 'the differential geography of profit'. The general image is of a capital market that has a specific role to play in financing the sort of risky new and small enterprise that tends to be shunned by conventional sources of investment finance. The venture capitalist, as entrepreneurial fund manager, seeks to reduce his risk actuarially by spreading across a portfolio of investments, each carefully screened for technological innovation, market relevance and managerial leadership. This, at least, is the prospectus he offers his investors (Janeway, 1986; Dixon, 1989).

Unlike in the United States, where the venture capital industry spans back several decades (Lorenz, 1989), in the UK its growth is almost entirely a 1980s' phenomenon. Although venture capitalism existed prior to the 1980s, it was not generally referred to as such (Cary, 1989), and was certainly not an identifiable sector of the capital market. For much of the period 1945–1980, almost the only organised source of venture capital was the Industrial and Commercial Finance Corporation, now renamed Investors in Industry (3i), which was set up in 1945 by the Bank of England and the major clearing banks to help meet British industry's long term capital needs. Even as recently as 1979 there were only 20 specialist venture capital organisations in the UK. But by 1989 there were more than 120 full-time members of the British Venture Capital Association, and at least a further 60 organizations involved in some way with venture capital financing.

Investment has shown a similar rapid growth. Whereas in 1984 (the first year for which there are reliable data) total investment by managed funds amounted to only £280 million, by 1989, having grown in line with the boom in the economy during the

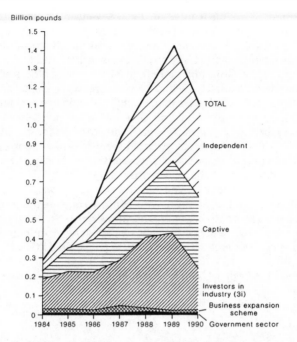

Billion pounds

Figure 7.4.1: The Growth of Venture Captial Investment (Managed Funds) by Type of Institution or Scheme, 1984–1990

second half of the 1980s, annual total investment had reached £1.420 billion. It then fell back to £1.106 billion in 1990 reflecting the subsequent onset of economic slowdown and recession (Figure 7.4.1). Although still the single largest individual source of venture finance, 3i no longer dominates the market as did in the early 1980s: its share of total investment has fallen from over 50 to 20 per cent, while the shares of independent and captive (subsidiary-based) funds have more than doubled, from less than 20 to over 40 per cent in each case. As a result of this growth, since 1984 more than £6 billion of venture capital funds have been invested, with a further £1 billion currently available for investment, giving a total venture capital pool of more than £7 billion. There can be no doubt, therefore, that the venture capital business is now established as a significant specialist division of the UK finance capital market. Annual investment is currently more than double the sum the Government is spending on regional policy assistance. In this respect, therefore, venture capitalism has a potentially important role to play in shaping the pattern of business enterprise and economic growth across the country.

THE REGIONAL STRUCUTRE OF VENTURE CAPITALISM

The significance of the venture capital industry for the regions is essentially twofold: first, the location of the industry itself is likely to be dependent on the pattern of regional economic development, and second, the investment flows undertaken by the industry will in turn have a key influence on shaping the geography of that development.

Probably the most striking feature of the UK venture capital market as it has emerged since the beginning of the 1980s has been its very high degree of spatial concentration. Like banking, currency trading and other financial and investment activity, the venture capital market is controlled primarily from London. More than 60 per cent of venture capital firms and more than 50 per cent of offices are located there (Martin, 1989; Venture Economics, 1990). The main provincial clusters of locally-based venture capital firms that exist are extremely small by comparison, namely Edinburgh (5% of UK firms), Birmingham (3%), and Glasgow, Cambridge, Belfast, Cardiff and Leeds (all with about 2%). Even more significant, the London-based organisations control around 80 per cent of the total national venture capital pool. This dominance of London derives in part from the established position of the city as a financial centre, with its nexus of financial institutions, expertise and networks. Of course, some of the larger London-based companies have branches in the regions, the most significant example being Investors in Industry (3i), with 18 offices outside the South East. But the general lack of an extensive network of organisations across the country and the spatial monopoly of London over the supply of venture capital have undoubtedly influenced the relative availability of venture finance for new enterprises in the different regions.

Table 7.4.1. The Regional Distribution of Venture Capital Activity, 1984-90

				per cent of Amount Invested			
	1984	1985	1986	1987	1988	1989	1990
South East	51	55	58	57	50	48	61
East Anglia	6	8	6	3	3	3	5
South West	4	7	5	7	4	7	3
East Midlands	5	3	3	8	7	8	6
West Midlands	5	8	3	4	9	6	6
Yorks-Humberside	0	4	4	7	6	4	5
North West	10	2	6	4	4	5	4
North	2	1	3	1	8	3	2
Wales	6	4	3	4	2	1	1
Scotland	11	7	7	5	6	15	7
Northern Ireland	0	0	0	0	1	1	0
Total	100	100	100	100	100	100	100

Source: Venture Economics, British Venture Capital Association and Investors in Industry (3i).
Notes: (1) Data refer to the venture capital organisations surveyed by Venture Economics in their annual review of investment activity for the British Venture Capital Association. Prior to 1987 these did not include investments made by 3i. To achieve continuity, the data for 1984–1986 were adjusted to incorporate estimates of 3i's regional investments calculated by the author using figures supplied by 3i.
(2) Column sums may differ slightly from 100 because of rounding errors.

Certainly thus far, the South East region has attracted the bulk of venture capital investment (Table 7.4.1). This area has received some 53 per cent of the funds invested by UK venture capitalists since 1984. Scotland has attracted the next largest share, about 8 per cent, though this represents but a fraction of the volume of investment that has gone to the South East. The other regions of Britain have received even smaller proportions of venture capital investment, and activity in Northern Ireland has been negligible. The regional distribution of venture capital investment has thus closely mirrored the locational structure of the industry itself. There is in fact a systematic relationship between the origin or supply of venture finance (the location of the venture capitalist) and its destination (the location of the investment). In value terms, London has been the source of the majority (about two-thirds) of national venture investments: it dwarfs all provincial centres. As a result, every region of the country is dependent to some extent on London venture capitalists for investment funds. But at the same time, London-based venture capitalists have shown a distinct preference for enterprises located nearer to London. Thus while London venture firms have been the origin for some 90 per cent of the venture capital invested in the South East, this share declines to around 60 per cent in the West Midlands, North West and Yorkshire-Humberside, 40 per cent in the Northern region, and about 20 per cent in Scotland and Wales (Martin, 1989). Thus, unless a region has a well-established nexus of venture capitalists of its own, then the further it is from London the more disadvantaged local enterprises and entrepreneurs appear to be with respect to accessing this type of risk capital; or to put it another way, the further a region is from London, the more important it is for that region to have its own circuit of venture finance.

Of course, to some extent the concentration of venture capital funds and investment in the South East region has been demand-induced: it was this area of Britain that led the economic boom during the mid and late 1980s, and which, as we have noted, experienced the highest rate of new firm formation. In the same way, the slower economic turnaround in northern Britain held back the rate of new firm formation and business expansion there, and this presumably depressed the demand for venture capital. To some extent, then, venture capitalism can be expected to follow and thus accentuate the geography of uneven economic growth (Thompson, 1989). However, to compound this process, the very nature of venture capitalism, as an entrepreneurial activity itself, has probably also militated against the northern regions. Venture capitalists invariably insist that good projects can expect financial support regardless of where they happen to be located. Yet, in practice, the spatial proximity of and scope for 'hands on' contact between venture capital fund managers and local client projects is considered of key importance. In other words, risk aversion is likely to be an increasing function of the locational separation between the venture capitalist and the investees seeking enterprise finance. Given the concentration of venture capitalists in the London area, this factor has arguably imparted a regional bias in venture investment in favour of the surrounding parts of southern England which, being within convenient travel distance and thus easy to monitor, have been viewed as rich in investment opportunities and 'low risk'. By comparison, northern regions have often been viewed as lacking in enterprise and 'high risk', if only because of the greater difficulty of direct contact with, and the lack of knowledge of, local investment opportunities on the part of London-based venture capital firms. Thus, in terms of both the demand for and supply of finance, the uneven spatial development of the venture capital industry over the 1980s reflected and reinforced the uneven geography of the 'enterprise economy'.

VENTURE CAPITAL INVESTMENT: MYTHS AND REALITIES

Two sorts of investment are often regarded as the very essence of venture capital activity: start-ups and new high-tech businesses. Both are seen as epitomizing the most exciting and risky aspects of supporting entrepreneurship and enterprise. And both, furthermore, are widely viewed by geographers and policy-makers alike as key sectors in regional economic development. A certain amount of myth and folklore surrounds these assumptions. Not all start-ups are of the first-time inventor or 'greenfield' variety, so beloved of transatlantic venture capital myth. Many new enterprises are formed by experienced people wishing to launch their own business in an industry they know well. Others are spin-offs from research bodies or large corporations, while still others may arise in response to the sub-contracting or sourcing needs of existing businesses.

Start-ups are undoubtedly the most fertile source of the 'big winners' of which all venture capitalists dream. But this area of the business world is also a graveyard of failed projects: new small firms have the highest death rate of any branch of the private corporate sector, and are particularly sensitive to business cycle downturns. And as far as 'high-tech' activity is concerned, during the first half of the 1980s almost every newly quoted company that appeared in the USM and Stock Market claimed to be 'high-tech' in some respect. In reality, while many of these were applying the latest technological advances, few were operating at the leading edge of research and development (R & D) of important new technologies. The number of firms engaged in such activity is small.

Table 7.4.2. Trends in Venture Capital Investment, by Financing Stage of Enterprise 1983–90

| | per cent of Amount Invested | | | | | | | |
	1983	1984	1985	198	187	1988	1989	1990
Start-up	15	17	13	16	8	5	6	7
Other Early Stage	10	9	6	7	5	5	9	5
Expansion	43	41	36	27	30	31	23	31
Buy-out/Buy-in	24	28	38	44	55	56	61	52
Secondary Purchase	7	5	6	5	2	3	1	5
Other	1	0	1	1	0	0	0	0
Total	100	100	100	100	100	100	100	100

Source: Venture Economics, British Venture Capital Association.
Note: (1) Column sums may differ slightly from 100 because of rounding errors.

Table 7.4.3. Venture Capital Investment by Industrial Sector, 1984–90

| | per cent of Amount Invested | | | | | | |
	1984	1985	1986	1987	1988	1989	1990
Consumer-related	23	20	20	28	35	43	35
Computer-related	20	9	11	5	4	5	6
Electronics	10	12	8	4	2	2	2
Medical/Biotechnology	6	4	9	5	2	3	4
Industrial Products	5	7	7	11	8	8	6
Communications	6	8	8	2	1	2	2
Transportation	2	3	8	4	3	5	9
Energy	4	1	0	1	1	1	0
Construction	2	4	2	5	6	7	6
Other Manufacturing	6	8	3	7	20	13	14
Financial/Other Services	16	9	13	28	19	11	15
Total	100	100	100	100	100	100	100

Source: Venture Economics, British Venture Capital Association.
Note: (1) Column sums may differ slightly from 100 because of rounding errors.

In practice, the proportion of venture capital finance invested in business start-ups and high-tech enterprise has been disappointingly low. Only a few specialist venture capital firms focus specifically on seed capital, R-and-D projects, or start-ups; most operate a much wider portfolio of investments. As a result, overall, start-ups have accounted for only a small fraction of total venture capital investment, well below 20 per cent during the early 1980s and falling to less than 10 per cent in recent years (Table 7.4.2). Other early stage investments have made up a similarly small amount. Likewise, venture capital support for business expansions has also fallen, from some 43 per cent of venture investment in 1983 down to 31 per cent by 1990. The counterpart of these downward trends in the shares of new and expanding enterprises has been the steady rise in the proportion of venture capital investment going to finance management buy-outs/buy-ins. Whereas in the early 1980s this type of activity attracted just under quarter of venture capital investment, by 1990 its share had increased to over 50 per cent.

This trend reflects the general boom in management buy-outs that has taken place since the early 1980s (see Lorenz, 1989; *Financial Times*, 1990; Wright et al, 1990). It also reflects the lower risk and quicker returns that are often associated with this form of investment as compared to start-ups. This concentration on management buy-outs has fostered considerable debate about the meaning and purpose of venture capitalism, about whether it has moved too far away from what many regard as its proper role of backing new small business ventures. Against this it can be argued that the boom in management buy-outs is no less part of the new 'enterprise culture' than is the boom in new small firm formation. Management buy-outs can assist the creation of smaller enterprises through the de-merger and break-up of larger corporations, they promote entrepreneurship, and they help to recombine management with ownership. In addition, where management buy-outs save parts of parent companies that would otherwise have been closed down, they can have a positive role to play in protecting local jobs. The problem is that management buy-outs can siphon off very large sums of capital, which arguably ought to be provided from elsewhere within the investment finance market, as is the case in the United States.

As the relative share of venture capital investment allocated to start-ups has declined, so too has the share devoted to 'high-tech' activities. In the early 1980s, high-tech activities were a major focus of venture capitalism: in 1984 the computer-related, electronics-related, medical-biotechnology, and communications sectors together accounted for more than 40 per cent of venture investment. By 1990, however, this share had fallen to only 14 per cent (Table 7.4.3). This relative shift away from high-tech enterprises has been due in part to the uncertain and less buoyant conditions in the computer and electronics industries, and in part to a channelling of investment into what became the major growth sectors after the mid-1980s, namely consumer-related activities (retail, leisure, products, services), and financial services. Nevertheless, the overall slow relative growth of venture capital investment in 'high-tech' enterprise has concealed some important regional differences. Most of the investment in this sector has in fact gone to those southern regions (South East, South West and East Anglia) that together already contained most of the country's high-tech industry (see Martin, 1989), and thus far venture capitalism appears to have done little to promote any substantial high-tech based development in the northern regions of the country.

INDIGENOUS SUPPORT FOR INDIGENOUS ENTERPRISE: BUILDING REGIONAL
VENTURE CAPITAL MARKETS

The picture that emerges, then, is one in which over the past decade a rapidly growing venture capital industry, itself a symbol of the new enterprise economy, has emerged as an important new source of finance for industry. The development of this new circuit of equity capital has not fully matched up to expectations, however. It has not functioned as a specialist source of funds for those enterprises, namely start-ups and high-tech ventures, which many believe face the most pressing 'equity gaps'. What the new venture capital market has done is to concentrate investment in the south-eastern and adjacent areas of the country where the venture capital industry itself is mainly located and where the 'enterprise boom' has been most marked.

The challenge facing the northern and peripheral regions of the UK is how to initiate a local synergism between venture capital activity and new economic enterprise. The development of local venture capital markets in the regions is obviously a key aspect of this challenge. According to some observers (Hamilton-Fazey, 1987, 1988), in the late 1980s venture capitalism entered a new provincial-based phase of development, with a number of London-based venture capital firms opening branches in the regions and with the appearance of a number of new locally-based funds. But as Table 7.4.1 suggests, the extent of these developments should not be exaggerated, and the realization of truly regionally focused venture capital funds is still some way off.

One strategy that has been suggested for closing the small firm equity gap in the regions is the promotion of 'informal' venture capitalism, that is risk capital provided by private individuals directly to new and growing businesses in which they have had no prior connection, a model based on a similar development in the United States (ACOST, 1990; Mason and Harrison, 1991). According to the Advisory Council on Science and Technology (ACOST), 'an active informal venture capital market is a pre-requisite for a vigorous enterprise economy' (op. cit., p.41). To increase this source of funds in the UK it would be necessary to change the tax system to make equity investment, especially in risky start-ups, much more favourable relative to institutional saving. Also, as Mason and Harrison argue, a network of local and regional financial marriage bureaux, subsidized by the public sector if necessary, would be required in order to bring local informal investors and capital-seeking entrepreneurs together. There is undoubtedly considerable scope for increasing the flow of informal risk capital; and the informality and inherent localism of this type of private direct investment are certainly attractive features. On the other hand, there is no guarantee that the apparent success of informal venture capitalism in the United States would be replicated automatically in Britain, where the whole culture of saving, investment and risk aversion is different. Moreover, it is also uncertain that it would do much to close the regional gap in equity capital supply. The local nature of informal venture capitalism (Mason and Harrison, op. cit.) implies that it will tend to vary with the local wealth base. This means that the South East and adjacent areas of Britain would be the areas likely to benefit most from this form of venture activity.

Other strategies for building regional and local venture spatial markets have been tried. A recent initiative by the British Venture Capital Association (1989) is based on establishing twelve regional seed capital funds with support from corporate backers and Government funding to cover management costs. The latter has not been forthcoming, however. Similarly, the three seed and start-up funds established in the UK under the European Community's Seed Capital Initiative have found it difficult to raise the necessary finance to contribute to their operating costs. These problems have prompted the argument that some sort of regional or local intermediary body, such as a regional enterprise board, would help to focus and co-ordinate local venture capital activity. Both the Scottish and the Welsh Development Agencies have established regional venture capital funds, amounting to £30 million and £35 million respectively. Likewise several of the enterprise boards originally set up by the metropolitan local authorities in the early 1980s now have independent venture capital funds, such as Lancashire Enterprises (with invested funds of £7 million), Merseyside Enterprise Board (£5 million), Yorkshire Enterprise (£13 million), West Midlands Enterprise Board (£12 million), Greater Manchester Economic Development (£3 million), and Greater London Enterprise (£4 million). Such locally-based and locally focused venture capital organisations have the advantage that they generally possess much more detailed knowledge of their local economies than do London-based venture fund managers, and are more able to identify and promote the flow of local projects for investment.

In fact local authorities more generally seem to be developing an interest in local venture capitalism. Of crucial significance in this regard is the potential of local authority pension funds in helping to build indigenous and locally focused venture capital markets in the regions. These local authority pension funds are estimated to be worth about £25 billion. Until 1974 statutory restrictions prevented local authority pension funds from holding unquoted investments in their portfolios at all. However, under current local government superannuation regulations up to 10 per cent of local authority pension funds can be invested in unquoted enterprises. This means that about £2.5 billion of local authority pension fund monies are available for investment in venture capital, making local authorities major potential players in the market (Pensions and Investment Resource Centre, 1989). Thus far, only a small part of this pool of monies, about £200 million, has been invested as venture capital. Nevertheless, there are already signs that local authorities in the West Midlands and the northern regions are taking the innovative lead in this new trend.

Local authorities in these regions have been attracted into venture capital investment not only in order to benefit from the high potential rates of return, but also because of the job creation potential of venture capital and the opportunity to target investments on their local areas. Furthermore, following the economic dislocations of the 1980s, many local authorities now realize they have an important role to play in local economic regeneration, and the use of pension fund monies for investment in local enterprises is seen as a key element in that role. However, the extent to which venture capital investment can be carried out as an in-house activity may be limited for many local authorities because of the operating costs and specialist expertise requirements associated with such funds. In these cases some sort of collaboration or partnership with local private sector venture capitalists would seem to be the most effective strategy. Also, of course, local authorities have to ensure that their use of pension funds monies for venture capital investment is consistent with meeting their pension obligations. For this reason, they will want to avoid overcommiting their venture capital investments to high-risk projects.

It is this issue of risk in relation to the new and small firm sector that has been so sharply highlighted by recent macro-economic events. In many respects the boom in new and small firms in the second half of the 1980s was unrealistic, encouraged by the exaggerated boom in the economy induced in part by the Government itself and by the over-enthusiastic flood of loan capital from the banks. The subsequent move by the Government to reduce the inflationary effects of that boom by raising interest rates then dealt a double blow to the small enterprise sector: a deep downturn in the economy combined with (excessively) high loan charges by the banks, which together resulted in a surge of small firm bankruptcies and failures. As far as the enterprise economy is concerned this experience suggests at least two important lessons. The first is that the successful development of new and small firm enterprise in the regions not only depends on favourable local circumstances and factors, including access to finance, but also requires a stable pattern of national economic growth, not one of 'boom and bust'. The second is that the advantages of equity capital relative to loan capital have become more apparent, particularly its long-term nature, the absence of crippling repayments or interest charges in the vital early stages of an enterprise, and in the case of much venture capital a closer interest by the investor in the management of the enterprise in question. Added to this, in the wake of the recent wave of bad debts by the small firm sector, the banks are almost certain to curtail their supply of loan capital somewhat in the future. There are likely to be increasing pressures, therefore, for more vigorous venture capital markets in the regions over the coming decade.

REFERENCES

Advisory Council on Science and Technology (ACOST) (1990) *The Enterprise Challenge: Overcoming Barriers to Growth in Small Firms*, London: HMSO.

Bank of England (1990) Venture Capital in the United Kingdom, *Bank of England Quarterly Bulletin*, 30, pp 78–84.

Braudel, F. (1982) *The Wheels of Commerce*, New York: Harper and Row.

Burrows, R. (Ed) (1991) *Deciphering the Enterprise Culture*, London: Routledge.

Cary, L. (1989) *The Venture Capital Report Guide to Venture Capital in the UK*, London: Pitman.

Department of Trade and Industry (1988) *DTI Department for Enterprise*, London: HMSO.

Dixon, R. (1989) Venture Capitalists and Investment Appraisal, *National Westminster Bank Quarterly Review*, November, pp 2–21.

Financial Times (1990) Management Buy-Outs, *Financial Times, Special Survey*, 6 September, pp 1–15.

Financial Times (1990) Venture Capital, *Financial Times, Special Survey*, 26 November, pp 1–10.

Hamilton-Fazey, I. (1987) A Network is Emerging, *Financial Times*, 4 December, p.7.

Hamilton-Fazey, I. (1988) Local Knowledge an Asset for the North's Players, *Financial Times*, 30 November, p 3.

HM Government (1931) *Report of the Committee of Finance and Industry (Macmillan Report)*, Cmnd 3897, London: HMSO.

HM Government (1971) *Report of the Inquiry on Small Firms (Bolton Report)*, Cmnd 4811, London: HMSO.

HM Government (1979) *Interim Report on the Financing of Small Firms (Wilson Report)*, Cmnd 7503,London: HMSO.

Janeway, W.H. (1986) Doing Capitalism: Notes on the Practice of Venture Capitalism, *Journal of Economic Issues*, 20, 2, pp 431–441.

Keeble, D.E. (1990) New Firms and Regional Economic Development: Experience and Impact in the 1980s, in Cameron, G.C. et al (Eds) *Cambridge Regional Economic Review*, Cambridge: Department of Land Economy and PA Economic Consultants, pp.62–71.

Lorenz, T. (1989) *Venture Capital Today*, New York: Woodhead-Faulker (Second Edition).

Martin, R.L. (1989) The Growth and Geographical Anatomy of Venture Capitalism in the United Kingdom, *Regional Studies*, 23, 5, pp 389–403.

Martin, R.L. (1991) Has the British Economy Been Transformed? Critical Reflections on the Policies of the Thatcher Era, in Cloke, P. (Ed) *Policy and Change in Thatcher's Britain*, Oxford: Pergamon. PP.

Mason, C. (1987) Venture Capital in the United Kingdom: A Geographical Perspective, *National Westminster Bank Quarterly Review*, May, pp.47–59.

Mason, C. (1991) Spatial Variations in Enterprise: The Geography of New Firm Formation, in Burrows, R. (Ed) *Deciphering the Enterprise Culture*, London: Routledge, pp 74–106.

Mason, C. and Harrison, R.T. (1991) *A Strategy For Closing the Small Firms' Finance Gap*, mimeo, Department of Geography, University of Southampton.

Pensions and Investment Resource Centre (1989) *Local Authority Superannuation Fund Venture Capital Investment in England, Scotland and Wales*, London: PIRC.

Rybczynski, T. (1989) Financial Systems and Industrial Restructuring *National Westminster Bank Quarterly Review*, November, pp 3–13.

Shilson, D. (1984) Venture Capital in the United Kingdom, *Bank of England Quarterly Bulletin*, 24, pp 207–211.

Thompson, C. (1989) The Geography of Venture Capital, *Progress in Human Geography*.. PP.

Wright, M., Thompson, S. and Robbie, K. (1990) Management Buy-Outs: Achievements, Limitations and Prospects, *National Westminster Bank Quarterly Review*, August, pp.40–53

Young, D. (Lord) (1990) *The Enterprise Years*, London: Headland Book Publishers.

CHAPTER 8

NEW TECHNOLOGIES AND THE REGIONS

8.1

High Technology Industry and the Restructuring of the UK Space Economy

David Keeble

Since 1980, UK industry and the country's space economy have both arguably under-gone radical restructuring. This restructuring has involved considerable rationalisation and closure of existing factories, widespread adoption of new production technologies and work practices, significant growth in numbers of new and small firms, and substantial inward investment by foreign multinationals (Keeble, 1987). High technology industry, as defined below in terms of especially rapid technological innovation in products and associated above-average research and development intensity, appears to have played an important role in this restructuring, along with the effects of the acute early 1980s recession and intensifying global competition. Indeed, some observers argue that Britain and other western capitalist countries have since the 1970s been experiencing a technological revolution, based particularly on microelectronics, computers and new information technology, which may herald a new fifth Kondratief long wave of innovation-related economic growth (Freeman, 1986; Aydalot and Keeble, 1988; Hall and Preston, 1988). For the UK, however, a major concern must be that the greatest positive impacts of any such technological revolution appear to be benefiting selected regions of the USA and Japan, rather than of Europe. Thus substantial high technology employment growth in the former two countries contrasts with decline in the UK (Hall, 1987).

HIGH TECHNOLOGY DEFINITION AND CHARACTERISTICS

The definition of high technology industry has generated considerable debate (Thompson, 1988), partly because of the term's association with particular media stereotypes and political ideologies (Morgan and Sayer, 1988, p.37), partly because of absurdly wide categorisation by some US researchers. The approach adopted here, as in other recent work (Begg and Cameron, 1990), emphasises the vital significance of research and development activity in generating new products and services which are technology-intensive and dynamic. These are often based on radical technological innovations, and involve a marked degree of rupture with previous technologies and forms of social and economic organisation (Aydalot and Keeble, 1988). This definition thus excludes sectors which use rather than manufacture high technology products, even when the use of high technology processes revolutionizes their production methods, as in the UK iron and steel industry during the 1980s (see Keeble, 1991, pp.45–46). In practice, recent analysis by the Chief Statistician of the Department of Trade and Industry (Butchart, 1987) following this approach has identified 19 Standard Industrial Classification (SIC) 4-digit high technology industries (Table 8.1.1) on the basis of above average research and development (R&D) intensity and proportion of scientists, professional engineers and technicians in the work force. This logical and up-to-date definition will be used here. It must be stressed that any definition will involve some internal heterogeneity of individual sectors with respect to technological intensity, as well as variations in technological sophistication and function between establishments in the same SIC activity heading but located in different areas. The latter are discussed later.

Table 8.1.1. High Technology Industries in the United Kingdom

UK Standard Industrial Classification Activity Code and Industry Description

2514	Synthetic resins & plastics materials	3453	Active components & electronic sub-assemblies
2515	Synthetic rubber	3640	Aerospace equipment manufacturing & repairing
2570	Pharmaceutical products	3710	Measuring, checking & precision instruments & apparatus
3301	Office machinery	3720	Medical & surgical equipment & orthopaedic appliances
3302	Electronic data processing equipment	3732	Optical precision instruments
3420	Basic electrical equipment	3733	Photographic & cinematographic equipment
3441	Telegraph & telephone apparatus & equipment	7902	Telecommunications
3442	Electrical instruments & control systems	8394	Computer services
3443	Radio & electronic capital goods	9400	Research & development
3444	Components other than active components mainly for electronic equipment		

Source: Butchart, 1987

Defined in this way, high technology industry in the UK is characterised by five more or less distinctive features. The first is very rapid technological change in products, leading to ever shortening product life cycles. In the global semiconductor industry, for example, extraordinarily rapid miniaturisation has doubled the capacity of RAM silicon chips approximately every two years since 1965, from 1k (1000) bits to 64k in 1979 and 256k in 1984 (Kelly and Keeble, 1988). This has been associated with a remarkable reduction in cost, from £40 to only £5 per 1 megabit (million bits) of storage capacity in only ten years, 1978–87 (Kelly and Keeble, 1990).

The result is a further feature of most high technology sectors – rapid growth in market demand and hence output. The incorporation of microelectronics and computers, for example, into every aspect of western economic and social life during the 1980s has been dramatic. Global sales of semiconductors increased by 122 per cent over the five years 1982 to 1987 alone (Morgan and Sayer, 1988, p.44). Sales of UK-manufactured electronic data processing and aerospace equipment grew in constant prices by +208 per cent and +75 per cent, respectively, between 1979 and 1989, to £5.7 and £7.8 billion, despite acute recession until 1983. Government expenditure on defence and health (pharmaceuticals) has been one important component of this growth.

A third significant characteristic of high technology industry is the vital importance of scientific research and development in competitive success. High technology firms thus exhibit a pronounced – and growing – dependence on brain power in the form of highly qualified research scientists, engineers, technicians and managers. In the UK electronics industry, for example, the number of professional engineers and scientists nearly doubled (+87%) between 1978 and 1987, in stark contrast to a decline of 17 per cent in the industry's overall work force (Green and Owen, 1989). The availability of such staff is thus an extremely important locational influence, both for large firms with major research laboratories such as IBM (Kelly and Keeble, 1990), and for small enterprises set up by 'boffin' entrepreneurs.

High technology industry in Britain is also characterised by considerable recent corporate restructuring. This has involved expansion both of foreign multinationals and new, small indigenous firms. Inward investment by large multinational companies, chiefly from North America and Japan, has been considerable and growing during the 1980s (Keeble, 1991). Such firms regard Britain as an excellent base from which to supply both the UK and wider European Community markets. In 1988–89, for example, new foreign direct investment in the UK totalled no less than £14 billion, a 66 per cent increase on 1985–86, and 39 per cent of all such investment in the European Community (Huhne, 1991). Britain is Europe's leading destination for both US and Japanese manufacturing investment, the latter involving 132 manufacturing companies employing 25,000 people by January 1990 (Yoshitomi, 1991). Much of this is in high technology sectors. In contrast, larger indigenous British firms have been losing market share, a major reason for the serious UK balance of payments deficit in electronics which has developed since 1980. Britain's last remaining major computer company, ICL, was forced to accept takeover in 1990 by the Japanese giant Fujitsu.

Recent growth in new and indigenous high technology firms is part of a general phenomenon of recent small firm expansion in Britain (Keeble, 1990a; 1990b). Usually established by highly qualified entrepreneurs, new high technology firms owe their inception to very rapid technological change and the new market opportunities and niches this creates (Keeble and Kelly, 1986: Kelly, 1987). Interestingly, such firms appear to be important in sectors with both high and low barriers to entry, such as biotechnology and computer services, respectively. The latter industry has witnessed a dramatic explosion in the number of small companies in the 1980s, the stock of computer service businesses growing by a greater volume (+13,000) and rate (+89%) than any other sector of the UK economy between 1985 and 1989 (Keeble, Bryson and Wood, 1991).

Table 8.1.2. High Technology Industry: Regional Trends in the 1980s

Employment in Full-Time Equivalents

	1981 '000	1989 '000	Change '000	1981–89 %
Wales	36.3	51.5	+15.2	+41.9
East Anglia	31.9	40.7	+8.8	+27.7
South West	105.4	115.2	+9.8	+9.3
Rest of South East	334.2	334.4	+0.2	+0.1
Yorks/Humber	54.4	54.3	-0.1	-0.1
Scotland	89.7	88.7	-1.1	-1.2
East Midlands	80.3	74.4	-5.9	-7.4
North West	148.5	133.9	-14.6	-9.8
North	54.5	48.7	-5.8	-10.6
West Midlands	108.6	93.1	-15.5	-14.3
Greater London	218.5	177.6	-40.9	-18.7
Great Britain	1262.0	1212.4	-49.7	-3.9

Source: Unpublished Census of Employment statistics from NOMIS.
Part-time staff are treated as 0.50 of full-time staff.

However, most such firms are small, and their rapid growth has not been sufficient to prevent overall national decline in high technology employment (Table 8.1.2).

The final feature of UK high technology activity, then, is its relatively poor international performance, as noted earlier, and equivocal contribution to UK economic development. On the negative side, a number of high technology sectors have been in balance of payments deficit in the 1980s, overall high technology employment is falling, not rising, as a result of increasing automation and the poor performance of indigenous UK companies, and recent levels of capital investment have simply mirrored manufacturing industry generally (Begg and Cameron, 1990). On the positive side, high technology manufacturing as a whole has a positive balance of exports over imports, production has increased rapidly (see above), and employment decline has been less than for total manufacturing (-11.6% as compared with -15%, 1981–89). Virtually all (95%) high technology jobs are full time, not part time, while a high and growing proportion are also highly paid. Finally, high technology employment growth appears to be most characteristic of those areas and regions which have achieved above average industrial and economic growth generally during the 1980s. This regional association suggests the possibility of a wider and more strategic importance for high technology industry than simple employment figures alone might indicate.

THE SPATIAL DYNAMICS OF HIGH TECHNOLOGY DEVELOPMENT

Historically, the origins of high technology industry – in electrical engineering, aircraft and pharmaceutical manufacturing – lie mainly in London and South East England, which still accounted for a dominant share (44%) of UK employment in 1981. The last decade has however witnessed significant regional shifts in the location of high technology production and employment, involving two different and distinctive types of growth area. One is outer southern England (see Figure 8.1.1), comprising East Anglia, which is the UK's second fastest growing region for high technology industry (Table 8.1.2), the 'western crescent' of outer South East England (Hall et al, 1987), and South West England (the third fastest-growing region). High technology development here often involves 'new industrial spaces' (Scott, 1988), with the development of both small and large technology-based firms in previously relatively unindustrialised towns and even villages. The 'Cambridge Phenomenon' is a particularly striking example of this (Keeble, 1989). The second type of growth area is very different, namely Wales and, to a lesser extent, Scotland ('Silicon Glen'). These old industrial regions are, of course, characterised historically by severe industrial decline, high unemployment, and regional policy assistance.

The nature of high technology development in these two types of growth region differs in important ways. In southern England, expansion has occurred typically in large firm headquarter, administrative and research functions, and in indigenous small and medium sized companies. In the assisted regions, on the other hand, most development has involved branch production units set up by large firms headquartered elsewhere, often to serve wider European markets. This is well illustrated by IBM, which operates a large production plant at Greenock in Scotland assembling personal computers and systems for the European market. Its main UK research establishment is, however, at Hursley in Hampshire, with a further production unit nearby at Havant on the south coast, which works closely with Hursley on new product development. IBM's previous London head office also decentralised to Portsmouth in 1976 (Kelly and Keeble, 1990, pp.31–34).

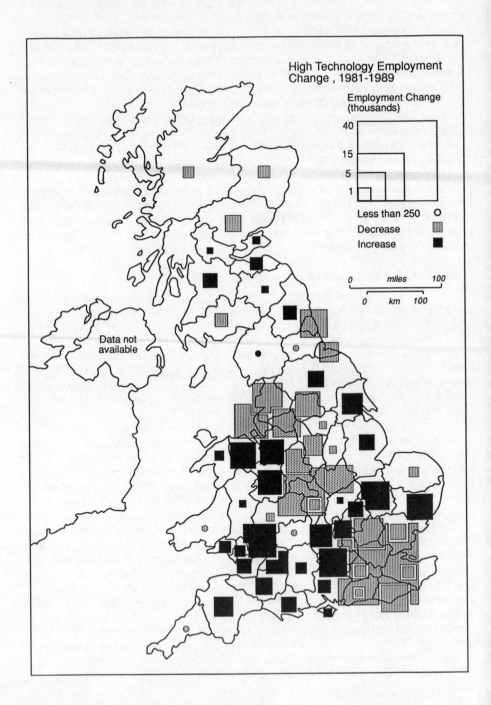

Figure 8.1.1: High Technology Employment, Absolute Change 1981–1989

The geography of high technology industry in Britain is thus characterised by a broad functional differentiation of activity between regions. This reflects both the investment decisions of large firms and a concentration of new small firm formation and development in southern England (Keeble and Kelly, 1986). In turn, this regional functional differentiation both partly reflects, and helps to perpetuate, a degree of 'spatial division of labour' between southern and assisted regions. A majority of managerial, professional and research-intensive functions and jobs are concentrated in southern England, with a greater focus on production jobs, involving lower incomes and qualifications, in the assisted regions (Massey, 1984, pp.136–53). This generalisation can, however, too easily become a stereotype, and it must be stressed that high technology firms in the assisted regions do provide highly qualified jobs (30% of IBM's Scottish employees are graduates), while a majority of UK production operatives work in southern factories.

Spatial dynamics at the sub-regional scale are even more dramatic. The recent and current pattern here is of a very marked urban-rural shift of high technology industry. All Britain's largest cities are losing high technology employment very rapidly (Figure 8.1.1). Greater London's employment alone fell by 41,000 jobs or 19 per cent, 1981–89 (Table 8.1.2). Conversely, high technology industry is growing in many smaller towns and rural areas. Indeed, there is a clear, consistent and striking gradient in recent high technology employment change between urban and rural counties of Britain (Table 8.1.3). This closely mirrors earlier and wider spatial trends in manufacturing industry in Britain and the European Community (Keeble, 1980; Keeble, Owens and Thompson, 1983). Rural county high technology growth is particularly evident in eastern England and central/northern Wales, together with much of the South West (Figure 8.1.2).

Table 8.1.3. High-Technology Industry and the Urban-Rural Shift in the 1980s

Employment in Full-Time Equivalents

	1981 '000	1989 '000	Change '000	1981–89 %
Conurbations (8)	475.3	399.1	-76.2	-16.0
More-Urbanised Counties (14)	319.7	308.9	-10.8	-3.4
Less-Urbanised Counties (21)	375.5	401.8	+26.3	+7.0
Rural Counties (20)	91.6	102.7	+11.0	+12.0

Sources: Unpublished Census of Employment statistics from NOMIS.
Urbanisation classification from Keeble (1980).

REGIONAL AND RURAL TRENDS IN HIGH TECHNOLOGY INDUSTRY: TOWARDS EXPLANATION?

These regional and spatial trends arguably reflect the particular and specialised needs of successful high technology firms, most notably for technological competitiveness and research leadership. This imperative in turn demands continuing and maximum access to highly qualified workers, because of their essential roles as researchers, development engineers and managers in large firms, and entrepreneurs and founders of new firms. Such individuals are in short supply, yet crucial for competitive success. Locationally, however, they and their families have spearheaded recent migration out of big cities to environmentally attractive small towns and rural areas for quality of life reasons (*Economist*, 1989; Bolton and Chalkley, 1989). They are also concentrated in

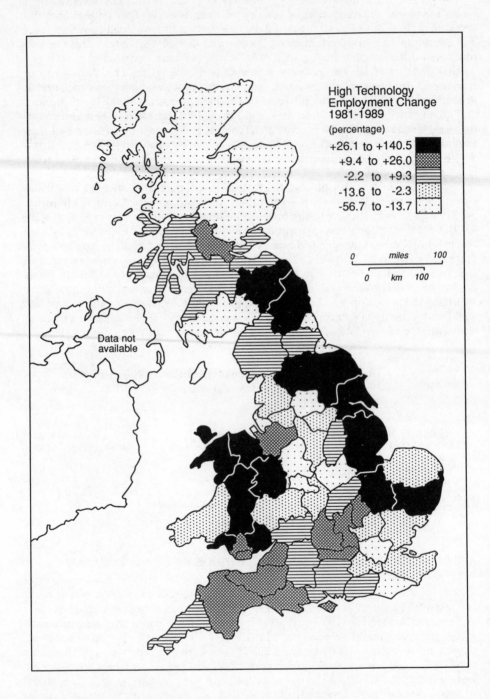

High Technology
Employment Change
1981-1989
(percentage)

+26.1 to +140.5
+9.4 to +26.0
-2.2 to +9.3
-13.6 to -2.3
-56.7 to -13.7

Data not
available

Figure 8.1.2: High Technology Employment, Percentage Change 1981–1989

southern England rather than elsewhere both because of its historic industrial structure and their own residential preferences. The attraction of highly qualified professionals to climatically or scenically favoured regions for quality of life reasons is of great importance in understanding current regional dynamics throughout Europe, as with the French 'Midi' or southern Germany (Keeble, 1991). In Britain, this is probably the chief single reason for the growth of new high technology enterprises in rural southern regions such as East Anglia, where not only are a majority of new firm founders inmigrants from elsewhere, but two-thirds report that the region's perceived attractiveness as a place to live was 'of great importance' in their decision to locate in this area (Keeble and Gould, 1985).

This key locational influence overlaps with another, namely the existence in particular areas of southern England, often for historic reasons, of significant local concentrations of scientific research activity. This includes both major universities – Cambridge, Oxford – and government research laboratories, many of which are in South East England, and notably its 'western crescent' (Hall et al, 1987). The remarkable growth of small high technology firms in the Cambridge region (600 companies, 20,000 workers in southern Cambridgeshire by 1989), for example, owes much to research links with, graduate recruitment from, and the prestige of its university (Keeble, 1989). The Cambridge Science Park, established by Trinity College in 1973, now houses 86 companies and 2800 workers. Such concentrations also often benefit from good communications with and general proximity to London. High technology firms often serve specialised and hence global markets, and need frequent access to London's international airports. Capital is also more readily available from City institutions to firms located in southern England (Martin, 1992). Lastly, the general urban-rural shift of high technology employment almost certainly also reflects urban space shortages and the need for attractive and spacious modern premises, in line with 'constrained location theory' (Fothergill, Kitson and Monk, 1985).

The dramatic expansion of high technology industry in Wales – and to a lesser extent Scotland – has been a key component in the 1980s' restructuring of the economies of these old industrial regions. Indeed, Wales recorded the UK's best regional manufacturing employment performance over the 1981–90 period, largely due to the growth of technologically-advanced companies (Keeble, 1991). The chief single reason for this is the attraction to multinational firms seeking a European base of regional policy financial incentives, together with the supportive activities of the government financed Scottish and Welsh Development Agencies. No less than 80 per cent of foreign-owned computer electronics companies in Scotland were powerfully influenced by such incentives in their location decision (Kelly, 1987, p.197). In South Wales, the remarkable growth of Japanese electronic consumer goods employment since the 1970s (Sony, Hitachi, Mitsubishi) is chiefly due to financial incentives and related government policies (Milne, 1990). A favourable labour market environment, in the form of readily available production workers in these regions of higher unemployment and good industrial relations, has also played some part. Some new small firms have also been set up in rural Wales and Scotland, sometimes as spin-offs from multinationals, but almost always in attractive residential environments.

HIGH TECHNOLOGY INDUSTRY AND THE 1990s

As noted earlier, high technology industry has been particularly prone to ideological and media stereotyping, and over-inflated claims of the benefits of 'sunrise industries' or 'silicon landscapes'. Nonetheless, and notwithstanding recent critical assessments (e.g. Crang and Martin, 1991), many localities in both southern and peripheral Britain have benefited from increased full-time employment in technologically advanced sectors during the 1980s. This has often also generated high local income and linkage multiplier effects on consumer and business services (Keeble, 1989). These gains are, however, being eroded by the severe 1990–92 recession, with its effects upon many small firms in southern England, while the serious weakening of regional policy since 1988 is bound to inhibit and reduce future investment in assisted regions such as Wales. The general lack of any clear national government policy towards high technology industry, unlike Britain's competitors, further militates against substantial national economic or employment growth in this area. European-wide restructuring in the context of 1992 and intensified Japanese competition is also likely to benefit European corporations in more centrally located regions, as with the Siemens-IBM £500 million joint venture announced in July 1991 to convert IBM's Corbeil-Essones plant near Paris to produce 16-megabit DRAM (Dynamic Random Access Memory) micro-chips. The UK's future role in and benefits from high technology industry are therefore at best uncertain and at worst destined to decline.

REFERENCES

Aydalot, P. and Keeble, D. (1988) High Technology Industry and Innovative Environments in Europe: An Overview, in Aydalot, P. and Keeble, D. (Eds) *High Technology Industry and Innovative Environments: The European Experience*, London: Routledge, 1–21.

Begg, I. and Cameron, G.C. (1990) The Regional Distribution of High Technology Activity: The Need for a New Policy Initiative, in G. Cameron, B. Moore, D. Nicholls, J. Rhodes and P. Tyler (Eds) *Cambridge Regional Economic Review*, Cambridge: Department of Land Economy and PA Cambridge Economic Consultants, 40–50.

Bolton, N. and Chalkley, B. (1989) Counter-Urbanisation – Disposing of the Myth, *Town and Country Planning*, 58, 249–250.

Butchart, R.L. (1987) A New UK Definition of the High Technology Industries, *Economic Trends*, 400, 82–88

Crang, P. and Martin, R.L. (1991) Mrs Thatcher's Vision of the 'New Britain' and the Other Sides of the Cambridge Phenomenon, *Environment and Planning D, Society and Space*, 9, 1, 91–116.

The Economist (1989) Demographic Trends: Rural Rush, *The Economist*, September 23, 43–44.

Fothergill, S., Kitson, M. and Monk, S. (1985) *Urban Industrial Change: The Causes of the Urban-Rural Contrast in Manufacturing Employment Trends*, London: Departments of Environment and Trade and Industry.

Freeman, C. (1986) The Role of Technical Change in National Economic Development, in A. Amin and J. Goddard (Eds) *Technological Change, Industrial Restructuring and Regional Development*, London: Allen and Unwin, 100–114.

Green, A.E. and Owen, D.W. (1989) The Changing Geography of Occupations in Engineering in Britain 1978–1987, *Regional Studies*, 23, 27–42.

Hall, P. (1987) The Geography of High-Technology: An Anglo-American Comparison, in J.W. Brotchie, P. Hall and P.W. Newton (eds) *The Spatial Impact of Technological Change*, London: Croom Helm, 141–156.

Hall, P., Breheny, M., McQuaid, R. and Hart, D. (1987) *Western Sunrise: The Genesis and Growth of Britain's Major High Tech Corridor*, London: Allen and Unwin.

Hall, P. and Preston, P. (1988) *The Carrier Wave: New Information Technology and the Geography of Innovation*, London: Unwin Hyman.

Huhne, C. (1991) A Sterling Performance in the Investment Race, *The Independent on Sunday*, February 10, p.11.

Keeble, D. (1980) Industrial Decline, Regional Policy and the Urban-Rural Shift in the United Kingdom, *Environment and Planning A*, 12, 945–962.

Keeble, D. (1987) Industrial Change in the United Kingdom, in W.F. Lever (Ed) *Industrial Change in the United Kingdom,* Harlow: Longman, 1–20.

Keeble, D. (1989) High-Technology Industry and Regional Development in Britain: The Case of the Cambridge Phenomenon, *Environment and Planning C, Government and Policy,* 7, 153–172.

Keeble, D. (1990a) New Firms and Regional Economic Development: Experience and Impacts in the 1980s, in G. Cameron, B. Moore, D. Nicholls, J. Rhodes and P. Tyler (Eds) *Cambridge Regional Economic Review,* Cambridge: Department of Land Economy and PA Cambridge Economic Consultants, 62–71.

Keeble, D. (1990b) Small Firms, New Firms and Uneven Regional Development in the United Kingdom, *Area,* 22, 3, 234–245.

Keeble, D. (1991) De-industrialisation, New Industrialisation Processes and Regional Restructuring in the European Community, in T. Wild and P. Jones (Eds) *De-industrialisation and New Industrialisation in Britain and Germany,* London: Anglo-German Foundation, 40–65.

Keeble, D., Bryson, J. and Wood, P. (1991) Small Firms, Business Services Growth and Regional Development in the United Kingdom: Some Empirical Findings, *Regional Studies,* 25, 437–457.

Keeble, D. and Gould, A. (1985) Entrepreneurship and Manufacturing Firm Formation in Rural Regions: The East Anglian Case, in M.J. Healey and B.W. Ilbery (Eds) *The Industrialisation of the Countryside,* Norwich: GeoBooks, 197–219.

Keeble, D. and Kelly, T. (1986) New Firms and High-Technology Industry in the United Kingdom: The Case of Computer Electronics, in D. Keeble and E. Wever (Eds) *New Firms and Regional Development in Europe,* London: Croom Helm, 75–104.

Keeble, D., Owens, P.L. and Thompson, C. (1983) The Urban-Rural Manufacturing Shift in the European Community, *Urban Studies,* 20, 405–418.

Kelly, T. (1987) *The British Computer Industry: Crisis and Development,* London: Croom Helm.

Kelly, T. and Keeble, D. (1988) Locational Change and Corporate Organisation in High-Technology Industry: Computer Electronics in Great Britain, *Tijdschrift voor Economische en Sociale Geografie,* 79, 2–15.

Kelly, T. and Keeble, D. (1990) IBM: The Corporate Chameleon, in M. de Smidt and E. Wever (Eds) *The Corporate Firm in a Changing World Economy: Case Studies in the Geography of Enterprise,* London: Routledge, 21–54.

Martin, R. (1992) Financing Regional Enterprise: The Role of the Venture Capital Market, in P. Townroe and R. Martin (Eds) *Regional Development in the 1990s: Britain and Ireland in Transition,* London: Jessica Kingsley.

Massey, D. (1984) *Spatial Divisions of Labour: Social Structures and the Geography of Production,* London: Macmillan.

Milne, S. (1990) New Forms of Manufacturing and their Spatial Implications: The UK Electronic Consumer Goods Industry, *Environment and Planning A,* 22, 2, 211–232.

Morgan, K. and Sayer, A. (1988) *Microcircuits of Capital: 'Sunrise' Industry and Uneven Development,* Cambridge: Polity Press.

Scott, A.J. (1988) *New Industrial Spaces: Flexible Production Organisation and Regional Development in North America and Western Europe,* London: Pion.

Thompson, C. (1988) Some Problems with R&D/SE&T-based Definitions of High Technology Industry, *Area,* 20, 265–277.

Yoshitomi, M. et al (1991) *Japanese Direct Investment in Europe,* Aldershot: Avebury.

Patterns of Research and Development

Jeremy Howells

There has been a remarkable growth in the knowledge and information intensification of the global economy, particularly centred on the advanced industrial nations of the world. In turn, research and technological innovation is seen as a key factor in maintaining international competitiveness through strengthening long-term economic growth prospects. This growth in knowledge and information intensification is reflected in the substantial increases in Research and Development (R&D) spending during the 1980s. For the OECD area as a whole Gross Expenditure on Research and Development (GERD) grew by no less than 6 per cent in real terms between 1981 and 1985. However the UK was very much an exception to this pattern having the lowest annual compound real growth of all OECD countries at just 1.6 per cent over the same period (OECD, 1989).

In addition, government financed GERD in real terms in the UK actually declined between 1981 and 1985 and was again the worst performer in the European Community (EC) over this period (Ireland was the only other EC country to reduce its government expenditure on research over this period). Similarly, in Higher Education Research and Development Expenditure (HERD) again the UK was one of the worst performers in the first half of the 1980s within the Community (compound real growth rate of 2.7% compared with 4% for the EC as a whole). During the first half of the 1980s and beyond, therefore, the UK has lagged well behind its EC partners in terms of funding of R&D and most research activity in Britain in real terms has witnessed only marginal growth or has actually contracted. This has had a significant bearing on the whole operation of the UK research and technology system over this period, reflected in the absolute decline of industrial R&D employment in Britain from 195,000 in 1981 to some 183,000 in 1988 (a fall of 6.1%). This is due to continue in terms of government financed R&D where expenditure in real terms is set to fall by 8.9 per cent between 1990–91 and 1992–93 (Cabinet Office, 1990).

Within this overall framework of decline in UK research employment, spatially R&D activity within Britain remains highly concentrated (Figure 8.2.1) reflecting former clusters of both public [1] and private research establishments. Using the latest Census of Employment data for 1989, the South East region had over 40 per cent (41.3%) of a total 97,200 thousand R&D jobs in Britain. [2] Indeed southern England as a whole (the South East, East Anglia and South West regions) has had a remarkably stable share of all R&D activity within the UK throughout the 1980s (1981 – 56.0%; 1989 – 56.7%). Unfortunately, the quality of the employment data for R&D makes it difficult to make an accurate analysis of employment change data between 1981 and 1989, even on a

1 See, for example, Buswell, R.J. Easterbrook, R.P. and Morphet, C.S. (1985) 'Geography, regions and research and development activity: the case of the United Kingdom' in Thwaites, A.T. and Oakey, R.P. *The Regional Impact of Technological Change* Frances Pinter, London, 36–66. Historical background given by Heim, C.E. (1988) 'Government research establishments, state capacity and distribution of industrial policy in Britain' *Regional Studies* 22, 373–386.

2 The Census of Employment uses a narrower definition of R&D than that employed by the Business Statistics Office which uses the OECD 'Frascati' definition.

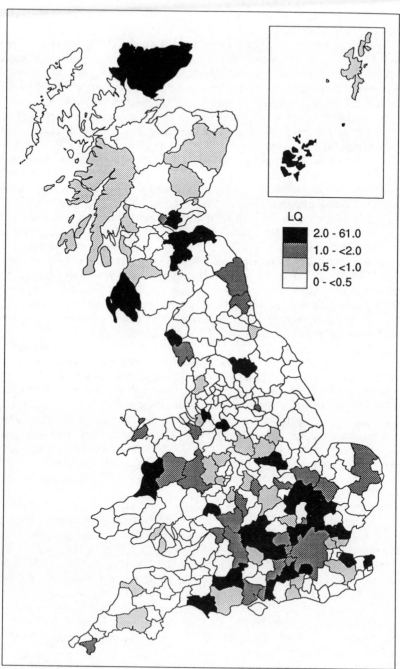

LQ

■	2.0 - 61.0
▨	1.0 - <2.0
░	0.5 - <1.0
□	0 - <0.5

* R&D employment location quotients (AH 9400) 1989

Figure 8.2.1: The Locational Pattern of R & D Activity in Britain

broad inter-regional basis. However there is some indication that there has been further decentralisation of R&D within southern England which has benefited the East Anglian and other adjacent counties.

The lack of growth in R&D activity in Britain during the 1980s was therefore a reflection of a number of macro, structural factors occurring in the UK economy, associated with the continued lack of international competitiveness of UK industry, cutbacks in government funding for R&D, as well as the more specific effects of industrial restructuring and inter-industry shifts in performance. A further element offsetting the rise of research employment has been the effect of labour productivity improvements as companies seek to stem the rising real costs of R&D (particularly development costs) and overcome some of the problems of trying to recruit scarce scientific and technical personnel. The more effective targeting of research effort together with the implementation of efficiency programmes and the benefits of increased automation of sampling and test procedures and the use of Computer Aided Design (CAD) are all important here.

An additional factor which may be holding down R&D spend in the UK is the growing impact of mergers and acquisitions. Recent studies in the US, for example, have indicated that mergers, acquisitions and other corporate restructurings (such as leveraged buyouts) lead to a reduced research spend at both a company and industry level. Thus acquisitions and other restructuring processes were shown to 'hurt' their respective industry R&D performance over time. Given that the UK has been a prime target in Europe of both domestic and foreign predators in recent years, the impact of mergers and acquisitions may have a significant depressing effect on overall levels of industrial research in Britain.

In a limited number of cases merger and acquisition activities have led to the outright closure of laboratories or the relocation of research establishments into a smaller number of more concentrated research sites. However, generally, corporate R&D networks have been very stable geographical systems as most companies have feared losing key research teams (which may have been built over very long time spans) through relocation or outright closure. This may be changing in the London metropolitan area where costs for carrying out research are increasing and where labour recruitment and retention for certain types of scientific staff is becoming a growing problem. As a consequence an increasing number of short distance (less than 50 miles) moves have been made to overcome these problems by decentralising laboratories within the South East region.

However, not all industrial sectors within Britain have been associated with static or declining research capabilities; there have been significant inter-industry variations. Thus a number of high technology manufacturing sectors, such as electronics, computers, aerospace and chemicals (as indeed within the OECD as a whole), have exhibited often dramatic growth in R&D effort. Thus the UK pharmaceutical industry, for instance, increased its expenditure on R&D in real terms by no less than 300 per cent between 1970 and 1982. The scale and complexity of industrial research has often changed dramatically within individual companies as a result. Companies have frequently had to move from operating R&D on a single site, or small group of closely connected sites, towards managing research across a much wider geographical spread of establishments.

This expansion in research activity has in turn been associated with the increasing internationalisation of R&D effort by firms. Glaxo, a major UK pharmaceutical company, provides a good example of such developments (Table 8.2.1). In 1968 it employed just over 750 in R&D, overwhelmingly centred on two sites in the UK. By 1978 employment had increased to over 1500 but with the main focus of R&D operations still centred on the UK. However, by 1988 employment had grown to nearly 5000, with only 53 per cent of total employment in R&D by this date being located in the UK. By 1992 with the relocation of its main research laboratory from Greenford in London to Stevenage in Hertfordshire, Glaxo will have a fully integrated international research operation.[3] Up until recently, therefore, the level of foreign R&D undertaken by companies has been limited, and largely restricted to US multinationals. However, this is now changing with UK and other European companies beginning to expand their overseas research capabilities in the late 1970s. More recently Japanese companies have started to establish research laboratories overseas, following on from their expansion in manufacturing facilities. In the UK for example, Nissan is establishing a new research facility in Cranfield (while retaining minor development and test facilities at its Sunderland car plant), while Canon has set up a R&D unit at Guildford and Yamanouchi a pharmaceutical research laboratory near Oxford.

Table 8.2.1. The Development of a Global R & D Network: The Case of Glaxo

Location	1968 % R & D employees [b]	1968 R & D centres [c]	1978 % R & D employees	1978 R & D centres	1988 % R & D employees	1988 R & D centres	1992 [a] % R & D employees	1992 [a] R & D centres
UK-based	97.3	2	89.3	2	63.4	3	60.9	3
Overseas-based	2.7	1	10.7	2	36.6	6	39.1	6
Total	100.0	-	100.0	-	100.0	-	100.0	-
Absolute	752	3	1591	4	4820	9	5586	9

[a] Projected figures
[b] Percentage breakdown of R & D employees between UK and overseas research centres
[c] Absolute number of designated R & D centres.

Source: Howells, (1990a)

This expansion in overseas research facilities is also associated with shifts in the role of overseas R&D units. In the past these units undertook modification and development work on innovations coming from the main domestic R&D establishments so as to make them acceptable for the 'host' market of the overseas unit. Increasingly, however, multinational companies are becoming what are termed as 'world market' companies where their products and markets are oriented towards a global framework. Host market modifications by overseas research units have therefore become less important and instead companies are establishing an integrated system of international R&D laboratories with particular overseas research units specialising in particular scientific and technical areas where that country has especial strengths. As such, multinational companies are becoming concerned with the availability abroad of specific types of research skills, seeking to locate laboratories on a world-wide basis in order to tap the increasingly scarce pools of scientific and technical talent.

A further element in this internationalisation process has been the growth in inter-firm and inter-institutional (industry-academic-government) research collaboration on a global basis, which has led to an increasing number of transnational linkages between organisations involved in research. Internationalisation of research is also having two wider implications on the geography of R&D activity. Firstly, research

3 See, for example, Howells, J. (1990a) 'The location and organisation of research and development: new horizons'. *Research Policy* 19, 133–146.

laboratories within a particular region or country may no longer be integrated with local production plants but may have closer ties with plants located elsewhere in the corporate network often abroad. Thus research is becoming increasingly locationally 'fluid' as both research contacts and administrative boundaries expand from often highly localised research systems to national and international networks. Second, related to this, regions and countries can no longer be seen as 'closed' geographical economic systems in terms of R&D, as such research inputs/outputs cannot be assumed to remain within a given regional or national framework.

A final factor which is helping to shape the organisation and location of R&D in Britain is the research process itself. A major element in the organisation and operation of corporate research revolves around the advantages (and disadvantages) of concentrated versus dispersed patterns of R&D. This decision centres on a number of key economic and technical criteria including benefits of scale and scope economies; the needs between internal and external communication and coupling arrangements in research; and the use of specialist equipment and staff. There have been two major forces which have had an increasing impact on R&D operations and which may have shifted the balanced towards more decentralised forms of research organisations. The first relates to the changing nature of research itself and its context within the firm. Research is becoming much harder, as R&D is directed towards more complex and ill understood areas of sciences, and more expensive as development costs in particular have risen. Against these rising development costs and lengthening development times there has been a shortening of product innovation life spans. In a whole range of industries as development times have increased, the rate of change in terms of the life span of new products is also speeding up. As a solution to these twin problems firms are seeking more decentralised R&D operations by dispersing laboratories to individual manufacturing facilities in order to more effectively control development costs, shorten the transition of an innovation from its development to full manufacture and market launch, as well as allowing improved contact with local customers. This pressure could also be associated with the growth in R&D 'externalisation' during the 1980s, where the increasingly blurred boundary between basic and strategic research, shorter lead times to commercialisation and the 'uncertain' technological environment have made industry more willing to fund external research.[4]

A potential factor which may facilitate this shift is the use of information and communication technologies (ICTs), in particular the growth of computer-communication networks. A growing number of companies are using computer-communication networks as a response to the growth of their R&D operations both at home and abroad. The development of these communication networks has reduced the potential duplication of research effort, as well as speeding up information flows and allowing

---

4 The growth in external R&D has also been related to the rise of new pervasive enabling technologies, in particular information and communication technologies (ICT), biotechnology and advanced materials. Based on earlier notions of long wave theory and business cycles, the emergence of a new set of technologies and industries do not emerge smoothly from existing firms and sectors but instead rely upon what Schumpeter terms the 'process of creative destruction', whereby much of the knowledge needed to implement such change must be sought from *outside* the firm which could be viewed as part of the rise of a new 'techno-economic paradigm' (Freeman and Perez 1988, 46). However, although these major shifts or changes in the techno-economic environment may be intuitively appealing in explaining the growth in external research collaboration by industry, yet there is little evidence more directly linking it with such growth. What evidence there is suggests that the growth of external R&D activity is associated with, rather than instead of, internal research effort (Freeman, C. and Perez, C. (1988) 'Technical change and the theory of regulation' in Dosi, G. Freeman, C. Nelson, R. Silkberg, G. and Soete, L. (Eds) *Technical Change and Economic Theory* Frances Pinter, London).

resource sharing between geographically separated research laboratories (thus helping to overcome some of the problems which have characterised the operation of decentralised R&D operations in the past). A key question is how far developments in ICTs in R&D will be more actively used to change the organisation and location of corporate research activities rather than as a mechanism which has tended to respond to and facilitate organisational and operational pressures (Howells, 1990). As such, companies may seek to develop communication networks in order to allow them to locate certain research activities closer to key customers, to tap pools of scarce scientific and technical labour, or to develop a more streamlined system of specialist research centres. Over and above this is the nature of information and a data flow transmitted over networks. Computer-communication networks can provide relatively cheap, fast and effective means of communicating structured, routine information between sites. However for more important, non-routine contacts involving key and substantive research issues, face-to-face meetings will undoubtedly remain the dominant form of communication for the foreseeable future.

Above all, R&D activity within the UK must be viewed within a more dynamic and open spatial system. Research flows and collaborative links within Britain will be increasingly operated as part of a global research system whose scale and complexity will continue to expand. The question of what local areas or regions will gain from such research will, however, become much harder, as the economic benefits of research being undertaken in one locality will no longer necessarily remain within that area or even country.

REFERENCES

Cabinet Office 1990 *Annual Review of Government Funded Research & Development* HMSO, London.

Howells, J. (1900b) 'The internationalisation of R&D and the development of global research networks' *Regional Studies* 24, 495–512.

OECD 1989 *R&D, Production and Diffusion of Technology OECD Science and Technology Indicators Report No.3.* Organisation for Economic Co-operation and Development (OECD), Paris.

Acknowledgements: Thanks go to Anne Green for her help. The map is based on Department of Employment Census of Employment data from the National On-Line Manpower Information System (NOMIS) programmed by Robert Nelson of the Geography Department, University of Durham.

The Regional Dimension to the Adoption of Innovations

Neil Alderman and Alfred Thwaites

Successful technological change and innovation in manufacturing is widely regarded as one of the keys to regional economic growth and development. Technology has become a crucial weapon in the armoury of firms seeking to gain or protect a comparative advantage in domestic or international competitive markets. The turbulent period of the 1980s has seen considerable change in the structure of manufacturing employment. Following the deep recession at the start of the decade, recovery in output has not been matched by a recovery in employment, implying considerable productivity gains. Technological advance has been an important component of this process of change, but the evidence of the 1980s suggests that this has not been a spatially even process.

Indeed, there are two basic perspectives on the role of technological change and innovation. The first, essentially optimistic, view sees technology contributing to economic and employment growth through the creation of new industries, by increasing the competitiveness of firms in existing industries, and through a wide range of multiplier effects in associated supplier and service sectors. The second, pessimistic, view regards technology as a displacer of employment, a vehicle for the deskilling of labour, and a source of increased competition between regions with divergent economic development tendencies. Whichever view dominates, one thing is clear: regions do not enter competitive market processes on an equal footing in technological terms.

The technological capacity of regions is all about the ability to generate new technology as well as the ability to adopt and use appropriate advanced techniques. According to Begg and Cameron (1988), ten years ago high technology industry (the major source of novel products and technologies) was concentrated in four regions of the UK: the South East, South West, East Midlands and North West. Eight of the nine manufacturing industries they identified were overrepresented in employment terms in the South East region outside London. The more peripheral regions of Scotland, Wales and the North were underrepresented in these sectors, particularly those employing the greatest numbers.

The regional pattern of innovation in terms of the introduction of advanced subcomponents, such as microelectronics, into the products of more traditional industries has exhibited similar characteristics, despite the fact that such industries are less concentrated in areas such as the South East. In terms of process technology, the aggregate regional patterns are less marked. The available evidence suggests that as technologies mature regional differences in the extent of their adoption become less significant. However, the ability to advance technologically seems more constrained in the indigenous sector than within parts of large corporate organisations, although within the peripheral regions there has also been a tendency for these latter plants to be more dependent on the transfer of technology from outside the regions than on local technology generation (Thwaites et al 1981, 1982).

As we enter the 1990s, there is little evidence to suggest that the regional picture has altered much. The 'shake-out' of manufacturing capacity during the 1980s may have led to an apparent improvement in the technological standing of the lagging regions, but this could simply reflect the fact that many of the technological laggards have gone. While some peripheral regions have increased the level of activity in some high technology sectors such as pharmaceuticals, these advanced sectors still remain spatially concentrated. Furthermore, a continuing structural problem for the peripheral regions is indicated by the high proportion of industrialists who claim their products are not suited to advanced innovation (Alderman et al, 1988).

By way of summary then, it is clear that the peripheral regions and parts of the industrial heartland of the West Midlands and Yorkshire, depending on the industrial sector, have experienced a disadvantage in technological terms relative to the core regions of the UK. Although the 1980s have seen new industrial structures emerging (a 'leaner', certainly, 'fitter', possibly, manufacturing base) with an enhanced level of technological change generally, regional disparities, particularly in the generation of new technologies, remain apparent.

Understanding the regional patterns of technological change in the 1990s calls for an understanding of the way the manufacturing environment is changing and for new approaches to academic research in this area. Geographers have tended to focus on two principal facets of innovation, namely product and process change, and most of the evidence for the regional dimension to technological change is based upon various measures of these two attributes. Increasingly, however, the critical question from the perspective of economic development (actual or potential) concerns the configuration and use of new technologies, not simply whether or not they are adopted *per se*. Innovation under such a definition clearly includes other forms of change in terms of managerial innovation or organisational structures and interrelationships. The key question for the 1990s is whether this broader process of technological change will serve to reinforce existing spatial patterns or bring about significant spatial re-adjustments.

The rapid globalisation of manufacturing activity we are currently observing seems set to continue, with the formation of an increasing number of strategic alliances in technology development as the costs of keeping ahead of the opposition escalate. Similarly, the trend towards increasing world trade will be enhanced in 1992 with the Single European Act removing barriers to trade and exposing many European enterprises to inter-regional competition within the European Community (Cecchini, 1988). Effective use of new technology will be a key element in the success or otherwise of individual regions, particularly in meeting new product standards or environmental legislation. Further challenges to regional economies are likely to arise as a result of liberalisation within Eastern Europe, with the growing opportunity for East/West trade and technology transfer. These countries are more likely to compete in terms of the traditional industries of steel, textiles or mechanical engineering upon which the economies of the less favoured regions are more dependent.

Changes in the pattern and nature of trade are being accompanied by a rapidly growing demand for high quality products, a trend that is filtering down to the lowliest supplier of sub-components. New technologies and innovations in control systems and organisational arrangements are becoming a necessary part of the process of meeting increasingly stringent customer demands for quality and reliability (Leonard and Sasser, 1982). The dominant corporate players in the economy are one of the driving forces behind this particular trend.

Another feature of the 1990s seems set to be a continued rise in the rate of technological change, coupled with market fragmentation and product differentiation, largely as a response of those major players in the economic system to the twin problems of over-capacity and increasing competition from the low wage, newly industrialising countries. A consequence of this is that product life cycles become truncated, production runs shorter and pressures increase for even shorter lead times in both manufacturing and design (PA Consulting Group, 1989).

Such changes as these are being met by means of a number of innovatory responses in terms of technology and organisation. Faster design times are being tackled through the introduction of computer-aided design (CAD) systems. The reduction of inventory costs and a tightening of delivery times is achieved through the introduction of just-in-time systems. Product quality is being realised through total quality concepts and techniques such as statistical process control (SPC). These forms of innovation are likely to become more prevalent during the 1990s. Such innovatory responses have knock-on effects through the industrial supply chain as an increasing number of firms, irrespective of industry, engage in a 'search for excellence'. This process concerns the critical question of where to obtain the most appropriate technology (in the sense of knowledge and expertise, as well as equipment) to meet the competitive market conditions faced by the firm. The implication is that the firm itself may not be the ideal producer of all the components, sub-assemblies or subsystems required for its product (for example, motors, pumps, fans, gears, etc.), implying an externalisation of activities previously undertaken in-house.

Externalisation can help reduce the risks associated with rapidly changing customer demands and the costs of carrying inventory, essentially by passing these on to the supplier. However it carries additional risks of its own in that, to guarantee quality and delivery, the standards of the purchasing firm must somehow be imposed upon the supplier. Thus, we are likely to see significant changes to the relationships between customer and supplier firms through the 1990s, in many cases mediated through the use of new technology, particularly computer networks, together with a trend towards reduced supplier bases. Under such circumstances, only those suppliers that are technologically competent and possess the right organisational structures are likely to become a part of these new networks.

The key research question is therefore what are the regional implications of these trends and relationships? At present our knowledge is limited. What is clear from the available evidence is that the majority of the key players in the manufacturing system in each region are well advanced in terms of their technological capability. It is the surrounding infrastructure of suppliers and subcontractors that are less well equipped to meet the demands of the 1990s. This is one important area where regional disparities exist and could worsen if their technological capability is not uprated, because increasingly local industry has to compete at an international level.

The key manufacturing players or 'drivers' in the system (for example a major vehicle assembly plant) also have an impact on a temporal dimension by placing demands on the system for increased speed of operation. While computer networking between firms can speed up the flow of information between them, in terms of physical goods or services the need for close proximity to the 'driver' may result in new clusters of activity around them. Whether such new agglomerations of manufacturing activity serving the needs of the drivers will indeed arise, as some commentators believe, is a matter for speculation (Schoenberger, 1987).

Although the changing relationships between firms may offer some prospect for renewed development in less favoured regions, the types of technological change and innovation referred to above are likely to exhibit conflicting impacts upon the regions. These new systems are part of a long term trend towards integration within the manufacturing sphere, widely referred to as computer integrated manufacture (CIM).

The pessimistic view of this process sees it as a movement from stand-alone pieces of equipment on the shop floor to 'islands of automation', leading ultimately to the fully integrated and potentially 'workerless factory'. The optimistic view sees CIM as the key to enhanced competitiveness and the source of future economic growth. In practice this concept is far removed from the reality facing the majority of firms today and is unlikely to be perfected this side of the turn of the century. The regional impacts are not easy to distinguish. On the one hand automation has the potential to reduce manufacturing employment, but on the other hand the need to achieve rapid responses to market and customer signals is bringing about a closer locational relationship between design activities and manufacturing, with potential benefits for those regions with dynamic parts of key enterprises.

The nature of the market demand to which the manufacturing establishments and enterprises of a region are exposed will therefore influence the diffusion of integrated systems. The spatial incidence of this type of innovation will be influenced by the location of different types of user firm. In this respect some regions may still face a structural problem if they lack the key dynamic drivers in the system. There is currently a lack of evidence as to the way that these new systems and relationships are developing spatially. Our research, and that of others, suggests that hardware limitations are not viewed as of such a serious nature as the challenges facing the development of software for complex integrated systems. Significant new manufacturing developments are likely to be seen in this field over the next ten years.

The evidence from the 1980s reveals no major regional shift in the pattern of technological change and innovation in British manufacturing industry. It is clear that manufacturing industry throughout Britain will face an ever growing series of competitive challenges. For the less favoured regions, one way of offsetting such challenges is to uprate the technological capability of local industry as well as to encourage the development of new industries. While recognising the importance of the presence and growth of high technology industry to the development of regions, one of the key factors emerging from the 1980s is the rapid pace of technological change in more traditional manufacturing sectors, where the operations of many firms are as 'high tech' as the next and it is only the sector to which their main product is classified that denies them this accolade. There is no reason why enterprises operating in traditional sectors in less favoured regions should not become world beaters through the application and use of appropriate technologies and innovation in organisational and management systems. This does not necessarily imply reducing support for high technology industries in such regions, but a recognition of the importance of more traditional manufacturing industries in the economic development process.

REFERENCES

Alderman, N., Davies, S. and Thwaites, A.T. (1988) *Patterns of Innovation Diffusion: Technical Report*. Newcastle upon Tyne: CURDS, University of Newcastle upon Tyne.

Begg, I.G. and Cameron, G.C. (1988) High technology location and the urban areas of Great Britain. *Urban Studies*. 25, 361-379.

Cecchini, P. (1988) *The European Challenge 1992*. Aldershot: Wildwood.

Leonard, F.S. and Sasser, W.E. (1982) The incline of quality. *Harvard Business Review*. 60 (5), 163-171.

P A Consulting Group (1989) *Manufacturing into the late 1990s*, London: HMSO.

Schoenberger, E. (1987) Technological and organisational change in automobile production: spatial implications, *Regional Studies*, 21 (3), 199-214.

Thwaites, A.T., Oakey, R.P. and Nash, P.A. (1981) *Industrial Innovation and Regional Development. Final Report to the Department of the Environment,*Newcastle upon Tyne: CURDS, University of Newcastle upon Tyne.

Thwaites, A.T., Edwards, A. and Gibbs, D.C. (1982) *Interregional Diffusion of Production Innovations in Great Britain. Final Report to the DTI/EEC.* Newcastle upon Tyne: CURDS, University of Newcastle upon Tyne.

Information and Communication Technologies and the Regions: An Information Economy Perspective

John Goddard

INTRODUCTION

In 1986 the Economic and Social Research Council (ESRC) established its Programme on Information and Communication Technologies (PICT). PICT's origins can be traced to an academic concern not only with the social and economic implications of information technology (IT) but also a concern on the part of policy makers with the role of information activities in economic development. Many major public decisions were having to be made in the absence of well-grounded research on the implications of various regulatory regimes. Current examples include policy towards international trade in information based services which are under discussion in the General Agreement on Tarrifs and Trade (GATT) round, on regulation of telecommunications considered in the recently completed review of the telecommunications duopoly in the UK, and on the regulation of information intensive-industries such as the media incorporated in the 1990 Broadcasting Act.

One reason for this knowledge gap has been that researchers and policy makers have placed most emphasis on the 'T' of 'IT' and neglected the role of information generation, capture and transmission or communication in economic growth and change more generally. This neglect was surprising given that the demand for IT derives from a growing demand for information (cf Cabinet Office, 1983).

This over-emphasis on technology and neglect of information is particularly apparent at the sub-national scale, where a great deal of attention has been paid to the location of information technology production (eg Hall et al, 1987). The success of high technology corridors such as the M4, fortuitously underpinned by state support for research laboratories and defence spending, has led development agencies to seek to create the conditions for high technology production in lagging regions and ailing cities – for example through the promotion of science parks and, in other countries if not the UK, the science park's big brother, the technopolis. Current academic debates on local economic development do consider the greater flexibility that new technology is bringing to the organisation of production in different regions and the possibility of creating industrial districts based on a new division of labour between small firms (eg Scott and Storper, 1988). However, attention has tended to focus on the *workplace* and not on the new flexible geography of multi-site *organisations* made possible by information and communications technology.

An information economy perspective would suggest that this emphasis fails to come to grips with one of the key dynamics in contemporary economic restructuring. It is as if the fundamental economic development issue in the nineteenth century related to the ability to build steam engines and not to the spread of steam power into a wide range of products and processes and the changes in the *systems* for organising production that the rapid improvements in communication made possible.

Partly because of a lack of previous research on the geography of the information economy many policy decisions are still being made with little understanding of their spatial implications. For example, few agencies promoting local or regional economic development were aware of – let alone engaged in – national debates on the regulation of telecommunications and broadcasting leading up to the review of the telecommunication duopoly and to the Broadcasting Act. One consequence of these regulatory changes is that cable franchises are being established in many cities but the first time local policy makers begin to appreciate the possible implications is when the franchise holder requests planning permissions.

National policy debates are often equally blind to spatial issues. Office of Telecommunications (OFTEL)'s formal interest appears to be confined to public telephones in rural areas; and although the Broadcasting Act supports the regional dimension of Channel Three the connections between broadcasting and regional development received little discussion of substance in the preceding White Paper. And yet the spread of Information and Communication Technologies (ICT) in conjunction with the 'informatisation' of the economy carries with it implications for the location of activities and the development of cities and regions in the UK as profound as the spread of railways, roads and electric power, newspapers and the telephone in relation to the development of the industrial economy.

A DEFINITION OF THE INFORMATION ECONOMY

The essence of the information economy from the geographical perspective can be captured in four interrelated propositions.

The first proposition is that although it has always been an important factor, information is coming to occupy centre stage as the key strategic resource on which the effective delivery of goods and services in all sectors of the world economy is dependent (Gillespie and Williams, 1988). Far from a transformation from an industrial to a post- industrial economy in which the emphasis is placed upon a shift from manufacturing to services, an information economy perspective would suggest that manufacturing and service activities are becoming equally dependent on effective information management. London and a few other large cities are – and always have been – foci for information processing and exchange functions; as information becomes more important in both production and distribution, so the pivotal role of these areas is reinforced.

The second proposition is that this economic transformation is being underpinned by a technical transformation in the way in which information can be processed and distributed. The key technical development is the convergence of the information processing capacity of computers (essentially a within workplace technology) with digital telecommunications (essentially a technology linking workplaces). The resultant technology of telematics is emerging as a key spatial component in the technical infrastructure of the information econ omy (Hepworth, 1987). Because of their historic role, metropolitan cities such as London are becoming the nodes or switching centres of this network based economy.

The third proposition is that the widespread use of information and communications technologies is facilitating the growth of the so called 'tradeable information sector' in the economy. This transformation embraces traditional information activities like the media and such new activities as on-line information services. Moreover, many information activities previously undertaken within firms can now be purchased from external sources at lower cost in the 'information market place' – the growth of the advanced producer service sector can in part be accounted for by the externalisation of information functions from manufacturing and other firms (Howells, 1988). While the use of ICT permits an increasing volume of inter-organisation transactions, inter-personal contact is still sufficiently important, particularly in relation to the development of new services and relationships, for the role of a few key cities to be further enhanced.

The final proposition is that the growing 'informatisation' of the economy is making possible the global integration of national and regional economies. As the arena widens within which this highly competitive process of structural change is worked out, so the pattern of winners and losers among cities and regions is likely to become more sharply differentiated. Far from eliminating differences between places, the use of information and communications technology can permit the exploitation of differences between areas, for example in terms of local labour market conditions, the nature of cultural facilities and of institutional structures (Castells, 1989).

RESEARCH FINDINGS ON THE GEOGRAPHY OF THE UK INFORMATION ECONOMY

With these propositions in mind research under PICT carried out at the Centre for Urban and Regional Development Studies at Newcastle University has sought to inject a concern for geography into the study of, and formulation of policy for, the UK information economy. The research has had three strands.

First, studies of the adoption of ICT in organisations in the public and private sector and in manufacturing and service industries linking this adoption to the geographical division of task between workplaces within and between organisations and relating this to the territories over which the organisations operate. Second, studies of the spatial development of the UK telecommunications system, focusing initially on BT itself as a complex organisation with its own inter-regional relations. And third, a geographical analysis of the development of a tradeable information sector par excellence, the audio visual production sector. These investigations have involved in-depth studies of individual organisations, survey research, analysis of secondary data and conceptual work on the relationship between ICTs and geographical change.

A number of conclusions are emerging from the research. First, ICTs, when taken together with other factors, are supporting a more uneven pattern of regional development within the UK. Information occupations and industries have grown dramatically in London and the South East in the past ten years, reflecting the capital's international as well as its national role. For example through the teeth of the 1979–83 recession the South gained 800,000 jobs in occupations concerned with the processing of information while other regions recorded net losses. Subsequently, between 1983 and 1989 London alone gained 273,000 jobs in the information intensive financial and business service sector, a 41 per cent increase. This growth has been underpinned by the rapid diffusion of computer networks; these networks are hubbed on London, serving to reinforce its dominant position in the national and international urban system. For example 40 per cent of organisations in the City of London have over 100 users of computer networks compared with only 15 per cent in the North East of England.

Second, there is only limited evidence so far of ICTs contributing to more flexible ways of organising the production of goods and the delivery of services in the way that could benefit smaller enterprises and indigenous development in declining regions. Computer networks are still used primarily for intra-organisational transactions and as a means of reasserting control over organisational processes; very few small firms are networked. For example the Government's Workplace Industrial Relations Survey of 1984 revealed only 5 per cent of single site workplaces were connected to a computer network compared to an average 26 per cent for all workplaces. However, there are cases of organisations which are using ICTs to create competitive advantage, reconfigure their corporate geography and change the way in which they manage territory. For example one case study company based in Doncaster has used a computer network to enable it to shift from a collapsed local authority dominated market for its products in the North of England to expanding retail markets in the South without building new facilities in the most expensive part of the country. Clearly ICTs have the potential for radically changing the face of Britain rather than simply reinforcing the old order.

Third, the intersection between sectoral and geographical considerations in relation to the development of the UK information economy is poorly articulated in the regulation of information industries or in public policy more generally. The fact that the competitive model of telecommunications regulation favoured by the current legislative environment is only fully realised in London and the South East and a few other leading urban centres is likely to be reinforced by the outcome of the duopoly review. The duopoly review suggests that telecommunications policy, like many other areas of public policy, is policy for the core area of the UK and a few places outside.

These points are clearly demonstrated in the PICT submission to the duopoly review. PICT recognises the advantage that competition has brought in the provision of a wide range of telecommunications services. However, these benefits are unlikely to be universally available, particularly in rural areas and peripheral regions where BT will remain a monopolist (PICT, 1990). New entrants into telecommunications, such as British Rail and the cable television companies, will heighten competitive pressures on BT in a few locations and market segments; this could be to the detriment of significant parts of the UK industrial capacity in the small firm sector and in domestic markets where costs of service provision are high and revenues low because they are off these main routes. In Scotland, for example, 60 per cent of households live in areas which have not received interest from cable franchises. These include significant urban centres such as Dunfermline, Ayr, Dumfries, Inverness, Kilmarnock and Sterling (Gillespie and Williams, 1990). The competitive threats in relation to BT's most lucrative large volume business market are therefore concentrated in London and the South East and a few other cities. With the potential of many more 'cream skimming' entrants into the telecommunications market (e.g. British Rail Telecommunications) it is not surprising that BT has restructured itself from a territorially to a functionally organised business – its primary divisions are now World Wide Networks, Business Communications and Personal Communications not regions.

A similar failure to fully embrace the spatial dimension in regulating the information economy is apparent in the sphere of broadcasting. Although the existing Channel 3 regional franchise areas are to be retained a process of concentration of ownership across regional boundaries remains possible. This would have significant implications for the fragile complex of independent television production beginning to emerge outside London based on regional programme purchasing and for sustaining regional cultural identities. Similarly, increasing commercial pressures on the BBC has already resulted in a concentration of production facilities; for example, Manchester now controls production for the North West, Yorkshire and Humberside and the North East regions.

CONCLUSION

At the national and local level, there is little evidence of, but an urgent need for, coherent planning for the information economy which integrates training, infrastructure provision, technology demand simulation measures etc, not only as a means of achieving more balanced regional development, but in order to ensure that the UK reaps the benefits of becoming a network-based economy.

The spread of ICTs and the associated emergence of more geographically flexible and market responsive organisations also raise important questions concerning methods of regulating the economy in a way which balances public and private interest. The old hierarchical order of national, regional and local governance and of sectoral and regional policy, has been irrevocably challenged. There are dangers of global integration proceeding hand in hand with regional and local disintegration, of islands of economic growth in the networked economy and economic decline off the network. These dangers may now need to be countered by a new era of re-regulation. This will require new skills in public administration and the drawing together of knowledge from a variety of sources. Better information flows between central and local government, between different departments of state and between the public and private sectors, often in a European context, will be increasingly necessary if even sharper regional disparities in the information economy are to be avoided. Regional policies for the information economy will certainly be different to those for the industrial economy or the enterprise economy.

REFERENCES

Cabinet Office (1983) *Making a Business of Information, Report of the Information Technology Advisory Panel*, London: HMSO.

Castells M (1989) *The Information City*, Oxford: Blackwell.

Gillespie A E and Williams H (1988) 'Telecommunications and the Reconstruction of Regional Comparative Advantage' *Environment and Planning A*,20,pp 1311–1321

Gillespie A E and Williams H (1990) *The Future of Telecommunications in Scotland*, Centre for Urban and Regional Development Studies, University of Newcastle upon Tyne (mimeo).

Hall P et al (1987) *Western Sunrise: The Genesis and Growth of Britain's Major High Tech Corridor*, London: Allen and Unwin.

Hepworth M (1987) 'Information Technology as Spatial Systems' *Progress in Human Geography*, 11, pp 157–80.

Howells J (1988) *Economic, Technological and Locational Trends in European Services*, Aldershot: Avebury.

PICT (1990) *Competition and Choice: Telecommunication Policy for the 1990s – a Response to the DTI Consultation Paper*, PICT, Social Studies Faculty Centre, University of Oxford (mimeo).

Scott A and Storper M (1988) 'Flexible Production Systems and Regional Development: The Rise of New Industrial Spaces in North America an Western Europe' *International Journal of Urban and Regional Research*, 12, pp 173–85

Acknowledgments: The chapter is based on research undertaken in the Centre for Urban and Regional Development Studies at the University of Newcastle upon Tyne as part of the ESRC PICT Programme. It is a shortened version of PICT Policy Research Paper Number 11 entitled *The Geography of the Information Economy*. The contributions of Andrew Gillespie, Mark Hepworth, Kevin Robins, John Taylor and Howard Williams together with James Cornford, Ken Ducatel, Irene Hardill, Steve Johnson and Pooran Wynarczyk are gratefully acknowledged. Any errors of fact or interpretation are of course the author's.

CHAPTER 9

EMPLOYMENT TRENDS AND THE REGIONS

9.1

The Changing Mix of Occupations and Workers

A. E. Green

CONTEXT

Over the last 250 years regional economies have become increasingly integrated into national and international economic systems. During the next decade the trend towards increasing openness of regional and national economies is expected to continue, notably with the creation of the Single European Market. However, the continued evolution of this integrated and international economy may well be supplemented by the development of smaller scale and self-sustaining local economies. There are likely to be conflicting trends towards greater distinctiveness and greater uniformity in local and regional industrial and occupational structures, contrary tendencies towards centralisation and decentralisation, and growth in both large and small firms as increased industrial concentration spawns new opportunities for small firms.

Within the context of seemingly counteracting trends and tendencies, all regions of the UK are expected to share the same main quantitative changes in labour demand and supply – albeit to varying degrees. Similarly, all regions are anticipated to witness the same main qualitative changes in the nature of work – as categories of work and leisure break down and distinctions between industries and occupations become blurred.

As regional industrial structures have *converged* towards a national average, so greater attention has been placed on regional differences in occupational structure: the so-called *spatial division of labour (Massey, 1984)*. A key distinction has been made between a disproportionately large share of higher-status and white-collar occupations in the southern regions of the UK, and of blue-collar and less-skilled occupations in northern regions, relative to the national average (Green and Owen, 1984). Table 9.1.1 illustrates this pattern of occupational specialisation at the regional scale using data from the 1987 Labour Force Survey.

OCCUPATIONAL CHANGE

The changing mix of occupations and workers represents the outcome of the interaction between labour demand and supply trends. During the 1990s the industrial structure of labour demand is projected to continue to alter in favour of the service sector and away from primary and manufacturing industries. As a result the pattern of occupational demand is also expected to change, with occupations employed in service industries favoured at the expense of those concentrated primarily in manufacturing industries. This is the so-called 'industrial effect' component of occupational change, i.e. that portion of occupational change attributable to changes in the industrial structure. At the same time, within individual industries, technological developments and changes in work organisation lead to changes in occupational structure. This is the 'occupational effect' component of occupational change, i.e. that portion of occupational change attributable to changes in occupational composition within industries. The 'occupational effect' may reinforce or counteract the changes due to the 'industrial effect' (Institute for Employment Research, 1989).

Table 9.1.1 Broad Occupational Structure by Region

Region	% of employees	
	high status white-collar *	blue-collar +
South East	34.0	29.6
East Anglia	30.5	38.3
South West	30.7	35.8
West Midlands	27.3	42.0
East Midlands	27.3	42.7
Yorkshire & Humberside	28.1	41.0
North West	29.6	37.6
North	28.7	38.8
Wales	29.5	40.6
Scotland	28.7	40.0
Northern Ireland	30.4	36.3
UK	30.5	36.3

* managers and administrators, professional occupations, associate professional and technical occupations
+ craft and skilled manual workers, plant and machine operators, other occupations

Source: 1987 Labour Force Survey

Over time, new occupations emerge and old occupations die out. An examination of the occupational categories used in the the early years of the twentieth century reveal a large number of industrially-specific occupations no longer in existence. Other occupations, quite commonplace today, would not be found. A new occupational classification – the Standard Occupational Classification (SOC) – has been developed for use in the 1990s, emphasising distinctions between occupations in terms of skill levels and entry qualifications (Thomas and Elias, 1989). It is no longer considered appropriate to define occupations on an industrial basis, since occupations are increasingly relevant across a whole range of industries. With developments in technology and industrial organisation new occupations are continually evolving.

LABOUR DEMAND

According to forecasts made in the mid 1980s, employment in the UK is expected to grow by 0.7 per cent per annum to the year 2000 (Institute for Employment Research, 1989). This aggregate picture disguises faster than average rates of growth in some industries and occupations and decline in others. In industrial terms, primary industries and utilities are expected to continue their long-term downward trend in employment. Further job loss is anticipated in manufacturing – albeit at a slower rate than in the 1980s. The construction sector is projected to remain fairly buoyant over the medium-term. Job growth is forecast in the service sector – with a substantial rate of increase in business services, large absolute gains in leisure and tourism, and modest increases in non-marketed servcies. Turning to the occupational dimension, the pattern of demand for skills is expected to alter significantly during the 1990s (Table 9.1.2). The main growth occupations (at the broadest level of disaggregation in the new SOC) are managers and administrators, professional occupations, and associate professional & technical occupations, with forecast job growth in the UK of 700 thousand, 500 thousand and 400 thousand, respectively, between 1988 and 2000. Employment loss is projected to be concentrated in plant and machine operative and other occupations, with anticipated declines of 170,000 and 60,000 jobs over the same period (Training Agency, 1989).

Table 9.1.2 Projected Employment Change by Occupation *, 1988–2000

Sub-group	absolute change (000s)	nnual average change (%)
Managers and administrators	+700	+1.7
Professionals	+496	+1.7
Associated prof. and technical	+437	+1.6
Clerical and secretarial	+303	+0.5
Craft and skilled manual	+79	+0.2
Personal and protective services	+327	+1.4
Sales occuaptions	+137	+0.5
Plant and machine operators	-174	-0.5
Others	-61	-0.2
Whole Economy	+2244	+0.7

* excludes HM Forces

Source: Institute for Employment Research (1989)

Considering these occupational projections in greater detail, forecast rapid growth in managers and administrators is fuelled to a large extent by the expansion of the service sector and the increase in self-employment. This positive 'industrial effect' is reinforce-ed by a positive 'occupational effect' as the proportion of managers and administrators increases within industries. There is growing recognition that the quality of such staff is vital to the success of all types of organisation. Professional occupations are also projected to become more important, both absolutely and relatively, during the 1990s. Within industries there is increasing 'professionalisation' of many types of work, alongside growth in industries in which professional occupations are concentrated. The scope of many professional occupations is widening – as requirements increase for the application of information technology in a variety of fields, work across disciplinary boundaries, and development of broader project management and human relations skills (Rajan and Pearson, 1986).

Alongside these professional occupations, associate professional and technical occupations, including legal and business-related technical jobs, are expected to under-go particularly rapid growth due to the expansion of business and miscellaneous services. With increasing competition for professional personnel, there are likely to be pressures for expansion of the scope of associate professional and technical occupa-tions. As is the case for professional occupations, growth is attributable to positive 'industrial' and 'occupational effects'.

The share of total employment accounted for by workers in clerical and secretarial occupations is expected to decline in most industries (a negative 'occupational effect'). In part this reflects the increasing use of information technology, which will also serve to alter the nature of those jobs remaining. However, the pattern of industrial growth in favour of service industries (a positive 'industrial effect') is such that the absolute numbers employed in such occupations will remain relatively stable during the 1990s.

In the case of craft and skilled manual occupations it is anticipated that a negative 'occupational effect' will be reinforced by a negative 'industrial effect', as the manufacturing sector continues its long-term decline. With technological advances and changes in work organisation, the nature and content of these occupations have changed. Growing emphasis is placed on multi-skilled craftsmen able to apply their skills using a range of technologies, to a variety of materials, and across a wide spectrum of functional areas – thus breaking down traditional job demarcations. By contrast, a modest increase is anticipated in personal and protective service occupations, explained largely by changes in industrial structure. Many of these jobs are of a part-time nature. During the 1990s it is likely that such staff will be required increasingly to develop broader-based social, product, diagnostic and entrepreneurial skills. The proportion employed in sales occupations is projected to remain static in most industries. A forecast modest overall growth is due to overall expansion of the economy. Finally, considerable job loss is anticipated in the case of plant and machine operatives and other occupations. These occupational groups include many semi-skilled and unskilled workers in manufacturing. Forecast severe employment decline is attributable to a negative 'occupational effect' reinforced by a negative 'industrial effect'.

LABOUR SUPPLY

The size and composition of the workforce is a function of two factors: first, the size of the population (subdivided by gender and age), and second, the activity rate, i.e. the proportion of the population in any subdivision which is in the labour force. The size and age structure of the population can be projected with reasonable accuracy over the short and medium term. Activity rates are more difficult to predict, since they depend upon the complex interaction of socio-economic forces, which in turn depend, at least in part, on the state of the economy (Department of Employment, 1988).

As labour markets tightened – particularly in southern regions – during the late 1980s, attention was drawn to the impending 'demographic time bomb' (National Economic Development Office/Training Commission, 1988). As a result of low birth rates in the 1970s, there would be a reduction in the number of young people entering the labour market in the early 1990s (Department of Employment, 1988). As the 'under 25' age group declines, middle-aged and older workers will account for for an increasing proportion of the workforce – more than offsetting the decline in young people in absolute terms. Indeed, it is anticpated that virtaully all of the projected 1 million increase in the workforce between 1988 and 2000 will be accounted for by middle-aged women. Beyond changes in the age structure of the labour force, the 'greying' of the UK population has implications for the organisation and nature of work. The growing burden of care responsibilities for elderly relatives will fall mainly on middle-aged and older workers. These extra commitments demand more flexible work patterns – not only associated with part-time work and flexible hours, but also with more frequent entries to and exits from the workforce, which in turn have implications for career structures and training patterns.

It is significant that virtually all of the increase in middle-aged workers in the 1990s will be women. The activity rate element in the labour supply equation is much more volatile for women than for men. It is the key factor in determining the size of the female labour force. A number of social and demographic factors have led to higher female participation in the labour force in recent years. Key factors favouring female participation include the shift in the industrial structure from manufacturing to services, and the change in work practices towards flexibility and part-time working. Women returners – women returning to the workforce following a break for child- birth and child-rearing purposes – constitute the largest element of labour supply available to employers to meet new demands in the 1990s (Training Agency, 1989). Over recent years a tendency has been evident for women to return to work sooner after the birth of the youngest child. There is also a growing tendency for women to return to work between births.

Increases in female employment are anticipated in all regions. In some of the more depressed areas with high male unemployment many women seek employment to boost household incomes. Similar motivations exist in some of the more buoyant regions with high housing costs and numerous suitable employment opportunities.

Many women returners seek part-time work – particularly in the first instance. The overwhelming majority of part-time jobs are held by females. Female and part-time employment is concentrated overwhelmingly in four occupational groups: sales, clerical occupations, personal services, and a variety of 'other' occupations. It is anticipated that while the number of full-time jobs declines, part-time jobs will increase by over 2 million, accounting for over one-quarter of all jobs by the year 2000. This increase reflects both changes in industrial structure in favour of those sectors which employ large proportions of part-timers, and rising shares of part-time employment in most sectors.

Alongside the rise in the number of part-time jobs is a growth in temporary employment. Some workers on temporary or short-term contracts see this as a second-best alternative to full-time employment. For other groups, such as the disabled, the long-term unemployed and some ethnic minority groups, the increase in temporary and part-time jobs offers entry routes into employment which might not otherwise have been open, or a widening of available employment opportunities. For those in secure full-time jobs, the availablity of temporary work opens up opportunities for secondment to gain experience and enhance career development.

Alongside the increases in the numbers of female workers and of part-time jobs, a growth in self-employment is anticipated, albeit at a slower rate than during the 1980s. Self-employment grew very rapidly in the 1980s, from just under 2 million in 1981 to more than 3 million in 1988. All regions shared in this increase in self-employment, with the more prosperous southern regions leading the way. Over the next decade, self-employment is projected to increase its share of total employment, with a further rise of 0.75 million between 1988 and 2000. It is very difficult to assess in detail how employment in small firms will change during the 1990s. Change is dependent on such factors as the general economic climate, the extent to which people facing an enforced job change see this as an opportunity of becoming self-employed, industrial and economic change, and government policy (such as the encouragement of the develop-ment of an 'enterprise culture' during the 1980s). It seems that attractions of inde-pendence, flexibility, choice and freedom are more important for most people than the financial motivations of self-employment (Hakim, 1989).

In line with the more knowledge-intensive nature of the economy, it is likely that there will be an increasingly highly qualified workforce during the 1990s. 'Staying on' rates among young people seem set to continue to rise: further decreasing the available stock of young workers in the short-term, but representing a valuable investment in human capital in the longer-term. Alongside high-level skills the tendency to devote greater attention to general employment skills and enhanced flexibility seems likely to continue in the 1990s. It is now recognised that a high level of 'general competence' – in skills such as literacy, numeracy, personal effectiveness, and technical, economic and business awareness, is needed as a foundation for occupational competence. The workers of the 1990s will need to be more flexible and have skills enabling them to cope with change.

CONCLUSION

During the 1990s employment is expected to rise most rapidly in higher skilled jobs in all regions.* Declines will continue in semi-skilled and unskilled manual jobs. These tendencies may in part be explained by the continuing growth of the service sector, and the decline in primary and manufacturing industries. Changes in industrial composition aside, the nature of jobs within all sectors will change significantly – with those with managerial and professional skills benefiting most from the changes. Supply-side changes mean that employers will increasingly have to seek women returners, and to offer flexible working arrangements to accommodate their other roles. With the need for flexibility to cope with change there will be greater emphasis on continuing training to develop general and specific competencies.

REFERENCES AND NOTES

Department of Employment (1988) 'New entrants to the labour market in the 1990s', *Employment Gazette* 96, 267–274.

Department of Employment (1988) 'Labour force outlook to 1995', *Employment Gazette* 96, 117–129.

Green, A.E. and Owen, D.W. (1984) 'The changing spatial distribution of socio-economic groups employed in manufacturing in Great Britain', *Geoforum* 16, 387–416;

Green, A.E. and Owen, D.W. (1989) 'The changing geography of occupations in engineering, 1978–1987', *Regional Studies* 23, 27–42.

Hakim, C. (1989) 'New recruits to self-employment in the 1980s', *Employment Gazette* 97, 286–297.

Institute for Employment Research (1989) *Review of the Economy and Employment 1989 – Volume 2: Occupational Studies*, Coventry: Institute for Employment Research, University of Warwick.

Institute for Employment Research (1989) *Review of the Economy and Employment*, Coventry: Institute for Employment Research, University of Warwick.

Massey, D. (1984) *The Spatial Division of Labour*, London: Macmillan.

National Economic Development Office/Training Commission (1988) *Young People and the Labour Market: A Challenge for the 1990s*, London: National Economic Development Office.

Rajan, A. and Pearson, R. (1986) UK *Occupation and Employment Trends to 1990*, London: Butterworths.

Training Agency (1989) *Labour Market and Skill Trends 1990/91*, Sheffield: Training Agency; Institute for Employment Research (1989) *Review of the Economy and Employment*, Coventry: Institute for Employment Research, University of Warwick.

Training Agency (1989) *Labour Market and Skill Trends 1990/91*, Sheffield: Training Agency.

Thomas, R. amd Elias, P. (1989) 'The development of the Standard Occupational Classification', *Population Trends* 53, 16–21.

---

* At the time of writing, researchers at the Institute for Employment Research, University of Warwick, were working on medium-term occupational projections by region. The results have been published in institute for Employment Research (1991), *Review of the Economy and Employment: Regional Assessment*, Coventry: Institute for Employment Research, University of Warwick.

The Growth of Service Activities and the Evolution of Spatial Disparities

J. N. Marshall*

INTRODUCTION

The last two decades have been characterised by a growing prominence of service activities in regional economies in Britain (Gillespie and Green, 1987; Howells, 1988; Howells and Green, 1988). This is, of course, part of a long-term trend; the proportion of total employment in service industries has increased throughout most of the twentieth century (Table 9.2.1). The recent shift towards services has been particularly sharp, however, because it has coincided with a contraction of employment in manufacturing industry (Table 9.2.2).

It has been argued in various quarters that the creation of service jobs could ameliorate the regional impact of deindustrialisation (see De Groot, Foy and Pearson, 1987). Indeed, it was with this view in mind that exportable services were incorporated into mainstream regional assistance in the 1984 revisions of regional industrial policy. However, the significance of service activities is only partly expressed in terms of their contribution to employment growth. The growth of employment in services underlines the fact that parts of the service sector can be an important engine of growth in the economy, contributing directly to regional exports (Polese, 1982). There has also been a deepening of the relationship between the service and manufacturing sectors such that the performance of the latter may be heavily dependent on the local service input (Marshall and Green, 1990). Services are clearly, therefore, a critical part of the supply capacity of regional economies (Wood, 1986; 1991).

Table 9.2.1. Employment Changes in Great Britain, 1861–1988

	Percentage of Total Employment in Service Industries
1861	28
1871	31
1881	33
1891	35
1901	35
1911	36
1921	41
1931	49
1951	46
1961	49
1971	53
1981	62
1988	69

Source: Thrift and Daniels (1987) & Department of Employment Gazette

* This paper draws upon work by the author carried out as part of a Centre for Urban and Regional Development Studies (CURDS) review of regional and sub-regional disparities for the DTI. The author wishes to acknowledge the advice and comments received from other members of CURDS.

Table 9.2.2. Employment Change by Sector in Great Britain, 1971–88 (thousands)

	1971 Absolute	Percent	1988 Absolute	Percent	Change Absolute	Percent
Manufacturing	7890	36.4	4995	23.1	-2.895	-36.7
Services	11388	52.6	14872	68.8	+3.484	+30.6
Other	2370	10.9	1741	8.1		
	21648	100	21607	100	-41	-0.2

Source: Department of Employment Gazette

Unfortunately, in Britain the growing prominence of services in the economy at large has been associated with a spatially uneven distribution of growth. The employment performance of the South East region improved during the 1980s relative to other regions largely as a consequence of the growth of service jobs, and vibrant growth in service activities has also occurred in regions adjacent to the South East, most notably East Anglia. This has largely reinforced the existing concentration of economic activity in the South of the country (Tables 9.2.3 and 9.2.4). Although the present recesion recession has arrested this drift to the South, it is not yet clear if this is more than a temporary phenomenon. It is also worth noting in passing that the position is somewhat different elsewhere in Western Europe, where the growth of service employment has been much more spatially decentralised (see Illeris, 1989; 1991).

PROBLEMS OF ANALYSIS

The growing prominence of services in regional economies has not been fully reflected in the literature on urban and regional development. Definitional and classificatory problems, as well as inadequacies in the statistical data base also cloud analysis (Allen, 1988a; Watts, 1987). To explore the dynamics of growth in service activities, and to understand the contribution of this growth to reinforcing spatial disparities in the economy it is necessary, first, to disaggregate service activities to explore the different processes underlying locational trends (Allen, 1988b; Daniels, 1985; Daniels and Thrift, 1987; Marshall et al, 1988); second, to appreciate the interdependence of services and other sectors of the economy (Wood, 1986; 1990) and, third, to recognise the differential regional effect of government policies towards the liberalisation of markets on the location of service activities.

Table 9.2.3. Employment Change in Service Industries by Region in Great Britain, 1971–88 (000S)

	Absolute Change	Percentage Change
South East	1239	27
East Anglia	219	69
South East	365	49
East Midlands	360	65
West Midlands	332	37
Yorkshire/Humberside	342	40
North West	163	12
North	141	24
Wales	97	21
Scotland	239	23

Source: Department of Employment Gazette

Table 9.2.4. Percentage Regional Employment Change in Service Industries, 1981–84

	1971–78				1978–81				1981-84			
	Pro	Con	Pub	Tot	Pro	Con	Pub	Tot	Pro	Con	Pub	Tot
SE	5.7	7.4	9.2	7.4	5.4	5.1	-2.2	2.9	4.8	4.5	3.8	4.4
E Ang	30.8	22.5	17.0	22.3	8.1	4.3	1.8	4.7	15.7	7.7	4.3	9.5
SW	33.6	33.0	25.2	30.2	6.7	3.5	-1.1	2.7	12.4	2.2	-1.8	4.3
W Mid	13.4	10.4	19.1	14.5	2.0	6.6	-2.7	1.8	13.3	2.7	-1.8	4.7
E Mid	27.2	28.3	38.0	31.6	5.4	8.5	-7.4	1.4	7.8	5.2	7.0	6.7
Y/H	11.4	22.1	22.9	19.4	6.0	-1.0	-3.2	0.1	10.5	4.5	-2.2	4.3
NW	-2.7	11.4	16.0	8.4	2.6	3.5	-4.7	0.3	-1.9	1.0	-1.6	-0.9
North	10.3	10.5	12.4	11.2	-2.2	0	-6.3	-2.9	7.7	-2.1	6.0	3.3
Wales	5.7	21.8	22.3	18.0	1.4	2.4	-1.0	0.9	4.5	1.9	-7.9	-1.5
Scot	4.6	14.4	18.3	13.1	3.7	4.6	2.5	3.6	5.8	-1.0	-4.5	-0.1
N Ire	8.2	18.6	42.4	26.6	-0.3	5.7	8.3	6.0	-	-	-	-
UK/GB	8.6	14.2	17.2	13.5	4.4	4.2	-2.1	2.0	6.3	2.9	0.6	3.4

Notes:

Pro= Producer Services
Con= Consumer Services
Pub= Public Services
Tot= Total

The definitions are those used by the Producer Services Working Party, see Marshall et al (1988).

Source: Marshall (1989b)

FINANCIAL AND BUSINESS SERVICES

The growth of financial and business services have been at the leading edge of the growth in service employment (Marshall et al, 1988). Changes in markets, the increasing technological sophistication of the production process and the growing contribution of services to business competitiveness have fuelled a strong demand for financial and business services (frequently labelled producer services) (Petit, 1986; Ochel and Wegner, 1987; Rajan and Pearson, 1986; Rajan, 1984; 1987).

Financial services have played a key part in this growth. Spurred on by government policies designed to create an open international market for financial services, foreign institutions have expanded in London. Despite concern over the impact of some of the provisions of the Financial Services Act the position of London as a global financial centre has been enhanced. The removal of exchange controls and restrictions on consumer credit, the abolition of the corset, new personal pension and health care arrangements, as well as a number of changes in taxation have fuelled a one off expansion of financial services (Hutton, 1991). Deregulation in financial services has also promoted competition between institutions such as the banks, building societies, insurance companies and estate agents, and this has encouraged innovation, but it has also produced, more recently, overcapacity and nationalisation.

Thrift, Daniels and Leyshon (1988) and Leyshon and Thrift (1989) indicate the scale of employment growth in financial services in major provincial financial centres. But the principle growth of financial services associated with the circulation of capital and the provision of corporate services has been funnelled through the City of London (Marshall and Gentle, 1992). Between 1981 and 1987 61,000 jobs were created in the financial sector in the capital, three times as many as in the previous decade. This, of course, has had substantial multiplier effects on a host of related accounting, legal and property services (Rajan and Frytt, 1989) (Figure 9.2.1), and has been an important factor behind the resurgence in the capital's economy in the 1980s (Thrift, Leyshon and

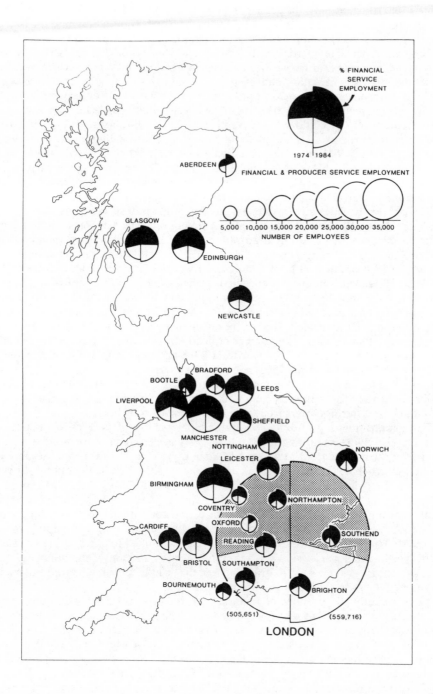

Figure 9.2.1: *Expansion of financial and producer service employment in provincial financial centres, 1974–1984 (Source: Leyshon and Thrift, 1989)*

Daniels 1987). Increasingly, the growth in London encouraged spatial decentralisation of back office and head office administration to the Greater South East, and the fastest rates of financial service employment growth in the country were recorded in places such as Letchworth, Haywards Heath, Basingstoke, Peterborough and Milton Keynes.

A related complex of large firm head offices close to Greater London, which contains substantial numbers of senior managerial staff, and has strong associated links with the local specialist supply sector, underpins the concentration of services such as consultancy, advertising and marketing in the Greater South East (Crum and Gudgin, 1977; Goddard, 1979; Goddard and Smith, 1978). Organisations supply the latter services to their clients on a national and increasingly international basis through a network of offices located in major national and regional centres (Marshall, 1983; Marshall et al, 1988). This works to the disadvantage of peripheral regions such as the North East of England because their demands are frequently serviced from regional capitals outside the area such as Manchester and Leeds (Marshall, 1983).

The last two decades have witnessed a reorganisation of service provision within large companies. Parallelling the decentralisation of financial services there has been a significant decentralisation of head offices from London. Spiralling rental levels, labour shortages and congestion problems in the capital encouraged relocation. The capital lost 50 headquarters from among the *Times Top 500* companies between 1971 and 1988. However, London continues to dominate as a head office centre with 54 per cent of the total *Times Top 500* company headquarters. Indeed, London's position as a control centre has remained untouched by the change. The 271 head offices remaining in London in 1988 controlled 74 per cent of the turnover of the Top 500 companies, slightly more than in 1971. The number of head offices in provincial centres outside the South and East declined (from 132 to 119) between 1971 and 1988, but the major change outside London in the 1980s has been the emergence of the M4 corridor as an important head office centre. Slough, Reading, Basingstoke and Bracknell are all now important head office centres on a par with Leeds or Edinburgh, and together in 1988 accounted for 28 headquarters from among the Top 500 companies.

The composition of the administration and support functions carried out by large firms has also changed during the last two decades as firms have rationalised in-house services and contracted out to the specialist supply sector. The details of this change are subject to debate (Marshall, 1989a), and the issue is clouded by the rigidly sectoral character of official statistics. The view taken here is that, during the 1970s and early 1980s, corporate reorganisation favoured the Greater South East. The steep decline in manufacturing in the Midlands and North of the country had a major impact on non-production work in manufacturing and on the related specialist supply sector (Harris, 1987). Though the specialist supply sector continued to grow for regions such as the North and North West, when account is taken of the contracting out of existing in-house services from manufacturing, little of the growth appears to be additional to the respective regional economies (Marshall, 1989b).

More recently the position of financial and business services in the provincial regions has improved. For example, Marshall (1988) and Marshall and Green (1990) document significant growth of business services in a number of provincial centres including Birmingham, Wolverhampton, Edinburgh, Newcastle, Leeds and Bradford; though growth remains strongest in the Outer South East and in adjacent Standard Regions, especially East Anglia and the West Midlands (Table 9.2.4).

There are a number of mechanisms behind this growth. First, the resurgence of manufacturing industry in the regions since the 1980s' recession. Second, more decentralised business structures have led to a reduction in the size of head offices, and possibly encouraged the development of in-house services adjacent to production sites, and facilitated stronger business links with the local service sector. Third, there have been opportunities for local service companies to take a larger share of the growing regional market in those spheres where major City based institutions have become preoccupied by the growth of national and international business. Fourth, the growth of the financial sector in London has fuelled relocation; financial back office, computer and even head office functions have been moved to the Outer South East, and Midlands. Fifth, major provincial conurbations such as Manchester, Leeds and Bristol have also gained from a reorganisation of large financial institutions, including the expansion of their regional offices (though it should be recognised that some of the functions presently located at regional offices were formerly provided by the local branch network elsewhere within the regions. It must also be noted that the multiplier effect of the financial sector is less strong in the provinces than the capital).

CONSUMER SERVICES

Consumer services supplying leisure, recreation and tourism markets have grown rapidly in the last two decades, but in consumer services as a whole, this growth is counteracted by employment declines in petrol stations, food retailing and a variety of small shops. Traditionally consumer services have been regarded as fairly evenly distributed across the country in relation to population and income levels. However, it has been increasingly recognised that the relationship between consumer service growth and local income and expenditure is becoming more complex (Marshall, 1989b). During the 1980s a number of urban initiatives have sought to develop local provision in a range of media, arts, tourism, recreation and leisure activities, and to use these activities as a catalyst in urban regeneration. Examples include the Albert Dock, Tate Gallery and Beatles museum developments in Liverpool; the Convention Centre, Symphony Orchestra complex and the National Ballet developments in Birmingham, as well as the Metro Centre and the adjacent Garden Festival site on Tyneside. These initiatives seek to encourage people to spend more of their money locally, to enhance the image of the area making it attractive to new businesses and tourists, as well as improving confidence in the local area and increasing the involvement of residents in the community.

There have been few economic assessments of the impact of such urban regeneration initiatives (Audit Commission, 1989; Myerscough, 1988), and studies are hampered by the intangible nature of the wider impacts. However, there does seem to be some scope for local proactivity in developing consumer service provision in less-favoured regions (European Economic Development Services, 1990). There is concern, though, that initiatives are encouraging 'old problems', such as the expansion of external ownership and control in consumer services (Robins, 1989). It must also be remembered that the 1980s were a uniquely favourable period for such initiatives because a substantial growth of personal disposable income, a decline in personal savings and an explosion of credit were all fuelling consumption. Such conditions do not prevail in the more stringent early 1990s.

Furthermore, notwithstanding the achievements of urban regeneration initiatives, a key fact which stands out from an analysis of the 1980s is that the decade was characterised by a spatially uneven growth of consumer service employment. Regions such as East Anglia, the South East and the East Midlands which witnessed the main growth of business-related services were also characterised by strong growth in consumer service employment. In contrast, the Northern region, for example, actually experienced a decline in consumer services between 1978 and 1984 (Table 9.2.4).

During the 1980s the benefits of the growth in consumer incomes were substantially experienced in the Greater South East. A combination of regional differences in the impact of the recession and recovery, spatial variations in wages growth and geographical variations in the impact of reductions in direct taxation promoted an uneven growth of personal disposable income and ultimately consumer service employment. A further major factor has been the effect of inheritance -the Greater South East, unlike much of the North, experienced substantial growth in homeownership during the 1930s at a time of low population birth rate. Much of this wealth, capitalised in housing, was passed on to a generation who already owned their own houses and whose children have left home. Much of this wealth passed directly into local consumption of services in the Greater South East, or into savings managed by local financial institutions established there. In contrast, in much of the North, the limited wealth available through inheritance suggests that service sector led urban regeneration may have not only contributed to limited employment growth but also to local displacement effects. However, the 1990s have not been so depressing with lower investment in housing in the North meaning that consumer spending has been more resilient to high interest rates.

THE PUBLIC SECTOR

Despite the fact that there has been little recent research on this subject, the public sector remains a major employer in the regions, its location there having been encouraged by a deliberate policy to relocate central government work away from London and a generally relaxed attitude during the 1950s and 1960s towards the growth of central and local government expenditure and employment. However, the present government's attempts to control the growth of the civil service, and expenditure constraints on local authorities have restricted the growth of public services everywhere. Privatisation of public utilities, a more managerial approach towards the running of public sector organisations and competitive tendering and associated contracting out have influenced both the growth and the location of public services.

While local authority manpower is linked to the distribution of population, civil service employment is concentrated in a relatively small number of local labour markets, and these are areas which are coming to depend critically on the fate of particular departments (Marshall, 1990). Manpower and budgetary constraints on the civil service have been associated with major employment declines in London, Newcastle, Edinburgh, Cardiff, Manchester, Leeds, Nottingham and Portsmouth (Table 9.2.5). The consequences of this reduction in civil service employment are particularly severe in provincial conurbations because the public sector is a more significant component of the local economy than elsewhere. However, employment decline is not ubiquitous in provincial centres, with Sheffield experiencing employment growth associated with the expansion of the Employment Group.

In the last few years civil service relocation has returned to the political agenda, as a consequence of cost pressures and recruitment problems in the the capital. However, in 1989 the economics of relocation favoured a broad belt of the country roughly between 80 and 170 miles from London. Further north the cost savings in salaries and rental levels achieved through relocation from Central London was eroded by the extra communication costs in a more peripheral location (Marshall, Alderman and Thwaites, 1991). Traditionally these costs have been reduced by decentralising self-contained

Table 9.2.5. Employment Change in the Main Locations for
non-industrial Civil Service Staff, 1979–1987

Administrative	Change 1979–87		Total
			Employees 1987
District	Absolute	% Change	
London	- 19 013	-14.1	116 012
Newcastle	- 4 055	- 23.1	13 481
Edinburgh	- 1 333	- 9.6	12 557
Glasgow	+ 58	+ 0.5	11 429
Cardiff	- 1 419	- 13.7	8 904
Birmingham	- 349	- 4.0	8 410
Plymouth	- 393	- 5.2	7 162
Manchester	- 2 339	- 25.1	6 979
Liverpool	- 866	- 11.5	6 634
Leeds	- 1 061	- 13.9	6 592
Sefton	+ 1 098	+ 21.7	6 159
Swansea	- 687	- 10.5	5 879
Bristol	- 578	- 9.1	5 804
Bath	- 838	- 13.5	5 369
Blackpool	- 49	- 1.0	4 921
Sheffield	+ 1 760	+ 56.9	4 855
Portsmouth	- 2 206	- 32.6	4 552
Durham	+ 568	+ 14.9	4 375
Southampton	- 843	- 16.8	4 161
Nottingham	- 1 352	- 24.6	4 141
Southend	- 874	- 17.4	4 069

Source: Marshall (1990)

blocks of clerical work. However, the recent round of relocations included a fuller range of functions, as a consequence of the intense cost pressures on the civil service in London.

The future of the civil service in the regions will also be shaped by the introduction of the new agency structure proposed in the Ibbs Report. It is likely that the reductions in costs required of agencies and other civil service departments and associated labour productivity improvements will continue to hold back civil service employment growth. The reorganisation of the major blocks of clerical work (decentralised to the regions in previous rounds of civil service dispersal) by the introduction of more distributed computer processing at the customer interface, could also mitigate against a further expansion of back office civil service employment in provincial cities. However, for selected locations the relocation of civil service work will counteract such trends. This is especially likely should relocation and reorganisation of the civil service interact, with relocation being used, as in the case of the DSS/DHS relocation to Leeds, to reinforce the separation of management and policy-making functions. However, on balance, it is unlikely that the most northerly regions will benefit much from this trend.

CONCLUSION

The over-representation of service activities in the hinterland of London, and the concentration of service growth in the southern half of the country, have made an important contribution towards the widening of regional disparities during the latter 1970s and 1980s. They have skewed job creation towards the more prosperous regions rather than locations of manufacturing decline. Furthermore, the skills of managerial and technical staff within business and the quality and range of their local financial and business service suppliers are significant influences on the competitiveness and capacity for successful adjustment to change of local industry. It follows, therefore, that the continued under-representation of service activities in less favoured regions is an important constraint on the ability of such areas to sustain economic growth.

Nevertheless, the current recession and associated high interests rates has taken the steam out of the finance-led growth in the economy, and this has for the forseeable future ameliorated the drift south of that sector. But at the same time the pressures that have pushed private and public office relocation ever further North during the 1980s have also abated. The 'choking off' of the Lawson-Thatcher boom at the end of the 1980s has truncated the participation of the North in that phase of growth.

REFERENCES

Allen, J. (1988a) 'Service industries: uneven development and uneven knowledge', *Area*, 20: 15–22.

Allen, J. (1988b) 'The geographies of service' in Massey D and J Allen (ed) *Uneven Re-Development*, London: Hodder Stoughton.

Audit Commission (1989) *Urban Regeneration and Economic Development: The Local Government Dimension*, London: HMSO.

Crum, R.E. and Gudgin, G. (1977) *Non-production Activities in UK Manufacturing Industry*, Regional Policy Series 3, Brussels: Commission of the European Economic Communities.

Daniels, P.W. (1985) *Service Industries: A Geographical Appraisal*, London: Methuen.

Daniels, P. and Thrift, N. (1987) 'The geographies of the UK service sector' *Working Papers on Producer Services No 6*, Service Industries Research Centre, Portsmouth Polytechnic.

De Groot, L., Foy, M. and Pearson, P. (1987) 'Service Employment Means Real Jobs,' *Local Economy*, 2, 55–59.

European Economic Development Services (1990) *Potential Economic Benefits arising from the Development of the Arts in Newcastle upon Tyne*, Wylam, Tyne and Wear: European Economic Development Services Ltd.

Gillespie, A. and Green, A. (1987) The changing geography of producer service employment in Britain, *Regional Studies*, 21, 397–411.

Goddard, J.B. (1979) 'Office location in urban and regional development', in Daniels, P.W. (ed) *Spatial Patterns of Office Growth and Location,*London: Wiley.

Goddard, J.B. and Smith, I.J. (1978) 'Change in corporate control in the British urban system, 1972–77', *Environment and Planning A*, 10, 1073–1084.

Harris, R.I.D. (1987) 'The role of manufacturing in regional growth', *Regional Studies*, 301–312.

Howells, J. (1988) *Economic, Technological and Locational Trends in European Services*, Aldershot: Gower.

Howells, J. (1989) 'Externalisation and the formation of new industrial operations: a neglected dimension in the dynamics of industrial location', *Area*, 21, 289–299.

Howells, J. and Green, A. (1988) *Technological Innovation, Structural Change and Location in UK Services*. Aldershot: Gower.

Hutton, W. (1991) *Good Housekeeping: How to Manage Credit and Debt*, Economic Study Number 9, London: Institute for Public Policy Research.

Illeris, S. (1989) *Services and the Regions in Europe*, Aldershot, Hants: Gower.

Illeris, S. (1991) The many roads towards a service society, *Norsk Geografisk Tidsskift*, 45, 2–9.

Leyshon, A. and Thrift, N. (1989) 'South goes North? The rise of the provincial British financial centre', in Lewis, J. and A. Townsend (ed) *The North-South Divide*, London: Chapman.

Marshall, J.N. (1983) 'Business service activities in British provincial conurbations' *Environment and Planning A*, 25: 1434–60.

Marshall, J.N. (1989a) 'corporate reorganisation and the geography of services: evidence from the motor vehicle aftermarket in the west midlands region of the UK', *Regional Studies*, 23, 139–150.

Marshall, J.N. (1989b) 'Private Services in an Era of Change', *Geoforum*, 20 (3): 365–379.

Marshall, J.N. (1990) 'Reorganising the British Civil Service: how are the regions being served?' *Area,* 22.3, 246–255.

Marshall, J.N., Alderman, N., and Thwaites, A.T. (1991) Civil service relocation and the English regions, *Regional Studies,* 25, 499–510.

Marshall, J.N. and Gentle, C. (1992) Regulatory change, corporate restructuring and the spatial development of financial services *Regional Studies* (forthcoming)

Marshall, J.N. and Green, A. (1990) 'Business reorganisation and the uneven development of corporate services in the British urban and regional system', *Transactions of the IBG,* 15,162–176.

Marshall, J.N. et al (1988) *Services and Uneven Development,* Oxford:Oxford University Press.

Myerscough, J. (1988) *The Economic Importance of the Arts in Britain,* London: Marton.

Ochel, W. and Wegner, M. (1987) 'The role and determinants of services in Europe', Occasional Paper 132, *FAST,* Brussels: Commission of the European Communities.

Petit, P. (1986) *Slow Growth and the Service Economy,* London: Frances Pinter.

Polese, M. (1982) 'Regional demand for business services and interregional service flows in a small Canadian region', *Papers of the Regional Science Association,* 50: 151–63.

Rajan, A. (1984) *New Technology and Employment in Insurance, Banking and Building Societies: Recent Experience and Future Impact,* Aldershot, Hants: Gower.

Rajan, A. (1987) *Services: a New Industrial Revolution?,* London; Butterworth.

Rajan, A. and Frytt, J. (1989) *Create or Abdicate: The City's Human Resource Choice,* London: Wetherby and Co.

Rajan, A. and Pearson, R. (1986) *UK Occupation and Employment Trends to 1990,* London: Butterworth.

Robins K (1989) 'Reimagined communities', *Cultural Studies,* 3, 145–165.

Thrift, N., Daniels, P. and Leyshon, A. (1988) *Location Behaviour of Large Professional Producer Service Firms in Britain,* Report to ESRC, London.

Thrift, N., Leyson, A. and Daniels, P. (1987) 'Sexy Greedy: The New International Financial System, the City of London and the South East of England' *Working Paper on Producer Services No.8,* Service Industries Research Centre, Portsmouth Polytechnic.

Watts, H.D. (1987) 'Producer services, industrial location and uneven development', *Area,* 19: 353–355.

Wood, P. (1986) 'The anatomy of job loss and job creation: some speculation on the role of the producer service sector', *Regional Studies,* 20, 37–46.

Wood, P. (1990) An integrated view of the economic role of services, in Teare, R. and Morgan, N. *Managing and Marketing Services in the 1990s,* London, Cassell.

Wood, P. (1991) Flexible accumulation and the rise of business services, *Transactions of the IBG,* 16,160–177

The Urban/Rural Shift

A. R. Townsend and A. G. Champion

URBAN/RURAL SHIFT AND NORTH-SOUTH DIVIDE

The Urban/Rural Shift in population and employment is a well-known feature of the US and the UK in the 1960s and 1970s and has been identified in a number of other developed countries (Champion, 1989). The general acceptance of the thesis of Fothergill and Gudgin (1982), that employment trends, particularly in manufacturing, varied systematically between heavy decline in London and the conurbations and growth in rural areas, sits oddly, at first sight, with the traditional RSA regional structure of Part II of this volume.

There were, however, sound reasons for paying prime attention to regional trends in much of the 1980s. The recession conditions of 1980 to 1982 and their aftermath restricted the opportunities for new investment and migration of population and thus appeared to restrain the central mechanisms of the Urban/Rural Shift. Work by Champion and Green (1989) at Local Labour Market level showed that 'North/South' differences had emerged more strongly in the 1980s relative to Urban/Rural trends.

The two dimensions were not, however, irreconcilable. It is possible that *both* are strengthening in their effects, if growth was concentrated more in the Rural 'South', and the worst conditions were focussed in the Urban 'North', i.e. in conurbations such as Clydeside, Tyne and Wear and Merseyside (longstanding foci of regional policy) and in Intermediate Areas such as Sheffield and Birmingham. A major ingredient of change was the levelling out of population and employment decline in London itself. This recovery in London's population change rate cannot be put down to a single demographic or economic factor, although relevant hypotheses must include the growth of financial sector jobs, the rundown of slum clearance and overspill programmes, and possibly trends in the birth rates of ethnic groups (Champion and Congdon, 1988).

Population and employment trends must clearly interact in a variety of ways. A comprehensive new review of the two variables had to await the availability of results of the 1987 Census of Employment in September, 1989, which may be most fully compared with data for 1981. The tables which follow have utilised on the National Online Manpower Information System (University of Durham) the classification of districts of England and Wales for OPCS (VS No.14/PP1 No.10, HMSO, 1989), extended to include Scotland by the present authors. This is a different geographical framework from that used by Fothergill and Gudgin (1982), and has some defects, most notably that these administrative units do not correspond exactly with the functional realities of the urban system and associated travel-to-work areas (Champion et al, 1984; Champion et al 1987, Chapter 1). Nevertheless, in aggregate the classification captures a substantial proportion of the between-place variation in urban status, demographic structure and socio-economic character.

POPULATION AND EMPLOYMENT TRENDS

Some key features of recent population and employment trends are shown in Table 9.3.1. This allocates the OPCS district types into four broader groupings, which in turn are divided between the 'North' and 'South' of Great Britain. Between 1971 and 1981, the 'large cities' reduced in population by ten per cent, and the 'remoter, mainly rural' areas expanded by that amount, with a fairly systematic spread of figures for other areas in between.

In the period 1981 to 1988, the range of population outcomes was narrower even allowing for the fact that the data relate only to a seven year period as opposed to a full decade. Trends were more moderate for most types of district, the main exceptions being the marked acceleration in the growth of 'resort, port and retirement' districts and the more rapid depopulation of 'other metropolitan districts'. The population data therefore suggests a weaker urban-rural shift in the 1980s than in the previous decade.

Employment trends for 1981 to 1987 exhibit a wider range across urban-rural types than those of population, 1981 to 1988. Across the country as a whole, 'large cities' and 'industrial districts' saw more rapid declines of employees in employment than in population, while 'prosperous sub-regions' experienced more rapid growth of employment than of population. Only for 'remoter, mainly rural' areas were the two rates relatively evenly matched.

The Urban/Rural Shift is also evident within the South and North separately. While for all four types, the southern representatives were in a stronger position than their northern counterparts, both halves of Britain exhibit clear urban-rural gradients for both population and employment change in the 1980s. It can also be seen that employment change was more positive than population change in only two cases, namely the southern 'prosperous sub regions' and the southern 'remoter, mainly rural' areas. Elsewhere in the South,and for all four types in the North, the ratio between total population and total employees deteriorated over this period, with particularly severe effects on the 'large cities' and 'industrial districts' of the North.

How does the Urban/Rural Shift of employment of the 1980s compare in magnitude with the range of performance of individual standard regions? The range of performance across nine district types in Table 9.3.1 extends from a decline of 8.7 per cent in 'principal cities' (Glasgow, Newcastle, Leeds, Sheffield, Manchester, Liverpool and Birmingham) to an average increase of 7.1 per cent in 'urban & mixed urban/rural' (for example, Shrewsbury, Huntingdon, Horsham Districts). In other data the range of performance among ten standard regions varied between the extremes of a 5.5 per cent decline in Scotland and an increase of 8.6 per cent in East Anglia. In all, the range of variation was of 14.1 percentage points among regions compared with 15.8 points among district types. When all allowances are made for the arbitrary content of both classifications, we may say that Urban/Rural variation was certainly no less than inter-regional variation. To some extent, of course, the two dimensions are inter-related since the North is more weighted towards larger cities and industrial districts and the South towards smaller urban centres and rural areas. This raises a leading question, whether the underlying causes are more regional or urban-rural in their pattern of operation.

THE IMPORTANCE OF 'DIFFERENTIAL SHIFTS'

In the past the proponents of Urban/Rural shift stressed that it was largely independent of industrial structure (Fothergill and Gudgin, 1982). This appeared to remain true in the 1980s. In Table 9.3.2, employment changes for 1981 to 1987 by district type

Table 9.3.1 Population Change, 1971–88, and Employment Change, 1981–87 by District Types, Great Britain

District type	Population 1988 000s	Population change 1971–81 000s	Population change 1971–81 %	Population change 1981–1988 000s	Population change 1981–1988 %	Employment 1987 000s	Change 1981–87 000s	Change 1981–87 %
Large cities	10,865	−1,292	−10.4	−264	−2.4	5,452	−240	−4.2
London (South)	6,735	−724	−9.6	−70	−1.0	3,506	−54	−1.5
Other principal cities (North)	4,130	−569	−11.6	−194	−4.5	1,946	−186	−8.7
Industrial	16,021	+102	+0.6	−122	−0.8	5,464	−185	−3.3
South	2,676	+119	+4.8	+65	+2.5	1,022	+11	+1.1
North	13,344	−16	−0.1	−186	−1.4	4,442	−196	−4.2
Other metropolitan districts	8,572	−125	−1.4	−130	−1.5	2,888	−140	−4.6
Industrial areas	7,448	+227	+3.2	+8	+0.1	2,576	−44	−1.7
Prosperous sub-regions	22,182	+1,059	+5.2	+690	+3.2	8,465	+310	+3.8
South	14,975	+826	+6.1	+601	+4.2	5,666	+324	+6.1
North	7,207	+233	+3.4	+89	+1.3	2,799	−13	−0.5
Non-metropolitan cities	5,431	−171	−3.0	−126	−2.3	2,826	−3	−0.1
Districts with New Towns	2,821	+351	+15.1	+137	+5.1	1,079	+43	+4.2
Resort, port & retirement	3,611	+185	+5.8	+242	+7.2	1,105	+42	+3.9
Urban & mixed urban\rural	10,319	+693	+7.5	+437	+4.4	3,455	+229	+7.1
Remoter, mainly rural	6,419	+558	+10.2	+368	+6.1	1,897	+90	+5.0
South	3,596	+341	+11.4	+248	+7.4	1,102	+74	+7.2
North	2,823	+217	+8.7	+121	+4.5	795	+16	+2.1
Great Britain	55,486	+427	+0.8	+673	+1.3	21,271	−41	−0.2
South	27,982	+562	+2.1	+843	+3.1	11,275	+339	+3.1
North	27,505	−135	−0.5	−170	−0.6	9,996	−380	−3.7

Notes: Due to rounding certain items do not sum to column totals;
'South' comprises the South East, South West, East Anglia and East Midlands; 'North' the rest of Great Britain.

Sources: OPCS, NOMIS

are subjected to shift-share analysis in the 'South' and the 'North'. That part of total change which is not accounted for by each industry performing at its national rate in each area is identified as the 'differential shift'. For instance, in Outer London, this shift would account for a 5.2 per cent reduction of employment, when national structure would have predicted an increase of 1.7 per cent. In all, the differential shift column demonstrates changes of the same general magnitude as 'total' change; that is to say that most variations on the Urban/Rural spectrum are occurring independently of the inherited industrial structure of the area groupings.

Table 9.3.2. Employment Trends by District Type, Percentage Change, 1981–1987

	South		North	
	Total	Differential Shift	Total	Differential Shift
Large Cities				
Inner London	- 0.0	- 9.2	-	-
Outer London	- 3.5	- 5.2	-	-
Other metropolitan cities	-	-	- 8.7	- 9.2
Industrial				
Other metropolitan districts	-	-	- 4.6	- 0.4
Industrial areas	+ 1.1	+ 6.3	- 3.5	+ 2.8
Prosperous sub-regions				
Non-metropolitan cities	+ 1.3	+ 0.6	- 1.9	- 3.7
Districts with New Towns	+ 8.8	+ 10.7	- 0.5	+ 4.8
Resort, port & retirement districts	+ 5.1	+ 3.3	- 0.3	- 2.7
Urban & mixed urban-rural districts	+ 8.8	+ 8.0	+ 1.8	+ 2.5
Rural				
Remoter, mainly rural districts	+ 7.2	+ 7.8	+ 2.1	+ 2.7
Total, Great Britain	+ 3.1	+ 1.5	- 3.7	- 1.5

Shift-Share Analysis conducted at the level of the 58 Classes of the Standard Industrial Classification 1980 on Census of the Employment data (NOMIS)

Looking at Table 9.3.2 in more detail, it is found that in the South, some of the largest departures occurred in Inner London, where a balance which was theoretically favourable, due to the weight of business and general services and finance, was offset by widespread differential shifts. In 'industrial areas' of the South, there were positive differential shifts in most sectors of the economy. In the North, much of the decline in 'other metropolitan districts' lay in structural dependence on manufacturing and mining. In 'industrial areas', the structural effects of heavy industry, engineering and mining were offset by positive shifts in mechanical engineering and most non-metal using sectors. The Northern New Towns suffered from an adverse industrial structure but gained from the attraction of a wide range of sectors. The important point is that there were negative differential shifts in the most urban areas, in London and in cities and metropolitan areas of the North, combined with positive differential shifts in the rural and mixed urban-rural areas, together with 'resort, port and retirement districts' of the South.

Table 9.3.3. Employment Trends by District Types, Percentage Change, 1981–4, 1984–7

	South		North	
	1981–4	*1984–7*	*1981–4*	*1984–7*
Large Cities				
Inner London	- 1.0	+ 0.9	-	-
Outer London	- 5.1	+ 1.7	-	-
Other principle cities	-	-	- 7.3	- 1.6
Industrial				
Other metropolitan districts	-	-	- 5.4	+ 0.8
Industrial areas		- 2.3	+ 3.5	- 4.9
Prosperous sub-regions				
Non-metropolitan cities	- 0.7	+ 2.0	- 3.2	+ 1.4
Districts with New Towns	+ 2.9	+ 5.8	- 2.6	+ 2.1
Resort, port & retirement districts	+ 1.0	+ 4.1	- 5.0	+ 4.9
Urban & mixed urban-rural districts	+ 3.9	+ 4.7	- 0.9	+ 2.7
Rural				
Remoter, mainly rural districts	+ 2.9	+ 4.1	- 0.3	+ 2.3
Total, Great Britain	+ 0.8	+ 3.0	- 4.6	+ 1.0

Source: NOMIS

CHANGES IN TOTAL EMPLOYMENT DURING THE 1980s

The dynamic nature of the 1980s resulting largely from the recovery of national employment levels from their low point of 1983, can be seen from a comparison of the two periods between Employment Censuses. Thus, the period 1981 to 1984 saw a 2.2 per cent reduction in national (GB) employment, with a strongly significant contrast between the South East and East Anglia on the one hand and the 'North', particularly the North West, on the other. The years from 1984 to 1987, however, saw a national increase of 2.0 per cent, with *less* significant contrasts at large, the most important lying between the South West and Scotland. In terms of our Urban/Rural types of district (Table 9.3.3), this transition saw a quickening of the rural growth of employment, as of population; the most significant contrast remained between 'principal cities' outside London (all in the North) and the 'urban and mixed urban/rural' areas of the South.

Even so, differences between district types were much less strong in the period of general recovery between 1984 and 1987, than in the aftermath of recession in 1981-84. Table 9.3.3 shows how, in the South, a mixed pattern of growth and decline in 1981-84 was turned into employment gains in every district type between 1984 and 1987. Even more dramatically, decline in every district type of the North from 1981-84 was replaced by growth everywhere except the principal cities (Glasgow etc.). The effect of this recovery was actually to damp down the Urban/Rural Shift; differences within columns for 1984-87 are less than for 1981-84.

MANUFACTURING IN THE 1980s

In relating these findings to established writing in the field, it is necessary to consider the manufacturing sector, which showed the most consistent Urban/Rural Shift in the 1960s and early 1970s. Table 9.3.4 demonstrates that in considering manufacturing we are essentially dealing now with variations in levels of employment *decline*, both in the

Table 9.3.4. Manufacturing employment trends by district type, Percentage change, 1981–4, 1984–7

	South				North			
	1981–4		1984–7		1981–4		1984–7	
	Total	Differential Shift	Total	Differential Shift	Total	Differential Shift	Total	Differential Shift
Large Cities								
Inner London	-14.9	-6.4	-20.5	-18.8	-	-	-	-
Outer London	-18.2	-6.9	-11.7	-8.2	-	-	-	-
Other principal cities	-	-	-	-	-20.5	-7.0	-10.1	-6.0
Industrial								
Other metropolitan cities	-	-	-	-	-15.9	-2.5	-2.9	+1.5
Industrial areas	-10.0	+1.9	+1.0	+3.8	-12.9	+0.2	+2.5	+8.0
Prosperous sub-regions								
Non-metropolitan cities	-10.5	+1.9	-8.1	-3.7	-9.7	+0.9	-6.1	-0.3
Districts with New Towns	-7.1	+4.0	-4.5	+0.2	-11.7	+1.9	+2.1	+6.4
Resort, port & retirement districts	-5.0	+5.4	-0.6	+2.8	-19.6	-8.1	+9.6	+14.7
Urban & mixed urban-rural districts	-4.2	+6.3	-3.4	+0.3	-8.2	+4.3	-4.1	+0.4
Rural								
Remoter, mainly rural districts	-3.2	+7.8	+0.1	+3.4	-5.9	+5.7	+3.9	+7.6
Great Britain	-9.3	+0.5	-5.8	-2.6	-13.4	-0.4	-2.6	+2.4

Shift-Share Analysis conducted at the level of individual classes 21–39 of the Standard Industrial Classification, 1980 on the Census of Employment data (NOMIS).

North and in the South, although there were some net gains of employment in the period 1984-87, more notably in the North than in the South. What remains striking, however, is a strong Urban/Rural gradient in terms of differential shifts. London and other principal cities showed negative shifts throughout, whereas the last four district types in the table all showed positive differential shifts in both periods with the sole exception of Northern resorts in 1981-84.

The urban-rural gradient is not consistent at this level of disaggregation. It is not generally true to say that differential shifts are more indicative of a greater urban-rural trend in 1984-87 than in the preceding three years. However, the evidence is that differential shifts contributed to a resumed urban-rural pattern of manufacturing job dispersal in this period. Space does not permit further comment on the causes of the pattern beyond reference to work such as Fothergill et al (1985). Viewed, however, in the wider context of labour and population trends, it is important to bear in mind the return of skill shortages in London and parts of the South East in the second part of the 1980s (see next section) and the very systematic nature of outward migration of population from cities to rural areas. The evidence of migration data derived from the National Health Service central register is that in most age groups the net flow of migrants from any one county has been firmly towards counties of lower population density.

CONCLUSION

The experience of individual district types is considered in Champion and Townsend (1990). Outline data from the Census of Employment, 1989 are now available. Over the two year period, September 1987 to 1989, prior to the current recession there were improvements in trends for all entries of Table 9.3.3 except for Inner and Outer London, and the northern 'resorts'. The 'remoter, mainly rural districts', which now have almost as high a proportion of workers in manufacturing as Britain as a whole, are not likely to make large net gains in total manufacturing employment. Multipliers from these gains, and the servicing of incoming migrants, are, however, seen as bases for employment growth in non-manufacturing sectors. The 'urban and mixed urban-rural districts' lie mainly in the South and profited increasingly from the dispersal and growth of financial offices: exemplars in the North are not seen to have a large enough population and economic base to contribute major economic growth to their respective regions. Districts with New Towns continued to achieve employment performances out of line with their neighbours. Structural effects may cause renewed employment reductions in Northern 'industrial areas' and 'other metropolitan districts', even where differential shifts are more moderate. The evidence suggests that 'other principal cities' are bound to suffer continued negative trends, while the 'recovery' of London itself is increasingly seen as a transitory phenomenon (Gordon, 1988; Law, 1988). The conclusion must be that Great Britain is undergoing both North-South and Urban-Rural differentiation of trends, and that regional studies must be constantly aware of this interplay.

Acknowledgements: to staff of the National Online Manpower Information System, University of Durham for the programming of Census of Employment data, and to Michael Blakemore for technical assistance in constructing files for district types

REFERENCES

Champion, A.G. (ed.) (1989) *Counterurbanization: The Changing Pace and Nature of Population Deconcentration,* London: Edward Arnold.

Champion, A.G., Coombes, M.G. and Openshaw, S. (1984) New regions for a new Britain, *Geographical Magazine* 56, 187-90.

Champion, A.G., Green, A.E., Owen, D.W., Ellin, D.J. and Coombes, M.G. (1987) *Changing Places: Britain's Demographic, Economic and Social Complexion* London: Edward Arnold.

Champion, A.G. and Congdon, P.D. (1988) An analysis of the recovery of London's population change rate, *Built Environment* 13, 193-211.

Champion, A.G. and Green, A.E. (1989) Local economic differentials and the north-south divide, in Lewis, J. and Townsend, A. (eds.) *The North-South Divide: Regional Change in Britain in the 1980s* (London: Paul Chapman), 61-96.

Champion, A.G. and Townsend, A.R. (1990) *Contemporary Britain: A Geographical Perspective,* London: Edward Arnold.

Fothergill, S. and Gudgin, G. (1982) *Unequal Growth: Urban and Regional Employment Change in the UK,* London: Heinemann.

Fothergill, S., Kitson, M. and Monk, S. (1985) *Urban Industrial Change: The Causes of the Urban-Rural Contrast in Manufacturing Employment Trends,* London: HMSO.

Gordon, I.R. (1988) Resurrecting counter-urbanisation: housing market influences on migration fluctuations from London, *Built Environment* 13, 212-22.

Law, C.M. et al (1988) *The Uncertain Future of the Urban Core* London: Routledge.

Public Expenditure, Public Employment and the Regions

J. Mohan

Public expenditure accounts for some 39 per cent of Britain's gross national product (GNP), and so its distribution might be expected to have considerable effects on the relative prosperity of the regions. The public sector also accounts for substantial numbers of jobs, and in some areas it is a key source of paid employment; regions such as North East England and South Wales have been termed 'state managed' (Hudson, 1988) or 'nationalized' (Cooke, 1987) regions, in that their economic prospects have become inextricably bound up with state policies and expenditures. But it would be unwise to focus solely on regions like the two cited, thus emphasising the state's direct role as an employer through the nationalised industries, because this would neglect the state's indirect role in supporting employment, through various 'hidden' subsidies and policies, which are also considered here.

PUBLIC EXPENDITURE

Relatively little is known about the overall regional incidence of public expenditure and taxation, apart from Short's (1981) work. No aggregate figures are available on the overall impacts of public spending by Standard Region, despite numerous calls for this (for instance Northern Region Strategy Team, 1977), but it is clear that some programmes, such as defence expenditures, are heavily concentrated into certain regions. The bias of defence procurement towards South East England has helped preserve that region's competitive advantage over the rest of the UK. Boddy and Lovering (1988) argue that the widening of the gap between 'North' and 'South' in the 1980s is related to 'the militarisation of the British economy'. Areas such as the M4 and M11 'corridors' and the outer South East in general (see Breheny et al, 1987) have benefited disproportionately from military expenditures, though defence industries are also prominent in the South West and North West of England and, more modestly, in Scotland. But Boddy and Lovering caution against the conclusion that defence expenditure is a hidden regional policy, because there is some dispute over whether defence industries can be regarded as autonomous sources of regional change or whether they merely reflect wider changes in the relative fortunes of the regions. It remains the case, however, that defence expenditures supported 11 per cent of manufacturing employment in the South East and South West Standard Regions in 1985, compared to as little as 1.3 and 2 per cent in Yorkshire and the West Midlands respectively, which clearly indicates the highly uneven impact of defence expenditures.

The gradual thawing of the 'Cold War' may mean that defence expenditures could be substantially reduced (though at the time of writing this would depend on the long - term outcome of the Gulf War). The announcement of the Ministry of Defence's 'Options for Change' exercise in the summer of 1990 seemed to herald a reduction in expenditures which would have considerable implications for communities where large employers depend on the production of military hardware, as well as for Britain's remaining naval bases, such as Plymouth, where substantial employment reductions have already taken place since the privatisation of the Devonport Dockyard in the late 1980s. Alternatively, this could open up the prospects for a 'peace dividend' in which resources released from defence expenditures could be used to socially useful ends and to promote Britain's manufacturing base in all regions. There are some dangers in this; as Lovering (1990) argues, a precipitate decline in defence spending could spell economic disaster because defence related industries are major export earners and sources of demand for high technology products, processes and personnel, so that rapid reductions in defence spending could seriously weaken the UK's manufacturing base. Instead, it will be essential to consider carefully how a conversion policy can be pursued so that domestic demand can be created for the kind of socially useful items that the defence industry could produce, thereby preserving the manufacturing base and securing employment in vulnerable areas (Lovering, 1990).

This apparent lack of strategic thinking in relation to defence expenditures is also evident with regard to the regional implications of major infrastructure schemes. Adequate infrastructure is essential if all regions are to be able to compete in the post 1992 Single European Market, but major investment decisions have been taken in preference to alternatives which might have promoted a more balanced distribution of economic activity. Good examples are decisions to invest in new airport facilities (e.g. Stansted) in the South East, rather than strengthening underused regional airports, and the apparent lack of commitment to high speed rail links to ensure that northern and western parts of Britain benefit from the Channel Tunnel. Growing private sector involvement in infrastructure planning is inimical to such strategic thinking, as recent discussions on extensions to the London Underground and on the East London River Crossing demonstrate; such decisions are made on a case-by-case basis, without any overall goal in mind (Whitelegg, 1989).

Finally, a less widely discussed aspect of public expenditure policy concerns the hidden systems of counter-regional subsidies and supports which benefit the South East of England disproportionately. Some of these, such as cuts in direct taxation since 1979, are the visible result of deliberate government decisions to prioritise their core supporters in the Conservative heartlands. Perhaps less obvious are the effects of tax relief on mortgage interest: because the South East has higher proportions of high rate taxpayers and because mortgages are typically at least £30 000, therefore attracting maximum tax relief, the South East and London accounted for 41 per cent of mortgage interest relief in 1986 (Low Pay Unit, 1987, cited in Hamnett, 1989). So mortgage relief can be seen as a geographically regressive as well as a socially regressive system. Other subsidies such as those to the British Rail 'Network South East' (some £200 million per annum, compared to £500 million for the whole of the provincial system) are similarly inducements to remain in or move to the South East. Finally it has been shown that the take-up of numerous government incentives to enterprise formation and development has been far greater in the South East than elsewhere. Martin (1989) has observed that the Government's emphasis on the 'enterprise economy' and on 'self help' as means of promoting regional regeneration is somewhat vacuous, outweighed as it is by these less visible subsidies.

In short, whether by accident or design, public expenditure and taxation policies have had the effects of benefitting the South East of England disproportionately through support for private sector economic activity and for high levels of consumption. In other locations, particularly those where defence industries and military bases are important, economic prospects are vulnerable to important political decisions about military futures.

PUBLIC EMPLOYMENT

The regional dimensions of public sector employment have received somewhat limited coverage (for an exception see Parry, 1985), but it can be shown that the contribution of the public sector to total employment varies from region to region and within regions, while the post-war growth in the public sector has now been halted. In addition the public sector is now experiencing in an acute form the consequences of the state-fuelled uneven growth of the British economy; as house prices have run ahead of public sector incomes, recruitment difficulties have reached unprecedented levels in large areas of South East England, while this problem is prompting government departments to seek relocation to lower cost areas with renewed urgency.

One consequence of the expansion of the welfare state from 1945 was a rapid growth of employment, notably in health care, education and local government, in all regions, until public expenditure cuts in the mid-1970s. One result was that public sector employment assumed considerable relative significance: in 1987, 36.2 per cent of all jobs in Northern Ireland were in the public sector, with the figures for Wales and Scotland being 34.6 per cent and 30 per cent respectively. This compares with 19.9 per cent in South East England and 23.7 per cent in East Anglia. These figures reflect three kinds of influences: the presence of regional departments of state in Wales, Scotland and N Ireland; the absolute decline in other sources of employment; and (though to a lesser degree than formerly) the importance of nationalised industries in these regions. However, these proportions, though high, are nevertheless lower than the corresponding figures for 1977 (Parry, 1985) suggesting that the public sector has been unable to help stem the tide of the relative decline of these regions. One reason for this has been public expenditure restraint which has compelled public employers to reduce staffing levels and/or to contract out work to the private sector; as a result, employment in the NHS, for example, has begun to fall in recent years. Such pressure for greater efficiency, taken together with regional resource allocation schemes such as the NHS's (which involves net transfers of resources away from London) have produced some quite dramatic reductions in employment: in 1984, for instance, there were some 33,000 fewer people employed in delivering health care in London than in 1978. The recent reforms of NHS and education provision, plus competitive tendering for local government services, will mean that future employment growth in these services will be strictly limited.

Despite releasing personnel in this way, there is evidence that the public services have had considerable difficulties in recruiting and retaining staff for some years now. No comprehensive survey of this problem is available, but (for the health service) agency staff expenditure is one index of the relative severity of the problem: in 1986–1987 13 district health authorities (DHAs) in London spent over 4 per cent of their budgets on agency personnel; for England as a whole the figure was approximately 0.7 per cent. In education the position is equally serious, perhaps most notably in inner London where local education authorities (LEAs) are almost routinely recruiting staff from Europe and Australasia in order to maintain services. Beyond this anecdotal evidence, the geographical distribution of advertisements for teaching posts indicates that, for maths and modern language teachers at secondary school level in 1990, turnover of teachers was substantially greater in the South East and in surrounding regions such as East Anglia, than elsewhere in England. For instance, up to 20 per cent of all posts in these subjects were advertised in some London Boroughs in the first four months of 1990 (Bryce, Lee and Mohan, 1991), a rate of turnover which was several times greater than that experienced in many northern LEAs.

In the long term these difficulties could begin to threaten the ability of the public sector to maintain levels of service provision, thus undermining the prosperity of the South East. It is particularly ironic that while statutory authorities are competing with one another for scarce staff in the South East, local authorities in the north are strenuously competing with one another for jobs. In addition, the problems of public service staff shortages in the South East are a function of the region's excessive growth and house price inflation, itself partly a consequence of the public expenditure and taxation subsidies available to the region. Present policy responses seem likely to involve some decentralisation of pay bargaining to the local level, but this will simply pit authority against authority in offering the best deal for teachers, nurses or any group of scarce staff, and seems to contradict declared government aims of cutting public expenditure.

One policy response which is not available to national services such as health care and education is to decentralise staff to locations where office and labour costs are lower, and there is evidence of a rapid increase in relocations by various government departments. This is not new, as many jobs were decentralised during the 1960s, in ways which helped 'reinforce the developing spatial division of labour within the economy' (Marshall, 1990, p.247) as largely routine jobs were moved while high-level positions remained within London. Compared to the planned decentralisation of the 1960s, present developments do not represent the working out of a grand, centralised design. Relocation is taking place due to decisions taken by individual departments, which is in line with the general devolution of management within central government. As such, according to Winckler (1990), current relocations in no way represent 'a coherent policy' on the part of central government. Press reports in late 1989 suggested that as many as 34,000 civil service jobs could move out of London by the year 2000. Among recent examples are the following: the transfer of Pay-As-You-Earn tax offices, employing some 400 people, to Cardiff, Edinburgh, Bootle, Glasgow and Livingston during 1988 and 1989, with a further 1200 posts to move by the end of 1992; a further 2000 Inland Revenue posts to be transferred to Nottingham in 1992; the building of the Customs and Excise VAT centre in Liverpool, involving a transfer of 250 jobs from the South East (presently on a split site – London / Southend); and others include moves by parts of the Department of Health (some 1650 jobs) to Leeds. Such moves are to be welcomed both on equity grounds and in terms of savings in public expenditure, though it is fair to say that many of these jobs could have been moved some years ago. Questions remain, though, about precisely which jobs will move: if jobs are largely routine and low grade, multiplier effects will be limited. Furthermore, relocations seem to be taking place in accordance with the residential preferences of staff rather than in accord with some criterion of 'need' for employment; the DoH's move to Leeds followed exhaustive assessment of the preferences of the staff involved, thus providing endorsement for Winckler's point noted above.

Such moves will have a beneficial impact, at least in terms of numbers of jobs created in or transferred to the regions, with attendant multiplier effects on local businesses. But policies in a key element of the public sector, the nationalised industries, have had precisely the opposite effect over the last decade, to the point where Hudson (1989) regards these sectors (notably coal, steel and shipbuilding) as having led the deindustrialisation of regions such as South Wales, central Scotland, and North East England. To put this into perspective, between 1978 and 1987 some 431,000 jobs were lost in Great Britain in the three sectors referred to; of this figure, 89,000, 60,000 and 59,000 jobs were lost in the Northern region, Scotland and Wales respectively, reflecting the highly concentrated nature of those industries in the public sector (Hudson, 1989; Department of Employment, 1989). The irony of this is that nationalisation was seen as one mechanism whereby mass unemployment on the scale of the 1930s could be avoided, yet the policies pursued in recent years have had precisely the effect of producing mass unemployment in numerous communities. The primary reason for this has been the Conservative Government's policies of reducing subsidies to such industries and requiring that they become profitable, usually as a prelude to privatisation, though such policies have also been pursued in order to support the Government's wider political goal of reducing union power. If these nationalised industries were in a narrow sense uncompetitive, a broader case could have been made for their retention, focussing on their importance to the nation's manufacturing base and on the importance of coal in a balanced, long term energy policy.

SUMMARY

The commentators drawn upon in this chapter have amply demonstrated that, in Cooke's (1987, p.191) words, that 'the nature of state intervention in regional development cannot …be compartmentalised', and that there are many ways, both direct and indirect, in which state expenditures and employment have an uneven regional impact. It is not overstating the case to argue that state subsidies to the South East are in part to blame for the present problems of 'overdevelopment' within the region, while the tax cuts which have likewise contributed to that overdevelopment have been paid for, in part, by savings in expenditure on nationalised industries and by receipts from privatisation of state assets. The case for a coordinated approach to all state expenditures and programmes, so as to give due consideration to all regional interests and claims on resources, is hardly new but it has been reiterated by several commentators and politicians recently. Balchin (1990) comments that many forms of public expenditure could and should be spatially discriminatory. As well as defence procurement, environmental and infrastructural expenditures could also be biased in favour of particular regions. Discriminatory expenditures on social programmes (housing, education and health care) could both provide employment and improve the 'marketability' of specific regions. There is a need for a full audit of the regional implications of public expenditure, one outcome of which would be to discriminate positively in favour of those regions disadvantaged by the present lack of strategic thinking in respect of public programmes.

REFERENCES

Balchin, P. (1990) Regional Policy: The North–South Divide London: Paul Chapman.

Boddy, M. and Lovering, J. (1988) 'The Geography of Military Industry in Britain', Area, 20, 41–51.

Breheny, M., Hall, P., Hart, D., and McQuaid, R. (1987) Western Sunrise: The Genesis and Growth of Britain's High–Tech Corridor London: Allen and Unwin.

Bryce, C., Lee, R. and Mohan, J. (1991) 'The geographies of teacher shortages in England and Wales: evidence from national advertisements' Area, 23 (2), 119–127.

Cooke, P. (1987) 'Wales', in Damesick, P. and Wood, P. (eds) Regional Problems, Problem Regions, and Public Policy in the United Kingdom Oxford: Oxford University Press, pp.191–217

Department of Employment (1989) '1987 Census of Employment' Employment Gazette, 97 (10), 545–558.

Hamnett, C. (1989) 'The political geography of housing in contemporary Britain', in Mohan, J. (ed) The Political Geography of Contemporary Britain Basingstoke: Macmillan, pp.208–223.

Hudson, R. (1988) Wrecking a Region: State Policies, Party Politics and Regional Change in North East England London: Pion.

Hudson, R. (1989) 'Rewriting history and reshaping geography: the nationalised industries and the political economy of Thatcherism, in Mohan, J. (ed) *The Political Geography of Contemporary Britain* Basingstoke: Macmillan, pp.113–129

Lovering, J. (1990) 'The Labour Party and the 'Peace Dividend': How to waste an opportunity' *Capital and Class*, 41, 7–14.

Marshall, N. (1990) 'Reorganising the British civil service: how are the regions being served?' *Area*, 22 (3), 246–255.

Martin, R. (1989) 'Deindustrialisation and state intervention: Keyensianism, Thatcherism and the regions', in Mohan, J. (ed) *The Political Geography of Contemporary Britain* Basingstoke: Macmillan, pp.87–112

Mohan, J. and Lee, R. (1989) 'Unbalanced growth? Public Services and Labour Shortages in European Core Region', in Breheny, M. and Congdon, P. (eds) *Growth and Change in a Core Region* London: Pion, pp.33–54

Northern Region Strategy Team (1977) *Strategic Plan for the Northern Region* Newcastle upon Tyne: NRST.

Parry, R. (1985) Britain: stable aggregates, changing composition pp.54–96 of Rose, R. et al (1985) *Public Employment in Western Nations* Cambridge: Cambridge University Press.

Regional Studies Association (1983) *Report of an Inquiry into Regional Problems in the UK* Norwich: GeoBooks.

Short, J. (1981) *Public Expenditure and Taxation in UK Regions* Farnborough: Gower.

Whitelegg, J. (1989) 'Transport Policy: Off the Rails?' in Mohan, J. (ed) *The Political Geography of Contemporary Britain* Basingstoke: Macmillan, pp.187–207

Winckler, V. (1990) 'Restructuring the Civil Service: Reorganisation and Relocation' *International Journal of Urban and Regional Research*, 14, 135–157.

PART IV

THE REGIONAL IMPACT OF NATIONAL POLICIES

CHAPTER 10

ECONOMIC AND SOCIAL POLICY DEVELOPMENTS

10.1

Impact of Infrastructure Investment Policy

Nigel Spence

THE NATURE AND ROLE OF INFRASTRUCTURE

The term infrastructure was defined recently (Diamond and Spence, 1989) as 'the collective and integrative basis for economic activity'. This overshort and somewhat glossy definition camouflages perhaps too many of the difficulties encountered in defining this term. In fact the word has come to mean many different things to interested commentators. Although it is usually thought of as a material item such as a transport facility or a piece of community infrastructure, most certainly it can also be thought of in non-material terms such as the educational or skill level of a workforce or the quality of public safety in an area. It is however perhaps best considered as possessing in varying quantities, according to type of infrastructure, some of the following characteristic attributes. Infrastructure provision usually involves high levels of capital expenditure. In many instances this expenditure is provided from the public purse although this notion of the publicness of infrastructure is becoming more and more blurred as the private sector plays a more important role. Much infrastructure, it can be said, is at least under public regulation or influence. Such costly public capital expenditure often only achieves low levels of productivity measured in conventional ways. It tends to service a wide variety of economic activities for a long time often at low or zero cost. Now it is not difficult to think of examples of infrastructure types which do not conform exactly to the characteristics outlined above but most exhibit many of such features. Infrastructure provision has an undoubted integrative function in the economy providing a sound social and economic foundation for production and facilitating the necessary transactions demanded by contemporary society.

Obviously some infrastructure is required for directly productive activities to take place. The simple point is that the costs incurred by such activities should be lower the higher the levels of infrastructure provision deployed. In the view of the Commission of the European Communities 'more and better infrastructure makes a region more attractive and cuts production costs for firms; it raises their competitiveness and also provides a permanent boost to the growth of business investment, employment opportunities and incomes' (Commission of the European Communities, 1987). Given such a view about the role of infrastructure provision in the well-being of economic activities it is not surprising that infrastructure has become a prime tool of regional development. Unfortunately the strategies of infrastructure provision are not quite so straightforward. There are basically two lines of approach (Hirschman, 1958). Infra-structure can be provided in advance of development in the hope that by improving the competitive advantage of a region development will subsequently follow. Or infrastructure can be provided after sufficient development has taken place secure in the knowledge that it will be well used on the day of provision. In the former strategy (excess capacity) the opportunity cost is clearly the foregoing of the investment potential that help for directly productive activities alone may achieve. In the latter (shortage) the opportunity cost is the foregoing of the investment potential stifled by an inadequate infrastructure.

The former strategy has undoubtedly been in the ascendency in policy making in Britain and Europe in the past but recently the wisdom of such a strategy is being more and more questioned. The purpose of this brief paper is to review some of these questions. In this review the current position of the state of infrastructure in Britain in Europe will be considered. This will be followed by illustration of some of the doubts that exist on the prominence of infrastructure in policy making. Finally the piece will conclude with a plea for caution when policies of this type are being evaluated. But first what exactly are the objectives of such policies?

THE OBJECTIVES OF INFRASTRUCTURE POLICY

The European Regional Development Fund is the principal, although not the sole, agent of regional policy in the European Community. It was started in 1975 'to correct the principal regional imbalances within the Community resulting in particular from agricultural preponderance, industrial change and structural under-employment'. Member states applied to the fund to obtain grants for physical investment projects in special assisted areas. These projects could involve the provision of infrastructure or direct financial assistance for investment by industry. Funds were apportioned amongst member states on the basis of a quota system. In 1979 a non-quota component to the fund was set up. This amounted to some 5 percent of the budget. It was designed to allow initiatives which were specifically Community oriented, not necessarily in the assisted areas and not necessarily confined to physical investment proposals. The last major reform of the fund took place in 1984 and was part of a much wider evaluation of the effectiveness of the Community's structural funds. Basically the fund is now instructed 'to contribute to the correction of the principal regional imbalances within the Community by participating in the development and structural adjustment of regions whose development is lagging behind and in the conversion of declining industrial regions'. Such an objective may be achieved in some five major ways. First, special Community Programmes may be supported the first two of which were related to improving access to advanced telecommunications services and exploiting indigi-neous energy potential in less favoured regions. Second, there is assistance for national programmes of Community interest involving assistance to industry and/or infra-structure initiatives designed to promote endogenous development potential. Third, measures to exploit endogenous develoment potential involving non-physical invest-ment assistance to industry are encouraged. Fourth, there is support for the traditional investment opportunities in infrastructure and industry widely interpreted. Finally it is possible for the fund to finance research studies, especially if they are of an evaluative nature. In addition, it may be noted that the fund may participate in the support in integrated operations which are particular initiatives of a coordinated character de-signed to benefit a specific region or sub-region.

It can be seen from the above that many of the possible avenues of support from the fund could involve infrastructure provision. The 1988 operating budget for the fund was 3.7 billion European Currency Units (ECU) somewhat less than 10 per cent of the overall budget (Comfort, 1988). Over the period 1975 to 1986 some 81 per cent of Regional Fund monies were allocated to infrastructure projects, 24,832 of them in total (Court of Auditors, 1988). In 1986 infrastructure related spending consumed the major fraction of the 3 billion or so ECUs at around 88 per cent. Before the 1984 reform there was a rule that the infrastructure slice should not exceed 70 per cent. After the reform the rule became a guideline that assistance to directly productive activities should aim to achieve a 30 per cent share. In practice these targets have proved difficult to achieve, it being altogether much easier to prepare and obtain funding for infrastruc-ture related spending. The result produces a paradox as is well illustrated in the case of the United Kingdom. Internal regional policy is almost wholly couched in terms of direct financial assistance to industry. In 1986 72 per cent of Regional Fund monies coming to the United Kingdom were for infrastructure projects.

In the United Kingdom the nature and objectives of infrastructure policy are by no means as clear. The publicly owned or privatised and publicly regulated infrastructure is an enormous asset yet there is no comprehensive, definitive and detailed record of the value, condition and cost of necessary repair for all facilities. Nor are there any consistent data on regional variations in the quantity and quality of infrastructure stocks. It is widely thought that a modern infrastructure must be a prerequisite for economic development. This belief underlies much of the infrastructure provision and infrastructure regulation by government.

Infrastructure is provided in a variety of diverse ways. There has come into existence a multiplicity of agencies with responsibilities for providing facilities. The result is a multiplicity of infrastructure policies. It is quite unrealistic to expect to be able to characterise overall infrastructure policy except in the most general terms. The reality is of a great variety of types of providers managing a great variety of highly variable stock in quite contrasting economic and social contexts.

Despite this variety there are a number of important common elements among the issues that face the infrastructure providers. First amongst these is the accumulating volume of obsolescent facilities despite important modernisation programmes. The combination of urban history and technical change has resulted in some severe current renewal and replacement needs. Second, this aspect assumes greater significance in the current economic context of policies to curtail and reduce public expenditure. There is little dispute amongst commentators in the field that overall investment in infra-structure has declined in recent years.

Within this context of an infrastructure dated in specific components and localities, and retrenchment in public sector investment, it must be recognised that industry has been radically restructured in recent times which has affected both its organisation and its location. This can be expected to materially affect the pattern of demand in terms of level, type and location of new infrastructure provision. In many instances this pattern of new demand does not coincide with the target areas for regional development. Yet the traditional regional development aspirations of infrastructure policy, for example in the provision of roads, remain to compete for the reducing public resources. These features make the fomulation and implementation of public policies for infrastructure provision a central issue in the national and regional development debate. Again many commentators percieve a switch of emphasis in recent times, need for provision now being interpreted more as satisfying current demand. Stategic provision in advance of demand is becoming a less visible policy strategy.

THE STATE OF INFRASTRUCTURE AND DEVELOPMENT

In its last periodic report on the social and economic situation and development of the regions of the Community the Commission again explored the wide disparities existing between regions over a range of indicators (Commission of the European Communities, 1987). It is shown that the recent aquisitions to the Community (Spain and Portugal) have really only served to widen these disparities. However also apparent is the intensity of problems existing in some more developed northern areas of the Community where structural adjustment difficulties are being faced. The report acknowledges that amongst a range of other factors infrastructure provision is one element which can be thought of as significantly influencing the comparative advantage and hence competitiveness of individual regions. The research confirms that the regions which are lagging in development terms are 'much more poorly equipped with infrastructures directly serving economic activities'.This is then a principal reason why so much of the Regional Fund and the Social Fund monies (and other structural funds to some extent) currently are spent on improving infrastructure provision. The regions of the Community differ a great deal in their infrastructure stock endowment. Those regions in the south and west are shown to still lag way behind the general levels of provision elsewhere—in some cases these discrepancies may amount to some 60 per cent of provision in other regions. The centrally located areas of highest development provide the contrast in the extremes of provision. The United Kingdom, it can be seen on this measure of stock or infrastructure capacity, comprises a most uniform pattern of provision intermediate between such extremes. However a critical variable here concerns the notion of capacity for this is in some ways a rather poor measure for certain purposes. Infrastructure use or more specifically the identification of infrastructure bottlenecks (both in terms of quality as well as quantity) are of greater research interest and perhaps policy relevance. (The aggregate infrastructure indicator is not fully explained in the report but is clearly based on earlier research (Biehl, 1982) which included a range of infrastructure types normalised for regional purposes by head of population and land area served.)

Regional development potential, according to Biehl is conceived of as a function of a set of resources which are fixed in location, costly to substitute and servicing a wide variety of directly productive activities. The natural resource endowment of a region is clearly one such potentiality factor. The regional population and its age and sex structure forms the basis for the labour force potential of a region. The geographical location of a region incorporates an accessibility potential. The position of the region in the international settlement system and the size and structure of the settlement system within the region both offer potential for variations in economic development.

The sectoral structure of the regional economy is often indicative of levels of economic development. Finally, and not the least important here, the nature of the capital stock of a region most certainly is a determinant of development potential.

Now the argument runs that if to these fixed location potentiality factors be added the correct mix of the mobile factors of production such as private capital, entrepreneurial flair and qualified manpower then the potential can be utilised. In a sense the potentiality endowment can be thought of as providing the limits for development, necessary but not sufficient for actual development success through regional infrastructure policy to be judged. To operationalise the above ideas Biehl uses the familiar notion of a production function but in a regional context. The basic idea is that physical infrastructure provision in a region is one of the potentiality factors which determines physical regional output and hence income, employment and development. Its contribution is measured by comparing the actual income of a region with its potential one using the production function as the analytical tool.

The researchers (Meadows and Jackson, 1984 in the case of the United Kingdom) pooled their judgement and experience to produce a ranking of infrastructure categories based upon 'relative degrees of infrastructureness'. The result was a high, medium and low categorisation for close on 100 infrastructure groups and subgroups on a checklist of eight infrastructure characteristics. On this basis measures of the levels of infrastructure capacity were derived for the regions of the country. These infrastructure types were analysed for their linkage with economic development for the two cross section years 1975 and 1980. The basic hypothesis was that disparities in levels of economic development should be traceable to the disparities in infrastructure provision and other potentiality factor endowments. Simple correlations between infrastructure and regional development are reasonably high in the case of the United Kingdom. Highest correlations are to be found with directly income generating infrastructure categories, such as transport and communications, showing high levels of publicness. However there were also significant correlations found with levels of educational provision and wider social facilities. More complex quasi production functions of various sorts were also calibrated. In all the higher the levels of infrastructure the higher the levels of economic development. If other potentiality factors are added to the equation such as location, agglomeration and sectoral structure then the contribution of infrastructure declines, as expected, but usually remains significant. Infrastructure, although important, is then shown to be only one of the potentiality factors crucial for regional development. Infrastructure usually provided a more powerful 'explanation', according to the statistical tests used, of regional development in terms of income and productivity than employment.

Overall, then, from this type of research in the United Kingdom two points seem to emerge. First the levels of regional disparity in provision are not particularly high, certainly not as high as those between the member nations of the European Community. Second, that although there are some apparent linkages with economic development these are not particularly high in terms relative to other factors or clear in the ways which they are operating. The basic question of causality remains. Little wonder then that the policies are becoming questioned more and more.

THE EMERGING POLICY DOUBTS

In an interesting review paper Comfort (1989) outlines what he sees to be the weaknesses of the current emphasis on infrastructure in European regional policy making and goes on to elaborate on possible alternatives. Although this does not purport to be true policy evaluation research it does pose some thought provoking ideas and opinions. First, the paper emphasises the possibilities of approaches other than infra-structure. The regulations permit them and the Commission encourages them. The second point resorts to intuition and is most certainly debateable. He argues that while equal provision of 'social infrastructure' is desirable over the regions of the Community equal provision of 'physical infrastructure' is not. In examples of the former he includes hospitals, schools and old people's homes and the latter roads, bridges, telecommuni-cations and electricity supply. Physical infrastructure provision should, he argues, 'correspond to demand and not to either the level of population nor to considerations of equity'. Most definitely an infrastructure-development policy of the 'shortage' variety this. Third is a related and equally debateable point, that although development is dependent on physical infrastructure, its advance provision is much more relevant to the attraction of inward investment and not the mobilisation of indigenous activity. Contemporary regional development he argues is much more a function of the latter. The final point made concerns the desirable scale of infrastructure initiatives. While conceding that a certain minimum of infrastrcuture provision is necessary in the modern global economy, he is of the opinion that public spending on big projects must be subject to the following three basic questions. Does the infrastructure contribute significantly to the development of the region concerned? What are the opportunity costs of the investment and especially could not a better rate of return be gained from incentives to private investment? And if infrastructure spending is essential could it be financed by loans rather than grants? It is not difficult to see reflections of such arguments in current attitudes of government towards such spending.

The alternatives to infrastructure and to a certain degree the conventional emphasis on assistance for manufacturing industry involve a range of policies currently being deployed in varying strengths in individual nations or in embyonic form by the Community. These include a variety of policies designed to nurture small and medium sized private enterprises (not restricted to manufacturing alone) especially by provid-ing assistance in the form of services usually of a business or a technical nature. However, they also include such initiatives as the improvement of vocational training, the improvement of local administration and the support of local development agen-cies. All good ideas these and the various current implementations of them seem to be providing some useful results. It should be recognised, however, that if infrastructure is broadly interpeted some of these alternatives could be categorised as such. Indeed Comfort in his paper makes this point in his description of a better supportive environment for infrastructure

In an important recent study the Court of Auditors of the European Community (Court of Auditors, 1989) have undertaken an evaluation of the infrastructure compo-nent of the European Regional Development Fund. It should be noted that although the research is not without its problems this is a real attempt to undertake a systematic evaluation of infrastructure policy. The basic approach which was adopted was to review the levels of use made of the infrastructure provided through the policy. The line taken is a simple one. Regional development benefits vary in direct proportion to the levels of use made of the new facilities, admittedly after a suitable period of time. Use in this sense was largely confined to economic use of the infrastructure after deducting an amount for what was called 'general' use. Similarly attempts were made to take account of the effects of diversion of activity from other infrastructure in the region, of substitution of activity from other infrastructure out of the region, of exportation which is the use of new infrastructure by economic agents outside the region, and finally of normal demand which is increased use which would have taken place anyway regardless of the new provision.

Notwithstanding a range of other provisos in this complex task the results are most interesting. (The data incidentally on the use of the new infrastructure was provided by survey of the member governments of the European Community). They show that a significant proportion of projects in which the fund has invested are not optimally utilised. In most cases utilisation rates are much less than 50 per cent of capacity. In some cases use was lower on the new provision than on the old. The effects on regional development then are thought to be weak.

The Court does emphasise that the research is not a thorough cost-benefit analysis nor does it include any evaluation of alternative projects. However despite these shortcomings the findings do provide further evidence for the often stated maxim that infrastructure is a necessary but not sufficient component in the regional development process. The study concludes that these disappointing results are due to the lack of an integrated regional development programme to associate projects with precise objectives.

THE POLICY EVALUATION PROCESS

It has been shown in this short paper that infrastructure is complex in terms of its make up and character. Its relationship with regional development is not well understood. Yet there has been a policy stance which anticipated development benefits from its provision. Such policy has been shown to be insufficient to overcome the development inequalities that still persist. The policy is now coming under close scrutiny. Now this paper is not seeking that this questioning not be undertaken nor that the status quo as regards infrastructure policy be maintained. It is, however, calling for a more thorough understanding of the processes by which policies such as these are evaluated.

Policy evaluation involves assessment made from several perspectives and it is necessary to distinguish clearly between them. Diamond and Spence (1983) have argued that evaluation of policy outcomes should be examined in terms of their effects, effectiveness, efficiency and efficacy. Effects are the measured impacts of the policy according to chosen indicators. Effectiveness is achieved when the outcome of the identified effects is congruent with the policy objective. Cost-effectiveness is a measure relating the effects to their direct costs as in the case of regional or infrastructure policy when cost-per-job created is used as an evaluative measure. However, even if there are no problems in identifying the relevant effects and costs in such assessments they are nevertheless not comprehensive in the sense that the real costs of the policy must include any losses created and diversion of resources incurred. This is the concept of efficiency. It is the aggregate effect of infrastructure policies on the economy as a whole, that is their contribution to the national output net of resource cost which is the measure of the efficiency of the policy. In the case of infrastructure the financial impact on the national exchequer is, because of the scale of spending, another evaluation perspective of considerable importance.

The maximisation of effectiveness and efficiency is not always possible in practice because any one public policy is affected by for example other policy objectives, consideration of administrative feasibility, international treaty obligations and of course political acceptability. All of these can and do provide constraints. A policy which although not maximising effectiveness and efficiency but which is the best possible compromise in the context of the constraints that operate is an efficacious policy. This is the broadest of all the evaluation measures of policy and is sometimes forgotten. But even at this level evaluative judgement is not without its difficulties. Take attitudes of business to infrastructure provision. In a recent survey (Diamond and Spence,1989) it was shown that businesses found it extremely difficult to identify the directly discernible job generation effects of infrastructure. Yet business did recognise the critical role of infrastructure in its operations. In a sense all jobs are dependent on general economic well-being of establishments which the survey shows to be partly a function of infrastructure provision. When it comes to spending public monies on infrastructure in a hypothetical context, businesses would allocate most to roads, but never more than half the budget. The second highest priority is spending on local public services. Less tangible non-public sector spending on telecommunications and utilities comes third in line, with provision for rail a poor fourth. When it comes to spending on infrastructure as opposed to direct financial assistance to industry, again hypothetically, on average only one quarter of the budget would be allocated to the latter. Many establishments in the South East would allocate nothing to industrial assistance but even in the North East infrastructure spending would still command half as much again of the budget as direct financial assistance to industry.

As far as the evaluation of infrastructure policy is concerned two things are clear – the research is still in its early stages and there is some way to go before judgements can be made with confidence.

REFERENCES

Biehl D. (1982) *The contribution of infrastructure to regional development.* Report produced by the Infrastructure Study Group for the European Community.

Comfort A.M. (1988) Alternatives to infrastructure? Possible ways forward for the ERDF: a perspective from Luxembourg. *Regional Studies* 22, 542-551.

Commission of the European Communities (1987) *The Regions of the Enlarged Community.* Third Periodic Report of the Social and Economic Situation and Development of the Regions of the Community. Luxembourg.

Court of Auditors of the European Community (1989) The European Regional Development Fund. Luxembourg.

Diamond D. and Spence N. (1983) *Regional Policy Evaluation.* Aldershot, Gower.

Diamond D. and Spence N. (1989) *Infrastructure and Industrial Costs in British Industry* London, HMSO.

Hirschman A.O. (1958) *The Strategy of Economic Development.* New Haven, Yale University Press.

Meadows W.J. and Jackson P.M. (1984) Infrastructure and regional development: empirical findings. *Built Environment* 10,4, 270-81.

Recent Developments in Vocational Education and Training in the UK

Meredith Baker and Peter Elias

INTRODUCTION

The conventional wisdom is that Britain under-trains its labour force, both compared with the standards of international counterparts and with the internal needs and challenges of an economy facing increased competition in the 1990s. The inadequacies of the British vocational educational and training system have been keenly debated over the last decade, both in the face of rising levels of youth unemployment and now, as we approach a significant downturn in the numbers of young people available for work (MSC, 1982; Sanderson, 1988; OECD, 1983; Finegold and Soskice, 1988; White, 1988, Fonda and Hayes, 1988; Keep and Mayhew, 1988; Coopers and Lybrand, 1985; Hart, 1989 and Davis, 1986).

First, we present an overview of training in Britain: How do we define training? Who receives training? How much? How has this changed over time? What are the regional dimensions? These are difficult questions to answer given the nature of training data in Britain. Nevertheless, we explore a variety of sources to glean an overview of the distribution of the different types of training in Great Britain at present. The evidence points towards an increase in job-related training in the recent past, most probably associated with the growth of professional, technical and sales employment and the higher levels of training associated with such occupations.

Following this we canvass the policy developments which have occurred in vocational education and training, focusing on the decade of the 1980s. Attention is paid to the regional evolution of these policy developments and their potential impact. The conclusions we draw from this broad analysis are that the future success of training policies will hinge on three factors: (i) the increased openness of the UK economy following the removal of European Community trade barriers in 1992; (ii) the marked fall in the number of young people entering the labour market; and (iii) the balance of incentives available to young people and the private sector to invest in skills and training. The regional impacts of these three influences will vary significantly, even in the absence of any explicit regional dimension to national policies affecting vocational education and training. It is argued that the formation of Training and Enterprise Councils (TECs) at the sub-regional level will not necessarily provide a regional dimension to policy initiatives in this area. On the contrary, a sub-regional framework for the delivery of training may exacerbate the existing North-West/South-East polarisation of human resources.

THE DEFINITION OF VOCATIONAL EDUCATION AND TRAINING

Definitional problems remain a major obstacle in the elaboration of information from various statistical sources on the provision, nature and extent of vocational training in the UK. This difficulty is not unrelated to prevailing views about the UK training system. At one extreme is the image of vocational training as a formalised system of apprenticeships, linked to the traditional 'craft' status of certain occupations. At the other extreme, training may be regarded as a period in which a person is less productive in his/her work than the experienced person, simply because certain procedures or tasks need to be learnt and rules need to be assimilated. Often without access to any formal programme of training, a new employee will be regarded as undergoing training – a process of 'learning-by-doing' at its crudest level.

Without a clear and consistent definition of vocational training over the period under investigation (1979–89), we present what amounts to a patchwork of evidence on the nature and extent of vocational education and training. For reasons made clear later, the situation is improving. National accreditation of vocational training courses and the development of a common 'language' for such courses and employer-based training programmes will undoubtedly lead to improvements in the monitoring of progress in this area. The interests of the European Commission and proposals for pan-European accreditation of training courses will also stimulate the generation of more information. Meanwhile, we adopt some of the more general and inconsistent definitions available from current statistical sources.

TRENDS IN VOCATIONAL EDUCATION AND TRAINING

'Training' is a self-defined variable in the Labour Force Survey coded in response to the question: Did you receive any job-related education/training during the last four weeks? The 1989 Labour Force Survey indicates that over 14 per cent of employees of working age in early 1989 received some form of job-related training (including on- and off-the-job training) in the four weeks prior to the survey. Using this same definition of exposure to training, this continues the steady annual improvement from the 9 per cent receiving job-related training in 1984 (Figure 10.2.1). Indeed, over the five years since 1984, it would appear that job-related training in Great Britain has undergone a sharp improvement, at least in sheer number terms. Between 1984 and 1989 there has been an increase of well over one million in the number of employees

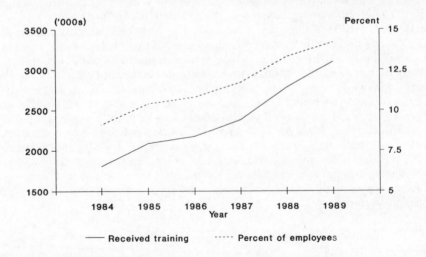

Source: Training Agency (1989); LFS 1989

Figure 10.2.1: Number of Employees of Working Age Receiving Job Related Training in the Four Weeks Before the Survey, Great Britain, 1984–1989

receiving job-related training in the one month reference period. Further evidence of the increasing trend towards training and retraining of existing employees is provided in case study evidence from field work still in progress (Rainbird and McGuire (personal communication)).

This increase is interesting, given the extent of the decline in the late 1970s of the traditional craft apprenticeship training route. Figures for the engineering industry show that since 1984 the annual craft trainee recruitment has hovered around the 6,000 mark, compared to levels of 20,000 or so during the mid-1970s. Figure 10.2.2 shows the sharp decline which took place in the recruitment of first-year craft trainees by the engineering industry between 1979 and 1983.

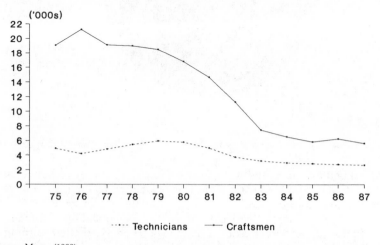

Source: Mason (1988)

Figure 10.2.2: Recruitment of First Year Craft and Technician Trainees by the Engineering Industry, 1975–1987

Taken together, these two diagrams characterise the dilemma we seek to address. Training by apprenticeship, a traditional approach to training covering a planned programme of training and work experience over three to five years, has declined dramatically. Yet, at the same time, the number of employees who have experienced some training related to their employment has increased equally dramatically. Where we lack knowledge is in terms of the quality of training that employees receive – its effectiveness in terms of earnings and career prospects for the individual – and in terms of productivity, labour stability and flexibility for the employer.

The problems inherent in the different definitions of training from the various statistical sources in Britain are underlined when we compare Figure 10.2.1 and Figure 10.2.3. On the one hand, Figure 10.2.1 shows that over 14 per cent of employees received job-related training in the four weeks prior to the Labour Force Survey. On the other hand, Figure 10.2.3 suggests that during 1986–87, almost half of all employees in Great Britain received some sort of training. A part of this difference lies in the different time periods covered by the two surveys, and part is also likely to be explained by the different definitions of training employed. Figure 10.2.1 is based on individuals' assessment of their own training experiences while Figure 10.2.3 is based on employers' assessment of their employees' training experiences. Moreover, definitional problems encountered within surveys are also underlined by the work of Rigg (1989) who

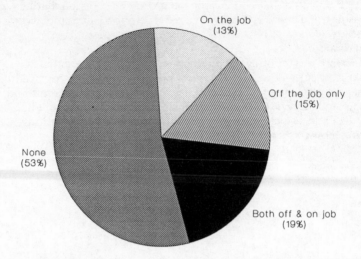

On the job
(13%)

Off the job only
(15%)

None
(53%)

Both off & on job
(19%)

Source: Training Agency (1989)

Figure 10.2.3: Percentage of Employees Receiving Training in the 12 Month Period 1986–87, Great Britain

analysed one of the components of the Funding Study: the survey of individual adults. Rigg reports that just under one third of the estimated population of employees aged 19–59 years reported to have received some vocational education or training in the three years prior to the survey. However, half of those who said they had not received any training during the period claimed that they had obtained other learning experiences at work. Rigg suggests that one or all of these 'other learning experiences' might be interpreted as on-the-job training.

THE DISTRIBUTION OF VOCATIONAL EDUCATION AND TRAINING

It is conceptually difficult, and perhaps inappropriate, to attempt to distinguish between vocational education and vocational training. The former terminology is used primarily to describe full-time, part-time or alternance (sandwich) courses organised by institutions in the tertiary education sector (universities, polytechnics, colleges of further and higher education, Scottish central institutions, etc). The latter relates mainly to employer-based training programmes which vary considerably in terms of content, quality, intensity and their management. Complicating this distinction is the fact that many employers will place employees into vocational courses in the tertiary education sector, thereby combining on- and off-the-job training. Off- the-job training provided by the tertiary sector cannot readily be separated into that which is vocational, in that it provides knowledge of direct relevance to a particular job, and that which is more general in content. For this reason, we have made no attempt to distinguish full-time students in terms of the vocational content of their studies.

Job-related training among employees accounts for the vast majority of training activity undertaken by individuals post-16 years of age (Figure 10.2.4). Following job-related training by employees, the full time education sector as a whole accounts for a large majority of those undertaking education and training. Government programmes by contrast account for a relatively small amount of training and education.

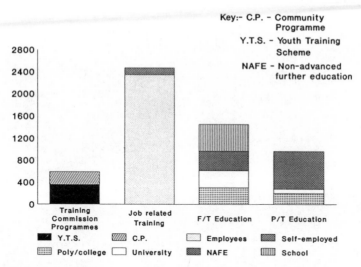

Source: Training Agency (1989)

Figure 10.2.4: Post-16 Education and Training

Greenhalgh and Stewart (1987) using 1975–76 data from the National Training Survey (NTS) show that women receive significantly less full time training than men when they first enter the labour market. This inequality is compounded in the case of married women by their intermittent participation in the labour force and when undertaking part-time work (see also Booth, 1991). However, courses taken outside working hours constitute the second most prevalent type of training, and this evening training is frequently undertaken by women. More recent figures from the Labour Force Survey indicate that women receive marginally less training while employed. However, approximately the same proportions receive job-related training during unemployment. Gender differences in the type of training received and the length of training are also important (Booth, 1991; Wickham, 1986).

Human capital theory suggests that the rate of accumulation of general or firm-specific human capital, via education and training, declines with age. This was confirmed by Greenhalgh and Stewart (1987) using NTS data, Booth (1991) using the 1987 British Social Attitude Survey (BSA), and is still the case in 1989 with 27 per cent of 16–19-year-olds receiving some form of training in the four weeks prior to the survey (Figure 10.2.5), compared with only 12 per cent of 35–49-year-olds and 6 per cent of 50–64 year-olds receiving some form of training. We note, however, that as the pool of young workers shrinks, more emphasis on the training or retraining of older workers may become evident.

Among 16–18-year-olds, the proportion in education and training has steadily increased since the late 1970s. In 1988 almost a third of 16–18 year-olds were in full time education compared to only a quarter in 1975. The growth in YTS since its introduction in 1979 has also been steady, accounting for 16 per cent of young people aged 16–18 on YTS by January 1988 (Training Agency 1989). Counterbalancing these increasing proportions has been the declining cohort of young people since 1979, which implies that these increases will not have been so great when measured in numerical terms.

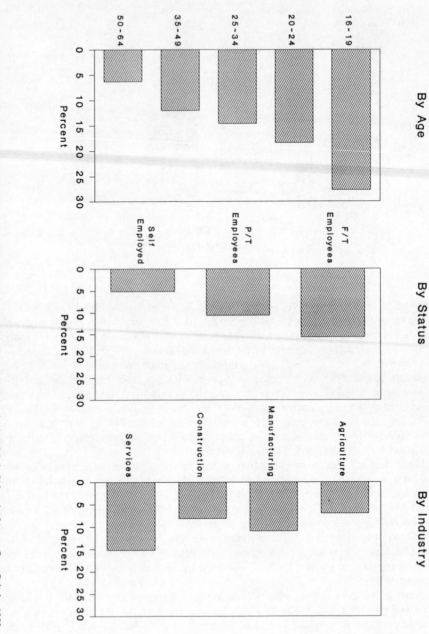

Figure 10.2.5: Percentage of Employed Labour Force of Working Age Receiving Job Related Training in the 4 Weeks Before the Survey, Great Britain, 1989

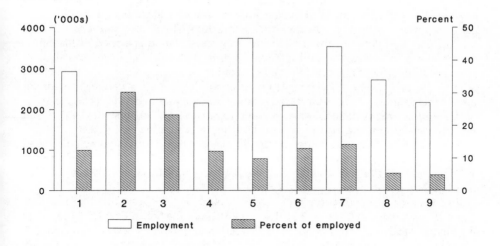

Employment   Percent of employed

KEY: 1. Managers and Administrators
      2. Professional Occupations
      3. Associate Professional, Technical
      4. Clerical
      5. Craft and Skilled Manual Occupations
      6. Personal and Protective Occupations
      7. Sales Occupations
      8. Plant and Machine Operatives
      9. Other Occupations

Source: LFS 1989

Figure 10.2.6: Percent and Numbers of Employed Labour Force Receiving Job Related Training by SOC Major Group in the 4 Weeks Before the Survey, Great Britain, 1989

Non-manual workers, especially professional and technical workers, receive more training than do manual workers (Figure 10.2.6). This accords with the findings of Greenhalgh and Stewart (1987) who show that men and single women are more likely to train the higher their occupational status compared to married women, and the findings of Booth (1991) where manual workers are 25 per cent less likely to be trained than their non-manual counterparts. Rigg (1989) also notes the concentration of training in non-manual occupations. Moreover the probability of receiving employer-provided training declines less with age for those in managerial and professional occupations. Greenhalgh and Stewart also found that, across all three groups (men, single women, married women), the higher the occupational status, the more likely employees are to obtain evening training.

Interestingly, a greater percentage of service sector workers obtain training than those in the agricultural, manufacturing or construction sectors (Figure 10.2.5). Given the structural shifts occurring in the British economy, with an increasing emphasis on services and an associated decline in the manufacturing sector, this may provide evidence of a shift in attitudes towards training. Indeed, it is tempting to conclude that the substantial increase in job related training since 1984 may in part be due to the training activities of the service sector and the strong growth of this sector in the post 1981 economic recovery. This may be compared with the findings of Rigg (1989) who suggests that industry appeared to have little effect on the likelihood of training once education was considered. On the other hand, Rigg (1989) also cautions that this finding may be related to the limited industry classification specified in his study. Furthermore, the work of Booth (1989) suggests that working in sectors such as agriculture, energy, transport and communication and other services was likely to increase the probability of receiving training, controlling for other variables. Approximately these same industries increased training probabilities in Booth's (1991) analysis of the 1986 survey of 1980 Graduates and Diplomates. She suggests that this result perhaps reflects demand-side factors in changing or expanding industries.

Job-related training also varies by employment status with part-time employees less likely to receive training than their full time counterparts (Greenhalgh and Stewart, 1987; Booth, 1989,1991). Furthermore, the self employed are less likely to have obtained training than part-timers (Figure 10.2.5).

Examination of the distribution of training by region suggests that there is some significant variation (Figure 10.2.7). Those workers in the South East (15%) reported the highest incidence of training in the reference month, with the lowest percentage of training observed in Scotland (10.6%). These differences are probably a function of regional differences in the sectoral distribution of training. However, Booth's (1991) analysis of the 1987 BSA Survey data suggests that the probability of receiving training does vary somewhat by region, controlling for sectoral influences. In particular, relative

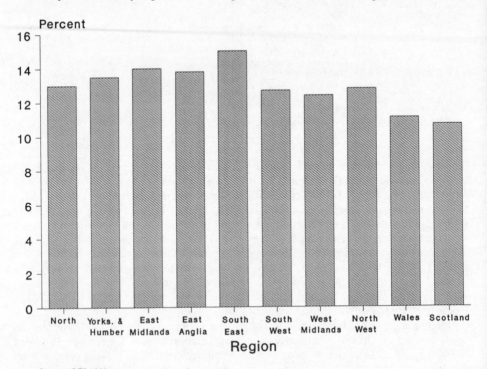

Source: LFS 1989

Figure 10.2.7: *Percentage of Employed Labour Force Receiving Job Related Training in the 4 weeks before the Survey, by region, Great Britain, 1989*

to living in the South, those who reside in Scotland are significantly less likely to receive training.

What then seem to be the main factors behind who receives training? While there are clear complementarities between higher educational qualifications obtained after leaving school and receiving training during employment, it is the occupation of an individual which appears to be a driving force determining employment-related training. Age is also an important determinant of the receipt of training, but evidence suggests that the decline in the probability of receiving training is less for those in non-manual occupations (Rigg, 1989). Women and part-time workers are also less likely to receive training (Booth, 1989,1991).

THE VIEW OF THE CRITICS

Having outlined the distribution of training in Britain, we now catalogue some of the major criticisms levelled at the vocational education and training system. Not necessarily in any order of importance, they include:

- the liberal bias of the secondary education sector which has been geared around a small number of academic elite. As a consequence Britain has traditionally placed a low emphasis upon vocational education within the secondary education system (Sanderson 1989).
- the lack of any well-recognised system of post- secondary formal vocational training contributes in turn to the low staying-on rates at schools after students attain the compulsory school-leaving age (Fonda and Hayes, 1988; White 1988, Finegold and Soskice, 1988; Keep and Mayhew, 1988).
- the craft apprenticeship system was synonymous with training. Job demarcations and other barriers to mobility meant a lack of training for other non-craft sections of the workforce (Keep and Mayhew, 1988).
- the traditional industrial relations system has not placed a strong emphasis on the value of training in collective bargaining (Keep and Mayhew, 1988).
- poor management attitude to training, possibly as a consequence of its own lack of training opportunities (Crockett and Elias 1984, Hart 1989).
- the short-term relationship between finance, profit and investment in physical capital, coupled with the myopia of British management has contributed to the low level of investment in human capital (Keep and Mayhew, 1988).
- the primary economic reason for the lack of training beyond craft levels has been the inadequate private returns to skills training in Britain (Daly et al, 1985; Prais and Wagner, 1988). Furthermore, the high level of youth pay may have depressed employers' demand for trainees (Jones, 1988).
- the lack of a nationally coherent system of VET both during and post-school, together with the lack of an adult training strategy, has also contributed to Britain's poor VET performance (Keep and Mayhew, 1988).
- the absence of statutory training and retraining provisions and entitlements, especially given the historical failure of voluntarism in employer provided training (Rainbird, 1990; Perry, 1976; Streeck, 1989).

In essence, critical appraisal has been uniformly negative, focussing around the low esteem afforded to vocationally orientated education and training. Set against these views is the patchwork of evidence which suggests that a major process of change may be under way. To gain further insight into the potential for change, we examine next the pattern of reforms in the system of vocational education and training.

REFORM OF THE SYSTEM OF VOCATIONAL EDUCATION AND TRAINING

The present Government has instituted a number of major reforms to the system of vocational education and training over the last decade. The focus of its policies has been based on the proposition that training is best left to the market, whilst recognising that training is the joint responsibility of both the Government and industry between the ages of 16 and 18.

Three distinct phases of education and training policies have been suggested (Finegold and Soskice, 1988). The first stage, that of 'preparation and market orientation', aligned with a non-interventionist training stance (1979–81) was characterised by budget cuts in education, together with the virtual dismantling of the Industry Training Boards and the adjacent collapse in apprenticeship training during the 1980 recession.

The second phase commenced with the introduction of the New Training Initiative (NTI) in 1981. The deepening recession and the sharp rise in youth unemployment compelled the government to reassess its non-interventionist training stance. Under the NTi, the Youth Training Scheme (YTS) was introduced, replacing the Youth Opportunities Program (YOP), by upgrading its training content, duration, and availability (it was made open to all minimum age school leavers not just the unemployed). YTS was subsequently increased to two years and apprenticeship routes through YTS were introduced. The Technical and Vocational Education Initiative (TVEI) was also launched during this phase, a major initiative which led to the introduction of technically and vocationally orientated modular learning programmes in schools for 14–18-year-olds. More recently, YTS has evolved into YT (Youth Training), emphasising the fact that the training of young people between the ages of 16 and 18 is viewed as a permanent feature of labour force entry.

The development of the further education (FE) sector with the introduction of the Certificate of Pre-Vocational Education (CPVE) was another initiative in the area of vocational training. Finally the National Council for Vocational Qualifications (NCVQ) was established following the De Ville Report (1985). The NCVQ has the task of rationalising all of the country's training qualifications into five levels with clear paths of progression between stages and national standards of competence and proficiency (Finegold and Soskice, 1988; Jessup, 1991).

An expansion of the focus of education and training policy is the dominant strategy under the third phase of recent reforms (1987 to date). The narrow concentration of education and training policy on the 14–18 age group has been broadened to include both general education (The Education Reform Act (ERA) 1987) and adult training (Training for Employment 1988). The development of City Technical Colleges under the ERA also signals the commencement of an alternative secondary school track funded directly by the Department of Education and Science with contributions from industry. The larger colleges of further education and polytechnics have been removed from Local Education Authority control, encouraging them to compete for students and strengthen their ties with employers.

The most recent innovation under this third phase comes with an added regional orientation. The establishment of Training and Enterprise Councils (TECs) was first heralded in Employment for the 1990s (HMSO, 1989). Based upon the premise that the major responsibility for training lies with the private sector with some limited government assistance, the TECs – whose members primarily consist of a majority of local industry representatives together with government representatives – emphasise training at the local level and flexibility with respect to the needs of the local economy. Linked with the TECs is the Business Growth Training Scheme which assists companies to develop a training strategy to meet their business objectives (Department of Employment, 1989). In 1991, TECs took over responsibility for the planning of work-related further education, courses which are offered primarily through Colleges of Further Education (Employment Department Group, 1991a). Planned reforms related to the developing role of the TECs include the issuing of Training Credit Vouchers to 16- and 17-year-olds planning a vocational education. Such vouchers will be redeemable via employers and training organisations which have established training courses approved by the TECs. Local authorities will lose control of sixth form and further education colleges, which will be supervised by separate funding councils for England and Wales, and all college governing bodies will have to include a representative of the local training and enterprise council (Employment Department Group, 1991b).

EVALUATION

While these major reforms to the system of vocational education and training over the past decade have gone some of the way to redressing the so-called training imbalance in the British economy, a major criticism of the reforms is their ad hoc nature and their apparent lack of coherence. For example, one of the primary objectives of the TVEI, the improvement of staying-on rates at secondary school, has clashed with YT. In effect, YT offers students a dual incentive to leave school at the minimum school-leaving age. First, because YT offers an allowance, and second, access to certain skilled jobs appears now to be routed through the YT apprenticeships (Finegold and Soskice, 1988). Such criticism may be misplaced, however, as evaluation of TVEI indicates that, while TVEI has been in operation, there has been almost a doubling of students taking balanced science and design and technology courses and that nine out of ten employers viewed the job performance of TVEI recruits favourably (Employment Department Group, 1991).

Ranson (1985) forecasts that these uncoordinated series of reforms will provide a three-tier, post-compulsory education and training system which will not generally raise the qualifications of those entering the work force. The top rung, the higher education sector, will continue to be confined to the academic elite. The middle tier, consisting of technical and vocational courses in full time FE, is unlikely to expand in the face of limitations on its funding and the lack of individual Educational Maintenance Allowances (to attract young people on to such full-time courses). The basic training route will continue to be the YT – a low cost option which it is suggested will not succeed in solving the skills problem (Finegold and Soskice, 1988, p.35). A number of reasons have been put forward. First, Jones (1988) suggests that the 2-year YT offers insufficient time for the development of higher level skills in many occupations. Second, many of the FE courses taken by trainees offer only basic qualifications (Jones, 1988). There have also been criticisms of the quality of training offered by YT providers; more than half of all YT providers failed to meet the quality standards set out by the Manpower Services Commission in May 1987 (Finegold & Soskice, 1988). Finally, in the face of falling numbers of school leavers, Finegold & Soskice (1988) note that employers have found it increasingly difficult to attract these leavers onto the scheme. As the numbers of school-leavers continue to decline into the 1990s, the success of YT lies in part with its ability to compete successfully with the alternatives offered to young people.

The unknown element in this process of rapid change and evolution in Britain's training system is the role of the TECs. This new system for the delivery of training, particularly to low-skilled and unskilled workers and to disadvantaged groups in the labour market, coupled with the creation of better links between education and training at the local labour market level, represents the most radical reform of the training system since the introduction of Industry Training Act of 1964. The very existence of 80–90 TECs across England and Wales (and 22 'local enterprise companies' in Scotland) imbues the geography of Britain's labour markets with a degree of importance not hitherto recognised.

CONCLUSIONS

The recent arrival of the TECs as the vehicle for local delivery of publicly funded training displays some desirable, as well as some potentially worrying, elements. In the light of the criticisms levelled at the UK vocational education and training system, the TECs represent an attempt to improve the responsiveness and flexibility of the local economy to the changing economic circumstances leading up to and following 1992. On the other hand, the arrival of the TECs also raises some questions about the efficient use of resources.

By delegating responsibility for planning and provision of publicly funded training to a large number of local bodies, the Government plans to overcome one of the main criticisms of a centrally administered scheme – that it never produced the right skills at the right time. The involvement of local industrialists on the TECs will, it is hoped, significantly reduce the lead-time between the identification of skill shortages and the provision of skills training. In so doing, the TECs offer flexibility as well as a decentralised focus for addressing issues of current skill shortages and future training needs and capacity at the local level.

In practice, however, it is questionable whether the efforts of 80–90 local bodies, each funding its own local labour market information-gathering efforts, each replicating the development work required to establish new training programmes and each vying for a larger share of the national allocation of resources for TEC funding, will necessarily better the efforts of what was a centralised system of training intervention with a devolved regional structure. Britain has a tiered structure of local labour markets which are spatially related via the occupational groups they serve. For instance, for professional, technical and certain managerial groups, the Greater London region constitutes one labour market. For operatives and unskilled workers, the spatial labour market may be better represented at the level of the Borough or below. The number and spatial allocation of TECs suggests that they will be bypassed by the former occupational groups.

Issues of the geography of Britain's system of vocational education and training arise also in consideration of a post-1992 Europe with a freer flow of human resources. The favourable location of the Southern and Eastern areas of Britain, in terms of their access to continental Europe, will provide accessibility both in terms of training opportunities for persons in Britain who feel that the existing system has 'failed' them in some way, and as an additional source of skilled, qualified human resources for employers who wish to satisfy particular skill shortages. Spatial access to superior training facilities in other European Community countries and to the product of such facilities will remove some of the pressure for reform in this vital part of the British economy, but simultaneously this will reduce the national stock of human capital and exacerbate the problem of human capital formation in the North and West.

Demographic trends are likely to play a significant role in the spatial provision of vocational education and training. Without a major re-evaluation of the scope for and access to retraining by older workers, certain areas within the UK will encounter a steady reduction in the demand for vocational education and training as the population of young persons continues to fall. Migration intervenes heavily in the spatial distribution of young people, so that the more attractive areas will find that demand remains high, whereas the less attractive areas will experience an apparent decline in the demand for training from young people. But the demand for job-related training by young people translates ultimately into the supply of trained labour to the workforce. These factors may not be apparent to a locally orientated producer of training programmes.

Finally, an issue which lies at the heart of our attitudes to training is the extent to which we view vocational education and training as a quasi-public good – not provided simply to benefit the trainee/employer relationship, but as part of our social capital. The apparent shift of focus over the decade of the 1980s toward training as an adjunct of the employee/employer relationship, and encapsulated within the philosophy underlying the formation of the TECs, is a development which causes concern among those holding the view that vocational education and training display positive externalities. The fact that TECs have now effectively taken control of work-related further education, an area in which local education authorities have seen their sphere of influence decline steadily over the past few years, is indicative of this same 'employer/employee' focus on training. This increasing emphasis upon the vocational education and training system, to provide skilled labour in areas of skill shortage, places rigid short-run demands upon a system which is also expected to lay the foundation for the range of general vocational skills required of a flexible labour force.

In our assessment of education and training reforms we are then left with three questions: How will these reforms stand up to the increased openness of the UK economy following completion of the European Internal Market after 1992? Given the marked fall in the number of young people entering the labour market, will these reforms provide the correct balance of training opportunities between young people and other workers? Finally, do these reforms provide the incentives to individuals and to employers in the private sector to invest in the level of skills appropriate for a rapidly evolving technical, professional and service oriented labour market? These are important issues which will require detailed investigation and evaluation over the 1990s, as TECs evolve their interventionary stance. In terms of the geography of human resource development, this new level of spatial interaction resurrects the subregions to the centre of the stage and places a renewed urgency upon our need to understand labour and product market linkages at the intra and inter-regional scale.

REFERENCES

Booth, A.L. (1989b). 'Earning and Learning: What Price Specific Training?' Discussion Paper No.8911. Brunel University London, November

Booth, A.L. (1991). 'Job Related Formal Training: Who Receives it and What is it Worth?' *Oxford Bulletin of Economics and Statistics*, 53 (3), 281–294.

Coopers and Lybrand Associates (1985). *A Challenge to Complacency: Changing Attitudes to Training*, MSC/NEDO: Sheffield.

Crockett, D. and P. Elias (1984). 'British Managers: A Study of Their Education, Training, Mobility and Earnings', *British Journal of Industrial Relations*, 22, 34–46.

Daly, A. et al (1985). 'Productivity, Machinery and Skills in a Sample of British and German Manufacturing Plants', *National Institute Economic Review*, February.

Davis, N. (1986). 'Training for Change' in P.E. Hart (ed) *Unemployment and Labour Market Policies*, Aldershot: Gower.

Department of Employment (1989). 'News Brief', *Employment Gazette*, January, 3–4.

De Ville, H.G. (1985). *Review of Vocational Qualifications in England and Wales*, London: HMSO.

Employment Department Group (1991a). *The Government's Expenditure Plans 1991–1992 to 1993–1994*. (CM 1506). London: HMSO.

Employment Department Group (1991b). *Education and Training for the 21st Century*. London: HMSO.

Finegold, D. and D. Soskice (1988). 'The Failure of Training in Britain: Analysis and Prescription', *Oxford Review of Economic Policy*, 4(3), 21–53.

Fonda, N. and C. Hayes (1988). 'Education, Training and Business Performance', *Oxford Review of Economic Policy*, 4(3), 108–119.

Greenhalgh, C. and M. Stewart (1987). 'The Effects and Determinants of Training', *Oxford Bulletin of Economics and Statistics*, 49(2), 171–89.

Hart, P.E. (1989). *Youth Unemployment in Great Britain*, Cambridge: Cambridge University Press.

HMSO (1989). *Employment for the 1990s*, HMSO: London

Jessup, G. (1991). *Outcomes: NVQs and the Emerging Model of Education and Training*. London: Falmer.

Jones, I. (1988). 'An Evaluation of YTS', *Oxford Review of Economic Policy*, 4(3), 43–71.

Keep, E. and K. Mayhew (1988). 'The Assessment: Education, Training and Economic Reforms', *Oxford Review of Economic Policy*, 4(3), i–xv.

Manpower Services Commission (MSC) (1982). *Youth Task Group Report*, London: MSC.

Mason, G. (1988). 'Trends in employment and training of Craftsmen and Craftswomen in the engineering industry'. *Engineering Industry Training Board Occupational Profile*, RM87 42. January. Watford: EITB.

Organisation for Economic Cooperation and Development (OECD) (1983). *Policies for Higher Education in the 1980s*, London: OECD.

Prais, S.J. and K. Wagner (1988). 'Productivity and Management: The Training of Foremen in Britain and Germany', *National Institute Economic Review*, February.

Perry, P.J.C. (1976). *The Evolution of British Manpower Policy from the Statute of Artificers 1593 to the Industrial Training Act 1964*. London: Eyre and Spottiswoode.

Rainbird, H. (1990) *Training Matters: Union Perspectives on Industrial Restructuring and Training*. Oxford: Basil Blackwell.

Ranson, S. (1985) 'Contradictions in the Government of Educational Change', *Political Studies*, 33(1), 56–72.

Rigg, M. (1989) *Training in Britain: Individuals Perspectives*. London: HMSO.

Sanderson, M. (1988). 'Education and Economic Decline', *Oxford Review of Economic Policy*, 4(1), 38–50.

Streeck, W. (1989). 'Skills and the Limits of Neo-liberalism: The Enterprise of the Future as a Place of Learning', *Work, Employment and Society*, 3(1).

Training Agency (1989). *Labour Market Quarterly Reports*, May and July.

White, M. (1988). 'Educational Policy and Economic Goals', *Oxford Review of Economic Policy*, 4(3), 1–20.

Wickham, A. (1986). *Women and Training*. Milton Keynes: Open University Press.

Acknowledgements: The authors would like to thank Helen Rainbird, Paul Ryan and Alison Booth for comments and suggestions on an earlier draft of this paper. The excellent clerical and word processing skills of Christine Jones, Barbara Wilson and Carol Dobson are acknowledged with thanks.

Social Welfare as a Dimension of Regional Development

S. E. Curtis

Much of the debate over regional development in Britain focuses on indicators of economic growth, industrial structure and employment. However, a wider definition of 'development' should take into account dimensions of social welfare which reflect regional variations in the outcome of social and economic development in the country.

Social welfare is an imprecise term and many alternative definitions could be offered. A working definition adopted here is the relative degree of well-being and quality of life of a group in a society. The concept must be considered as relative because in every society, expectations will depend on the living standards, rights, and privileges enjoyed by the majority of its people, at a particular point in time, and on the political ideology of its social institutions. Our view of welfare is therefore is a value laden and variable concept. Criteria for assessing social welfare vary, as do views on how far our society should ensure geographical and social equality in welfare.

In Britain there is a tendency to put industrial-economic objectives before others when making regional policy and evaluating the outcomes of policy implementation. Also implicit in much current policy is the view that a reduction in social and regional inequalities in socio-economic conditions is not a very high priority, compared with the need to promote national economic growth. It is argued that a healthy national economy will lead to trickle-down effects of benefit to poorer populations and that national growth is most likely to be achieved through the operation of market forces, which must be allowed to function more freely. However, the statistics on low income show that the poor have gained less rapidly than the wealthier members of our society as a result of application of this approach in the 1980s (as illustrated in a House of Commons report from the Social Services Committee (1990)). During the 1980s, economic policy tended to divert attention away from the persistent inequalities in important aspects of social welfare which any just and comprehensive policy for social and economic development should seek to redress. These inequalities remain important issues for the 1990s.

VARIATIONS IN SOCIAL WELFARE

The definition of social welfare offered above is broad and only a few selected aspects of welfare can be explored here. Different aspects of social welfare are so intricately linked, (in processes often summarised by the 'cycle of poverty'), that it is misleading to focus on one single dimension of social deprivation. However, the following discussion highlights certain aspects of social welfare which seem important and which deserve higher priority in socio-economic policy making at the national and regional scales in Britain.

HEALTH DIFFERENCES

One of the clearest and most disturbing dimensions of regional welfare differences within Britain is the health divide, which remains a major challenge to be faced in the 1990s. Health differences in Britain are widely documented (Townsend, Davidson & Whitehead, 1988) and are, for example, the subject of much work in medical geography. Table 10.3.1 shows the persistence of regional differences in Standardised Mortality Ratios. These indicators show a broad North-South divide with northern and parts of the country doing less well than southern regions. The latest decennial supplement on geographical patterns in mortality for the period 1979 to 1983 has recently published by the Office of Population Censuses and Surveys (Britton, 1990). It shows that deaths due to specific causes also show persistent geographical differences. Mortality due to Ischaemic Heart Disease shows a similar pattern to general mortality. Lung cancer is one of the diseases which shows a particularly high mortality rate in inner urban areas compared with the surrounding region, even in the wealthier South East. Typically these areas of high urban mortality are also the most deprived socio-economically.

Table 10.3.1.. Standardised Mortality Ratios (SMR*) by Region in England

Standard Region	SMR in 1975	SMR in 1985
South West	92	90
East Anglia	90	92
South East	95	94
(Greater London)	97	95
(Rest of South East)	94	93
East Midlands	98	100
West Midlands	103	104
Yorkshire and Humberside	104	105
North West	109	111
North	110	112
England	99	99

Source: Armitage, R. (1987) English Regional Fertility and Mortality Patterns, 1975–1985, Population Trends,47, p16–23

* The SMR expresses the number of deaths occurring in each region in a given year as a percentage of the deaths which would have been expected if the area was experiencing national morality age-sex specific mortality rates in that year. SMR of 100 is the ratio for England and Wales in the year in question.

Heart diseases and cancers used to be commonly referred to as 'diseases of affluence', because of their links with aspects of lifestyle common in wealthy nations. We have had some success in reducing mortality due to these diseases, although there is a lot more that could be done. There is now evidence to show that for the more privileged members of our society (non manual workers) the rates of mortality due to these diseases are improving more rapidly than for poorer people (manual workers) (Marmot & McDowall, 1986). These diseases are becoming, within countries such as Britain, diseases of poverty rather than affluence and they are symptomatic of important differences in social welfare.

Health inequalities are evident in levels of illness as well as death rates. Reported morbidity levels due to chronic diseases show worse trends for manual than for non-manual workers (OPCS, 1984). Several studies have also shown that populations living in more deprived parts of urban areas report comparatively high levels of emotional distress and mental illness, as well as physical illness (see, for example, Curtis, 1990; Giggs, 1973).

As we move into the 1990s with the National Health Service reforms already beginning to take effect and the planned changes to the community care system due to become operational in 1993 the issue of health inequalities becomes even more important. Concern has been expressed that the changes will make inequalities in access to health care more marked, to the disadvantage of those with chronic illness and those with limited incomes. Even if these concerns prove to be unfounded, it is crucial to the efficient operation of the new health care system that the purchasers of health care (District Health Authorities) are able to identify and quantify the needs of their local population for health care in order to arrange suitable contracts with the providers (hospitals and community health services provided by public and independent agencies). Health authorities are seeking to improve their knowledge of health differences and health care needs in different geographical areas in order to carry out this task.

There has been discussion over whether the poor levels of health in less privileged areas is because of the impact on health of living conditions in deprived areas or because of a 'healthy migrant effect' (healthier people move to more wealthy areas) combined with a 'drift effect' (those in poor health drift towards deprived areas). However, the balance of evidence seems to suggest that the effects of migration do not explain all the regional differences in health observed and that stressful, difficult and sometimes hazardous conditions in deprived areas are deleterious to health (Fox & Goldblatt, 1982).

Regional health inequalities are linked to other basic aspects of social welfare and, although there is a clear social class differential in health indicators, the regional differences are not fully explained by geographical variations in the social class structure of the population. Other indicators of living conditions such as housing status, car ownership unemployment also show strong associations with mortality and morbidity. The British Medical Association has recognised the importance of various aspects of social deprivation for ill health and have pointed to housing conditions as one of the most fundamental associations (BMA, 1987).

VARIATIONS IN HOUSING QUALITY

Housing quality is therefore another significant aspect of welfare, not only because it is, in its own right an important element of the quality of life, but also because of its association with other dimensions of welfare such as health. Various authors have considered the factors which contribute to poor housing quality. These include lack of basic amenities such as water supply and sewerage, overcrowding, dampness and coldness, poor access to facilities, employment and amenities and lack of privilege with respect to tenure rights and obligations. Home ownership is on many counts the most privileged form of tenure. The division between home owners and those in rented property, which has been referred to as the socio-tenurial polarisation of our population, extends to differences in morbidity and mortality.

More general home ownership is held up as one of the objectives of the present government and home ownership has increased over the last 10 years. However, the proportion of home owners in the population remains highest in southern parts of the country (over 70% of households are home owners in the South West region and in the South East outside London compared with 64% in the UK on average). This high rate of home ownership for southerners is, however, being bought at a high price. Hamnett (1989) has shown that the cost of home ownership is much higher in the South East than elsewhere, even allowing for the comparatively high wage rates in the region. This is one of the penalties of rapid economic growth and concentration of population in the south east. It is a factor which acts as a serious brake on labour mobility between regions.

Within the South East, also, housing tenure has become an important element in the division between the rich and poor. This division is visible in its most extreme forms in London, where we find the most expensive privately owned housing and also the highest levels of homelessness. Table 10.3.2 shows data on the rate of registration of homeless families by local authorities, which is highest in London. (With about 11% of the national population, London has 30% of the registered homeless households.)

Table 10.3.2. Homeless Families in England (1988)

Region	homeless families accepted onto local authority lists per 1000 households in 1987
North	7.1
Yorkshire and Humberside	4.9
East Midlands	5.1
East Anglia	4.0
South East	7.1
Greater London	11.0
Rest of South East	4.0
West Midlands	6.2
North West	7.4
England	6.2
Wales	4.4
Scotland	5.8
Great Britain	6.1

Source: Regional Trends 1989

These data relate to the 128,000 families accepted by local authorities in 1987 as homeless and qualifying for local authority housing provision. (Often the provision made is very inadequate housing in bed and breakfast institutions). These families represent only part of the total extent of homelessness. Figures on single homeless people, for example, are more difficult to obtain, partly because they often do not qualify for acceptance onto local authority housing lists. In 1989 the National Federation of Housing Associations examined 'hidden homelessness' and estimated that in London there were at least 3000 single people sleeping rough 19,000 squatting, 25,000 in bed and breakfast hotels, hostels or short life housing and 74,000 overcrowded and unwillingly living in other people's houses. The figures on homelessness therefore show a worsening situation which has reached its most serious proportions in areas of Britain which showed most rapid economic growth in the 1980s. For about 10 per cent of homeless households the reason given for their homelessness is their inability to continue mortgage payments. This is an increasing problem which reflects the damaging effects of high interest rates combined with high costs of housing in areas like the South East.

It is one of the failures of government policies that the need for affordable housing has not been met and has not seemed to be a high priority in regional development schemes. Some moves have been made recently to stem the rising levels of homelessness in areas such as London, with £1 billion allocated to acute housing problems, about a quarter of which was to be spent in the South East. Housing Corporation funds for 1992–3 have been set at double the 1989–90 levels. However, this will not be sufficient to ensure that housing needs will be met in the 1990s. It has been estimated that between 3.2 and 4 million new homes will be needed. The UK spends a small proportion of its gross domestic product (GDP) on housing (only 3.7% in 1987 compared with, for example, 5.1% in W. Germany). Furthermore Britain is relying increasingly on private sector house building, which has not in general met requirements for social housing. The new developments in the Isle of Dogs, in London's Docklands, for example, have mainly been expensive properties for incomers to buy rather than cheaper and rented properties to meet the needs of the local population.

EDUCATION AND EQUALITY OF OPPORTUNITY

Another issue underlying much inequality in social welfare concerns the lack of equal opportunities for particular groups in our society. One of the means available to governments to attempt to ensure more equality of opportunity is through provision of services such as education which are intended to promote equality of access to qualifications, the passports to good employment and income prospects in adulthood. There has been considerable debate over whether positive discrimination in the education system in favour of children from deprived backgrounds can effectively mitigate all the disadvantages they face. On the other hand, a good deal of evidence suggests that factors such as poor resourcing and institutionalised racism in schools are likely to be worsening some children's chances of a good education.

Some aspects of current education policy seem likely to exacerbate the differences in school achievement between pupils in different social and ethnic groups by increasing the inequalities between different parts of our education system. Burdett (1988) argues that we are heading towards a tiered education system with independent schools and a small number of city technology colleges forming the most privileged sectors and the local authority managed schools at the bottom of the pile. Furthermore, the independent sector, which is being strongly promoted in measures such as the Education Reform Act of 1988, shows strong tendencies towards spatial polarisation in the South and East of the country and in those localities where it is already well established. These trends, added to the serious lack of resources in the state education sector, acknowledged by the Schools Inspectorate, and the fact that intervention in the form of educational priority funding and preschool service provision no longer feature prominently in programmes to reduce urban deprivation, do not bode well for the ability of the education system to ensure that children in deprived areas get the best possible opportunities from their education.

CONCLUSIONS: A QUESTION OF PRIORITIES

The fact that economic policies and regional development seem to have been pursued without incorporating social welfare and quality of life as fundamental objectives of development reflects a limited view of the aims of a society like the one we live in and also a failure to understand, or at least to acknowledge, the underlying processes which bring about inequalities in health and quality of life between different parts of the country. The pursuit of growth in a market driven economy without due regard to the social welfare outcomes of this growth seems an unacceptably limited objective for public policy either nationally or regionally and seems to put us out of step with our partners in Europe. For example, the European member states of the World Health Organisation (including Britain) have agreed a programme which aims for Health for All by the Year 2000 (WHO, 1989). The programme includes 38 targets which include objectives of reducing health inequalities between regions, taking government action to improve aspects of lifestyle and environment which are damaging for health. During the 1980s, many European countries announced national versions of a Health for All programme. Britain was not among them, although it is claimed that government policies are in line with 'Health for All' objectives. It is difficult to escape the conclusion that this lack of commitment to Health for All goals reflects a fundamental reluctance to make welfare and quality of life basic aims of socio-economic policy in this country. Similarly, there seems to be need for a comprehensive housing policy in Britain to address all aspects of housing need. We also need to be looking critically at the fact that although ethnic minority populations are most concentrated in our inner cities, yet policies for urban economic regeneration have done very little to change the situation for ethnic minority groups. Injustice remains endemic in our social and commercial institutions because of economic deprivation, racism and sexism. Surely we will not realise greater equality of social welfare until this becomes a priority objective and is treated as a meaningful measure of success of development policies, rather than a side-issue.

REFERENCES

BMA (1987) *Deprivation and Ill-Health, British Medical Association Board of Science and Education Discussion Paper,* London: BMA.

Britton, M. (Ed) 1990. *Mortality and Geography: a Review in the Mid 1980's, England and Wales,* OPCS Series DS9. London: HMSO.

Burdett F. (1988) A Hard Act to Swallow? The Geography of Education After the Great Education Reform Bill. *Geography.* 73, 3, pp 208–215.

Curtis S. (1990) The use of survey data and small area statistics to assess the link between individual morbidity and neighbourhood deprivation, *Journal of Epidemiology and Community Health,* 44, p.62–68.

Fox A. and Goldblatt P. (1982) *Socio-demographic Mortality Differentials: Longitudinal Study 1971–75,* Series L.S. 1, London: HMSO.

Giggs J (1973) The distribution of schizophrenics in Nottingham, *Transactions of the Institute of British Geographers,* 59, p55–76.

Great Britain, Parliament (1990) Low Income Statistics: Social Services Committee 4th Report, House of Commons Paper 376, 9.5.1990, London: HMSO.

Hamnett, C (1989) The Owner Occupied housing market in Britain: a North South Divide p97–113 in Lewis and Townsend (eds) *The North South Divide in Britain in the 1980s,* London: Paul Chapman Publishing.

Marmot M. and McDowall, M. (1986) Mortality decline and widening social inequalities, *Lancet,* 1986, ii, p274–276.

OPCS (1986) *General Household Survey 1984,* London, OPCS, HMSO.

Townsend, P. Davidson, M. and Whitehead, N. (1988) *Inequalities in Health: the Black Report and the Health Divide,* Harmondsworth: Penguin.

WHO (1989) *Monitoring of the Strategy for Health for All by the Year 2000: Part 1 The Situation in the European Region 1987–8,* Copenhagen: World Health Organization.

Social Policy Developments: Housing

M. P. Kleinman

WHERE WE ARE STARTING FROM

The Conservative Government has entered the 1990s with a relatively coherent overall view of the way it wishes to see the British housing system develop (Monk and Kleinman, 1989). This view reflects both the neo-liberal orientation of the Government in theory, and its centralising tendencies in practice. As spelt out in the 1987 Housing White Paper, and subsequent legislation (1988 Housing Act and 1989 Local Government and Housing Act), this view comprises the following elements:

i. continued support for owner occupation to enable an even greater percentage of households than currently (65%) to become home owners.

ii. the development of the so-called independent rented sector, comprising profit-seeking private landlords and non-profit-making, but commercially minded, housing associations, as the main vehicle for meeting additional demand for rental units.

iii. a major change in the role of local authorities from being direct providers of housing to enablers of housing provision.

iv. support for existing council tenants who wish to 'opt out' of the local authority sector and have a different landlord acquire their estate. Alongside this, council rents will be brought more into line with market rents.

v. the principle that, as the major benefit from housing improvement and renewal above a minimum standard goes to the private owner, the costs should similarly fall to the owner-occupier and not the tax payer.

The general thrust of government policy is thus fairly clear. As for areas of concern, we can identify several, some of which are hardy perennials of the housing scene, while others are products of the specific circumstances of the 1990s.

First, there has been increasing interest in the relationship between house prices and mortgage finance on the one hand, and inflation and the money supply on the other. There are two issues here – one basically statistical, the other relating to macro-economic theory. The statistical concern relates to the way owner-occupiers' housing costs are incorporated into the Retail Price Index (RPI). At present, a simple measure of mortgage interest costs is used. This leads to the somewhat paradoxical position that, if interest rates are raised by the Chancellor as a way of bearing down on inflation, the change feeds through, via mortgage rates, and hence mortgage costs, into the RPI, giving an immediate short-term boost to inflation. This has led to some calls (not just from Chancellors of the Exchequer) for an alternative measure of owner-occupiers' housing costs to be included in the RPI, which reflects the net return to owner-occupied housing) and not just monthly mortgage payments.

A more fundamental issue is the effect that deregulation of mortgage finance has had on the economy. It has been argued that the deregulation of the market for mortgage finance, and the greater competition among lenders that resulted were a considerable source of inflationary pressure in the later 1980s, both directly through the greater availability of credit and indirectly through the 'wealth effect' of increased house prices. Associated with easier credit availability has been the phenomenon of equity withdrawal – i.e. the process whereby indebtedness rises by more than additional investment in housing.

Equity withdrawal can occur in a variety of ways. For example, owner-occupiers with no mortgage debt die and their houses are bought by mortgagors; owner-occupiers moving house increase their mortgage by more than the difference in house values; and owner-occupiers increase their existing debt to spend on items other than home improvements. Moreover, the 'wealth effect' means that even without an increase in net indebtedness, consumption will rise. As Ermisch puts it:

> The fact that [households] know that they can easily borrow on the basis of their housing wealth if necessary (note the spread of lines of credit based on housing equity) may make them more willing to draw down their liquid assets or use consumer credit to finance consumption when house prices increase. (Ermisch, 1990 pp.14–15)

Muellbauer is in no doubt about the importance of these housing market changes for overall economic policy. Referring to the partial elimination of credit rationing and the wealth effects of house price increases, he argues that

> Much of the explanation for the decline of the personal sector savings rate in the 1980s and the boom in consumer imports is to be found here. (Muellbauer 1990, p.49)

This greater importance flows in part from the continuing rise in owner-occupation over the last two decades, from 49 per cent in 1969 to 66 per cent in 1989, coupled with rising asset values and credit deregulation. In addition, increases in mortgage rates are increasingly taken into account by workers and unions in wage negotiations with employers. For both these reasons, the housing market will continue to be an area of concern for government macro-economic policy in the 1990s.

The second broad area of concern relates to North/South issues. Throughout the 1980s, house price differentials between the North and South widened. In 1975, prices in London were 57 per cent higher than in the Northern region, according to the Nationwide Building Society. By the first quarter of 1987, London prices were 142 per cent higher. At the beginning of 1988, the price of a semi-detached house varied from £101,000 in Greater London and £90,000 in Hertfordshire to £28,000 in Cleveland and £26,000 in South Yorkshire. The effect of these widening North/South house price differentials has been both to reduce labour mobility (and hence raise unemployment rates nationally) and also to push up wages in the tight labour markets of the South. The nature of the rented housing market in Britain has also contributed to labour mobility problems, with both the small size of the private rented sector, and the relative inflexibility of council housing being factors (Hughes and McCormick, 1981; Whitehead and Kleinman, 1990).

Third, fierce political battles have been fought over the issue of housing land availability, and the location of new housing developments in the booming South East. In particular, Consortium Developments, representing nine of the largest housebuilders in the country, announced plans to build a series of 'new communities' often on Green Belt land. The housing land debate has produced curious strategic alliances. On the one hand there is the spectacle of the volume builders incongruously invoking the rights of the huddled masses of the inner city yearning to be free in the greensward of the Outer South East. On the other hand, the virtues of the town and country planning system and the sanctity of local democracy are being belatedly championed by solidly

Conservative communities, who had not previously been known for their vociferous objections to, for example, the abolition of the Greater London Council (GLC) or the imposition of non-elected planning authorities in the Merseyside and London Dock-lands.

Fourth, issues relating to access to, and conditions within, the rented tenures remain important. Mass owner-occupation and the sale of council houses have increased fears about the 'residualisation' of council housing, as rented housing – particularly public rented housing – becomes dominated by the elderly, the poor, ethnic minorities and the excluded. At the same time, the reduction in new building and losses from the existing rented stock through the Right to Buy policy, has led to a shortage of affordable housing and an increase in homelessness. Moreover, towards the end of the 1980s, it became clear that lack of affordable housing was an issue not only in London, but in many parts of the South.

PROSPECTS FOR THE 1990S

The demographic underpinning of the housing market in the 1990s will differ in important ways from that of the last two decades. Changes in the age distribution of the population will mean net household formation will fall from 146,000 p.a. in 1981 and 197,000 p.a. in 1991, to only 139,000 p.a. by 2001 (Kleinman and Whitehead 1989, Department of the Environment 1991). The total number of households will continue to grow so that by the end of the century there will be over 20 million households in England, compared with 18 million in 1981. But the type of households will change. There will be more smaller and older households; more single parent households; and fewer households headed by a married couple. The number of households in this latter category will actually *fall* over the 1990s from 10.72 million in 1986 to 10.14 million in 2001.

As a result of these demographic changes, the emphasis within the private housing market will shift away from new construction for additional demand and the needs of first time buyers, towards a greater concern with replacement demand (both rehabili-tation and perhaps also renewal), improvement of existing properties and the needs of middle-aged and elderly, often fairly well off households. The equity locked up in houses owned outright by older households will represent a potent source of consumer demand both within the housing market and elsewhere. Opportunities for suppliers will range from leisure-orientated retirement complexes for the more active and newly retired through to 'very sheltered' housing schemes incorporating nursing and other care. Throughout the housing market there will be greater emphasis on quality and value added, rather than sheer numbers.

In the 1990s, owner-occupation will continue to be supported by both major parties as the tenure which the majority of the population both aspire to and can reasonably expect to attain. However, the fervency with which home ownership has been pro-moted as a panacea to all housing ills, particularly over the last decade, will decline. In part, this will reflect the fact that owner-occupation as an investment will not perform as spectacularly as it did over the 1974–1988 period.

The Labour Party has clearly accepted owner-occupation as the mass tenure, and, importantly, the principle of council house sales. However, if returned to power in the 1990s, Labour is likely to place at least some emphasis on the provision of an adequate supply of rental housing. Given Labour's justified lack of faith in the private rented sector's ability to perform anything other than a marginal role aimed at specific needs, such as job mobility, this will mean an increase in social housing expenditure. This will be channelled through housing associations as well as local authorities, although Labour may require greater local accountability and democracy from associations.

The Conservatives, though seeking to minimise the role of social housing, and particularly local authorities, are unlikely to increase substantially the tax privileges of owner-occupiers. Indeed, it is more likely that they will seek to divert such petty capitalist instincts away from the housing market and towards industry and commerce through greater tax reliefs on direct and indirect investment in equities.

Deregulation, and perhaps also the impact of 1992, will continue to cause concern in terms of the relationship between housing wealth and housing debt on the one hand and inflation on the other. Whether the current policy of reliance solely on interest rates will continue, or be replaced by alternative policies, such as direct credit controls, is impossible to say, depending as it does on the wider question of macro-economic policy in general, and issues such as the timing of progress towards greater European monetary union, etc.

During the 1980s, there was increasing attention and concern about growing regional disparities and the 'North/South' issue. The extent to which this will continue into the 1990s depends on a number of factors. As far as house prices are concerned, it may be the case that the widening of North/South differentials during the 1982–88 period was simply part of a cyclical pattern, in which regional differentials increase during the upswing of the national house price cycle, and decline during the down-swing. Such a pattern appears to hold for the period from the mid-1960s to the mid-1980s. But recent work by Holmans (1988) shows that such stability in regional house price differentials was not always the case; between 1956 and 1965, differentials between the South East and the North widened considerably (Holmans 1988).

It therefore remains an open question as to whether the 1982–88 period will resemble 1965–82 or 1958–65 (Ermisch 1990). In the 1980s, the effectiveness of regional policy has been considerably eroded, and there has been a continuation both of high levels of unemployment and sharp regional differences in unemployment rates. In addition, the general policy shift away from intervention and towards laissez-faire, and from a manufacturing to a service-based economy, has tended to favour the South. For all these reasons a structural (i.e. non-cyclical) shift in the North/South house price differential is at least plausible.

Will this pattern be maintained in the 1990s? The abolition of rates will boost Southern house prices more than Northern ones (and a return to it will have the reverse effect), while the construction of the Channel Tunnel and the completion of the European internal market will boost demand more strongly in the South East than elsewhere. On the other hand, congestion costs in the South will impact both directly on the 'quality of life' and indirectly via wage rates. Together with greater social and political division between North and South, this may lead to a reversal of policy, with stronger regional assistance to the North, encouragement of migration of firms and population from the South, and constraints on at least some types of economic activity in the South.

Under these circumstances, there would be greater convergence of house prices between North and South. Shortages of rented housing will persist, despite the reduction in household formation in the second half of the 1990s. In its most acute form, this means continuing high levels of homelessness. These problems will continue to be most acute in London, but will be by no means confined to the capital. Additional social housing provision will not be enough to meet housing needs (Kleinman, 1990).

Local authority new building will fall virtually to zero. Housing associations' activity will increase, but not to anything like the levels necessary to offset the decline in local authority provision; moreover, rents of housing association properties will drift upwards in real terms, in many cases, becoming unaffordable by the working poor. Inner city rehabilitation will be particularly squeezed, as local authorities will not have the resources to undertake this work, while increasingly cost-conscious, risk-bearing housing associations will be drawn towards less risky and cheaper new build schemes.

Continuing shortages of rented housing and homelessness in London will lead to increasing reappraisal of the question of 'who lives where?' This will mean implicit or even perhaps overt encouragement for the homeless to return to (or be exiled to) regions with less housing pressure. Apart from the human costs of such a policy, there are obvious inconsistencies with policies to encourage labour mobility to the faster-growing regions.

More generally, the issue of affordability will surface not only in acute pressure areas such as London, but in a range of rural, suburban and ex-urban communities. In areas of high house prices and strict constraints on development, concern about housing opportunities for local people – both 'sons and daughters' and essential service and industrial workers – will come into political conflict with green-tinged parochial restrictions.

London and the South East will continue to grow. As Peter Hall has pointed out, the area of maximum growth has continually moved outward through this century, from central core to outer ring to the regional fringe (Hall, 1989). The 1980s growth areas included some more than 100 miles distant from central London. Current projections for population growth show that most of the strongest growth areas in the 1980s and 1990s – places such as Bournemouth/Poole, Swindon and Milton Keynes/Northampton – are in the 'Greater South East' rather than the 'Rest of the South East' (ROSE) proper. This process is only being partially offset by reurbanization and the rediscovery of central London by the urban middle class.

Hall argues that a new generation of new towns in the South East will be needed. Though these will be developed primarily by private rather than public agencies, the public sector will be needed as an 'equal and co-operative' partner. Hall argues that between 1980 and 2000 another 1.5 million homes are necessary. Of these, no more than 250,000 will be in London, leaving 1.25 million for ROSE and the South East fringe. This will mean establishing a new generation of new towns, and devoting to urban development part of the large surplus of agricultural land (perhaps a quarter of current agricultural land will no longer be needed for food production) that will emerge by the end of the century.

In the 1970s and 1980s, the housing debate became dominated by the politics of tenure and the clash between central and local government. While these trends are likely to continue into the 1990s, there is also some evidence that the debate may be moving on to more fundamental questions such as overall investment, efficiency, and access to adequate housing. In addition, the 1990s may see rapid movement towards a more integrated Europe founded on principles of social justice as much as economic liberalism. If this does occur, the UK pattern of an increasingly well-housed majority co-existing with a badly-housed or homeless minority may come under attack both internally and externally.

REFERENCES

Department of the Environment (1991) *Household Projections, England, 1989–2011*, London:HMSO.

Ermisch, J. (1990) 'The Background: Housing Trends and Issues arising from them' in Ermisch J (ed) *Housing and the National Economy*, Gower: Aldershot.

Hall, P. (1989) *London 2001* Unwin Hyman: London.

Holmans, A.E. (1988) 'House Prices' Department of the Environment, mimeo.

Hughes, G.A. & McCormick, B. (1981) 'Do council housing policies reduce migration between regions' *Economic Journal, 91*, 919–937.

Kleinman, M.P. & Whitehead, C.M.E. (1989) 'Demand for New Housebuilding, 1986–2001' in Cross and Whitehead (eds) *Development and Planning 1989*, Policy Journals: Newbury.

Kleinman, M.P. & Whitehead, C.M.E. (1992)'A Medium-Term Forecast of Housing Output' University of Cambridge, Department of Land Economy, forthcoming.

Kleinman, M.P. (1990) 'The Future Provision of Social Housing in Britain' in van Vliet, W. and van Weesep, J. (eds) *The Changing Role of Government in Housing* London: Sage Publications.

Monk, S. & Kleinman, M. 'Housing' in P. Brown & R. Sparks (eds) (1989) *Beyond Thatcherism* Milton Keynes: Open University Press.

Muellbauer, J. (1990) 'The Housing Market and the UK Economy: Problems and Opportunities' in Ermisch, J. (ed) *Housing and the National Economy* Gower: Aldershot.

Whitehead, C.M.E. & Kleinman, M.P. (1990) 'The Viability of the Privately Rented Housing Market' in Ermisch J (ed) *Housing and the National Economy* Gower: Aldershot.

Health and Health Services

Graham Bentham

At its inception in 1948 there were high hopes that the National Health Service would eliminate the inequalities in health that had scarred Britain in the 1920s and 1930s. No longer would inability to pay be a barrier to sick people receiving good quality medical care. Nor would living in a deprived area carry the additional burden of lack of access to health care. Planning would ensure that a comprehensive health service was available to residents of all parts of the country and this would be free at the point of delivery. The NHS inherited a motley collection of existing health services and buildings. Some of these were the product of charity, some were municipal services which were often direct descendants of nineteenth century workhouses and others were the product of market forces. What the NHS had to work with was a collection of hospitals and activities, not a rationally planned health service. Inevitably, this meant that in many cases the wrong services were being provided for the wrong people in the wrong places. Tudor Hart (1971) summed up the situation in terms of what he called an inverse care law: that the availability of good medical care tends to vary inversely with the need of the population served. More than 40 years on it is possible to examine whether the NHS has been able to move towards a more equitable pattern of health care.

There is no doubt that the inertia resulting from the historical legacy of buildings and the vested interests of professional groups have exerted a profound influence on the evolution of the service. Nevertheless, some progress has been made towards a more equitable pattern. One success story has been the development of an effective system of primary health care with the general practitioner as its pivot. Before the Second World War the geographical distribution of GPs was extremely uneven. Those practising in poorer areas needed large numbers of patients on their lists to make a living from the low fees or insurance premiums that could be afforded by a deprived population. Other GPs achieved higher incomes from lower workloads by catering for a wealthier clientele concentrated in the more prosperous parts of the country. The result was a perverse geographical pattern where the areas with the greatest needs had the lowest numbers of doctors per head. If nothing had been done the position of GPs as independent contractors to the NHS would have guaranteed the persistence of this unacceptable situation.

One of the innovations of the NHS was the establishment of a body known as the Medical Practices Committee charged with the task of controlling the distribution of GPs throughout the country (Haynes, 1987). It has done this by a combination of negative controls and positive inducements. The country has been divided up into practice areas and where these are considered to have enough doctors the committee has the power to reject new applicants to practise in such locations. At the other end of the scale are so-called designated areas which are regarded as under-doctored. Here applications to practise are generally granted without question and financial incentives are given. This policy has worked best during the periods when there has been a large supply of new medical graduates to be steered into the less attractive areas. The achievements of this policy can be seen in Table 10.5.1 which gives regional data on GP list sizes. There is no obvious indication of an under-doctored 'North' and a more favoured 'South' although the relatively even distribution of GPs needs to be seen in the context of marked regional differences in health care needs. It is instructive to compare this pattern with the data on dentists also given in Table 10.5.1. Here, there has been no machinery geared towards an evening out of the geographical distribution of services and the result is much greater regional inequalities.

Table 10.5.1 The Regional Distribution of General Practitioners,
Dentists and Hospital Beds in 1987

Regional Health Authority	Average GP list size	Persons per dentists	Hospital beds per 1000 population
Northern	2002	3851	7.5
Yorkshire	1985	3558	7.1
Trent	2060	4127	6.2
East Anglian	1952	3695	6.3
NW Thames	2065	2244	6.6
NE Thames	2078	3028	6.9
SE Thames	2069	2779	6.4
SW Thames	2103	2389	7.1
Wessex	1922	3232	6.0
Oxford	2007	3220	4.9
Southwestern	1872	2947	6.7
West Midlands	2010	3893	6.2
Mersey	2012	3436	7.4
Northwestern	2081	3493	7.1
Wales	1849	3636	7.7
Scotland	1630	3324	10.9
N. Ireland	1835	3035	10.2

Source: Regional Trends , 1989

It should be stressed that the regional data on primary care hide some important problems that operate at a more detailed geographical scale at both ends of the urban/rural spectrum. There is evidence that primary health services in some inner city areas compare unfavourably with those elsewhere. A report on the situation in London (London Health Planning Consortium Study Group, 1981) found a catalogue of problems. Premises were unfit. There was a large proportion of elderly doctors. Some practices had very small lists (just enough to qualify for NHS allowances) but were unwilling to accept new patients. It was found to be difficult to contact many doctors during the working day and there was considerable reliance on deputising services. Whereas in most of the country virtually everyone is registered with a GP, non-registration rates amongst the mobile inner city population tended to be much higher. Such people are not only denied ready access to primary care but also to the more specialised services access to which is gained by GP referrals. Remoter rural areas also have their problems. Here the dominant concern is over physical access to health care. Following national trends GPs have been combining to form group practices most of which are located in the larger villages and small towns. The consequence has been that many surgeries in smaller villages have closed and many people now find themselves living at greater distances from the nearest surgery than was the case in the past. Increasing car ownership and affluence have meant that this poses few problems for the majority of people. However, for those without ready access to a car, particularly the poor, the old and the chronically sick, getting to the surgery can pose severe problems (Bentham and Haynes, 1985). This can mean that the very groups with the greatest need for care face the greatest difficulties in meeting those needs.

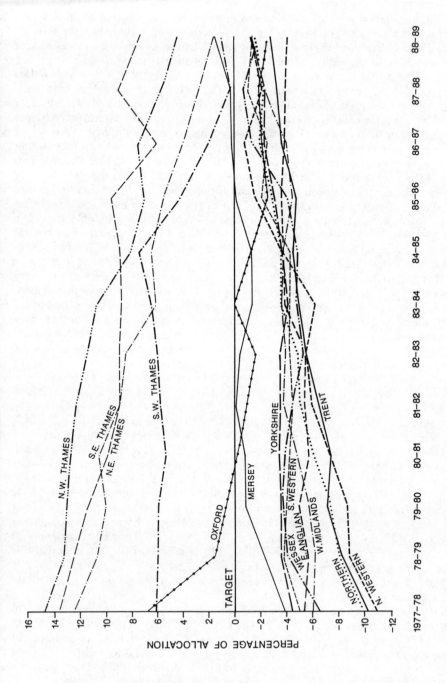

Figure 10.5.1: Allocation of Resources Within the NHS Since 1976.

As far as hospital services are concerned, in the early years of the NHS, resource allocation to different areas largely reflected their existing volume of services. In its turn this pattern of services dictated the numbers of patients treated in different regions. The result was the persistence of a pattern in which services were often in greatest supply in places where needs were least. What was called for was a system of resource allocation according to need. A version of such a system was implemented following the report of the Resource Allocation Working Party (RAWP) in 1976 (Department of Health and Social Security, 1976). The RAWP method establishes for each region target allocations of capital and revenue resources. These targets are based on an assessment of factors such as population size, age and sex structure and health status (as indicated by mortality rates) thought to affect health care needs. When these target allocations were compared with the actual share of resources going to each region considerable discrepancies were found. The four Thames regions and Oxford were shown to be most favoured with the Northwestern, Trent and Northern regions coming off worst. Rather than imposing a once and for all adjustment the actual policy has been one of incremental change with annual allocations of additional resources being greater for regions below target than for those above. Figure 10.5.1 shows that since 1976 there has been a marked reduction in inequalities at a regional scale. However, at more detailed geographical scales it has been alleged (Yudkin, 1978) that the system has worked to the disadvantage of deprived inner city areas. Here there is evidence that financial pressures have led to the closure of smaller hospitals serving a socially deprived population whilst more glamorous acute services have been maintained. Such trends will be intensified by the encouragement being given to health authorities to sell valuable inner city sites and concentrate services on cheaper out of town locations. Another important side effect of the reallocation of hospital resources is its impact on the demand for labour in different areas. It has been said that in Europe the NHS is second only to the Red Army in the size of its workforce. Its policies are therefore likely to have marked impacts on the labour market and often these have worked against other initiatives that have sought to bring new jobs to declining regions and to the inner cities.

In 1989 the Government published the White Paper 'Working for Patients' which represents the most radical rethink of the NHS since its inception, with an emphasis on the injection of market forces into this public service. Since April 1991 large GP practices have been able to apply to manage their own budgets which can be used to obtain treatment for their patients from any hospital in the country. Hospitals have the option of becoming hospital trusts independent of local health authorities. These authorities can buy services for their residents from wherever they can be provided most efficiently. Patients will be encouraged to travel longer distances to hospitals that have spare capacity or cheap prices. Hospitals capable of attracting more patients will grow whereas the less popular will decline. The Government's intention is that this will encourage greater efficiency but it is inevitable that this will also mean greater inequality in the geographical pattern of services, as will the emphasis on a greater role for the private health care sector.

It is possible to conclude that the NHS has achieved some welcome reductions in regional inequality in health service provision although some important problems still remain and political pressures may lead to a reversal of these trends. The architects of the NHS were in little doubt that reducing inequalities in access to health care would lead to a lessening of social and geographical inequalities in health status. Unfortunately all the evidence points to a failure to fulfill this ambition. The Black Report published in 1980 (Townsend and Davidson, 1982) provided overwhelming evidence that manual workers and their families in Britain continue to suffer more illness and disability than their non-manual counterparts. Furthermore, rather than lessening over time there are worrying signs of a widening of inequalities in health. Whilst there is now widespread agreement that these inequalities in health are real there is still disagreement about their causes. Some commentators have argued that the working class suffer poorer health because they smoke and drink more and eat a less healthy diet. The message here has often been that they have only themselves to blame for poor health because of their choice of an unhealthy lifestyle. Others have strenuously disagreed with this diagnosis and have pointed instead to the role of social and economic inequalities as factors affecting health. The argument is that lower social groups have worse health because of the poorer conditions under which they work and live and because of the pressures on them to consume unhealthy products.

Table 10.5.2 Standardised Mortality Ratios From all Causes by Region

		Standardised mortality ratio		
	Males		*Females*	
Region	1959–63	1979–83	1959–63	1979–83
North	107	112	108	110
North West	113	111	111	110
Wales	108	107	105	105
Yorkshire & Humberside	107	106	106	105
West Midlands	103	104	103	104
East Midlands	96	99	99	101
South East	94	94	94	94
South West	92	90	96	93
East Anglia	89	88	94	92

Source: Office of Population Censuses and Surveys (1990) *Mortality and geography: a review in the mid-1980s*, England and Wales, HMSO, London

The debate about social inequalities in health is echoed in a growing recognition of marked geographical variations in health status. Table 10.5.2 shows that there has been no reduction of the North-South divide in mortality rates. In fact the gap between the Northern region and the regions of southern England was wider in the early 1980s than 20 years earlier. Data on morbidity show a similar pattern of regional differences. For example, the General Household Survey shows that in 1986 54 per cent of persons aged 45–64 years in the North West region reported some longstanding illness whereas the figure in East Anglia was only 36 per cent. Similarly, 16.2 per cent of the population in the Northern region are disabled as compared with 12.1 per cent in the South East. Small area studies have revealed even more striking evidence of geographical variations in health with some parts of our major cities displaying mortality rates which are a disgrace to an affluent society. In part this is simply a reflection of the concentration of a socially and economically deprived population in some regions and in the inner cities. However, there is also strong evidence for regional variations in health within each social class pointing to the existence of geographical variations over and above those that might be expected from the social mix of different areas. This means that some people face a double disadvantage based not only on their social circumstances but also on where they live. Unravelling the interactions between health, social and economic conditions and geography remains a challenge for research. What is clear is that the economic and social processes that are the focus of this book play a large part in the creation of inequalities in health.

REFERENCES

Bentham, G. and Haynes, R. (1985) 'Health, personal mobility and the use of health services in rural Norfolk', *Journal of Rural Studies*, 1, 231–9

Department of Health (1989) *Working for patients*, London: HMSO.

Department of Health and Social Security (1976) *Sharing resources for health in England: report of the Resource Allocation Working Party*, London: HMSO.

Hart, J. T. (1971) 'The inverse care law', *Lancet*, 1, 405–412.

Haynes, R.M. (1987) *The geography of health services in Britain, Beckenham: Croom-Helm.*

London Health Planning Consortium Study Group (1981) *Primary health care in inner London, London: London Health Planning Consortium.*

Townsend, P. and Davidson, N. (1982) *Inequalities in health: the Black Report*, Harmondsworth: Penguin Books.

Yudkin, J.S. (1978) 'Changing patterns of resource allocation in a London health district', *British Medical Journal*, 2 1212–15.

PART V

POLICIES FOR THE REGIONS IN THE 1990s

CHAPTER 11

THE POLICY CONTEXT AND LOCAL POLICY CAPACITIES

11.1

The Macro-economic Context to the Regional Problem

Graham Gudgin

INTRODUCTION

The longevity and persistence of regional problems in the UK make them unusual among countries at a similar level of development. Certainly when compared to the USA it is surprising that the same regions have been relatively depressed throughout most of this century. While other countries, and notably Italy, have lagging regions which have never fully or successfully industrialised, the UK is again unusual in that it has a long-standing problem in regions which were formerly by-words for industrial progress. It is also surprising, given the stability of the problem, that it is not better understood. During the era in which Keynesian ideas dominated economic thinking in the UK the emphasis tended to be on the role of industrial structure. Some industries in national or international decline just happened to be located in the northern half of the UK or in Wales. Even though every empirical study found industrial structure to be only part of the explanation, the residual factors remained largely a mystery.

This structural explanation was never very convincing. Some declining industries like shipbuilding and much of textiles were almost wholly located in northern regions and it was difficult to disentangle cause and effect. The deeper questions of why the lagging regions had lost their nineteenth century adaptability, their ability to shed old industries and develop new ones, were rarely asked. As the major declining industries (including coal) withered away to almost nothing, such structural arguments lost what force they had, and have been replaced with only partial and eclectic explanations.

Subsequently, some pointed to the role of a division of labour, with peripheral regions getting production-dominated branch plants (or more recently back offices) with few higher order managerial functions. This however was only ever a partial factor and was as much a consequence as a cause of regional weakness. Others pointed out that major urban areas were losing jobs and population to less urbanised areas in many parts of the world. The heavily urbanised industrial regions of northern England, Scotland and to some extent Northern Ireland were thus prime candidates for economic decline. Conversely much of the rural lowlands of the UK were in the South and these have consequently prospered. This again was only ever a partial explanation and a comparison of similarly urbanised areas across the UK has tended to show the familiar pattern of higher growth in the South.

A large number of additional partial factors have been investigated. Geographers have pursued an eclectic examination of factors influencing changes in employment and hence demand for labour including enterprise (measured through new firm formation), and innovation (measured through Research and Development (R&D) awards etc). Economists, sticking closely to their central paradigm have tended to focus on labour supply and to ask why people in depressed regions have not acted more flexibly either to reduce their wages or to move to other areas, thus tending to equalise unemployment across regions.

The burden of this chapter is to argue that it is difficult to understand the regional problems of the United Kingdom by focusing on micro-economic aspects alone, whether on the demand side or the supply side. National and international macro-economic factors are an important part of the story which cannot be fully comprehended without them.

ORIGINS OF THE REGIONAL PROBLEM

Regional problems in the UK date from around the end of the first world war. The loss of export markets caused by the disruption of war was compounded by an over-valued exchange rate after 1925 and the collapse of the world's free-trade system into trade protection from 1931. Both of these changes had their strongest impact on those regions, chiefly in the North, which produced either primary products or manufactures for export. Until 1914 and into the inter-war period a substantial proportion of UK exports consisted of the low value-added products of textiles and coal. Regions in the North and the periphery which lost markets for such products were not particularly well placed to generate replacement industries in the new technologies of the motor, electrical and chemical industries. This was part of the national failure to graduate fully from first generation industrial revolution products to those based on late 19th and 20th century science. This was a failure which affected most sectors and regions but inevitably had its greatest impact on those regions which had industrialised earliest and furthest.

The period of trade protection, which lasted from 1931 well into the 1960s, had a major influence on the nature of the modern regional problem. The growing British industries of the period served either domestic UK markets, or external markets with few competitors. The importance of home markets in a new era, when the widespread availability of electricity relaxed locational constraints, meant that locations in the South and Midlands were as favourable or more favourable than those further North. The northern regions remained over-dependent on the traditional industries, including shipbuilding, initially at the cost of high unemployment and sometimes huge out-migration flows. Most of these industries had been located in these regions one hundred years earlier. By the time replacements were needed the technological and institutional contexts had changed completely.

FULL EMPLOYMENT AND TRADE PROTECTION

The period after 1930 quickly moved from one marked by high unemployment to one of full employment. Keynesian demand management techniques, operated within a context of international trade protection and international capital controls, were the main factors permitting the maintenance of full employment through to the late 1960s, although of course the boost given by war production greatly speeded up the process and demonstrated its efficiency. Regional problems were largely forgotten as national full employment returned, shortages came to dominate and war-time and early postwar production was directed into peripheral locations. This remained the position through the 1950s. Closely controlled trade protected home producers, while foreign markets were initially willing to buy as much as could be produced.

Nonetheless, technological changes were rapid, leading to the obsolescence of some industries, especially once postwar reconstruction was complete. The displacement of coal by oil brought the first re-emergence of potentially serious regional problems. The older coalfields of Wales, the north of England and Scotland all suffered serious job losses in the 1960s. However, in an era of generally full employment with labour shortages in some regions it was possible for government to organise effective regional policies. These involved financial assistance and controls to induce firms to move longer distances into areas of unemployment rather than into nearby rural areas as had been the practice in the 1950s. The policy, it could be argued, was virtually costless to the Exchequer since the removal of labour supply constraints allowed additional national real output, and hence higher tax revenues at an acceptable level of inflation.

RETURN TO FREE TRADE

Current regional problems really stem from two macro-economic changes, both international. The first was the phasing out of trade protection and the re-introduction of free trade. The second was the collapse of the international Keynesian orthodoxy, and its associated commitment to full employment, following the oil price rise of 1973. The two changes were connected and had profound effects on the UK, chiefly on its weaker regions.

The reintroduction of free trade proceeded under American influence at the General Agreement on Tarrifs and Trade (GATT) rounds from the 1950s, but only gathered speed once postwar re-organisation was complete. As late as 1959 the British Government was still responsible for purchasing some raw materials and allocating them to companies. A decade later in 1970 many trade barriers had been relaxed and imports of finished manufactures were beginning to enter the UK in large volumes. Ominously for some producers, Japanese engineering products rapidly gained an increasing share of the market, with the British motorcycle industry the first to disappear under the competitive onslaught.

With imports increasing faster than exports, balance of payments crises became the dominating issue of macro-economic policy. When the 1968 devaluation failed to cure the problem something akin to panic set in within the Treasury. The deepest postwar deflation followed, taking unemployment over the one million barrier in 1971 for the first time since the 1930s. The controversial decision to join the European Economic

Community (EEC) in 1973 gave free trade a further important boost but by then other, wider, changes were altering the international macro-economy out of all recognition.

THE GREAT SLOWDOWN

Before 1974 the world economy of industrialised (Organisation for Economic Co-oper-ation and Development (OECD)) nations had grown at a rapid rate. Aggregate Gross Domestic Product (GDP) in the OECD economies expanded at almost 5 per cent pa. Some nations, notably Germany and Japan, grew faster through increasing their share of world trade. Others, especially the USA and UK, grew more slowly as they lost shares in world trade. However, the aggregate economy of all the industrial nations together hardly faltered.

Rapid growth came to a sharp end in 1973 coinciding with the quadrupling of the international oil price by the Organisation of Petroleum Exporting Countries (OPEC). Since 1973, the GDP of the OECD nations has expanded on average by almost exactly half its former rate. While the pattern of winners and losers in international trade has remained similar to before 1973, all countries have experienced slower growth. The causes of the slowdown remain controversial but the most plausible factor has been deflationary policies adopted by several key nations to avoid the deficits which were the inevitable corollary of the OPEC trade surpluses. Nations which have attempted to unilaterally maintain their former growth rates were soon forced to deflate. Initially this included most third world economies, but socialist France and even the USA have subsequently had to cut short expansions to avoid unsustainable deficits.

Pre-1973 growth rates were sufficient to maintain full employment in all industrial countries despite rapid technological change leading to fast productivity growth. Even in the relatively sluggish UK economy pre-1973 trend growth at 3 per cent pa was sufficient to generate almost 2 million new jobs in 25 years, even though the economy-wide output per head was rising at 2.5 per cent pa.

Since 1973 only the most competitive economies have maintained full employment through their ability to raise their shares of world trade. Most of these have been in the Far East. European economies have in contrast mostly experienced high levels of unemployment throughout the period. The USA has done rather better, partly through a depreciating dollar exchange rate, rising external debt, and stagnating real wages in many sectors (partly achieved through a return to almost 19th century levels of immigration). As a result GDP in the USA has expanded faster than in Europe, but average incomes have not increased at all in two decades.

THE UK SINCE 1973

The UK has mirrored Europe in its rise of unemployment even though the timing of increases has sometimes been temporarily out of phase with the continent. GDP growth in the UK since 1973 has fallen to under 2 per cent pa, a rate which would have been insufficient to create new jobs at pre-1973 rates of productivity increase. However, since 1973 the economy-wide trend rate of increase in labour productivity has fallen to 1.5 per cent pa partly due to the importance of the service sectors in growth.

Until 1987, growth in UK GDP was only 1.5 per cent pa. Consequently, employment (including self-employment) was no higher in that year than in 1973. However, by 1987 the UK was already 12 months into its largest consumer and credit boom in the postwar period and perhaps this century. An unprecedented 2.1 million jobs were created between mid-1986 and mid-1990. Until 1986 unemployment had increased in almost every year after 1973. The number of unemployed adults in 1986 was 2.7 million higher than the 1973 figure of 460,000 (on common definitions). Four years later, in mid-1990, the total was 1.5 million lower, but had begun to rise once more. At the time of writing, in early 1992, the number of unemployed has risen back to 2.1 million above the 1973 level.

In summary, growth in the UK economy has slowed since 1973 in line with the wider international trend. This led to stagnant employment and rising unemployment, until the economic boom of 1986-89. The boom itself was unsustainable in that it involved a widening balance of payments deficit which reached a record 4 per cent of GDP by 1989. The need to restore external balance, and to reduce wage inflation within the European Exchange Rate Mechanism (ERM), which the UK joined in late-1990 to cure its persistent inflation problems, will mean slow growth and few additional jobs for most of the 1990s. Unemployment is also likely to remain above 2.5 million for much of the decade.

THE REGIONS IN THE PERIOD OF SLOW GROWTH

Slow growth and rising national unemployment since 1973 have exposed the under-lying weaknesses in the regional economies of northern England and the periphery of the UK. Until 1973 those regions had been able to remain at close to full employment for two reasons. First, the flow of factories and jobs from the South and Midlands has already been mentioned. An estimated 250,000 jobs were transferred in this way as a response to regional policy measures.

The second factor was migration. Large population outflows from Scotland, North-ern Ireland, Wales and from the regions of northern England, prior to 1973, disguised the fact that local job creation was insufficient to keep pace with local population increase. The outflows were made possible by the availability of jobs in the regions of the South and Midlands.

After 1973 employment growth slackened in most regions, North and South. Shortages of jobs became more acute in the northern and peripheral regions, and migration flows were damped down by the lower availability of jobs in the South and Midlands. Unemployment has risen everywhere. High unemployment became en-demic in much of the northern half of the UK and has never subsequently disappeared. Continued population outflows from the North, albeit at a lower level, also ensured that unemployment rose even in those regions like East Anglia and the South West where job creation outpaced natural increase in the labour force.

Because the most severe job losses occurred after 1979 the blame has sometimes been ascribed to the Conservative governments of Mrs Thatcher. It is doubtful, how-ever, that the outcome would have been much different under any alternative admin-istration. International slow growth since 1973 has meant that no economy as small and as open as the UK has been able to buck the trend. For a short period from 1974 to 1979 it seemed that the consequences might not be dramatic. However, in retrospect it appears that private sector employers were hoarding labour at the expense of stagnat-ing productivity and plunging profits. Few, it seems, realised that the long-term trend in expansion had changed.

The second post 1973 recession, which arrived in 1980, appears to have convinced many firms that they had to accommodate to the new reality. As a result the backlog of redundancies and closures reduced employment in manufacturing by 20 per cent within three years. Because the crisis was international in origin, it was the export industries which were most affected. This led to major losses in all manufacturing areas, affecting the northern regions particularly, but involving the industrial midlands almost as much.

COMPETITIVE WEAKNESSES

Slow growth in world markets has exposed the lack of international competitiveness in British industry. While external markets were growing rapidly, the falling UK share of those markets did not have disastrous consequences on the labour markets of the main industrial regions within the UK. Slow external growth means however that the economy is no longer able to sustain full employment.

If British industry were sufficiently internationally competitive, the industrial regions of the UK would be able to grow up to the point where constraints of labour or space prevented further expansion. This however does not make the UK depressed regions unique since most EC nations have some regions in a similar position.

It remains true, however, that the regions in the northern half of the UK have a longstanding competitive weakness relative to the southern regions and perhaps also the midlands. In part, this reflects the metropolitan nature of those sectors in which the UK has remained internationally competitive. Chief among these are banking, finance and insurance, all centred in London but increasingly dispersed throughout London's hinterland, which has now come to include large parts of East Anglia and the South West as well as the South East beyond London. These industries have been sustained by recruitment from Britain's elite universities and have not been hampered by Britain's notable deficiencies in industrial training.

Where manufacturing industry has also recruited intensively from Britain's small graduate base the results have also been respectable, as in chemicals or computers. This has assisted the South more than the North, partly because of the residential preference of white collar and scientific staff for locations away from heavy or declining industrial centres. More generally, Britain's well attested weaknesses in management qualifications and workforce skills have had their major detrimental effect on the regions which have traditionally depended on manufacturing.

The aim of the Thatcherite revolution of the 1980s was to arrest the decline in Britain's relative competitiveness. It is clear that weaknesses in education and training were initially neglected, and have only begun to be tackled seriously in the 1990s. However, in other respects major advances appear to have been achieved. The best measure of industrial competitiveness is a country's share of world trade. After falling for decades, the UK share of world exports stopped falling in 1983 and since then has been on a stable or even slightly upward trend (Figure 11.1.1). This improvement could be largely a reflection of productivity gains made during the expansion of output in the 1980s boom in domestic demand. It is still too early to know whether it will survive the 1990s recession and a subsequent decade of slower growth. The initial signs are that unit labour costs rose rapidly during the first year of recession, but since then wage settlements have risen slowly at a time when German wage inflation has accelerated due to the demand stimulus associated with reunification.

If the improvement in the UK share of world trade does prove durable then the main reasons are likely to have been a shift in power from trades unions to management leading to much a lower incidence of industrial disruption. Although it is difficult to measure, this change appears to have been associated with a widespread increase in management confidence and determination to succeed. The rapid spread of improved quality standards (as in the widespread adoption of BS5750), just in time delivery and similar world-class practices were all part of more competitive attitudes. Many of these

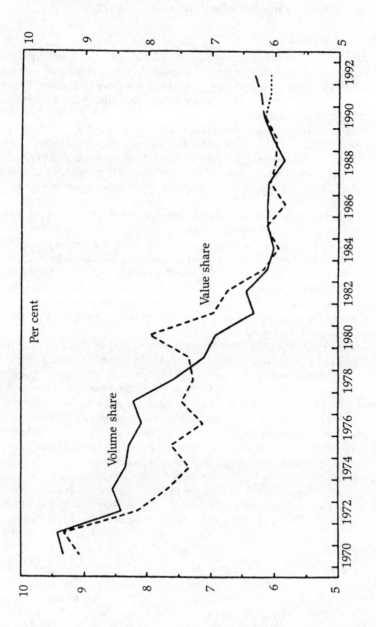

Figure 11.1.1: UK Share of World Trade in Manufactures

attitudes had their origins in the example set by the phenomenal success of Japanese manufacturing, and the boom in Japanese inward investment into the UK in the 1980s helped to spread these ideas more rapidly. Around a quarter of the 400 Japanese plants established in Europe in the 1980s were located in the UK. The two major car plants, Nissan and Toyota, which are beginning full production in the 1990s, promise to spread Japanese manufacturing practice even further over the decade.

EUROPEAN INTEGRATION

As a country with agricultural strengths and industrial weaknesses, the UK's experience of joining an EEC with agricultural protection but industrial free trade was predictably mixed at first. The strongest industrial sectors including chemicals and aircraft, were able to gain from a larger open market, but other industries suffered from rapidly rising import penetration.

The need to survive in a more open trade regime underpinned the industrial reforms of the 1980s, and will necessitate further reform in the 1990s particularly in management and workforce skills. While the cost of increased openness has been high, and has included the abandonment of full employment, in the long term free trade appears to be having the expected consequence of forcing improvements in competitiveness.

The moves to remove many of the remaining impediments to trade by 1993 should continue this process. The removal of border controls, and many detailed product regulations, will allow the most competitive firms to increase their European market share at the expense of other firms. Improved communications including the Channel Tunnel, together with fixed exchange rates will add to the process. The indications are that British companies as a whole will be able to absorb these changes without aggregate loss of markets. However, individual companies and industries will gain or lose. Traditional British weaknesses, including textiles and clothing, are likely to decline while the science-based industries expand.

Significant improvements in cost competitiveness in most northern and peripheral regions over the 1980s should provide a sound basis for future competitiveness. The least cost-competitive regions remain the Midlands, despite major improvements in the West Midlands in the 1970s and 1980s. A plethora of family-owned firms in traditional industries may still experience some decline before full competitiveness is gained. In Northern Ireland labour productivity remains low, and firms appear to have been protected by a generous grant regime. Moves away from largescale capital grant aid will need offsetting reforms in operating efficiency. In the South of England most will depend on the future of financial and other exportable services. If London and the South can retain their pre-eminent position as a financial centre in a more open Europe then prosperity will be assured. Industry will continue to decentralise from the South East, but the speed will depend on costs of land and labour relative to other regions. These in turn will reflect cost pressures from expansion in the service sector.

CONCLUSION

In the long term, the economic success of the UK and its constituent regions depends on competitiveness in producing tradable goods and services. Macro-economic fiscal and monetary policy have had more influence on the timing of cyclical fluctuations than on the secular trend. The illusory potential of a floating exchange rate had little influence as long as devaluations tended to be fully offset by rising wages.

The likely move to a single European currency in the 1990s, or perhaps later, should involve little difficulty in its fixed exchange rate aspect. Many businesses will welcome the removal of exchange rate uncertainty, and will adapt their costs and efficiency to match the new reality. The more serious danger will come with loss of control over interest rates. Interest rates will be set on a Europe-wide basis by an European Central bank. Interest rates may reflect average European conditions or even worse may be dominated by German conditions. In either case, they may be inappropriate for conditions in some UK regions. This has been the experience of regions like Northern Ireland (and earlier the Republic of Ireland), where high interest rates determined in London, have not reflected local needs to stimulate higher levels of economic activity. However, if UK inflation rates converge on those in Europe, as they must, the imposition of European interest rates should only intermittently handicap most UK regions. This handicap should be out-weighed by the benefits of full integration into a market of 350 million and perhaps eventually 500 million people.

1992 and Relations with the EEC

R. Ross MacKay

'There is abundant evidence that those embarking upon the course of regional integration should not rely on simple beliefs about the benevolence of "invisible hands".' (Padoa-Schioppa, 1987, p.21).

INTRODUCTION

The Single European Market is designed as an area without frontiers in which the free movement of goods, persons, services and capital is encouraged. The European Community of 12 countries is potentially the largest internal market in the world. Population is 1.3 times population in the United States and 2.6 times the population of Japan. According to the official review of 1992 (European Economy No. 35, March 1988, the Economics of 1992) that potential and power remain dormant as long as the Community remains fragmented and divided by non-tariff barriers (ntb's) to trade. The gross domestic product (GDP) of the 12 is approximately .95 US GDP and 1.8 Japanese GDP. The official review implies that this combined purchasing power remains irrelevant as long as non-tariff barriers protect the inefficient and restrict and confine exchange.

According to the review, potential economic gain from 1992 comes to between 5.8 and 6.4 per cent of Community GDP. The gain is 'not trivial': indeed it is 'large enough to make the difference between a disappointing and very satisfactory performance for the Community' (European Economy, No. 35, p.20). The internal market could raise annual potential growth of the Community, 'by around 1 percentage point' up to 1992, with prospects for buoyant growth further into the 1990s (European Economy, No. 35, p.19).

The estimates of benefits, while optimistic, are duly qualified. The most important benefits are the most difficult to quantify. The gains are rough orders of magnitude, rather than precise forecasts. There is, nevertheless, a possibility of bias. The estimates derive from studies approved and sponsored by the Commission. Potential gains are assessed on the assumption that all ntb's are effectively eliminated. The problems of implementation are considerable. They are not considered relevant to the returns from 1992. They will influence results.

The move to a Single European Market is expected to reallocate markets and redistribute production in favour of the most efficient and best situated firms. In addition to greater concentration of industry, it implies growing divergence at regional level. The gains from trade are expected to concentrate at the centre of the Community in the more prosperous regions: transient and long-term unemployment emerge at the periphery.

This unfortunate (but acknowledged) side-effect of 1992 occurs against the background of the following broad trends:

(1) a more difficult environment for regional policy, involving high unemployment, decline in manufacturing, public expenditure cuts

(2) reduced expenditure on regional aid at national level

(3) growing regional divergence in the years of slower growth and rising unemployment which followed the oil price rises of 1973 and 1979

(4) additional divergence in prosperity at regional and national level following enlargement of Community.

This note outlines the evidence on growing divergence at regional level, explains why 1992 is likely to add to disparity, and considers appropriate responses.

The European Economic Community has consistently recognised the importance of reducing regional inequality. The present step towards closer union, the single European market, is backed by measures to strengthen 'economic and social cohesion'. The Structural Funds[1] are planned to double by 1993. There is, however, no happy relationship between emergence and growth of the Structural Funds and regional equality. The forces which contribute to inequalities prove too powerful for the Structural Funds in the 1970s and 1980s. 1992 will contribute to divergence and it emerges at a time when the returns from the traditional forms of regional policy prove disappointing.

REGIONAL DIVERGENCE WITHIN THE COMMUNITY

Economic evolution is by nature uneven. It disturbs existing structures, it unsettles established communities, it is not a process of gentle transformation. But growth and change do not necessarily imply regional divergence. Within the European Community, the period of high growth and low unemployment up to 1973 was one of convergence. Regional differences in income and opportunity tended to diminish. The years of slow growth and high unemployment – from 1973 – witnessed divergence.

The Third Periodic Report on the Regions of the Community (hereafter the Regional report) provides detail. The period 1960–73 was associated with a process of convergence in terms of productivity, income per head and unemployment. Convergence applies between and within countries. Following the oil price crises of the mid-1970s, a new and difficult phase of economic transformation appeared. Economic growth fell to lower levels, the shift away from manufacturing accelerated, unemployment rose and the impact was concentrated on particular groups within society. In the years of low growth regional inequality increased. Growing divergence is apparent across a range of indicators. There is a core-periphery pattern to disparity, although some central regions (e.g. Ruhr, West Midlands) experienced severe industrial decline.

Figure 11.2.1 is taken from the Regional Report. Community unemployment doubled between 1973 and 1979: unemployment doubled again between 1979 and 1985. As unemployment climbed through the Community, the differences in unemployment between and within countries grew substantially. Regional disparities in unemployment (see Figure 11.2.1) increased with unemployment.

The increase in unemployment was greatest in those regions where unemployment was already high. Between 1976 and 1985 (Regional Report, p.62) unemployment rose by 4 percentage points in the 25 Community regions with the lowest unemployment rates. The increase in the 25 regions with highest unemployment was 13 percentage points. The unemployment gap at extremes of Community tripled in only 10 years.

---

[1] The Three Structural funds are Regional, Social, Agricultural Guidance. Regional and Social each account for about 7 per cent of Community budget expenditure, Agricultural Guidance for 2 per cent. The Community also supports regional convergence through the European Investment Bank.

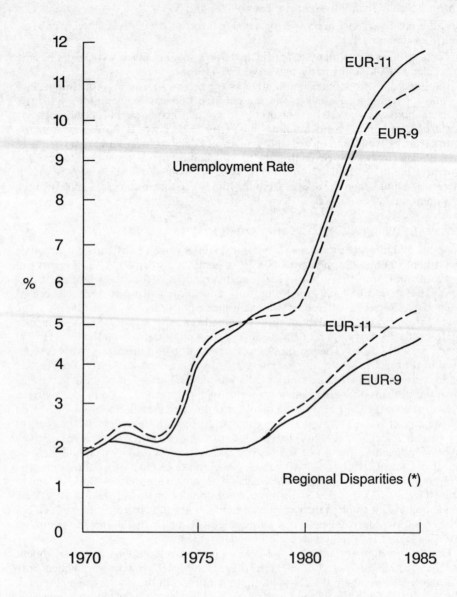

Source: Commision on the European Community (1987) Third Periodic Report on the Social and Economic Situation and Development of the Regions of the European Community

(*) Standard deviation weighted by the regional shares of the labour force

Figure 11.2.1: Trend of Unemployment in the Community

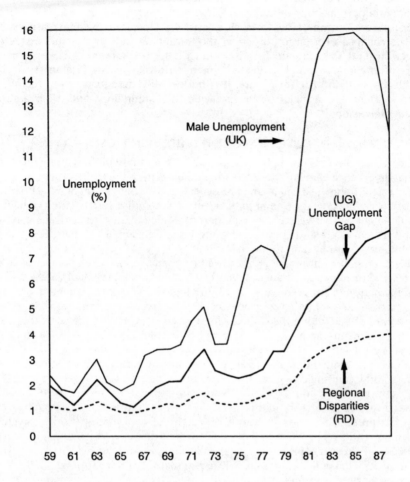

UG = Unemployment Gap = Male Unemployment rate in Inner Regions less
Male Unemployment rate in Outer Regions.
Inner Regions are South East, East Anglia, East Midlands, West Midlands,
South West.
Outer Regions are Scotland, Wales, Northern Ireland, North, North West,
Yorkshire and Humberside.
RD = Regional Disparity = Standard deviation weighted by regional share of
labour force.

Source: Historical Abstract of labour statistics, labour statistics, employment gazette

Figure 11.2.2: Trend of Male Unemployment in the United Kingdom, and Unemployment Gap

Unemployment in the 1980s took its characteristic form from employment relationships that were expected to provide continuity. The employment relationship involved an 'obligation of permanent, continuing employment' (Piore, 1987, p. 1845). With ties of this form severed, communities lost their *raison d'être*. Unemployment increase resulted from the collapse of a large portion of the traditional industrial structure. A gap emerged around the individual and around the local community. That gap is the essence of unemployment. The unemployment that follows is not voluntary. It does not reflect a sudden taste for leisure. It is not usefully described as productive job search. It is one of the major problems facing the Community, and it has a strong regional dimension.

REGIONAL POLICY AND DIVERGENCE – THE UNITED KINGDOM

Low growth and recession contribute to both community-wide unemployment and regional divergence. Similar effects are identifiable within the United Kingdom.

Figure 11.2.2 shows (1) male unemployment in the United Kingdom, (2) regional disparity (calculated as for Community regions – see Figure 11.2.1 – and (3) the male unemployment gap between Outer Regions (Scotland, Wales, Northern Ireland, North, North West, Yorkshire and Humberside) and Inner Regions (South East, East Anglia, East Midlands, West Midlands, South West).

Male unemployment in the UK increased from an average of 2.2 per cent between 1955–66, and to 14 per cent between 1980–88. As male unemployment rose so did the unemployment gap between Outer and Inner regions. The unemployment gap averaged 2.1 percentage points between 1959–76 and 5.5 percentage points between 1977–87. The growing divide within the United Kingdom concentrates on the years from 1979. The unemployment gap grew in every year between 1979 and 1988. By 1988 an extra 8 out of every 100 men were unemployed when we compare Outer with Inner regions. Although both the unemployment gap and regional disparities are sensitive to unemployment, they continued to grow in spite of unemployment decline in 1987 and 1988.

In the Community and the United Kingdom regional disparities were contained and even reduced prior to the mid-1970s. Convergence is, in part, a product of regional policy. For present purposes we can distinguish between three periods of regional policy intervention. The 1950s to early 1960s were years of weak regional policy, the mid-1960s to 1976 years of active regional policy impact, and the years from 1977 years of reduced regional policy emphasis. In 1975 regional aid came to approximately £1.300 million (1980 prices), or 0.7 per cent of GDP. By 1985 regional aid amounted to approximately £400 million (1980 prices), 0.2 per cent of GDP. In real terms regional aid lost two thirds of its value in ten years.

In all but two years between 1952 to 1963 (weak regional policy) and 1977 to 1988 (reduced regional policy) the Assisted Regions (Scotland, Wales, Northern Ireland, North) had an employment deficit: in all but two years of weak or reduced regional policy their share of national employment fell. The total deficit in the period of weak and reduced policy came to 674,000 jobs. In the years of active regional policy (1964 to 1976) the Assisted Regions had an employment surplus (their share of national employment increased) in 8 out of 13 years. The total surplus in the years of active regional policy came to 153,000 jobs.

The balance of employment shifts to Assisted Regions in the years of major regional policy emphasis: it shifts away from those regions when regional policy is relatively unimportant. That regional policy contributes to this contrast cannot be doubted.

A regional policy consistent with the circumstances of a particular stage in economic evolution delivered results. However, the traditional forms of regional policy evolved in conditions which no longer hold. The strategy depended on guiding manufacturing expansion away from regions of full employment to regions with unused resources. The growing opportunity gap between Outer and Inner regions reflects the reduced emphasis on regional policy and a more difficult political and economic environment.

THE INTERNAL MARKET AND REGIONAL DIVERGENCE

At its inauguration, the European Economic Community recognised the importance of 'reducing differences between regions and mitigating the backwardness of less favoured regions' (Treaty of Rome, 1958). The Commission remains consistent in recognising the attractions of regional convergence. The Padoa-Schioppa report (1987, p.25) describes 'economic benefits' as the 'cement of an economic community'. If those benefits fail to reach all parts, the Community lacks stability. Movement towards closer political and monetary integration is unlikely if economic benefits fail to reach the periphery. The declared objectives of the Single European Act include 'reducing disparities between the various regions and the backwardness of the less-favoured regions'. The objectives are backed by budgets. Resources to the three Structural Funds are planned to double by 1993: the proportion of Community Budget taken by the Funds rises from 17 per cent of payment (1986) to around one third.

The renewed commitment to regional convergence is a response to acknowledged difficulties. From 1973 differences between the regions in unemployment and income have grown. The removal of non tariff barriers is expected to add to divergence. Enlargement of the Community, the expansion from 9 to 12 nations, contributes to regional disparity. Spain, Portugal and Greece provide problem regions that are different in nature and degree from declining industrial areas in other parts of the Community.

The Regional Report claims that regional disparities are now stronger within the Community than in the United States. Comparing the European Community with the US, regional disparities are twice as high measured in terms of income, and three times as high measured in terms of unemployment. Within a land area more limited than the United States, regional differences are more pronounced. The search for 'economic and social cohesion' includes regions and localities with different life styles, living standards, structures and expectations.

Other problems emerge. Reducing non-tariff barriers has two effects. It differentiates between superior and inferior locations and sources of material and labour. It reallocates market areas and redistributes production in favour of the most efficient and best situated firms. This implies geographic specialisation and concentration of production, a process more likely to benefit the core than the periphery of the Community.

The second effect follows from concentration and expansion of production. Internal and external economics of scale and scope develop in particular locations, providing advantages which are more than temporary. Concentration provides its own momentum, with economic returns unevenly distributed. The argument for 1992 is that efficiency in production requires an extended and enlarged market area. That extension promotes selection as to location of production. It also progressively differentiates between superior and inferior locations and develops strategic trade routes.

The argument for 1992 implies that there is no natural process of convergence at regional level. Indeed, removal of non tariff barriers adds to divergence. It favours the most efficient enterprises, it develops favoured locations. There are, as the Padoa-Schioppa report (p.5) underlines, 'serious risks of aggravated regional imbalance in the course of market liberalization'. The authors emphasise that the most important returns rely not on direct gains from trade, but on the process of restructuring which follows from competition. The significant returns involve dynamic change.

The dynamic returns involve rationalisation and concentration on the most efficient producers. This restructuring involves losses in employment. Those losses may or may not be temporary. The benefits are estimated at equilibrium. The equilibrium assumption or postulate is 'that all resources released in rationalisation' (European Economy, No.35, p.156) find alternative employment. The labour displaced transfers to activities where the locality has a comparative advantage. Given redeployment, trade and exchange bring benefits in return for adjustment problems that are presumed to be minor.

The equilibrium assumption describes an economy where individuals have control over their own destiny – whether employed, or unemployed. That control is difficult to reconcile with economies where resources are specialised and effective competition often demands considerable scale. The equilibrium assumption is difficult to reconcile with the economic logic which lies behind the drive to the Single European Market.

The argument for 1992 emphasises the importance of internal and external economies of scale. Effective competition requires an internal market larger than the national markets provided by the United Kingdom, Germany, France or Italy. The economic system so described is not a series of small scale gambles where ease of entry and exit into production characterise all important markets. Those displaced by rationalisation face real problems. Those problems will often extend through time.

The equilibrium assumption is thus heroic, particularly so in a Community with an unemployment rate close to 10 per cent. It is difficult to reconcile with regional differentials which are substantial and growing. It is inconsistent with the emergence of long-term unemployment as a major Community problem. The review of 1992 (European Economy No.35, p.156) recognises that the new equilibrium may 'take quite a few years'; five is apparently sufficient for most adjustment, ten for almost all. The benefits are estimated at equilibrium, and ignore adjustment costs.

CONCLUSION

There are, at any one point, forces and pressures which contribute to regional convergence and forces and pressures which create divergence (Myrdal 1957; Hirschman 1958). The evidence indicates that the forces which contribute to regional inequality tend to gain in relative strength in periods of low growth (and high unemployment).

1992 provides a dilemma. The argument for 1992 is that only a large internal market can provide growth: only the Single European Market can deliver the potential benefits of market exchange. On the other hand, the process of integration adds to regional inequality. The removal of non-tariff barriers has an effect similar to reducing distance. Market areas extend, competition is introduced from distant sources. The dynamic gains (the important returns) involve restructuring. The process of selection adds to regional inequality. Concentration provides its own momentum, with economic benefits unevenly distributed. 'Removal of existing barriers to the free moment of goods, services and capital will benefit first and foremost the stronger and more attractive regions' (Regional Report, p.viii).

The means to faster growth provides, at least in the short run, the threat of growing inequality. The combination of market enlargement and market opening provides a sharp challenge within a Community where stability requires convergence.

The dilemma evolves against a difficult environment for regional policy. Given the decline in manufacturing there are fewer potentially mobile projects. They provide fewer jobs. Regional policy, in Britain and other countries, has tended to concentrate on manufacturing. Most of the direct assistance to enterprise has been aimed at manufacturing. In most countries, regional policy success occured in those earlier years when employment trends in manufacturing were more favourable. The location of the service sector has been less susceptible to influence; either because services needs to be performed within the local area they benefit, or because their locating factors, such as centrality, are not favourable to the high unemployment regions which policy seeks to promote.

In Britain, and in other European countries, public expenditure constraints have led to severe cuts in regional policy spending. Throughout Europe there is doubt as to the relevance of the old forms of regional policy and concern regarding its effectiveness (cost per job). These uncertainties and difficulties combine to reduce national involvement in regional policy. The Community desire to contain regional inequality is not, therefore, backed by growing commitment at national level.

One Community response has been to increase adjustment assistance. The three Structural Funds grow. However, given the introduction of Portugal and Spain, even doubling the Funds may not add to expenditure in the parts of Britain 'seriously affected by industrial decline'. The priority areas are 'less developed regions', the poorest part of Community. Additional expenditure does not necessarily mean more aid to Britain's Assisted Areas. Moreover, there are real problems in developing a truly effective regional policy at Community level. The most obvious and persistent difficulty is the vexing question of additionality. The Community insists that expenditure via the Structural Funds makes a difference. The Funds should add to existing national expenditure, provide extra projects and have an effect on the type of project receiving aid. The Funds are not intended as simple budget transfer: a substitution of Community money for internal expenditure.

A report from the House of Lords (Reform of the Structural Funds, 1988) provides a useful summary of additionality within the United Kingdom: (1) aid to industrial projects will not reach the firm, (2) local authority receipts from the European Regional Development Fund (ERDF) will reduce capital borrowing by a corresponding amount, (3) aid for electrification of a railway line will reduce expenditure elsewhere in the railway system, (4) our unusual system distributes part of ERDF outside Assisted Areas (Q.372, House of Lords,1988). 'The vast majority of United Kingdom schemes applying for ERDF aid would have been implemented anyway, regardless of whether or not they receive a grant' (House of Lords 1988, p.9). The United Kingdom claims national, not local, additionality. The Community contributes to the overall level of expenditure, but has next to no impact on its nature (or location). National additionality is impossible to disprove. It appears doubtful given the decline in regional policy expenditure: additionality has become a charade. The selection of projects by British officials and their careful scrutiny by European counterparts, serves no useful purpose.

The long-term response will require policies broader than the support provided by the Structural Funds. Those policies may emerge if the Community is successful in adding to growth. The forces that reduce regional inequality tend to be stronger in prosperous societies. This is partly because the state's ability to introduce national integration policies remains weak in times of economic difficulty. The more important the welfare state, 'the stronger will be both the urge and the capacity to counteract the blind market forces which tend to result in regional inequalities' (Myrdal, 1957, p.41). Within the Community, the social dimension of the market has a strong regional dimension.

The long-term response may, almost certainly will, require a mechanism for automatic fiscal transfer on the lines suggested by the Macdougall Report (Commission, 1977). As the Community budget grows in real terms and as a proportion of Community GDP, inter-regional transfers within the Community also grow. The Community budget is now approximately 1 per cent of GDP and is dominated by agriculture. Effective transfer will require both a different balance of Community expenditure and a higher level. Fiscal transfer may have greater meaning in federal states, or at least in countries which recognise the need for devolution and decentralisation. The above connects to the relationship between different levels of government and to decentralisation of responsibilities. The European Commission, in moving towards 1992, emphasise that the right level of government is the lowest level at which a function can be efficiently executed. This principle of subsidiarity (never entrust to a large unit what can be better achieved by a smaller one) is one which the British Government embraces in its dealings with the Community, but one which it consistently rejects in its control and management of Britain's internal affairs.

One consequence of a programme designed to enhance individual choice is an increase in the power of central government: also apparent is decline in the influence of local communities and intermediate institutions. In the name of the market, power is centralised: 'The ambit of government may be limited, but its scope has become infinite' (Bogdanor, 1985, p.135).

And yet decentralisation of responsibility links to the theme of indigenous growth. The Government seeks a regional policy which delivers self-generating growth, but to develop an economy while disregarding the needs of its people can only lead to unbalanced development. Indigenous development is impossible without participation. Growth from within the regions is difficult to reconcile with an administration which seeks to centralise control and ensure that it remains remote and divorced from the regions. In this respect the United Kingdom may yet learn from the Community. The Community connects the theme of indigenous growth (supply-side improvement) to a principle of subsidiarity designed to enlist involvement at local and regional level.

Finally, in developing a Community policy which seeks convergence, it is important to emphasise the role of human capital. The uneasy co-existence of a labour surplus and a labour shortage could create a conflict which if not dealt with will increasingly threaten regional, national and Community economic development. Given the present rate of technological change and the rapidly changing structure of regional economies, there is an increased need for a labour force with flexible skills. Economic development results in goods, but it starts with people and their education, training and opportunities. Without these three all resources remain latent, untapped, and inefficiently utilized.

REFERENCES

Bogdanor V. (1989), 'The Constitution' in (ed) Kavanagh D. and Seldon A., *The Thatcher Effect*, Oxford: Oxford University Press.

Commission of the European Communities (1987). *Third Periodic Report from the Commission on the Social and Economic Situation and Development of the Regions of the Community.* Com (87) 230 Final. Brussels (referred to as Regional Report in text).

Commission of the European Communities (1988), *European Economy*, No. 35, March 1988, 'The Economics of 1992'.

Hirschman A.O. (1958) *The Strategy of Economic Development*, New Haven: Yale University Press.

House of Lords (1988), Select Committee on the European Communities, Reform of the Structural Funds, HL Paper 82, London: HMSO.

Myrdal, G.M. (1957) *Economic Theory and Underdeveloped Regions.* London: Duckworth.

Padoa-Schioppa T. (1987), *Efficiency, Stability and Equity. A Strategy for the Evolution of the Economic System of the European Community.* Oxford: Oxford University Press.

Piore M.J. (1987), 'Historical Perspective and the Interpretation of Unemployment', *Journal of Economic Literature*, Vol XXI, ps 1834-1850.

Regional Problems and Policies: An Overview

J. Taylor

This chapter focuses on the causes and consequences of regional economic imbalance and suggests some possible ways in which the Government can help to reduce the substantial disparities in economic performance which have become a permanent feature of the UK spatial economy.

THE CAUSES OF REGIONAL ECONOMIC DISPARITIES

The existence of regional economic disparities and their growing significance during the 1980s is well documented and the evidence will not be paraded here (Armstrong and Taylor, 1988; Martin, 1988; Smith, 1989; Balchin, 1990; Taylor, 1991). It is sufficient to point to the very considerable widening and persistence of disparities in unemployment between the northern and southern regions during the early 1980s (see Figure 11.3.1).

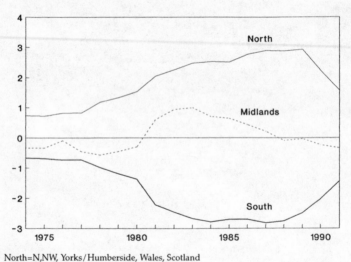

Note: North=N,NW, Yorks/Humberside, Wales, Scotland
Midlands = E. Mids, W. Mids; South = SE, EA, SW

Figure 11.3.1: Regional Unemployment Disparities in the UK 1974–90

Why do some regions perform better than others over very long periods of time? Perhaps the most commonly-cited factor is that some regions are endowed with faster growing industries than others. This factor has been especially important in determining the South East's growth rate. Industry mix is only part of the story, however, since the same industry grows faster in some regions than in others. This indicates the existence of factors other than industry mix in determining a region's economic performance. One of these factors is entrepreneurial activity since the birth rate of new firms is far higher in the South than in the North. Indeed, the birth rate of new firms (as measured by VAT registrations) is inversely related to distance from London. The South East and surrounding regions have several built-in advantages for new firm formation which are less in evidence in the North (Storey and Johnson, 1988).

A further factor which can be expected to affect a region's economic performance is the quality of its workforce. The South East is able to attract a disproportionate share of highly skilled and highly educated workers, which makes it a more attractive location for the high skill sector of UK industry. The South East thus benefits from a virtuous circle whereby highly skilled workers chase highly skilled jobs.

Loss of control over decision-making in areas of high unemployment has been suggested as another reason for their poor performance. The northern regions have generally been losing their managerial control due to acquisitions by firms located in the South East, the latter being the prime location of head offices. In addition, there has been a significant inflow of branch plants into the high unemployment regions due directly to regional policy, which has therefore turned out to be a double-edged sword in so far as branch plants are generally more vulnerable to recessions and company reorganisations than are independent plants. Moreover, branch plants often generate fewer local spin-offs than independent firms and tend to concentrate on lower level functions such as processing (Harris, 1988).

MARKET FORCES AND REGIONAL DISPARITIES: THE FAILURE OF MARKETS TO CLEAR

If there were no frictions to the free movement of capital and labour, regional economic disparities would be quickly eliminated through automatic responses in the factor markets. Labour would migrate from low wage to high wage areas and capital would move in the opposite direction. Indeed, if wages and prices were perfectly flexible, adjustments would occur through appropriate wage adjustments. Markets would clear very quickly. Wages would fall in areas of excess supply and increase in areas of excess demand, thus eliminating regional unemployment disparities. Although there is evidence that the adjustment process works in the predicted direction, the speed of the adjustment is far too slow to make a significant dent in regional economic disparities. In this sense, there is market failure.

There are two main reasons why regional economic disparities are not responsive to market forces. First, neither labour nor capital is perfectly mobile. Low-paid workers, for example, are extremely immobile because: the financial costs of moving are high; living costs are higher in low unemployment areas (e.g. there is a strong negative correlation between house prices and the unemployment rate across UK counties); many unemployed workers live in subsidised housing; and the unemployed are generally less knowledgeable about employment opportunities in other regions. There is also a great reluctance to move to other regions because of the consequent uncertainty. Very similar arguments apply to firms. They have a strong preference for the certainty of their present location rather than the uncertainty and disruption associated with moving to other locations. This geographical inertia is strongest in small firms since these normally have very close economic ties with other firms in their own locality. Second, the regional wage structure is generally insensitive to regional unemployment disparities – with the obvious exception that wages respond to situations of local excess demand. Walsh and Brown (1991) demonstrate that regional earnings disparities have actually narrowed during the 1980s in spite of the widening gap in unemployment rates between regions.

What are the policy implications of the failure of markets to clear? The obvious answer is that markets should be induced to work more efficiently by removing supply-side rigidities. The main candidates are: to replace national wage bargaining with local wage bargaining; to reduce housing subsidies in order to encourage outward migration from high unemployment areas; to operate less restrictive planning controls in the South East in order to reduce house prices there; to encourage the construction of low cost housing in the South East (both public and private); and to impose congestion taxes on firms in the South East in order to encourage capital to move northwards. Exactly how the Government can encourage local wage bargaining, other than by introducing this in the public sector, is not clear. Neither is it clear that encouraging a greater flow of people out of high unemployment areas will be equili-brating, since any increase in net migration into the South East will inevitably increase the pressure on existing facilities through the extra demand which migrants take with them into a region. Moreover, the regions losing population will experience further reductions in demand and leave behind underutilised social overheads. Do we really want to see an even greater concentration of the population living and working in the South East?

THE CONSEQUENCES OF REGIONAL DISPARITIES IN ECONOMIC PERFORMANCE

Persistent disparities in the economic performance of regions are generally regarded as being undesirable. There are four main reasons for this. First, if regional disparities in living standards are sufficiently great, this causes dissatisfaction and leads to claims that the distribution of income and wealth is unfair.

Second, regional disparities in economic performance result in massive underutili-sation of resources in some regions, the most obvious example being persistently high rates of unemployment in the northern regions relative to those in the South. The problem with the underutilisation of resources is that this represents a lost opportunity to produce output. And labour is not the only underutilised resource since there is ample land available for industrial and commercial development, as well as for housing and recreational use, in the northern regions without encroaching on green belts.

Third, regional disparities in growth have resulted in exactly the opposite problem in the South East. Land, buildings, roads, rail networks, and social overhead capital more generally are all suffering from excess demand at peak periods. The congestion that results from this overutilisation of resources translates into an immense loss of time for residents of the South East and a never-ending attempt to relieve the conges-tion by heavy investment in new facilities.

Fourth, persistent regional disparities in the economic performance of regions result in a higher level of inflationary pressure for the economy as a whole than would otherwise be the case. There is surely no doubt that the sharp increase in inflationary pressure at the end of the 1980s was the direct result of labour shortages in the tight labour markets of the South East. The intense competition between firms for scarce labour led to a steady increase in wage inflation after 1988 in the South East and this has been transmitted to other regions through inter-plant wage bargaining and na-tional wage agreements.

REGIONAL POLICY OPTIONS

Regional policymakers are faced with three broad alternative (but complementary) strategies. These are as follows: the geographical redistribution of industry from prosperous to depressed areas; stimulating economic development *within* the depressed areas; and regenerating depressed areas through improving their socio-economic infrastructure.

Redistribution of industry policy began in earnest during World War II when strategic and defence objectives led to strict controls on industrial location in order to achieve a wider geographical spread of industry (following the recommendations of the Barlow Report in 1940). The wartime controls on the location of industry were extended into the post-war era and were the primary instrument of regional policy until the 1960s, when investment and labour subsidies were introduced on a large scale. The purpose of location controls and investment grants was to achieve a closer geographical match between labour demand and labour supply. The aim was to reduce inflationary pressures and increase national output at the same time.

Several empirical investigations have indicated that both location controls and financial incentives achieved a good deal of success in diverting industry to (and creating jobs in) the Assisted Areas during the 1960s and 1970s, though it is now widely recognised that regional policy has been conspicuously less successful than many of its proponents had expected (Moore, Rhodes and Tyler, 1987; Twomey and Taylor, 1987). Perhaps the most damning criticism of the redistribution of industry policy was that it was far too expensive for the number of jobs which actually resulted from it. There are two reasons for this. First, for many years subsidies were paid to firms investing in highly capital-intensive projects. Indeed, considerable amounts of government subsidy were received by firms which were investing in labour-saving capital equipment. Government grants therefore induced *reductions* in employment in these cases. Second, many firms receiving investment grants would have invested in the assisted areas even without these subsidies. In other words, a substantial proportion of government grants have been 'deadweight' spending (Wren, 1989).

The redistribution of industry policy had other weaknesses in addition to being expensive. It has been argued that investment incentives are not appropriate for encouraging job creation in areas of high unemployment. Labour is the factor in excess supply and so labour is the factor that should in principle be subsidised. A further criticism is that the policy was directed almost entirely at the manufacturing sector. Little thought was given to the potential importance of service sector industries as a means of creating jobs in depressed areas until the policy reforms of the 1980s. Criticisms were also directed against controls on the location of industry, in spite of considerable success in diverting industry from the South East to the assisted areas in the 1960s and 1970s (Twomey and Taylor, 1985). Location controls were abolished in 1982 on the grounds that they were leading not only to firms having to locate in less profitable locations but also to a lower level of national investment. Firm evidence in support of these two arguments for scrapping location controls was not, however, provided.

Although the criticisms of redistribution of industry policy need to be taken seriously, they should not go unchallenged. The attack on regional investment incentives has several weaknesses. First, cost per job should take into account the jobs created *indirectly* in other industries through production linkages as well as those *directly* related to the investment project. Second, some investments actually prevent job losses rather than create additional jobs, such as a new capital-intensive method of production which maintains a firm's competitiveness even though it results in some job losses. Third, some investments may induce further investment in the region by other firms which would not otherwise have expanded their productive capacity. Fourth, cost per job estimates of investment incentives vary enormously according to the type of incentives being assessed. Wren (1989,1990) shows that the cost per job estimates were very high under the pre-1984 policy regime because of the high concentration of awards to capital-intensive projects. The revised Regional Development Grant (RDG) scheme (1984), which included a cost per job limit of £10,000, resulted in a sharp reduction in cost per job – but was abolished in 1988 in spite of this. Fifth, the appropriate measure in cost per job calculations is the net exchequer cost and not the *gross* costs of the policy (Armstrong and Taylor, 1985). Any drawbacks to the exchequer resulting from lower unemployment benefits and higher taxes should be deducted from the gross exchequer outlays. Finally, subsidizing investment helps to improve the industrial structure of a region, and hence its long-term competitiveness, since new investment will incorporate the latest technology.

The 1980s saw a switch away from traditional regional policy based upon the geographical redistribution of industry to one which emphasised the importance of *indigenous growth*. Although this policy switch coincided with a corresponding switch in political ideology (from state interventionism to free market conservatism), there was a more fundamental reason for the policy change: namely, the 1980–83 depression. This caused investment to fall sharply in the early 1980s – particularly in the manufac-turing sector – and the consequence was a corresponding fall in mobile investment. In addition, high levels of unemployment in *all* regions meant that firms had less incentive to move to high unemployment areas. Equally important was the realisation that in a period of high unemployment in *all* regions, redistribution of industry policy was simply shuffling jobs around; no additional jobs were being created. The policy therefore collapsed. A further factor which raised the profile of indigenous economic development policies was the sudden realisation by local authorities that they had a role to play in creating jobs in their own areas.

The consequence of this policy switch was an increasing interest in encouraging the growth of small firms. By creating the right economic conditions (e.g. low inflation, lower taxes, less government intervention, fewer state-owned companies), the Gov-ernment expected the small firms sector to prosper and by so doing create a more dynamic and competitive economy. The depressed regions were thus expected to regenerate themselves from within rather than relying on the inward movement of industry from outside.

Needless to say, relying on the small firms sector to restore the economic fortunes of the depressed areas has not been strikingly successful in terms of the number of jobs created. A major drawback of relying on small firms to generate indigenous growth is that small firms generally remain small. Very few small firms grow to any significant size and a high proportion go out of business within a year or two of coming into existence (Storey and Johnson, 1988). Moreover, the conditions for new firm formation are far more favourable in the South than in the North. Greater wealth, a better educated workforce, a greater proportion of workers in small firms, a favourable industry mix, easier access to finance and continuous net inward migration are all likely to contribute to making the South a more likely location for new start-ups. If small firms policy is to be more successful in reducing regional disparities, it is clear that it will have to be made far more regionally discriminating than is presently the case.

Investment in *infrastructure* is the third main arm of regional policy. Depressed areas are often saddled with a relatively poor infrastructure. This applies not only to the physical infrastructure (such as housing, recreational amenities, educational facilities and industrial property) but also to the socio-economic fabric of regions. The skills of the workforce, for example, are poorer in depressed areas because of an absence of growth industries and a higher incidence of long-term unemployment. In addition, the resident population of depressed areas generally has poorer educational qualifications as a consequence of the out-migration of the most highly educated workers who are in the best position to seek out opportunities in more prosperous regions.

The consequence of a poor economic and physical infrastructure is clear: private investors are deterred from committing themselves to long-term investment projects. This suggests an important role for the Government if depressed areas are to be made attractive to private investors. Extensive public funding of training programmes is needed, for example, in order to up-grade skill levels in depressed areas. This cannot be done on a shoe-string since training is inevitably expensive if trainees are to acquire skills which are attractive to potential employers (including those firms seeking to move out of the labour-scarce South).

Improving the *physical* infrastructure of depressed areas is also essential if investment is to be attracted into these areas. First, improvements in social overhead capital (such as roads, railways, telecommunications etc) will reduce production costs for private sector businesses and raise their competitiveness. Second, public investment in a region's physical environment (including clearing derelict land and constructing better recreational facilities) makes it a more attractive place in which to live and work. Thirdly, public expenditure on the physical infrastructure acts as a confidence booster for private sector investors since it reflects the Government's commitment to an area. Private investors are more likely to invest in an area if they believe it has a sound economic future.

The case against the preferential treatment of depressed areas in the provision of public funds for investment in infrastructure is that *all* investment, regardless of whether it is public or private, should be allocated to projects which yield the highest returns. There can be little doubt that the very high levels of congestion in the South East would yield high immediate returns to further investment in the transport network. The returns to investing in depressed areas, by contrast, are likely to accrue over a much longer time horizon. But it could also be argued that the provision of more infrastructure in the North will help to stem the migration from North to South, thus reducing the pressure on existing facilities in the South East.

WHICH WAY FROM HERE?

If a serious onslaught on regional economic disparities is to made, there is no alternative but to strengthen regional policy. This would require several changes to current policy, the most urgent of which are as follows.

(i) Investment incentives need to be significantly strengthened. Abolishing the RDG in 1988 was a mistake and should be reversed (but with a higher cost per job limit than previously). Regional Selective Assistance should be retained but more funds should be made available in order to provide greater financial incentives to firms investing in Assisted Areas. Extra financial incentives should be made available, for example, for supporting investment in Research and Development (R&D).

(ii) The newly installed business rates system is a potentially powerful regional policy instrument. Rates should be made sufficiently regionally discriminating such that they significantly reduce the attractiveness of locations in the South East and improve the attractiveness of locations in depressed areas.

(iii) Small firms policy needs to be strengthened by making it more discriminating in favour of the high unemployment regions. It is particularly important to find ways of stimulating the new firm formation rate in the North. Exactly how this can be achieved is no easy matter, but one priority would be to find ways of bridging the funding gap faced by small and medium-sized firms in the assisted areas. More public funds could also be made available to help finance the introduction of new products and new processes by small and medium-sized firms. In addition, there needs to be closer monitoring and evaluation of small firms receiving grants and loans so that potential fast growers can be identified.

(iv) A more comprehensive training and retraining programme needs to be developed for school leavers and for the long-term unemployed in order to raise skill levels in depressed areas.

(v) Local authorities should be encouraged to extend their involvement in the economic development of their own areas. Much valuable experience has been gained by local authorities in the 1980s in their many and varied attempts to stimulate economic development (Miller, 1990). The central government needs to recognise the essential role of local authorities in the development of their own localities.

(vi) There should be a more stringent policy towards the acquisition of companies located in Assisted Areas to stop the loss of managerial control and managerial functions to firms located in the South. This would take the form of an automatic referral to the Monopolies and Mergers Commission of the potential acquisition of independent regionally-based companies. The depressed regions need greater protection against predators whose allegiance to these areas is questionable.

(vii) Regional development agencies (similar to those in Scotland and Wales) should be set up in all regions. Their functions would be: to coordinate the activities of a wide range of government and private agencies involved in economic development; to construct development strategies for the region; to promote the region more effectively, especially to international investors; to develop training programmes in conjunction with the private sector; to encourage the creation and growth of financial institutions in order to attract investment into the region; and to evaluate regional development policies so that their effectiveness can be improved. These regional development agencies would receive their income from central government, probably in the form of a block grant so that Whitehall would be responsible for setting the broad priorities for the regional allocation of funds. The individual agencies would then be given freedom to use their own initiative (and local knowledge) in constructing appropriate policies for their own regions. Competitive bidding between the agencies for mobile investment would have to be closely monitored and controlled to prevent a waste of scarce public funds.

(viii) Far more attention needs to be paid to the regional distribution of government expenditure. All government departments, for example, should be required to estimate the regional impact of their expenditure programmes. They should also be required to decentralise their activities to 'northern' locations where it is economically efficient (in the broadest sense) to do so.

(ix) Finally, far more needs to be spent on regional policy. Expenditure on regional industrial assistance sank to miserably low levels at the end of the 1980s – a clear reflection of the government's lack of commitment to dealing with Britain's regional problems (Figure 11.3.2). If the policy measures suggested above are to be taken seriously, this will involve a sharp reversal in regional policy expenditure in the 1990s. The UK Government could do worse than follow the lead taken by the European Community in its determination to increase the proportion of its budget allocated to the Structural Funds in order to help to offset the harmful regional consequences of greater economic integration in the 1990s.

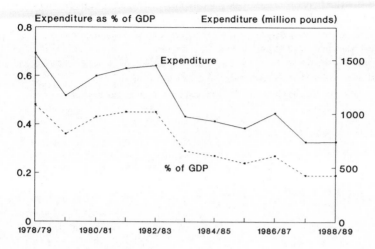

Source: Hansard, 29 November, 1989, p. 286

Figure 11.3.2: UK government expenditure on regional preferential assistance to industry, 1978/79–1988/89

CONCLUSION

Two points need to be hammered home. First, there is no simple or single cure for Britain's regional problems. A wide 'range of policy instruments are required if a significant reduction in regional economic disparities is to be achieved. Second, regional economic disparities are a permanent feature of all market economies. They are an inevitable consequence of a world economy which is continuously changing. Regional policy must therefore be regarded as a *permanent* feature of economic policy in much the same way that macroeconomic policy is permanent and continuously under review.

REFERENCES

Armstrong, H. and Taylor, J. (1985) *Regional Economics and Policy*, Oxford: Philip Allan.

Armstrong, H. and Taylor, J. (1988) *Regional Policy and the North-South Divide*, London: Employment Institute.

Balchin, P.N. (1990) *Regional Policy in Britain: The North-South Divide*, London: Paul Chapman Publishing.

Harris, R.I.D. (1988)'Market structure and external control in the regional economies of Great Britain', *Scottish Journal of Political Economy*, 35.

Martin, R. (1988) 'The new economics and politics of regional restructuring: the British experience' in *Regional Policy at the Cross-Roads: European Perspectives* (edited by L. Albrechts et alia), London: Jessica Kingsley.

Miller, D. (1990) 'The future of local economic policy: a public and private sector function' in *Local Economic Policy* (edited by M. Campbell), Poole: Cassell.

Moore, B., Rhodes, J. and Tyler, P. (1986) *The Effects of Government Regional Economic Policy*, Department of Trade and Industry, London: HMSO.

Smith, D. (1989) *Britain's Growing Divide: North and South*, Harmondsworth: Penguin.

Storey, D.J. and Johnson, S. (1988) *Are Small Firms the Answer to Unemployment?* London: Employment Institute.

Taylor, J. (1991) 'Regional economic disparities: causes and consequences', in *Reducing Regional Inequalities* (edited by A. Bowen and K. Mayhew), London: Kogan Page.

Twomey, J. and Taylor, J. (1985) 'Regional policy and the interregional movement of manufacturing industry in Great Britain', *Scottish Journal of Political Economy*, 32, November, pp.257–77.

Walsh, J. and Brown, W. (1990) 'Regional earnings and pay flexibility' Working Paper No.9008, Department of Applied Economics, University of Cambridge.

Wren, C. (1989) 'The revised Regional Development Grant Scheme: a case study in Cleveland County of a marginal employment subsidy', *Regional Studies*, 23(2), April, pp.127–137.

Wren, C. (1990) 'Regional policy in the 1980s', National Westminster Bank Review, November.

Regional Development Agencies in the United Kingdom

M. W. Danson, M. G. Lloyd, and D. Newlands

INTRODUCTION

A regional development agency has been defined as 'any publicly financed institution outside the mainstream of central and local government administration having powers designed for the specific purpose of promoting industrial development (including non-manufacturing activities) in regions that are generally designated as problem or priority areas' (Yuill and Allen, 1982, p.1). This, however, is perhaps too narrow a definition since, in addition to economic functions, many agencies have responsibilities for the environmental, and even social, development or regeneration of the region concerned. Regional development agencies are not new. For example, the Rural Development Commission (previously the Development Commission) was established as long ago as 1909 to address problems of rural development in Britain and, perhaps the best known agency, the Tennessee Valley Authority (TVA) in the US, was set up in 1933. However, most regional development agencies have been created since the Second World War and agencies now exist in most developed countries. This paper reviews the experience of regional development agencies in England, Scotland, Wales and Northern Ireland and speculates as to their future role in UK regional policy.

Until recently, regional development agencies occupied a relatively marginal position within the overall framework of regional policy in the UK, but interest has greatly increased with the demise of traditional regional policy. Nevertheless, there has still been relatively little discussion of the specific advantages of this particular institutional form.

Market failure in such areas as new firm formation, the development of advanced technology, and the provision of industrial infrastructure, all of which have pronounced regional dimensions, provides a justification of government intervention but not of regional development agencies as such. The reasons why their functions have not been pursued directly by central government itself have been explored by Wannop (1984). Discussing the origins of the Scottish Development Agency, he notes that:

> The principal arguments for a new agency to displace the externally directed Department of Industry had been economic ones…the case lay in the much increased intervention and financial support to United Kingdom industry by both Labour and Conservative Governments from the early 1960s, which had grown to such a degree as to require judgements on industrial performance and management which were beyond the experience of civil servants to provide creatively. Without removing Ministerial accountability, an agency with a board appointed from outside the Civil Service was seen as the means of introducing innovation and sensitivity to such Scottish industrial restructuring as the Government could encourage (Wannop, 1984, p.315).

There is then the further issue of the relative advantages of regional development agencies by comparison with an increased economic role for local authorities which is another alternative to direct central government intervention. In discussing four areas – promotional activity, major firm rescue operations, the retention of local ownership in key companies, and the promotion of new sectors – Cameron (1985) argues that development agencies permit appropriate levels of resources and expertise to be mobilised and avoid the dangers of duplication of effort and competitive subsidisation.

Although these economic factors are relevant, the increasing reliance upon development agencies is best explained by political considerations. As argued by Damesick and Wood (1987, p.262):

> Existing regional development agencies are the creatures of central government, reflecting its reluctance to put resources directly in the hands of local authorities... This mode of intervention has been deployed and sustained in Scotland and Wales essentially because of its advantages, from central government's viewpoint, as a way of responding to well articulated regional interests there, rather than because it is intrinsically superior to alternative arrangements.

As a consequence, development agencies have evolved as a politically acceptable form of supply side response to regional economic problems in the United Kingdom.

ENGLAND

The Development Commission began, in 1909, as an agency for the whole of Britain. It ceased to have responsibility for the Scottish Highlands and Islands in 1965, and for the rest of Scotland in 1975 and for Wales in 1975 as separate development agencies were created in those areas. Since 1975, therefore, the Commission has been the development agency for the rural areas of England. Its objectives have been fairly consistent. These are to combat rural depopulation, improve the economic and social structure of rural areas, and create employment. However, 'the nature and scope of its activities have changed considerably over the seventy five years of its existence' (Tricker and Martin, 1984, p.507). Initially, it had a variety of agricultural policy responsibilities and was also concerned with road building in rural areas. After 1945, many of these responsibilities were hived off and the Commission was left to concentrate on the promotion of rural employment and community development. On the other hand, it developed some new policy instruments. In particular, from the late 1950s onwards, it pursued a factory and workshop building programme in areas experiencing rapid depopulation but also thought to have the potential for future recovery.

Since 1984, and somewhat against the trend of the evolution of regional policy in Britain in the 1980s, the powers of the Commission have been extended to include the provision of direct financial assistance to firms through grants, loans and guarantees. Assistance is concentrated in Rural Development Areas (RDAs), selected according to criteria of employment opportunities, population structure and existing facilities. In recent years, the Commission has 'stressed the importance of simultaneously strengthening the economy of rural areas and supporting the social fabric of the rural communities' (Tricker and Martin, 1984, p.513). There have been some economic successes. Green (1986) has argued that RDAs have benefited from improved policy co-ordination, a greater flow of innovative ideas, and increased resources. However, the Commission's activities have had scarcely any impact upon the social problems of rural England.

SCOTLAND

There are two regional development agencies in Scotland, the Highlands and Islands Development Board (HIDB), which has now become Highlands and Islands Enterprise and the Scottish Development Agency (SDA), which has now become Scottish Enterprise. The HIDB was established in 1965 but underwent substantial changes in the 1980s, particularly as a result of the review undertaken by the Industry Department for Scotland and the Treasury (Industry Department for Scotland, 1987a). The review set out the limits to freedom of action of the HIDB very clearly: 'The Board, in pursuing any intervention in the market, should aim to encourage the private sector wherever possible, should justify the costs of any intervention against specified objectives and should aim to share in rewards as well as risks' (Industry Department for Scotland, 1987a, p.2). The HIDB was given several new objectives. These included the encouragement of entrepreneurship, the fostering of increased private sector involvement in the development of the area, and the disposal of land, property and investment when the opportunity arose.

The SDA was established in 1975 to be responsible for economic development in the whole of Scotland, apart from the area covered by the HIDB. Like the HIDB, it was closely scrutinised by the present Government in the 1980s. The result was either that the Government has dictated changes in the SDA's policy objectives and working arrangements or that the SDA itself responded to the changing ideological circumstances within which it had to operate.

There was a marked change in the SDA's economic development strategy following the election of the Conservative government. New investment guidelines were introduced in 1980. The SDA's objectives were made more commercial and selective with an emphasis on identifying and facilitating the opportunities for business development of Scottish entrepreneurship, support for growth sectors, including the promotion of new technology, the improvement of industrial efficiency and competitiveness, and the regeneration of local economies in different parts of Scotland. The previous obligations to maintain and safeguard employment and to promote industry democracy were dropped. As a consequence of these changes, the SDA developed a 'modified market' approach to economic regeneration in Scotland, an approach which stresses the development of competitive and efficient business and the leverage of private investment (Moore and Booth, 1986).

More recently, there was a further review of the SDA by the Industry Department for Scotland and the Treasury. As with the HIDB, the SDA 'should only be involved where the market alone will not produce the outcome desired by policy; and its intervention should wherever possible seek to achieve its ends by improving the working of the market and should not create dependency' (Industry Department for Scotland, 1987b, p.7).

The Government has embarked upon a further major reform of economic development and training functions in Scotland (Industry Department for Scotland, 1988; Danson, Lloyd and Newlands, 1989). A new body, Scottish Enterprise, has been created from the SDA and the Scottish operation of the Training Agency, formerly the Manpower Services Commission. Scottish Enterprise took over from the SDA in April 1991. Initially, the more strategic functions of the SDA and the Training Agency are to be retained by Scottish Enterprise at the centre but the new body is to subcontract its business development and training roles to local business led agencies, known as Local Enterprise Companies (LECs). In the Highlands and Islands, another new body, Highland and Islands Enterprise, has been created which is very similar to Scottish Enterprise in its powers and methods of operation and will contract out business and training services to LECs in the Highlands and Islands. There is a total of 22 LECs throughout Scotland. The first of these began operations in June 1990 with annual budgets of between £5 million and £70 million.

Of the board of ten members of Scottish Enterprise, it is required that at least six have a business background. Similarly, for the local agencies, 'two-thirds or more of the membership would be expected to be from the senior ranks of private sector business' (Industry Department for Scotland, 1988, p.15). The White Paper did not anticipate any significant role for local government. The experience and commitment of Scottish local authorities to economic development and to training initiatives was not acknowledged.

It is unclear which specific strategic functions will be retained by Scottish Enterprise at the centre and what the relationship between the central organisation and the local offices will be in practise. The continued support of central strategic functions received hardly any attention in the White Paper. It is possible, therefore, that the creation of coherent sectoral strategies and the environmental improvement of Scotland's cities, which count among the SDA's past achievements, will suffer as a result of the new reforms.

The attraction of inward investment into Scotland by Locate in Scotland, a joint venture of the Scottish Office and the SDA, is not affected by the Scottish Enterprise proposals. However, with increased awareness of the adverse effects of foreign investment and of 'the branch plant syndrome', the attraction of new inward investment will probably receive less emphasis (Young, 1989).

WALES

The Welsh Development Agency (WDA) and the Development Board for Mid Wales (now Mid Wales Development) were both established in 1975. As in Scotland, there is a geographical separation of economic development powers, with the WDA having responsibility for South Wales, while the WDA's environmental remit applies to the whole of the country.

The initial remit of the WDA included four principal objectives: the encouragement of economic development, the promotion of industrial efficiency and competitiveness, the provision, maintenance and safeguarding of employment, and the improvement of the environment. The WDA proposed an economic and industrial plan as a framework for its spending but this brought it into immediate conflict with the Welsh Office which reserved for itself sole control over Welsh economic planning decisions. As a result, 'the promised long term strategy was an early casualty' (Eirug, 1983, p.378).

In its first years, the WDA pursued a relatively active industrial investment policy, prompting its description as 'a fairly adventurous merchant bank' (Eirug, 1983, p.378). However, the requirement by the new Conservative government that the WDA should achieve a commercial rate of return on its investments has led to a contraction of direct investment as well as the indirect devaluation of employment generation as an objective of WDA policy. Other functions such as environmental improvement and factory building became relatively more important although, like other regional development agencies in the UK, the WDA has been required to involve the private sector more explicitly in its site development and factory building role. Over time, 'the WDA has moved somewhat from being a "state enterprise" form of agency, drawing its funds from the public sector, towards a more strongly "entrepreneurial" style of activity' (Cooke, 1987, p.210). In a similar arrangement to that in Scotland, the attraction of inward investment into Wales is the responsibility of WINvest, a body jointly operated by the Welsh Office and the WDA.

Contemporary with the introduction of Scottish Enterprise, a parallel White Paper proposed the establishment of Training and Enterprise Councils (TECs) in England and Wales (Department of Employment, 1988). However, TECS are to have fewer powers than the Local Enterprise Companies being introduced in Scotland and, unlike the SDA, the WDA is to survive largely unchanged. Wales may accordingly benefit from a closer integration of training and economic development functions but without any reduction of the WDA's central strategic powers.

NORTHERN IRELAND

The Northern Ireland Development Agency (NIDA), like the SDA and the WDA, was created in 1975. It incorporated the functions of the Northern Ireland Finance Corporation which provided loans, guarantees and equity capital to industrial firms threatened with closure or contraction. The NIDA was established with a strong investment banking function but its powers were narrower than those of the Scottish and Welsh agencies. The provision of factory sites and premises, and powers of environmental improvement and land renewal, remained the responsibility of separate Departments in the Northern Ireland Office. As a consequence, when the interventionist strategy of the mid-1970s ended with the election of the Conservative government, the NIDA, unlike the SDA and the WDA, did not have the basis for adaptation and could not survive in the new political climate (Harrison, 1986).

The NIDA was wound up in 1982 and its functions were transferred to a new Industrial Development Board (IDB) within the Northern Ireland Department of Economic Development. Under the IDB, the emphasis has shifted from the provision of general financial incentives to the formation and support of individual company plans. More attention is now given to the improvement of firms' efforts in marketing, research and development, and technology transfer. Attempts have been made to target inward investment more effectively, especially by the selection of key sectors.

Despite these improvements, the IDB does not provide a fully co-ordinated approach to industrial development in Northern Ireland. Responsibility for inward investment is divided among several divisions of the IDB. The IDB still lacks certain significant powers. In particular, employment promotion and industrial development in the small firm sector remain the separate responsibilities of the Local Enterprise Development Unit (LEDU).

FUTURE PROSPECTS

Regional development agencies in the UK have always represented an addition to, rather than replacement of, the system of regional aid. Nevertheless, there has been insufficient recognition that this particular institutional form may involve the pursuit of widely varying policies in practice. Over the last ten years, regional development agencies in the UK have experienced a complete transformation of their powers and functions. Employment has been downgraded as an objective of policy. Interventionist powers, particularly of direct investment in the private sector and of factory building, have been curtailed. Regional development agencies have become much more market-oriented, seeking to support private business and encourage entrepreneurship. They have been required to involve the private sector in most of their own economic development functions and to dispose of land, property and investments. Investment guidelines have been made more commercial and selective, and stress the leverage of private investment.

Regional development agencies continue to change. Labour training and economic development functions have been brought closer together. In England and Wales, there is still a fairly loose relationship but, under the Scottish Enterprise proposals, they are to be much more closely integrated in Scotland. However, if Scottish Enterprise is typical of future prospects, the likelihood is that regional development agencies will witness a further erosion of their strategic economic roles which represented one of the principal reasons for their establishment. There will be fewer means of tackling continued market failure in such areas as labour training, property provision and indigenous economic development. It is unlikely that the importance of industrial structure, ownership and control will be recognised. While Local Enterprise Companies in Scotland and Training and Enterprise Councils in England and Wales may possibly provide a better delivery of services in non innovative areas, a strategic viewpoint is essential with regard to measures to promote the adoption of new technology. In addition, with private business playing an ever greater role, there are growing fears of a loss of public accountability with regard to regional economic development functions in the UK.

REFERENCES

Cameron, G. (1985), 'Regional economic planning – the end of the line?'. *Planning Outlook*, 28, 8–13.

Cooke, P. (1987), 'Wales' in Damesick, P. and Wood, P. (eds), *Regional Problems, Problem Regions, and Public Policy in the United Kingdom*. Oxford: Clarendon Press.

Damesick, P. and Wood, P. (1987), 'Public policy for regional development: restoration or regeneration?' in Damesick, P. and Wood, P. (eds), *Regional Problems, Problem Regions, and Public Policy in the United Kingdom*, Oxford: Clarendon Press.

Danson, M., Lloyd, M. G. and Newlands, D. (1989), '"Scottish Enterprise": towards a model agency or a flawed initiative?'. *Regional Studies* 23, 557–563.

Department of the Employment (1988), *Employment for the 1990s*, London: HMSO.

Eirug, A. (1983), 'The Welsh Development Agency'. *Geoforum* 14, 375–388.

Green, C. (1986), 'Rural Development Areas – progress and problems'. *The Planner* 72(5), 18–19.

Harrison, R. (1986), 'Industrial development policy and the restructuring of the Northern Ireland economy'. *Environment and Planning C*, 4, 53–70

Industry Department for Scotland (1987a), *Review of the Highlands and Islands Development Board, Report of a Review Group to the Secretary of State for Scotland*, Edinburgh: HMSO.

Industry Department for Scotland (1988), *Scottish Enterprise: A New Approach to Training and Enterprise Creation*, Edinburgh: HMSO.

Moore, C. and Booth, S. (1986), 'From comprehensive regeneration to privatisation: the search for efficient area strategies' in Lever, W. and Moore, C. (eds), *The City in Transition*. Oxford: Clarendon Press.

Tricker, M. and Martin, S. (1984), 'The developing role of the Commission'. *Regional Studies* 18, 507–514.

Wannop, U. (1984), 'The evolution and roles of the Scottish Development Agency'. *Town Planning Review* 55, 313–321.

Young, S. (1989), 'Scotland v Wales in the inward investment game'. *Fraser of Allander Quarterly Economic Commentary* 14(3), 59–63.

Yuill, D. and Allen, K. (1982), 'European regional development agencies: an overview' in Yuill, D. (ed), *Regional Development Agencies in Europe*. Aldershot: Gower.

Urban Policy Initiatives: Trends and Prospects

Paul Lawless and Graham Haughton

INTRODUCTION

For more than 20 years a form of urban policy has operated in the United Kingdom. For a decade, from the mid-1960s onwards, a period of what can be seen as urban experimentation was effected by both Harold Wilson's Labour government and Edward Heath's Conservative administration. During this period about a dozen separate urban experiments were introduced (Lawless, 1979). Most of them have little contemporary relevance. Two schemes, however, the Community Development Projects initiated by Labour in the late 1960s and the Inner Area Studies commissioned by Peter Walker, then Secretary of State for the Environment in 1972, were to have a longer term impact. They examined the causes for, and suggested possible solutions to, deprivation within the major conurbations. Although they were far from unanimous in their views, two central themes emerged from many of these experiments: urban poverty was widespread and not confined to definable pockets of deprivation and the root cause of deprivation was the contraction in economic opportunities for many inner city residents.

These lessons were to be taken on board by the 1974–1979 Labour government, In 1977 the only White Paper ever published on the older conurbations, Policy for the Inner Cities (HM Government, 1977) emerged. In many respects the White Paper was to prove of considerable significance to the evolution of inner city policy. It argued that economic problems were crucial for the older cities and their inhabitants; that therefore the older conurbations should receive economically orientated, as well as social support; and that a permanent phase of inner city policy should be introduced. These principles were to guide the development of urban policy for more than a decade.

URBAN POLICY 1977–1990

Although relatively few policy innovations were discussed in the White Paper it nevertheless heralded an era of substantial development in terms of urban intervention. Both the Labour government between 1977 and 1979 and Mrs Thatcher's administrations thereafter were to implement a range of urban initiatives. At least ten separate inner city policy areas can be identified (Lawless, 1988a). Many of these can be subsumed however within three major themes: co-ordination, enterprise and development. Not all initiatives it should be said fall into this categorisation and there are overlaps. But a brief comment on each area should provide a flavour of British inner urban policy in the late 1970s and throughout the 1980s.

Efforts to co-ordinate government intervention within and towards the older conurbations characterise a number of urban projects. The Partnerships for instance, created by the Labour government in seven of the most deprived inner urban areas in England in the late 1970s, were designed to bring together pertinent central and local government departments, and other interested organisations, in order to tease out a co-ordinated strategy towards the cities. The City Action Teams and Task Forces established by Conservative governments in the 1980s were intended, among other functions, to enhance the integration of public and private sector activities within the cities. It is well worth noting that in contradiction to this 'co-ordination' drive was the short-sighted decision to abolish the metropolitan counties (Greater London Council (GLC), Greater Manchester Council (GMC), etc.) in 1986, which has left a telling vacuum in the ability of the larger urban areas strategically to think and plan at a sub-regional level.

During the 1980s Mrs Thatcher's administrations increasingly promoted the notion of enterprise within the cities. A nostrum widely advocated by these Conservative governments was the idea that one cause for urban economic decline was the excessive degree of public sector intervention, regulation and control within the cities in the post-war period, which had apparently dampened down private enterprise and initiative. To overcome this problem a number of urban projects were introduced. Enterprise Zones for example, of which there were 25 in the United Kingdom by 1987, were designated to enhance activity in economically deprived areas such as the inner cores of the older cities. This was to be achieved through reducing physical controls via a more liberalised planning regime and by financial incentives such as rate relief for ten years and 100 per cent capital allowances for industrial and commercial property.

Finally, a third theme which increasingly came to dominate the evolution of urban policy in the 1980s was the question of development. From the mid-1980s onwards this aspect of inner city intervention came to figure much more prominently. Urban Development, Urban Regeneration, (later assimilated as City Grant) and Derelict Land Grants were introduced and modified to subsidise and thus enhance private sector development within the older urban cores. Local authorities had to maintain registers of vacant and thus potentially developable land. And most important of all, Conservative administrations in the 1980s introduced Urban Development Corporations (UDCs). These are appointed by central government to effect the redevelopment of extensive areas of derelict urban land. They are independent bodies which may, but do not have to, collaborate with elected local councils. By 1988–89 UDCs, collectively funded to the tune of more than £250m per annum, had been established in the derelict dockland areas of London and Liverpool, the Black Country, Teeside, Tyneside, Trafford Park, Cardiff Bay, Leeds, Manchester, Bristol and Sheffield.

URBAN POLICY 1977–1989: A BRIEF CRITIQUE

Urban policy has been subject to two types of evaluation. At one level the Department of the Environment has commissioned a range of studies designed narrowly to investigate the operation of specific programmes or schemes. Some of these evaluations proved positive in their assessments. That undertaken into urban development grant argued, for instance, that this programme had helped substantially to raise private sector investment in the cities (Department of the Environment, 1988). Equally so evaluations of mainstream Urban Programme funding suggested that it had been important in helping to effect environmental improvements and employment creation projects (Department of the Environment, 1986a and b).

At a deeper level of analysis however most commentators assessing the wider impact of inner city policy on the older urban cores have tended to be more critical in their observations (Haughton and Roberts, 1990; Lawless, 1989b; 1989; Robson, 1988; Stewart, 1987). Urban policy still really cannot be regarded as a comprehensive programme designed to enhance the economic and social fortunes of the older urban areas and those living within them. In England especially, and Wales to a lesser extent, it has consisted of a series of ad-hoc projects initiated not because of any overwhelming evidence that they might alter things for the better but because they reflected the particular ideologies of different governments and key politicians within them. In Wales, the publication of 'The Valleys' in 1988 as a key strategy document appears to mark the emergence of a more co-ordinated series of urban-related policies. The urban policy picture in Scotland and Northern Ireland is rather less fragmented. In Scotland, the Scottish Development Agency (SDA) has adopted a much more co-ordinated approach involving both local and regional strategies – its replacement with a more localised delivery mechanism under the Scottish Enterprise banner, announced in 1988, may however see a diminution of this relatively co-ordinated approach. In Northern Ireland things are different again, most notably in the way in which housing provision is a much more central, integrated feature, entirely outside local authority control. In addition, regional policy, assisted by large amounts of European money, is much more pivotal to, and integrated with, urban development than on the mainland. In terms of pure urban policy, the main element is the Belfast Action Team, set up in 1986 with a small annual budget of only £500,000.

To return to England again where most urban innovations have occurred, it remains clear that urban policy has proven a relatively autonomous policy arena. Key issues having an impact on many people within the older urban cores such as housing, education, policing and transport have never figured particularly prominently. Indeed the whole question of social welfare, which was seen by some of the urban experiments such as the Inner Area Studies and the Community Development Projects as crucial, has been steadily relegated in importance throughout the 1980s across the nation. Increasingly the poor are supposed to benefit by 'trickle-down' effects from major property developments. It is unlikely that many will actually do so and it is significant that no government research has been commissioned to test this fundamental tenet of Ministerial ideology and policy. Related to this and also under-researched by Government departments, are racial issues. The 1989 Gifford report on Liverpool demonstrates the continuing deep-seated and pervasive nature of racial discrimination. There remains an unwillingness by Government to conceive of the nature, scale, scope and causes of racial problems, so that inevitably the policy response has been inadequate, ad hoc and under funded.

A number of other fundamental criticisms or urban policy might briefly be mentioned. It has not proved especially innovative. The Urban Programme, which in one guise or another has been around for more than twenty years, has increasingly tended to fund standard schemes which would have been resourced out of main stream expenditure had financial cut backs not occurred. There is little within the urban dimension moreover to suggest much in the way of strategic urban, sub-regional and regional vision. Broader questions affecting the cities have tended to be ignored. Issues such as relationships between conurbations and their regions, the impact of new technologies on the cities, the role of leisure and tourism within the older urban cores and many other strategic considerations have received little official comment or guidance. And finally it is clear, as official observers point out (House of Commons Environment Committee, 1983), that the implementation of inner urban policy has not been characterised by a consensual form of co-ordination between different agencies and organisations. Perhaps not surprisingly, bearing in mind the importance accorded inner urban problems by a wide range of political commentators, the implementation of inner urban policy has frequently been epitomised by inter and intra-institutional conflict (House of Commons Committee of Public Accounts, 1990).

URBAN POLICY: INTO THE 1990S

Speculating on the future direction of particular policy areas is never easy. In the case of inner urban policy there are a number of unknown factors which make prediction especially complex. It may be for example that urban economic decline moderates to some extent in the 1990s as at least some conurbations increase jobs within higher order service sectors and in areas such as tourism, sport and leisure. As a result of these kinds of considerations the inner urban problem might conceivably diminish in the public eye and political debate. Equally so urban disturbances, a marked feature of the 1980s may well re-occur, thus reinforcing the problems of the older urban cores within the litany of contemporary ills. And over-arching everything, and making prediction so complex, is the central issue of power. A Labour, or at least a non-Conservative, national government elected in the 1990s probably would wish to effect some changes in the scale and direction of inner urban policy.

It remains clear that the 1990s may still be dominated by Conservative administrations. These may well wish to present a slightly softer hue than was evident for much of the 1980s. But policy development in areas such as inner city intervention would probably reflect and indeed accentuate many of the themes emerging from Mrs Thatcher's administrations elected in 1979, 1983 and 1987.

If the perpetuation of Conservative rule into the 1990s does occur, it seems probable that a number of key trends will come increasingly to dominate the administration of inner city policy. The privatisation of policy will become more obvious. During the 1980s the private sector was given a greater role within the implementation of urban policy; Urban Programme submissions were often vetted by local chambers of commerce for example from the early 1980s. In the 1990s the market will come increasingly to dominate inner city policy. For example numbers of public-private sector 'partnerships' are likely to be increased. But as observers of the privatisation of urban policy in both the United States and Britain make clear, this increasing emphasis on market investment in the cities serves to enhance property development whereas questions of equity, poverty and distribution remain relatively neglected (Barnekov, Boyle and Rich, 1989).

Two other trends apparent within inner urban policy in the 1990s are likely to have an impact on urban intervention in the coming decade: central control and a diminishing role for local authorities. Throughout the 1980s central government has used inner city policy to increase its influence over the physical and economic restructuring of the cities. This is most obvious with the Urban Development Corporations. These are appointed by central government and in general have adopted strategies designed to encouraged commercial, retail and high quality residential development. Activities which have traditionally sustained the cities and their labour forces, notably manufacturing industry and cheaper housing, have been largely eschewed. Central governments in the 1980s were able in essence to effect urban regenerative strategies which too often ran counter to the aspirations of communities and their elected representatives. It seems improbable that the 1990s will see much of a reduction in this process.

Continuing central domination may occur through the creation of more development corporations, perhaps the establishment of a national urban development agency and constant central supervision of inner city funding. In parallel to this, continuing efforts by central government to bring local authorities to heel may well accelerate the deterioration of public service provision, as central funds are cut-back or cut-off. And finally, and as an inevitable corollary of what has gone before, local government will become increasingly marginalised in the implementation of inner city policy. Increasingly, decisions relating to the direction and funding of urban policy will be made by organisations which may have local government representation, but which will be controlled by central government and local business leaders. The emergence of Scottish Enterprise and Training and Enterprise Councils (TECs) provides an important example of new local delivery mechanisms for policy, which diminish the role of local authorities and enhance that of the private sector. TECs may well be setting a precedent for inner city policy.

Speculating on what probably will occur in the 1990s assuming continued Conservative rule should not prevent some consideration of what might occur to urban policy given a more favourable environment. Urban policy needs to be more strategic in its vision. The broader issues affecting cities and their developments need to be addressed. Some of these have been alluded to above. But to give another pertinent example, little consideration has been given to relationships between the major conurbations and enhanced infrastructural investment in roads, rail and the Channel Tunnel. It needs too to be more integrative in its approach. Urban policy largely deals with the administration of specific, and small urban budgets. Important issues for many in the cities such as housing and education receive little attention. There should be much more concern for these kinds of issues especially as they affect specific groups notably the poor, the disabled, women and ethnic minorities. Policing of the cities too is one of the most important problems facing many in the inner cities and should formally form a much greater part of the urban debate. And in general, underlying all of this, is the central question of equity. Too much of what has happened in recent years has only benefited property developers, land owners, financial institutions and the better off. More deprived sectors in society merit something too from the urban dimension, through new housing, improved social facilities, and better paid jobs. Urban policy needs an enhanced community dimension; in particular issues of race have yet to be tackled in anything other than an *ad hoc* fashion.

Moreover, it is not simply a question of re-orientating urban policy towards new objectives; its administration and financing need to be reorganised too. There probably is a case for the creation of urban development agencies given specific physical, economic and social tasks but operating in an altogether more consensual fashion than has proved the case with at least some of the urban development corporations. The Scottish Development Agency as it operated in the mid-1980s offers an apt model in that it adopted wider objectives than mere physical development in its urban regeneration programmes and it operated in collaboration with local government (Morison, 1987). A similar model would make sense for many English cities, where there is a compelling case for integrating their individual urban development strategies into appropriate regional and sub-regional strategic frameworks. Finally and inevitably, questions of financing loom large. Urban policy funding in the 1980s amounted to a few hundred million pounds a year at a time when many urban councils were losing substantial resources through government cut backs in capital allocations and revenue support. The urban problem quite simply merits far greater funding than has occurred to date. As is so evident in many European cities resources allocated to urban housing, transport, education, and development can dramatically improve the environmental, social and economic conditions within older conurbations to the benefit of all sectors of society. British urban policy is hardly in a position to claim this.

REFERENCES

Barnekov, T., Boyle, R. and Rich, R. (1989) *Privatism and Urban Policy in Britain and the United States*, Oxford: Oxford University Press.

Department of the Environment (1986a) *Evaluation of environmental effects of economic development projects funded under the Urban Programme*, London: HMSO.

Department of the Environment (1986b) *Assessment of the employment effects of economic development projects funded under the Urban Programme*, London: HMSO.

Department of the Environment (1988) *An Evaluation of the Urban Development Grant System*, London: HMSO.

Haughton, G. and Roberts, R. (1990) 'Government urban economic policy in England, 1979–89: problems and potential' in Campbell, M.*Local Economic Development*, London: Cassel.

H M Government (1977) *Policy for the Inner Cities, Cmnd 9571*, London: HMSO.

House of Commons Committee of Public Accounts (1990) *Reorganising its Inner Cities.*London: HMSO.

House of Commons Environment Committee (1983) *The Problems of Management of Urban Renewal, Appraisal of the recent initiatives in Merseyside*, London: HMSO.

Lawless, P. (1979) *Urban Deprivation and Government Initiative*, London: Faber.

Lawless, P. (1988a) British Inner Urban Policy: A Review, *Regional Studies* 22, 531–542.

Lawless, P. (1988b) British Urban Policy Post 1979a: A Critique, *Policy and Politics* 16, 261–275.

Lawless, P. (1989) *Britain's Inner Cities, Second Edition*, London: Paul Chapman Publishing.

Morison, H. (1987) *The Regeneration of Local Economies*, Oxford: Clarendon.

Robson, B. (1988) *Those Inner Cities*, Oxford: Clarendon.

Stewart, M. (1987) Ten years of inner city policy, *Town Planning Review*, 58, 129–141.

Emerging Constraints in the South East

Michael Breheny

For 50 years or more, the 'North South Divide' has been shorthand: for southern affluence and complacency, and northern depression and envy. Suddenly, however, this simple distinction is less clear. True, the North still has genuine problems. But in some places, at least, prospects do now look better, and increasingly the benefits – particularly the quality of life – of the North are being appreciated and promoted. The major change comes in the South: it is the realisation that the very success of the region – the basis of its relative comforts – is reaching the point where it produces distinct discomforts.

This realisation of the South East's inadequacies also comes at a bad time: at the very time that other prosperous, leading regions in Europe are gearing themselves up for the post 1992 competitive market. As the South East suffers, and government intervention is minimal, the French, for example, are developing public investment-led strategic plans 'To make Paris and the Ile-de-France the economic and cultural capital of Europe in 1993'(Pommel, 1989).

On an almost daily basis the media report on the South East's problems: road and rail congestion, high business costs, high housing costs, environmental problems, recruitment difficulties and so on. The phrase 'overheating' is used regularly. This rather vague term implies that economic growth pressures – not relieved by any significant public intervention – are such that major disbenefits begin to accrue. Many of these discomforts have existed in London for some time, but what is new is their appearance in the Rest of the South East (ROSE).

This relatively sudden switch from comfort to discomfort arises – arguably – because of the coincidence of two events. On the one hand the South East has been growing economically and physically at a very rapid rate; on the other, public investment, which was previously used as a way of coping with such growth, has been gradually withdrawn. Possibly coincidence is the wrong word, because both of these events are consistent with government policy. What the government has not bargained for is both the inability of 'the market' to cope with the consequences of such growth and the backlash from those who suffer as a result.

The reasons for and nature of the South East's growth in recent years are poorly understood. The large majority of academic research has gone into studies of our depressed regions. Only now is the South East begining to receive the attention it warrants. Although we know that the burgeoning service sector, along with the more modest but significant high tech sectors, have been focussed on the South East, and that much of this growth has been decentralised from London, we do not fully understand either the region's role in the changing international economy or the decentralisation process.

What is now more obvious to us than the reasons for the South East's growth are its consequences. Given more space, we could attempt to review the whole range of such effects. However, in order to convey the scale of the problem, it will suffice to consider just four sets of consequences. Two of them – transport inadequacies and labour shortages – are plain to see. The third – social polarisation – tends to be hidden relatively, but is no less significant for that. The fourth is, in effect, a consequence of the consequences: the backlash from disaffected residents.

TRANSPORT: ROSELAND GRIDLOCK?

Suddenly, in London and much of the outer South East transport is the issue. The recent Central London Rail Study was produced in response to widespread and intense complaints about congestion and woefully inadequate public transport services in the capital. In a city that had learned to live with congestion for centuries, these concerted complaints give a measure of the magnitude of the problem. After years of 'starvation funding', the public transport system is inadequate for the task. New road and rail investments are needed desperately.

It is this lack of investment in infrastructure, with the resulting congestion and squalor, that has led Peter Hall to refer to London as having the features of a Third World city (Hall, 1989).

Ironically, the very congestion that has driven many businesses and households out to the edges of the region now threatens to engulf them there. Again, this is a new feature of the South East's discomforts. While traffic problems have been recognised in many towns in the outer South East for some time, these problems are now reaching major proportions. Rapid growth in towns like Reading has taken place with virtually no additional investment in infrastructure. While efforts are now being made, it is often a case of 'too little, too late'. The parallels with Cervero's 'Suburban Gridlock'(Cervero, 1986) in the United States are all too obvious: a case perhaps of 'Roseland gridlock'.

The Channel Tunnel rail route controversy – coinciding as it has with much debate about the effects of 1992 – has focused attention on the inadequacy of British investment in transport infrastructure. The reluctance of BR and the government to tackle the high speed train issue in Kent, never mind across the rest of the country, is in marked contrast to the advanced planning of the French, German and Spanish governments in developing comprehensive high speed systems to ensure their spatial competitiveness in the European market.

OVEREMPLOYMENT

Following quickly behind years of nationally high unemployment, the South East now has a genuine shortage of workers, in some sectors and some areas. The lack of skilled workers is hampering many companies. In the Thames Valley, for example, there is a constant shortage of skilled workers in the electronics sector. Recent reports suggest that the civil service in London is operating at three quarters of its establishment level because of recruitment problems. The catering industry recruits in Ireland, and police forces in the north of England. Such recruitment drives are usually unsuccessful because of the prohibitive costs of moving into the South East.

The 'overheating' of local labour markets is usually reflected in low unemployment rates. Areas with unemployment rates of 3 per cent or less – areas 'without dole queues' according popular press reports – are regarded as having full employment. A rate lower than this will usually imply problems of mobility and recruitment. It is interesting to compare the change over the last year in the number of travel to work areas (TTWA's) that satisfy this 3 per cent criterion.

In September 1988, eight TTWA's had unemployment rates of 3 per cent or less; seven of them in the South East. By September 1989, 33 TTWAs could be included in this category; 18 of them in the South East region. Of these 18, eight had rates of 2 per cent or less, as shown in Table 11.6.1. We can conclude that these local labour markets are 'overheated' with all of the problems of recruitment, high house prices, strong development pressures, and congestion.

Table 11.6.1: Travel to Work Areas with Unemployment Rates of 3 per cent
or Less in the South East, September 1989

Andover	2.0
Aylesbury & Wycombe	1.9
Basingstoke & Alton	1.9
Bedford	2.8
Bicester	2.0
Chelmsford & Braintree	2.8
Chichester	2.1
Crawley	1.3
Guildford & Aldershot	2.0
Hertford & Harlow	3.0
Milton Keynes	2.8
Oxford	2.3
Reading	2.1
Slough	2.4
Tunbridge Wells	1.8
Watford & Luton	3.0
Winchester & Eastleigh	1.6
Worthing	2.5

Source: Department of Employment Gazette

THE NIMBY BACKLASH

The very obvious disbenefits of living in areas where these development consequences pile on top of each other has served to focus the minds of those who are as yet safe, but under threat. Protesting is back in fashion. The government's own supporters in the outer shires of the region are now making their anguish felt as they come under increasing pressures for more and more growth – either from local housing proposals or from major developments.

What started out as localised grumbles have burst into major issues. The NIMBY attitude has spread from a few localised outbursts against specific development proposals to a general concerted movement in much of the outer South East. The remarkable and unexpected scale of opposition to the alternative Channel Tunnel rail routes through Kent is an obvious example.

Other major wrangles are about to break, because ironically while this backlash grows stronger, the argument in favour of development also seem to become more powerful. There is little doubt that the Channel Tunnel rail link will have to be built, Kings Cross will have to be expanded, Heathrow will have a fifth terminal, Stansted will have to become one of the world's largest airports, and we will have a number of small new towns. This argument states that in many cases 'there is no alternative'. This TINA declaration, often voiced by the Prime Minister, can be contrasted with the prevailing NIMBY attitude[4]. In many cases, the collective local NIMBY attitude will prevail, and development will be fended off. However, in other cases NIMBY versus TINA will be a head-on collision. Interesting times lay ahead.

POLARISATION

Peter Hall, in his book *London 2001* (Hall, 1989), focuses on two polarising trends in the South East, one social, the other spatial; and both of which we do not fully understand.

The 1980's have seen a widening of the social divide between an increasingly affluent, largely service class – conveniently labelled as the 'yuppie' syndrome – and an 'underclass' that becomes increasingly marginalised by the 'job twist' that removes unskilled work and escalates the qualifications required for almost any job. The decline of the production sectors and the government's 'rolling back' of welfare provision have exacerbated the division. The group immediately above this underclass in the pecking order – those in employment, but on low wages – also struggle. There are many people in the South East who live on wages set nationally, who do not receive any London weighting, but who have to survive with much higher living costs. How do these people 'get by'?

The social divide is also paralleled by a spatial divide, with continued decline of population in London itself – albeit now at substantially reduced rates – and rapid decentralisation of growth to the outer parts of the South East. Indeed, the areas of the most rapid growth are now beyond the official boundaries of the region; in the adjacent counties, at the edge of what is now being called the 'Greater South East'. People living in such areas have been the main beneficiaries of the South East's success. However, as we have seen, these people are now beginning to feel the downside of success.

THE COSTS OF DEREGULATION

One of the interesting features of the NIMBY debate is that many residents of ROSE – presumably largely Tory voters and hence passive supporters of deregulation – have rediscovered the planning system. They appreciate that growth pressures are causing many of their problems, but there is also a sudden realisation that the consequences of such growth are felt most sharply when they are not controlled by the planning system. So, just at the time when the government is reducing the power of that system, its own traditional supporters are rediscovering its merits.

There is an implicit assumption in the attitude of the government to planning: that the business community welcomes moves towards a non-plan regime. In the case of big business, there is ample evidence that this is not true in principle or practice. On the practical front, there are very serious complaints on the part of large corporations in the South East that the consequences of largely unplanned growth have a detrimental effect on their operations. If we take the central Berkshire area, for example, two of the largest – and importantly high tech – employers have complained bitterly of congestion and of high land and property prices. David Baldwin, UK Managing Director of Hewlett Packard, expressed his concerns in 1986. While having a major commitment to the company's South East operations, he did warn that he had '…a growing concern about the high cost of living in this part of the world. We are always competing…with locations in Europe, and comparing France with Germany…and if this part of the world becomes so expensive then we simply won't continue to develop here' (London Weekend Television, 1986).

Hewlett Parkard's competitors, Digital, have more recently expressed the same concerns. Geoff Shingles, UK Managing Director says that traffic jams are costing his company a fortune in lost working time: somewhere between half and one million pounds a year he estimates, plus the penalties of 'sheer frustration'. He says that 'knowing what we know today, we would not have come to Reading'(Reading Business Report, 1988). The increasing strength of these two opinions probably reflects the deterioration in conditions in the intervening two years.

On the question of principle, David Baldwin, in the same interview expressed his desire for stronger strategic planning – indeed, national as well as regional planning –

that would coordinate infrastructure investment, land availability, industrial requirements and training.

It is now beginning to dawn on many people that paradoxically the South East is now facing strategic issues of an unprecedented scale and speed at the very time that the last remaining traces of the strategic planning system are being dismantled (Breheny, 1987). The rebellion in Kent over the Channel Tunnel rail routes started in January 1989, the same month that the government published the 'Future of Development Plans' White Paper confirming the abolition of structure plans. The recent draft Planning Policy Guidance (PPG) on 'Structure Plans and Regional Planning Guidance' (Department of the Environment, 1989) suggests that structure plans may be reprieved, but we are still a long way short of a strategic planning system to match the scale of the task.

Despite appearances to the contrary, much of the South East has been unhealthy for some time. In recent years its apparent success has introduced chronic stress. The Government's new medicine has been greater deregulation: of the planning system, of infrastructure provision, of finance. If the South East is the government's major test case of this medicine, then the clinical trial has been a failure. Some of the supposedly enthusiastic patients – be they businesses or Tory voters – object in principle to the cure offered. Even those that agree in principle are finding that the side effects are unbearable. Occasionally, other medicines will be offered to ease these side effects – as with the additional £500m on the Channel Tunnel rail routes. But there is little evidence that the experiment will be halted. As we experiment, the French plan.

REFERENCES

Breheny, M. and Hart, D., (1989) Conflicting Attitudes on the Expansion of Stansted Airport, *Town and Country Planning*, 58, 2, 47–49.

Breheny, M., (1987) The State of the Region – Economic Developments in the South East of England, paper to TCPA conference on The Future of the South East, London, April.

Cervero, R. (1986) *Suburban Gridlock*, New Brunswick, NJ: Rutgers University Center for Urban Policy Studies.

Department of the Environment, (1989) *Draft Planning Policy Guidance: Structure Plans and Regional Plannin Guidance*, London: DOE.

Hall, P. (1989) *London 2001*,London: Unwin Hyman.

London Weekend Television, transcript of interview for the programme Tomorrowland, dated 2.9.86.

Pommelet, P., (1989) Roissy et Massy dans le Project Regional d'Amenagement, *Cahiers de l'Institut de l'Amenagement et d'Urbanisme de la Region d'Ile-de-France*, 89, 27–31.

Reading Business Report, November 1988.

An earlier version of this paper was published under the title 'Southern Discomfort: The Costs of Success in the South East' in *The Planner*, 75, 5, 1989, 14–15.

Part VI

EPILOGUE

CHAPTER 12

AGENDA FOR THE NINETIES

Peter Townroe and Ron Martin

While regional economic policy has a high political profile at the level of the individual parliamentary constituency and the single town or city, in the national political arena regional policy has to shout for attention among many competing voices. Too often, it could be argued, regional policy in Britain has been deployed at the centre to meet visible and apparently short term economic problems (high rates of unemployment, large plant closures, inadequate stocks of factory building, etc), but using weapons that are essentially those of medium and long term economic adjustment. The political pay off extends beyond the Parliamentary cycle. This may be why the political noise comes from equity arguments, but the real achievement has come from efficiency gains and the deployment of policy to pull up the long run scale and productivity of economic resources in the lagging regions.

Over the past three decades a fundamental restructuring has been taking place in the economies of those parts of the United Kingdom which used to be referred to as the 'Depressed Areas'. While restructuring involves a renewal process that can never be complete in a dynamic economy, the economies of these areas (variously defined as 'Development' or 'Assisted' in the past) have experienced a fundamental change since the early 1960s. In employment terms, the reliance on the staples inherited from the industrial revolution of the nineteenth century has gone. In some areas jobs are no longer offered in shipbuilding, in coal mining, in steel manufacture, in textiles; while in others the significance of these sectors has shrunk dramatically. What is left is largely unprotected in terms of sectorally focused policy measures and has to compete on national and international markets.

At the same time, the economies of these same Assisted Areas have received huge investments in supporting infrastructures and services of all kinds: 'hard' infrastructure of roads, airports, mains utilities, industrial estates, etc., and 'soft' infrastructure of schools, hospitals, houses, leisure facilities etc. This investment has been a necessary support to the ebb and flow of British regional economic development policy which in the main has offered various brands and dimension of financial carrot, both to existing companies and to prospective incoming investors. Restructuring has taken place.

Policy has played an important role in this. Is a regionally focused economic development policy still needed therefore in the United Kingdom?

Underlying the papers in this volume is an acceptance of the argument put forward in the first chapter: that British governments will continue to need to offer a regional policy package that involves regionally differentiated expenditures for the foreseeable future. The acceptance of this broad proposition comes from the large group of specialist analysts who have contributed to successive earlier chapters. This acceptance does not have to mean more of the same in terms of measures, although for many it does mean more in terms of public expenditure than the allocations of recent years. But if the appropriate package of regional policy measures is to look rather different in the United Kingdom in the 1990s and beyond, wherein lie the desirable new emphases? The beginnings of an answer to this question are embedded in the chapters of this book. While it was never the intention of this compilation to conclude with a political or policy manifesto, a number of threads can be drawn together to point the way forward.

The geographic impact of changes in the fortunes of the national economy across the United Kingdom modified through the 1980s. The 1979 to 1982 national economic recession hit the Development Areas particularly hard. The manufacturing sector of many towns and cities in these regions was terribly exposed by uncompetitiveness and by the short-termism of financial policies and financial institutions. Unemployment soared, and the North-South divide of the nation which had been closing on many indicators in the late 1960s and early 1970s started to widen again. The South came out of the recession more rapidly than the North, without having suffered to the same extent. The South East region reasserted itself as the growth core of the British economy and it led through the mid-1980s, pulling up other regions behind it, but with an increase in inter-regional differentials in employment and incomes.

However, when compared with previous decades, the North-South divide of the 1980s was formed in a new context. The structure of the national economy changed, pushed by the uneven impact of the recession. The manufacturing sector moved further away from the old staples towards products requiring high levels of knowledge inputs in both their design and their production. What many now call the 'Post-Fordist' era started to arrive, with consequences for labour demand, for the need for local services, for new buildings, for changing organisational structures. At the same time European markets and European competition increased in importance. With improving communications, the manufacturing sector continued to be the driving force behind the urban-rural shift, with the consequent rise of the economies of the Southern smaller self-standing towns, complemented by an increasing number of comparable centres outside of the older industrial cities of the Midlands and the North, and Scotland and Wales and Northern Ireland.

In terms of employment growth, a major feature of the 1980s was the expansion in the banking, insurance and finance sectors and in related business services of all kinds. This expansion pulled a rising proportion of women into the labour market, many on a part-time basis. It also supported growth in many of those same self-standing smaller and medium sized towns that had been receiving manufacturing sector investments. The urban-rural shift was apparently reinforced.

However, by the end of the decade it was apparent that yet a further geographical rebalancing was starting to take place. Service sector growth, involving the business and financial services but also distribution and leisure-related jobs, was occurring strongly in the major cities. The resident populations of these cities which had been falling for over two decades started to stabilise. British cities joined the experience of many cities in Western Europe in experiencing a resurgence. The many measures of British central government urban policy had a role in this, in contrast to the financial penalties to many major urban local governments in their rate support grants in the early 1980s, but these measures complemented strong economic forces in most (but not all) of the major cities.

The most recent recession, which really began to bite in 1990, has had a different geographical impact to the recession of a decade before. The steepest relative rates of increase in unemployment have occurred in Southern England. This is a recession of high interest rates, not of an uncompetitive sterling exchange rate. Many indebted service sector businesses have been hard hit, alongside manufacturing companies of all kinds: hi-tech and low-tech, successful and unsuccessful, large and small. The common denominator is the extent of borrowing on the balance sheet. This underlines one of the directions in which regional policy could usefully develop.

It has been widely argued that the English regions need regional development agencies, somewhat on the model of Scottish Enterprise (what used to be the Scottish Development Agency). These agencies would have a core of public sector funding but with private sector borrowing also on their main balance sheets as well as involvement ('gearing') with private sector investors in individual projects. They would have an especial significance in the current type of recession; as well as playing what is now a well defined medium and long term regional economic development role. By taking a longer term view than the British banks and other financial institutions deem possible, and by building upon an agreed strategy for their region, each development agency could help selected companies through a recession, by means of equity participation and managerial expertise where necessary.

More widely than the current recession, four other more structural considerations are important in thinking about the design of British regional policy over the coming years. The first is the *growing significance of Brussels*. The regional economic development policy of the European Economic Community (EEC) became more important with the accession of Greece, Spain and Portugal to the Community. Moves to widen membership of the Community still further, to form associations with the nations of Eastern Europe, and to proceed towards monetary union, will all increase the demand for larger financial transfers to lagging regions. These transfers are channelled through regional agencies or regional governments, rather than through the regional policies of central governments; and they are increasingly complemented by other programmes of the Community requiring a regional dimension (e.g. in technology, in competition policy, in environmental policy). British regional policy has to relate to and to build upon these programmes. They are no longer peripheral.

The second structural factor, currently under much political debate, involves *changes in the structure and finance of local government* in the United Kingdom. The issues of tiers, boundaries, functions, autonomy and finance need not be rehearsed here, but the outcome of this debate will influence that on the role and status of regional development agencies and the need for central government policies directed at investors in lagging regions. The outcome is also, obviously, important for the development of central government urban policy, with the regional dimension of inner city regeneration being clear. Major inner city investments (shopping centres, leisure facilities, large industrial employers) have a wider spatial consequence.

More indirectly, a less discussed context for future regional policy in the United Kingdom, but one which has clear echoes in the debate over the future of local government, is a *changing public acceptance of degrees of inequality*. In the 1980s, the distribution of living standards of households in the United Kingdom has widened, rightly or wrongly, to surprisingly little general public disquiet. Given improved base-line standards in public and private services and rising real incomes for the vast majority of households, it could be argued that social dissatisfaction at living in a lagging region has, on average, declined in recent years. This is so, even though both spatial inequality and differences by social groups have widened. A minority suffers but it is a minority; and one of the political dynamics of regional economic development policy is removed. This is an untested proposition, but if there is substance to it, it pushes the concerns of future regional policy very much in the direction of efficiency rather than equity.

All across Europe it is clear that *efficiency, in economic growth and job creation terms,* is to be promoted by freeing up market forces and then supporting the technology necessary for competitiveness. Programmes of technological enhancement to industry in each region are now widespread within the EEC. They involve public sector support to research and development in companies, support for consultancy, funding of technology transfer from research institutes and universities, and a heavy emphasis on the building up of human capital. Inequalities in education provision and educational achievement between regions are becoming less acceptable, and the local delivery of relevant training and retraining is receiving a new stress. This developing context has yet to be fully linked into regional economic development strategies in the United Kingdom.

In conclusion, given these contexts and the changes taking place in the United Kingdom economy, we may conclude that future British regional policy should exhibit five characteristics. It should be *problem oriented,* with the identification of problems taking a long term view and coming up from the local level. It should be *multi-faceted,* in that the policy will not simply divide regions into 'prosperous' or 'lagging' but will be capable of attacking different structural weaknesses in the economies of different regions and sub-regions and be able to promote different potentials for growth and expansion.

Third, policy needs an emphasis on *innovation*. The ongoing innovatory capability of each region will determine its trade with other regions and its ability to sustain increases in living standards comparable with those in other regions. Each regional economy needs an ability to generate and to absorb new ideas and new technology. Regional policy therefore necessarily will tend to have an emphasis on the *use of indigenous resources,* taking the emphasis away from inter-regional redistribution towards enhancing growth capabilities based on resources within each region. And the policy package will need to be *flexible,* but without losing strategic sense. It will need to foster information flows and technology rather than movements of capital alone, to use programmes rather than projects, to target the service sectors in the regional economies as well as those in manufacturing, and to encompass small firms and suppliers of intermediate goods and services as well large multi-national companies.

The institutional mechanisms required for this kind of regional policy sit uncomfortably with the past practice of executive action falling largely to a central government department with regional outpost offices. There is a need for devolution. The new model has been taken furthest in Inner City policies, with collaboration between private and public sectors and between local and central governments, and networking between the agencies and institutions involved in development at the local level. Movement towards regional and sub-regional agencies, closely linked to restructured local governments, would bring the United Kingdom more closely into line with its major partners within the European Community, while allowing more localised interventions by what is essentially a central government policy.

Local interventions need to be integrated and coordinated between levels of government, as well as between relevant government departments and with necessary private sector agencies (e.g. the major utilities in the United Kingdom). One aspect of coordination comes in the mixture of sources of finance that are brought to bear in regional development policies. Leverage of private capital by public sector pump priming looks to be a continuing and necessary theme in the next decade.

As the European Community reduces barriers to trade, seeking to harmonise exchange rates and to move towards a common currency, it seems clear that domestic experience with unemployment and regional imbalance will require both a nation state and a Community response. The periphery of the Community cannot be allowed to become more peripheral and it is desirable that all regions contribute fully to the output and the economic welfare of the full Community. Regional policy expenditure will have a key macro economic role, driven by a political imperative.

Index

References in italics indicate tables.